From World War to Postwar

NEW APPROACHES TO INTERNATIONAL HISTORY

Series Editor: Thomas Zeiler, Professor of American Diplomatic History, University of Colorado Boulder, USA

Series Editorial Board:
Anthony Adamthwaite, University of California at Berkeley (USA)
Kathleen Burk, University College London (UK)
Louis Clerc, University of Turku (Finland)
Cindy Ewing, University of Toronto (Canada)
Petra Goedde, Temple University (USA)
Francine McKenzie, University of Western Ontario (Canada)
Lien-Hang Nguyen, University of Kentucky (USA)
Jason Parker, Texas A&M University (USA)
Glenda Sluga, University of Sydney (Australia)

New Approaches to International History covers international history during the modern period and across the globe. The series incorporates new developments in the field, such as the cultural turn and transnationalism, as well as the classical high politics of state-centric policymaking and diplomatic relations. Written with upper level undergraduate and postgraduate students in mind, texts in the series provide an accessible overview of international diplomatic and transnational issues, events, and actors.

Published:
Decolonization and the Cold War, edited by Leslie James and Elisabeth Leake (2015)
Cold War Summits, Chris Tudda (2015)
The United Nations in International History, Amy Sayward (2017)
Latin American Nationalism, James F. Siekmeier (2017)
The History of United States Cultural Diplomacy, Michael L. Krenn (2017)
International Cooperation in the Early 20th Century, Daniel Gorman (2017)
Women and Gender in International History, Karen Garner (2018)
International Development, Corinna Unger (2018)
The Environment and International History, Scott Kaufman (2018)
Scandinavia and the Great Powers in the First World War, Michael Jonas (2019)
Canada and the World since 1867, Asa McKercher (2019)
The First Age of Industrial Globalization, Maartje Abbenhuis and Gordon Morrell (2019)
Europe's Cold War Relations, Federico Romero, Kiran Klaus Patel, Ulrich Krotz (2019)

United States Relations with China and Iran, Osamah F. Khalil (2019)
Public Opinion and Twentieth-Century Diplomacy, Daniel Hucker (2020)
Globalizing the US Presidency, Cyrus Schayegh (2020)
The International LGBT Rights Movement, Laura Belmonte (2021)
Global War, Global Catastrophe, Maartje Abbenhuis and Ismee Tames (2021)
America's Road to Empire: Foreign Policy from Independence to World War One, Piero Gleijeses (2021)
Militarization and the American Century, David Fitzgerald *(2022)*
American Sport in International History, Daniel M. DuBois (2023)
Rebuilding the Postwar Order, Francine McKenzie (2023)
Soldiers in Peacemaking, Beatrice de Graaf, Frédéric Dessberg, and Thomas Vaisset (2023)

Forthcoming:

China and the United States since 1949, Elizabeth Ingleson

From World War to Postwar

Revolution, Cold War, Decolonization, and the Rise of American Hegemony, 1943–1958

BY ANDREW N. BUCHANAN

BLOOMSBURY ACADEMIC
LONDON • NEW YORK • OXFORD • NEW DELHI • SYDNEY

BLOOMSBURY ACADEMIC
Bloomsbury Publishing Plc
50 Bedford Square, London, WC1B 3DP, UK
1385 Broadway, New York, NY 10018, USA
29 Earlsfort Terrace, Dublin 2, Ireland

BLOOMSBURY, BLOOMSBURY ACADEMIC and the Diana logo
are trademarks of Bloomsbury Publishing Plc

First published in Great Britain 2024

Copyright © Andrew N. Buchanan, 2024

Andrew N. Buchanan has asserted his right under the Copyright,
Designs and Patents Act, 1988, to be identified as Author of this work.

For legal purposes the Acknowledgments on p. xvi constitute
an extension of this copyright page.

Series design by Catherine Wood
Cover image: People's Liberation Army soldiers in action during the weeks
leading up to the establishment of the People's Republic of China, 1949.
World History Archive/Alamy Stock Photo.

All rights reserved. No part of this publication may be reproduced or transmitted
in any form or by any means, electronic or mechanical, including photocopying,
recording, or any information storage or retrieval system, without prior
permission in writing from the publishers.

Bloomsbury Publishing Plc does not have any control over, or responsibility for,
any third-party websites referred to or in this book. All internet addresses given
in this book were correct at the time of going to press. The author and publisher
regret any inconvenience caused if addresses have changed or sites have
ceased to exist, but can accept no responsibility for any such changes.

A catalogue record for this book is available from the British Library.

A catalog record for this book is available from the Library of Congress.

ISBN:	HB:	978-1-3502-4021-6
	PB:	978-1-3502-4020-9
	ePDF:	978-1-3502-4023-0
	eBook:	978-1-3502-4022-3

Series: New Approaches to International History

Typeset by Integra Software Services Pvt. Ltd.
Printed and bound in Great Britain

To find out more about our authors and books visit www.bloomsbury.com
and sign up for our newsletters.

To those around the world who heeded Tan Malaka's call:
One-hundred percent Merdeka (freedom)!

CONTENTS

List of Illustrations xiii
Acknowledgments xvi

Introduction 1
    A Note on Text and Terminology 9
    For Further Reading 9

1 The United States at the Dawn of the "American Century" 11
    The Scale and Scope of America's Military Victory 13
    Global Networks of Predominance and Connectivity 14
    Shaping the Postwar World: Regimes of Military Government 17
    The United States and the World War 18
    Planning for Hegemony 19
    America's Wartime Economy 22
    The United States Reorganizes the World Economy 27
    Washington Structures Its Political Hegemony 31
    The Apex of American Power 35
    For Further Reading 36

2 Hegemony Qualified: The Soviet Union, Eastern Europe, and the Deepening Cold War 37
    The Wartime Devastation of Eastern Europe and Moscow's Plans for the Postwar 38
    The Russian Revolution and the Rise of Stalinism 39
    Truman, Trieste, and the Shaping of US Policy 43
    Eastern Europe in the Immediate Postwar 45
    Germany: The Central Question 50
    Washington Steps Up the Pressure 53

Moscow Tightens Its Grip 55
American Pressure Intensifies: H-Bombs and NSC 68 59
The Crisis of Stalinism 60
'Peaceful Coexistence' 63
For Further Reading 65

3 Hegemony Qualified: The Chinese Revolution and the War in Korea 67

The Great American Mutiny 67
China in 1945 69
China in American and Soviet planning 73
The Chinese Revolution 75
The CCP Consolidates Control 80
War in Korea 82
The War in Korea and the Transformation in China 87
For Further Reading 92

4 Hegemony Qualified: Anti-Colonial Revolt in South and Southeast Asia 93

Japan's Great East Asia Co-Prosperity Sphere 96
Wars of Indonesian Independence, 1945–50 97
Popular Revolt and Postwar Crisis in Southeast Asia 102
The Bloody End of British India 109
New Nation-States and Alternative Solidarities: The 1955 Bandung Conference 113
Communism in South and Southeast Asia 115
Organizing American Hegemony in South and Southeast Asia 118
For Further Reading 124

5 Hegemony Transferred and Hierarchy Reorganized: Western Europe, Japan, and the British Dominions 127

War, Revolution, and Political Restabilization in Italy 127
Democracy, Disarmament, and the Restoration of Political Equilibrium 131
Variations on a Theme: Postwar Political Stabilization Japan, France, and Belgium 137

The Key to Europe: Partition and Political Stabilization in Germany 141
The Greek Civil War 142
The Second Phase of Postwar Stabilization, 1947–50 143
Washington's Remilitarization Drive 148
Britain: Relative Decline and Hegemonic Transition 151
The 'Dedominionization' of Australia, Canada, and New Zealand 154
Organizing the Postwar World 156
For Further Reading 158

6 Hegemony Expanded: The Middle East and Africa 159

War and the Crisis of Colonial Rule in North Africa and the Middle East 159
Revolutionary Crises in Postwar Iran, 1945–53 162
Oil, the Cold War, and the United States in the Middle East 166
The Partition of Palestine 168
The 'Tripartite Aggression' or Suez Crisis, 1956 171
War and Postwar in Sub-Saharan Africa 175
The 'Second Colonial Conquest': Planning for Postwar Empire 177
Cold War Contexts: Washington Underwrites Colonial Empire 179
Roads to Decolonization 181
Shifts in American Policy toward Africa 184
South Africa: Anchor of Imperial Power 185
For Further Reading 188

7 Hemispheric Bedrock: Latin America and the Caribbean 191

The 1946 Haitian Revolt 191
Good Neighbors 193
Washington's Wartime Relations with Brazil, Mexico, and Argentina 196
The Consolidation of Washington's Regional Hegemony, 1944–48 199
A Latin American Front in the Postwar Labor Insurgency 202
Populism, Communism, and the United States 205
The Window of Democracy Closes 208
From Development and Modernization to Intensified Neocolonialism 212
The Caribbean Colonies 215

The Cuban Revolution 219
For Further Reading 221

8 Bringing It All Back Home 223
An American Front in the Postwar Labor Upsurge 223
The Deepening Cold War, Loyalty Oaths, and the Defeat of the Progressive Party 226
The Chinese Revolution and the Rise of McCarthyism 228
The National Security State and the Imperial Presidency 231
Eisenhower and the 'Middle Way' 232
Innovation, Modernization, and the Cold War University 234
High Art and Soft Power 237
The Civil Rights Movement—A Second American Front in the Postwar Upsurge 241
Constructing the Good War 245
For Further Reading 247

From World War to Postwar: Some Conclusions 249

Index 257

ILLUSTRATIONS

1.1 With American sailors looking on, the Japanese delegation arrives aboard the USS *Missouri* for the surrender ceremony that marked the formal end of the Second World War, September 2, 1945. (Bettmann/Contributor) 12

1.2 Women welders at the Ingalls shipyard in Pascagoula, Mississippi, 1943. (Spencer Beebe, Department of Labor, Image 86-WWT-85-35) 24

2.1 The 1956 Hungarian Revolution: Mass demonstration in central Budapest against Soviet control, October 25, 1956. (FOTO: FORTEPAN/Nagy Gyula, CC BY-SA 3.0 via Wikimedia) 63

3.1 American soldiers demanding rapid demobilization march on US headquarters in Manila, January 6, 1946. (Photo: Army Signal Corps, Image SC 248840, National Archives) 68

3.2 People's Liberation Army soldiers assemble for the assault on Shanghai during the closing phases of the Chinese Revolution, May 21, 1949. (Photo: Keystone/Hulton Archive/Getty Images) 78

4.1 Indonesian anticolonial revolutionaries armed with sharpened bamboo spears and Japanese rifles rally in Java, 1946. (Collection Nationaal Museum van Wereldculturen Coll.nr. RV-1971-271) 94

4.2 Royal Indian Navy sailors from HMIS *Talwar* march in central Mumbai, February 19, 1946. (Photo: The Times of India Group) 110

5.1 Young Italian partisans prepare to combat German snipers during the liberation of Pistoia, northern Tuscany, December 9, 1944. (Photo: Keystone/Getty Images) 129

5.2 Led by the aircraft carriers *Randolph* and *Midway* and the cruiser *Salem*, warships of the US Sixth Fleet at sea in the Mediterranean during the Suez Crisis, August 6, 1956. Headquartered in Naples, the Sixth Fleet gave the United States a large and permanent military presence in the Mediterranean. (Photo: Bettmann/Getty) 150

6.1 Iranian prime minister Mohammad Mosaddeq addresses a crowd of supporters shortly after the nationalization of the oil industry and the ejection of Anglo-Iranian Oil Company personnel from the Abadan refinery, October 19, 1951. (Photo: Keystone-France) 165

6.2 British troops on patrol in Port Said, Egypt, during the Suez Crisis, November 10, 1956. An oil refinery burns in the background. Despite rapid military success, the operation was a political disaster for the British and French governments. (Photo: Bettemann/Getty) 173

7.1 General Juan Perón addresses a mass rally of his supporters, Buenos Aires, Argentina, January 1, 1955. (Photo: Keystone/Hulton Archive/Getty Images) 205

7.2 A group of Jamaican men read a newspaper onboard the SS *Empire Windrush*. They were among the 800 West Indians who disembarked at London's Tilbury dock on June 22, 1948. (Image: Hulton Deutsch) 218

8.1 Striking members of United Auto Workers Local 15 on picket line duty outside General Motors' Fisher Body plant in Fleetwood, MI, November 24, 1945. Picket signs announce the union's demand for a 30 percent wage hike. (Photo: Bettmann/Getty) 224

8.2 A crowd of five thousand African Americans rally in the First Baptist Church during the Montgomery, Alabama bus boycott, February 27, 1956. Rally participants expressed their redoubled commitment not to ride city buses until the company ended its segregationist policies. (Photo: Bettmann/Getty) 245

ACKNOWLEDGMENTS

I would like to thank all the friends and colleagues who have discussed this project with me over the past couple of years. I am particularly grateful to those who have read and commented on parts of the manuscript: they include Andrea Barrett, Goran Musić, Bill Hovlund, Ruth Lawlor, Sarah Osten, Nicole Phelps, and Susanna Schrafstetter. I am deeply grateful to commissioning editor Maddie Holder and series editor Tom Zeiler for their commitment to this project, and to Bloomsbury's production and marketing staff in Britain and India: it has been a pleasure to work with you all. Above all, and as ever, my heartfelt thanks go to Mary Nell Bockman for her constant support, encouragement, and astute criticism.

Introduction

Writing barely a month after American troops entered Rome in June 1944, James Dunn, director of the Office of European Affairs at the US State Department, argued that Italy was now entering its "post-war period."[1] It was a bold claim. German troops still occupied northern Italy, and it would take another year of hard fighting—and a popular insurrection—to drive them out. Meanwhile, southern Italy was occupied by Allied troops, and while control of some regions had been handed back to the Italian government formed after the ouster of Mussolini the previous summer, large areas remained under Allied Military Government. But despite these harsh realities, Dunn pointed to an important truth. After capturing Rome, the Americans had engineered a bloodless coup that toppled the government of Pietro Badoglio and replaced it with one led by socialist Ivanoe Bonomi. The Allies had recognized Badoglio's government when they invaded Italy in fall 1943, but the fact that most of its members had been active Fascists discredited it in the eyes of many Italians. In contrast, the new Bonomi cabinet, which included leaders of all the major non-Fascist parties including the Communists (PCI), commanded broad popular support. Dunn and his colleagues hoped that with Washington's encouragement—and substantial economic aid—the new government would lay the foundations of a democratic, capitalist, and pro-American Italy: in this sense, Italy was indeed entering a postwar period, even as the war raged on.

Dunn's comments underscore the fact that in Italy, as elsewhere in the world, the passage from world war to postwar was not going to be a simple leap from one exclusive state to another. Instead, there would

---

[1] James C. Dunn to General Hilldring, Army Civil Affairs Division, July 6, 1944, quoted in Andrew Buchanan, *American Grand Strategy in the Mediterranean during World War II* (Cambridge: Cambridge University Press, 2014), 191.

be complex and uneven *processes* of transition in which postwar relations emerged in some places while fighting continued unabated in others. Thus, while large-scale military conflict might come to a rapid halt with the signing of a ceasefire, political turmoil, including insurrections and popular revolts produced by wartime dislocation, might actually intensify. In this sense, while Italy's postwar began in 1943, it continued into the hotly contested politics of the years that followed the formal end of the fighting and was not consolidated until the American-sponsored defeat of the Communist Party in the 1948 general election The process of transition from war to postwar therefore *combines* the top-level resolution of interstate conflict with the bottom-up expression of popular agency as ordinary people marched into the spaces created between the ending—or at least the weakening—of the old order and the incomplete establishment of the new. The postwar therefore emerges not as a temporal condition—literally the time after the war—but as a fluid period of contingency, movement, and opportunity as well as a time of completion and consolidation.

Historians of the First World War have already been grappling with the transition from war to postwar, recognizing in particular that the abrupt end of the fighting on the Western Front at 11:00 am on November 11, 1918, was not replicated on the war's sprawling Eastern fronts. Here, broad swaths of the former Austro-Hungarian, German, Ottoman, and Russian empires continued to be roiled by violent conflicts, including revolutions, civil wars, and foreign military interventions, well into the 1920s.[2] In fact, precisely because they involve the all-out mobilization of people and resources, large modern wars cannot end neatly and cleanly: the American Civil War, for example, was followed directly by a violent struggle over the reconstruction of the former Confederacy that continued until 1877, while the 1870–71 Franco-Prussian War produced a short-lived revolutionary government—the Commune—in Paris. While it is easy to see wars as clear-cut things with precise timelines, to do so is to short-circuit a deeper understanding of war as an accelerator of political, social, and economic changes that can only be consolidated into a stable postwar order as these war-driven crises are resolved over time.

The Second World War reprised these complex processes of transition from war to postwar on a truly global scale, with profound consequences for the shape of the new world order that emerged from the crucible of war. In Southeast Asia—a geopolitical region given shape by the Allies' wartime command structure—European and American colonialism had been shattered by Japanese advances at the start of the Pacific War, and the defeat of Japan in summer 1945 triggered a powerful wave of

---

[2]See Robert Gerwarth and Erez Manela, "The Great War as a Global War: Imperial Conflict and the Reconfiguration of the World Order, 1911–1923," *Diplomatic History*, Vol. 38, No. 4 (2014).

anti-colonial revolts stretching from Indonesia to French Indochina and the Philippines. In Korea, a popular insurrection asserted national unity in the face of Japanese, American, and Soviet occupation. The Japanese surrender found China deeply divided, with some areas remaining under Japanese occupation while others were dominated by the rival armies of the Guomindang (GMD) government and the Chinese Communist Party (CCP). Despite being the war's major victor, the United States had little military presence in China, and, with rebellious soldiers demanding rapid demobilization, Washington was unable to rush large forces into the country. As a result, for China the end of the world war brought not peace, but renewed civil war, popular revolution, and—within four years—the victory of the CCP.

In Europe, large-scale fighting ended in spring 1945 with the utter defeat of Germany, but here, too, the transition from war to postwar was marked by popular uprisings and guerrilla wars. With the exception of Greece, where civil war continued until 1949, insurgencies in Western Europe were quickly curbed by national elites acting with the active support of the victorious Allies and with the indispensable help of local Communist parties acting on Moscow's instructions. In Eastern Europe, however, guerrilla campaigns against Soviet forces in Ukraine, Poland, and the Baltic States continued into the early 1950s as Moscow struggled to consolidate its control over the region and to integrate it into its socialized economy. These complex and protracted political transitions from war to postwar unfolded amid economic devastation and extreme social dislocation on an unprecedented scale.[3] In Europe alone, some thirty million 'Displaced Persons' were on the move, their ranks swelled by Holocaust survivors, former forced laborers, and prisoners of war; in China, meanwhile, ninety million people ended the war as internal refugees displaced by fighting and by war-induced famine and flooding.[4]

The ragged endings of the Second World War in both Europe and Asia, along with the social and political crisis in the Middle East, Latin America, and Africa that accelerated under the impact of war, all help to illuminate the true character of the global war itself. Contrary to the carefully cultivated popular perception, the Second World War was not a single unified event with a self-evident timeline, clearly defined sides, and a transparent moral story of good versus evil. Instead, the *world* war was constituted out of a series of large regional struggles, each of which had their own specific causes and dynamics. Germany, Italy, and Japan were loosely linked in the Axis alliance, but their wars of imperial expansion aimed at conquering

---

[3]Keith Lowe, *Savage Continent: Europe in the Aftermath of World War II* (New York: Picador, 2012).
[4]Yasmin Khan, "Wars of Displacement: Exile and Uprooting in the 1940s," in Michael Geyer and Adam Tooze (eds.), *The Cambridge History of the Second World War*, Vol. III (New York: Cambridge University Press, 2015), 277.

autarkic regional empires in their own parts of the world rather than at challenging for global predominance. These wars included Italy's grab for territory in the Balkans and East Africa, Japan's invasion of China and its drive into Southeast Asia and the central Pacific, and Germany's war of colonial conquest in Eastern Europe, a struggle that included a ferocious drive to smash the Soviet Union and overturn its socialized economic system. Meanwhile, from 1939 Britain and France battled German and Italian expansionism in Europe, the Mediterranean, and North Africa while hoping to contain Japan in Southeast Asia. For London and Paris, these were wars to defend their existing empires from Axis invasion, and with the invaluable support of its colonies, Britain fought on after the defeat of France in 1940.

These large regional wars finally achieved global coherence in a forty-five-month 'central paroxysm' that stretched from the Japanese attack on Pearl Harbor in December 1941 to the atomic bombings of Hiroshima and Nagasaki in August 1945.[5] This period of intense worldwide war was defined by the formal participation of the United States, the only country with both the ability and—increasingly—the will to wage war simultaneously in *both* Europe (including the Mediterranean and North Africa) *and* the Pacific. Moreover, from the beginning Washington fought not to defend the existing international status quo, but to establish a new world order under its leadership.[6] Once fully mobilized, America's enormous economic resources enabled it to fight a matériel-heavy 'air-sea' war of strategic bombing and expansive naval power whilst at the same time producing the vast quantities of oil, food, and equipment needed to sustain Moscow's ground war against Germany and to supply its British, Chinese, and other allies.[7] America's military victories in the Mediterranean, Europe, and the Pacific laid the basis for its worldwide predominance, while its powerful universalizing claim to be fighting for the freedom of all humanity underscored the globality of the central paroxysm while simultaneously reinforcing Washington's claim to moral and political leadership.

As a result of its wartime victories, the United States also got to shape the master narrative of the *world* war, crafting in both popular culture and academic historiography the story of a single, simple, and clearly defined thing with which we are all familiar. Recently, historians have begun to chip away at these long-standing notions of 'the war' to good effect. There is now a substantial English-language literature of the long war in China—beginning with Japan's 1931 invasion of Manchuria—and

---

[5] The term is borrowed from Gerwarth and Manela's analysis of the First World War, see "The Great War as a Global War," 787.
[6] On the formation of American global strategy, see Stephen Wertheim, *Tomorrow, the World* (Cambridge, MA: Harvard University Press, 2020).
[7] On "air-sea war," see Phillips Payson O'Brien, *How the War Was Won* (Cambridge: Cambridge University Press, 2015), esp. 484–5.

comprehensive new work on India's war.⁸ Historians have tackled the global dimensions of the Axis alliance and its colonial-autarkic projects in Eastern Europe, the Mediterranean, and East and Southeast Asia.⁹ Synthetic histories have also expanded the war's spatial and temporal frames, with Evan Mawdsley's popular textbook pegging the start of the world war to Japan's 1937 invasion of China.¹⁰ Others have approached the war's globality from different directions, including from the viewpoint of the British Empire and through the lens of oceanic space and maritime power.¹¹ Nevertheless, while many historians now accept that the world war grew out of a series of large regional wars that began well before 1939, it has proved much more difficult to expand the temporal framework beyond the summer of 1945. To many, the final defeat of Nazi Germany, the dropping of atomic bombs on the cities of Hiroshima and Nagasaki on August 6 and 9, and the rapid Japanese surrender that followed still seem to establish a clear and unambiguous break between war and postwar. This approach inevitably reduces the ongoing wars in China and throughout much of Southeast Asia—as well as the complex transitions in Europe, the Middle East, Latin America, and sub-Saharan Africa—to simple aftermaths of the global war. In contrast, this book sees them as key constituent elements of processes that deepened even as the fighting between the great imperial powers came to an end.

The end of the *world* war in summer 1945 did resolve some key questions of global power, announcing the victory of the United States over its rivals in Germany, Italy, and Japan and its increasing predominance over its British and French allies. But while world war's central paroxysm ended abruptly

---

⁸On China, see Rana Mitter, *China's War with Japan, 1937–1945: The Struggle for Survival* (London: Penguin, 2013); Hans van de Ven, *China at War: Triumph and Tragedy in the Emergence of the New China* (Cambridge, MA: Harvard University Press, 2017); S. C. M. Paine, *The Wars for Asia, 1911–1949* (Cambridge: Harvard University Press, 2011): on India, see Tarak Barkawi, *Soldiers of Empire: Indian and British Armies in World War II* (Cambridge: Cambridge University Press, 2017); Yasmin Kahn, *The Raj at War: A People's History of India's Second World War* (London: Bodley Head, 2015); Srinath Raghavan, *India's War: World War II and the Making of Modern South Asia* (New York: Basic Books, 2016).
⁹Daniel Hedinger, "The Imperial Nexus: The Second World War and the Axis in Global Perspective," *Journal of Global History*, Vol. 12 (2017); Stephen G. Fritz, *Ostkrieg: Hitler's War of Extermination in the East* (Lexington, KY: University Press of Kentucky, 2011); Timothy Snyder, *Bloodlands: Europe Between Hitler and Stalin* (New York: Basic Books, 2012).
¹⁰Evan Mawdsley, *World War II, A New History* (Cambridge: Cambridge University Press, 2009). See also Richard Overy, *Blood and Ruins: The Great Imperial War, 1931–1945* (London: Penguin UK, 2021); Thomas W. Zeiler, *Annihilation: A Global Military History of World War II* (Oxford: Oxford University Press, 2011); Andrew Buchanan, *World War II in Global Perspective, 1931–1953* (Hoboken: Wiley, 2019).
¹¹See Ashley Jackson, *The British Empire and the Second World War* (London: Hambledon Continuum, 2006); Craig L. Symonds, *World War II at Sea: A Global History* (Oxford: Oxford University Press, 2018); Evan Mawdsley, *The War for the Seas: A Maritime History of World War II* (New Haven: Yale University Press, 2019); Paul Kennedy, *Victory at Sea: Naval Power and the Transformation of the Global Order in World War II* (New Haven: Yale University Press, 2022).

with the surrender of Japan, much of the fighting did not. Indeed, as the idea of ragged endings suggests, outside of those areas under direct occupation by American and other allied forces, many armed conflicts escalated at the start of the 'postwar.' In many places, wartime dislocation unleashed popular struggles for decolonized and more just and egalitarian futures, accelerating and deepening existing social conflicts and opening unstable power vacuums in which the legitimacy of capitalism—and of colonial rule in particular—was challenged. In many places, revolution seemed to be on the order of the day.

American policymakers took the link between war and revolution seriously. Their views had been shaped by the experience of the 1917 Russian Revolution and the subsequent revolutionary overturns of the German and Austro-Hungarian empires in 1918–19, and they feared similar crises would follow the Second World War. Instead, as we shall see, Allied forces in Western Europe were able to work *with* Moscow and the local Communist parties that looked to it for guidance to establish stable pro-US regimes. Thus, the alliance of convenience that had brought the United States and the USSR together to fight Germany in summer 1941 also brought Washington considerable benefits when it came time to stabilize the postwar order in Europe. In China and Southeast Asia, however, the United States had a much weaker grip, and here revolutionary uprisings that combined social questions like the distribution of land to peasant farmers with anti-colonial resistance to the reimposition of European imperial rule exploded after the formal end of the great power war.

This book is about the ways in which the ragged endings of the long world war shaped the contours of the postwar world. It argues that by breaking down the conceptual barriers between the categories of war and postwar and by emphasizing elements of continuity and connectivity as well as of change, we can form a clearer understanding *both* of the Second World War *and* of the postwar world that followed. Once we see that 1945 was both an abrupt break *and* a moment of continuity, then it becomes clear that the crushing military victories won by the United States in Europe and the Pacific—surely among the most decisive in history—did *not* guarantee Washington the complete global hegemony that it sought. Instead, US predominance was qualified from the very beginning by what it failed to accomplish during the war, registered most notably in the rapidly deepening crisis in China, in the great wave of anti-colonial revolts in Asia, and in the expansion of Soviet power in Eastern Europe. These developments either created or threatened to create substantial geographic zones in which capitalism did not operate and where, as a result, the fundamental economic foundations of American predominance were absent. Washington's rapid plunge into Cold War with the Soviet Union and its parallel efforts to contain the revolution in China and to tame the wave of anticolonial insurgencies in Southeast Asia were a direct response to these qualifications to its hoped-for hegemony. Moreover, the 'cold' character of the 'war' with the USSR was a reflection not of the great strength of the United States, but rather of the constraints placed on its capacity to use military force—that is to launch hot wars—by the outcome of the Second World War. Far from being a synonym for America's hegemonic project, as some have suggested, the Cold War was an expression of the challenges to that project in the years following the formal end of the Second World War.[12]

Viewed from this vantage point—as this book seeks to do—the ragged endings of the Second World War splice into the equally ragged beginnings of the postwar. This period was shaped *both* by Washington's drive to consolidate the global predominance won during the war's central paroxysm *and* by the roadblocks to this process posed by the extension of Soviet power, by the Chinese Revolution, and by anticolonial revolt. The capitalized Cold War, driven by Washington's desire to roll back (or 'contain') the expansion of Soviet power in Eastern Europe and then to topple the Stalinist regime in Moscow, now emerges as one part—or one front—in a broader global process. Given the political, military, and ideological weight placed on it by both sides, the Cold War was certainly a key component of the global postwar, but it neither subsumed developments in other parts of the world nor did it simply spill over into China and the newly named Third World.

This approach challenges much of the established historiography of the Cold War, itself a voluminous and hotly contested field of historical investigation that often claims—either directly or by implication—to be *the* history of the postwar. As Odd Arne Westad outlines in a useful summary of the field, Cold War historiography has passed through a number of clearly defined phases since the 1950s.[13] In the early postwar, orthodox Western narratives placed the blame for the conflict squarely on Soviet expansionism; later, revisionist historians writing in the shadow of the war in Vietnam assigned equal—or possibly greater—responsibility to the United States. Then in the 1990s 'post-revisionists' mined newly opened East European archives in a more nuanced attempt to restore Soviet—or possibly just Stalin's—culpability.[14] Nevertheless, while post-revisionists like John Lewis Gaddis deployed new evidence in support of earlier orthodoxies, many key issues, including the question of whether Soviet policy was fundamentally offensive or defensive, remained ambiguous. Since turn of the century, historians have focused on new concerns, often centered on questions of ideology and culture and on

---

[12] Odd Arne Westad, "The Cold War and the International History of the Twentieth Century," in Melvyn P. Leffler and Odd Arne Westad (eds.), *The Cambridge History of the Cold War* (Cambridge: Cambridge University Press, 2010), Vol. 1, 11.
[13] Westad, "The Cold War and the International History of the Twentieth Century."
[14] See John Lewis Gaddis, *We Now Know: Rethinking Cold War History* (Oxford: Oxford University Press, 1997); see also Richard Ned Lebow, "We Still Don't Know," Feature Reviews, *Diplomatic History*, Vol. 22, No. 4 (Fall 1998), 627–32.

the relationship between the US-Soviet Cold War and developments in the so-called Third World. Here, Odd Arne Westad blazed a trail with studies of the Cold War in the global South, while others dug deeply into its impact on specific countries and regions.[15]

This book builds on these important studies, but by rooting the narrative in the ragged endings of the Second World War in aims to offer a more integrated and truly global account of the emergence of the postwar world. In doing so, it takes two apparently contradictory approaches, offering a genuinely global review—giving due attention to regional specificities and dynamics—while at the same time highlighting the emergence and consolidation of a new American-led world order. For this reason, the book opens and closes with chapters focused on the United States and on the construction of American global predominance, with Chapter One looking at the United States in 1945 while Chapter Eight considers both global and domestic aspects of the consolidation of the new world-system during the 1950s. The intervening chapters discuss the transition from war to postwar in various regions, including the Soviet Union and Eastern Europe; China and Korea; Southeast Asia; Europe, Japan, and the British Dominions; the Middle East and sub-Saharan Africa; and Latin America and the Caribbean. Within this framework, the book highlights conscious human agency, showing that other outcomes were possible and that the consolidation of American hegemony inevitably rested on the foreclosure of numerous alternative futures.[16] In this light, Washington's 'rules-based' international order, consolidated in the decade after 1945, emerges not as the teleologically inevitable outcome of the war but rather as the product of contingent circumstance and of the actions of real people, many of whom hoped—and fought—for very different outcomes. Grasping this does not require a flight of counterfactual fancy; instead, it simply demands that we take seriously the fears of James Dunn and his colleagues as they struggled to birth a new American-led order amid a world marked by continuing economic and social dislocation, popular revolution, and struggles for national independence.

---

[15] See Ode Arne Westad, *The Global Cold War: Third World Interventions and the Making of Our Times* (Cambridge: Cambridge University Press, 2007) and *The Cold War: A World History* (New York: Basic Books, 2017); Lorenz M. Lüthi, *Cold Wars: Asia, The Middle East, Europe* (Cambridge: Cambridge University Press, 2020); Tanya Harmer, "The Cold War in Latin America," in Artemy M. Kalinovsky and Craig Daigle (eds.), *The Routledge Handbook of the Cold War* (Abingdon, Oxford: Routledge, 2014); William A. Booth, "Historiographical Review: Rethinking Latin America's Cold War," *The Historical Journal*, Vol. 64, No. 4 (Sept. 2021).

[16] See Ruth Lawlor and Andrew Buchanan, "Hopes Foreclosed and a World Remade: The Long Endings of World War II," in Lawlor and Buchanan (eds.), *Essays on the Greater Second World War* (forthcoming from Cornell University Press).

A Note on Text and Terminology

In the text, I have kept the use of footnotes to a minimum in the interests of readability, citing only direct quotations and specific facts. This introduction ends with a list of recommended titles that will give the reader insight into the global questions under consideration here, and each chapter concludes with a bibliography highlighting books and articles that allow specific regions and topics to be explored in greater depth.

Given the nature of the times under discussion, the words 'communist' and 'communism' occur frequently throughout this book. In many histories this term hides an ambiguity, conflating a narrow meaning—members and adherents of parties loyal to the Soviet regime in Moscow—and a broader meaning that embraces radical revolutionaries in general. I have sought to clarify this ambiguity by using a capitalized 'Communist' when referring specifically to official pro-Moscow parties and policies and using lower-case 'communist' to denote revolutionaries—many of whom were bitter opponents of Stalinism—in general.

For Further Reading

Andrew N. Buchanan, *World War II in Global Perspective, 1931–1953: A Short History* (Hoboken: Wiley-Blackwell, 2019).
Daniel Immerwahr, *How to Hide an Empire: A History of the Greater United States* (New York: Farrar, Straus and Giroux, 2019).
Melvyn P. Leffler and Ode Arne Westad (eds.), *The Cambridge History of the Cold War* (Cambridge: Cambridge University Press, 2010), Vol. 1.
Lorenz M. Lüthi, *Cold Wars: Asia, The Middle East, Europe* (Cambridge: Cambridge University Press, 2020).
Arnold A. Offner, *Another Such Victory: President Truman and the Cold War, 1945–1953* (Stanford, CA: Stanford University Press, 2002).
Odd Arne Westad, "The Cold War and the International History of the Twentieth Century," in Melvyn P. Leffler and Odd Arne Westad (eds.), *The Cambridge History of the Cold War* (Cambridge: Cambridge University Press, 2010), Vol. 1.
Ode Arne Westad, *The Global Cold War: Third World Interventions and the Making of Our Times* (Cambridge: Cambridge University Press, 2007).

CHAPTER ONE

The United States at the Dawn of the "American Century"

Sitting atop the gun turrets of the battleship USS *Missouri* with their legs swinging over the armored sides, American sailors enjoyed a grandstand view of the fleet that filled Tokyo Bay. It was September 2, 1945, and the world war was finally over. American warships, from hulking battleships to sleek destroyers rode at anchor, while 400 B-29 Superfortresses roared overhead. Over the previous months these aircraft had razed every major Japanese city in a relentless bombing campaign that culminated in the nuclear annihilation of Hiroshima and Nagasaki. The bombers were followed by wave after wave of the carrier-based aircraft: the fighters, torpedo-planes, and dive-bombers that had destroyed the Imperial Japanese Navy in a series of sprawling naval battles from the Coral Sea and Midway to the Philippine Sea and Leyte Gulf. Twelve submarines joined the assembled fleet, representatives of the wolf-packs that had prowled the western Pacific, cutting the sea routes to Japan and starving its economy of fuel and raw materials. Their efforts, along with those of the bombers, had effectively destroyed Japan's ability to wage war. The warships were joined at anchor by ships of the fleet train, the supply vessels, fast oil tankers, troop transports, landing craft, and hospital ships that had kept the warships fueled, armed, and fed, enabling them to remain at sea for long periods and giving them their unprecedented strategic reach.

This mighty armada had been assembled to witness the Japanese surrender, and no one watching could doubt the overwhelming scope of America's victory. In neat business suits and full-dress uniforms, the Japanese delegation came aboard the *Missouri* just before 9:00 a.m. Tieless and in a workaday uniform, General Douglas MacArthur, the newly designated head of the American-led occupation of Japan, addressed the ceremony. Surrounded by the physical manifestations of American power,

FIGURE 1.1 *With American sailors looking on, the Japanese delegation arrives aboard the USS* Missouri *for the surrender ceremony that marked the formal end of the Second World War, September 2, 1945. (Bettmann/Contributor.)*

MacArthur expressed the pious hope that a "better world" would emerge from the "blood and carnage" of war.[1] It would, he emphasized, be a world constructed as the United States wanted it, and in case anyone missed the point, the flag flown by Commodore Matthew Perry's 'black ships' when they entered Tokyo Bay in 1854 to open Japan to American trade hung from

---

[1]Douglas MacArthur, quoted in John Dower, *Embracing Defeat: Japan in the Wake of World War II* (New York: Norton, 1999), 41–2; See also Susan L. Carruthers, *The Good Occupation: American Soldiers and the Hazards of Peace* (Cambridge: Harvard University Press, 2016), 82–7.

the *Missouri*'s armored walls. It had taken nearly a century, but the contest between Japan and the United States for predominance in the western Pacific was finally over.

The Scale and Scope of America's Military Victory

By the time of the Japanese surrender, the idea of rebuilding the world under American leadership would have appeared to the *Missouri*'s sailors as the natural consequence of their overwhelming military victory. Yet just five years earlier this claim to global hegemony, with its intertwining of worldwide economic and military power and politico-moral leadership, was virtually unheard of, even in Washington's elite policy-making circles. The scope and scale of the American power upon which this new world role rested were reflected in the lived experiences of the sailors. Work on *Missouri* began in the Brooklyn Navy Yard in January 1941 and was completed just three years later: the speed with which the massive battleship was built testified in microcosm to the vast wartime expansion of American industrial capacity. The *Missouri* joined the Pacific Fleet in December 1944, operating from a massive anchorage and supply base at Ulithi Atoll that had been built from scratch after deporting the indigenous inhabitants. In early 1945, the *Missouri* pounded the Japanese-ruled Okinawa, paving the way for the US invasion and occupation that transformed the island into a place of military bases, airfields, and supply dumps. From here, *Missouri* raided a now nearly defenseless Japan, bombarding coastal steel mills and adding to the destruction delivered from above by the B-29s. The battleships long periods at sea were made possible by under-way refueling techniques copied from the Japanese and perfected by the navy's purpose-built fleet of fast oilers and supply ships.

The crew of the USS *Missouri* participated in some of the major operations of the Pacific War, but these military successes were just one part of America's worldwide victory. By the time Japan surrendered, its Axis partners in Italy and Germany had already been defeated and placed under Allied military occupations. Washington's land armies had made an important contribution to these victories, but its allies in the Soviet Union and China had borne the brunt of the ground combat against Germany and Japan. Meanwhile, America's economic predominance and its air - and seapower had been critical to the war's *global* outcome. Buoyed by America's booming economy, *Missouri*'s sailors enjoyed access to unprecedented military abundance. Shipboard sailors, along with US personnel on military bases, ate well-prepared meals that delivered up to 5,000 calories per day, and even the C-rations consumed by frontline troops were far more nutritious than the modest diets available to their enemies, with starvation or diseases associated with malnutrition causing some 60 percent of Japanese military deaths.[2] After lobbying to have ice-cold Coke declared a wartime necessity, the Coca-Cola company built bottling plants close to the front lines to keep soldiers well supplied. In ships and on land bases, troops also had access to libraries featuring the latest best-sellers, while first-run movies were air-dropped to frontline soldiers and shown on the hanger decks of aircraft carriers. No American soldier could have been unaware of this enormous material superiority: at a time when Germany and Japan were struggling to keep aircraft assembly lines running, slightly damaged American aircraft were often junked and replaced by brand-new planes, while hundreds more deemed surplus to requirements were flown to 'boneyards' on remote Pacific islands and bulldozed into pits.[3]

The scope of American military abundance was underscored by the development of nuclear weapons. Begun in 1942, the two-billion dollar Manhattan Project required not only the work of thousands of scientists but also the mobilization of two massive industrial efforts, one in Tennessee producing material for the uranium option (the bomb dropped on Hiroshima) and one in Washington supporting the plutonium option (the Nagasaki bomb). In contrast, while Germany conducted a modest nuclear research program, Berlin entirely lacked the industrial resources to produce a useable weapon. For American leaders, the moral obstacles to attacking civilian populations had already been overcome, tentatively in Europe and then with enthusiasm in Japan, but some top commanders still opposed the atomic bombing of Japanese cities on the grounds that Tokyo had already been brought to its knees by conventional bombing and naval blockade. After the atomic bombs were dropped, however, it was clear that nuclear weapons gave the United States access to entirely new levels of military capacity based on scientific secrets that Washington fondly believed would be theirs alone for the foreseeable future.

Global Networks of Predominance and Connectivity

In addition to its enormous firepower on land, sea, and in the air, by the end of the war the American military enjoyed unprecedented global reach. In September 1945, Washington controlled a worldwide network of around two thousand bases and 30,000 other military facilities that included

---

[2]Lizzie Collingham, "Food as Global Commodity and Local Scarcity," in Michael Geyer and Adam Tooze (eds.), *The Cambridge History of the Second World War*, Vol. III (New York: Cambridge University Press, 2015), 163.
[3]Ian W. Toll, *Twilight of the Gods: War in the Western Pacific, 1944–1945* (New York: W. W. Norton, 2020), 417.

hotels, ski resorts, and golf courses as well as the more obviously useful ports and airfields, radar and communications stations, supply dumps, barracks, and repair shops. The Joint Chiefs of Staff had begun planning for a worldwide network of postwar bases in November 1943, and while many facilities were deactivated in 1945, others remained in service or were mothballed for future use. Reflecting the sea - and airpower-centric war waged by the United States, many of these bases were deigned to project American power into the heartlands of Eurasia while exercising control of the world's waterways from the Atlantic, Pacific, and Indian oceans to the Mediterranean and—increasingly—the Artic seas. In the Pacific, military leaders refused to cede territory conquered during the war, leading to the construction of an array of bases on American-ruled Guam and Hawai'i, on occupied Okinawa, and in the Philippines, granted formal independence under US protection in 1946. In the islands of western Pacific—including the Mariana and Marshall islands, Micronesia, and Palau—the United Nations-sponsored Trust Territory of the Pacific Islands disguised what was in effect American colonial rule, made manifest in the construction of yet more bases, airfields, and nuclear test sites.

This far-flung web of military bases was embedded in new networks of global connectivity, developed during the war to move soldiers and supplies to distant war fronts and to ship Lend-Lease supplies to America's allies. These wartime transportation routes underpinned America's postwar military predominance while simultaneously sketching out the trade routes of a globalizing economy. This relationship between wartime necessity and postwar power began to take shape in summer 1940—well before Washington entered the war—when President Roosevelt asked Pan American Airlines president Juan Trippe to establish an air route connecting the United States to the Middle East and India via airfields in the Caribbean, Brazil and British - and French-ruled Africa. Named after the city where the aircraft flying it made landfall in the British-ruled Gold Coast (Ghana), the Takoradi Route carried critical supplies to British-Imperial forces in Egypt. As British officials feared, these new airfields and the experience of operating them also laid the basis for America's postwar domination of civil aviation. Other new air routes followed, some crossing the North Atlantic via Greenland, Iceland, and the Azores, and others reaching out across the Pacific using island-hopping routes that made extended transoceanic navigation commonplace.

New sea routes worked by American-built Liberty ships complemented these aerial highways. Convoy routes across the North Atlantic carried critical food, fuel, and military matériel to Britain, while other sealanes carried Lend-Lease supplied to the Soviet Union via the Arctic Sea, the Persian Gulf, and across the Pacific. American ships also kept US forces worldwide supplied with troops, fuel, and munitions, and at times American-run ports in Naples and Marseilles were reckoned the busiest in the world as they hustled to supply Allied armies fighting in Europe. As they learned how to unload vehicles, weapons, and stores across open beaches and through makeshift anchorages, American engineers developed the techniques of palletization, containerization, and roll-on/roll-off loading that later facilitated a rapid expansion in the scale and the pace of postwar commercial shipping. Again, wartime experience and postwar predominance were intimately linked.

These new aerial and maritime highways conveyed a powerful impression of American modernity and technical proficiency as they announced the physical infrastructure of a coming world order. Many soldiers had firsthand experience of these operations. In Europe, the US army assigned nearly 80 percent of its soldiers to the movement and distribution of matériel and other non-combat duties, while the Navy and Air Force had even longer logistical tails.[4] Military logistics transformed environments on a gigantic scale as ports were either built from scratch—like Ulithi Atoll—or else massively expanded; roads and railroads were driven through deserts, jungles, and across mountain ranges; and entire Pacific islands were turned into airfields, their runways made from hard-packed coral. Much of the work was carried out by US military engineers using powerful modern equipment, but their mechanized efforts were complemented by the physical toil of tens of thousands of colonized laborers—universally referred to as 'natives'—who moved dirt, broke rocks, and dug ditches by hand.[5] American engineers watched and learned from European colonial administrators, copying their methods of 'handling' local workers and often absorbing their racist attitudes toward people they held to be lazy, untrustworthy, and backward.

Prewar trade in Asia, Africa, and the Middle East had been largely conducted by European trading companies with decades of experience and extensive networks of local contacts, but as these connections were ruptured by war, Americans established new arrangements at breakneck speed. The physical movement and distribution of Lend-Lease supplies played a major role in this process, plugging American abundance into local ports, warehouses, and transportation systems. American officers worked through the North African Economic Board and the Middle East Supply Centre (MESC) to keep native populations pacified by ensuring regular supplies of food, fuel, and trade goods. Run by a Cairo-based bureaucracy, MESC also pursued a developmental agenda that aimed at reducing the demand for imported goods by promoting local industry and agricultural modernization. This work connected American officers and engineers to local officials and businessmen from Iran and Iraq to Egypt and the Levant. By 1944, American exporters were keen to break free from these bureaucratic wartime organizations while continuing to build on the invaluable networks

---

[4]John J. McGrath, "The Other End of the Spear: The Tooth-to-Tail Ratio (T3R) in Modern Military Operations," Occasional Paper 23, The Long War Series (Fort Leavenworth, KS: Combat Studies Institute Press, 2007), 105.
[5]Andrew Friedman, "US Empire, World War 2 and the Racialising of Labour," *Race & Class*, Vol. 58, No. 4 (2017), 27.

of contacts they had developed, and a top-level trade mission headed by diplomat and lawyer William Culbertson recommended moving quickly toward unregulated free trade throughout the Mediterranean and the Middle East.

Shaping the Postwar World: Regimes of Military Government

The scope of Washington's victory was also evident in the armed occupations and American-led military governments that oversaw the transition from war to postwar in Italy, Germany, and Japan. The US military had long experience of military governance, which had been central to its mission of Native dispossession and westward expansion in North America and to the exercise of American foreign policy in the Philippines, the Caribbean, and Central America in the early twentieth century. Nevertheless, the task of occupying, rebuilding, and politically reorganizing large capitalist nation-states was significantly more complex, and the Army prepared for it by opening a School of Military Government at the University of Virginia in May 1942. The school trained the thousands of civil affairs officers who administered military government at local, regional, and national levels, imbuing them with the idea that their mission was benevolent, progressive, and clearly differentiated from models of European and Japanese imperialism and colonialism. However, while the United States avoided direct territorial annexation—except in Micronesia—military governance necessarily involved the radical denial of national sovereignty and the assertion of Washington's right to impose such political, legal, and economic structures as it saw fit. The precise form of American predominance was different in each of the Axis countries: in Italy, Washington waged a protracted campaign to supplant Britain as the leading Allied power; in Germany, American resources quickly ensured Washington's dominance within the three western zones occupied by US, British, and French forces; while in Japan General MacArthur was the proconsular head of what was, with the exception of a modest British Commonwealth Occupation Force, an all-American occupation. In all three states American officials worked to establish governments, administrative and judicial bureaucracies, and economic systems conducive to their emerging hegemony.

Military occupations offer none of the compelling battle narratives central to most military history, a fact that helps to explain their almost complete omission from most histories of the Second World War. Nevertheless, the experience of military government, reflected in press coverage and in cultural productions like John Hersey's best-selling novel and 1945 movie *Bell for Adano*, helped to shape contemporary American perceptions of the Second World War as a 'good war' fought for the benefit of humanity. In this light, American-led military occupations were foundational not only to the practical construction of a new world order but also to the liberal internationalism that gave it ideological coherence. Occupation also framed the experience of millions of soldiers, whether assigned directly to military governance or posted to bases in occupied territory, and many validated their military activity in similarly benevolent terms. Their bases and camps became points of contact and exchange, joining military personnel to local people in numerous and complex ways, ranging from prostitution to the hiring of local workers to perform on-base cleaning and construction. Supply bases—like the sprawling complex of warehouses around Naples—kept local black markets functioning by funneling guns, cigarettes, food, and clothing to underworld gangs. Meanwhile, encouraged by officials who produced handy pocket-sized guidebooks, many soldiers spent time sightseeing, layering the hierarchical assumptions of the tourist gaze onto the explicit power relations embedded in military occupation. Much of this, along with information about art shows, opera performances and movie screenings, the location of officers' clubs and facilities for enlisted men, and details of local religious services, was printed in the army newspaper *Stars and Stripes*, local editions of which—in yet another show of abundance—were published in every major theater of operations.

The United States and the World War

For much of the long world war that began with Japan's invasion of Manchuria in 1931, the United States was not a combatant, and by the time Tokyo's attack on Pearl Harbor brought it into the war in December 1941 several key military turning points had already passed. By 1940, a volatile coalition of Chiang Kai-shek's governing Guomindang (Nationalist Party) and Mao Zedong's Communist Party had fought the Japanese invasion of China to a halt, leaving Tokyo in control of many of the major cities but with only a marginal grip on the countryside. Meanwhile, American aid and a worldwide imperial mobilization enabled Britain to fight on after the fall of France in June 1940 and to block Italian expansionism in Egypt and the Horn of Africa. After the German invasion of the Soviet Union in June 1941, the Red Army bore the brunt of the land combat against Germany for the remainder of the war, fighting first for survival and then, with increasing mastery of mobile warfare, for victory. Axis assaults on China and the Soviet Union were thus blunted *before* the large-scale military engagement of the United States. Moreover, the savagery of the fighting, the genocidal violence that accompanied it, and the waves famine and disease that it generated, ensured that these Eurasian bloodlands were the site of the bulk of the war's death and destruction. The Soviet Union alone mourned twenty-seven million deaths, a combined civilian and military casualty list that exceeded that of the United States sixty-five times over.[6]

These facts challenge many commonplace ideas about the character of the Second World War. They suggest that, far from being a single clearly defined thing with self-evident start and end points, the Second World War is best understood as an overlapping series of large regional wars that remained essentially separate until given a degree of global coherence by America's entry into the struggles in both eastern and western Eurasia in December 1941. Only the United States had the military-industrial capacity and the political will to fight a genuinely worldwide war for global predominance. Despite Nazi bluster, *global* predominance—as opposed to the creation of a European empire from the Atlantic to the Urals—was never on Berlin's practical agenda, while Italy and Japan envisioned themselves as major regional powers leading colonial-autarkic blocs in the Mediterranean/North Africa and China/Southeast Asia. The fact that the United States joined large regional wars in which enemy land forces had already been contained—or, as in the December 1941 Battles of Moscow, were at that moment being contained—profoundly shaped the war it fought. Washington was able to utilize its enormous productive capacity to fight a machine-heavy 'air-sea war' to defeat Japanese maritime expansionism in the Pacific, dominate global sea - and airspace, and bring Germany and Japan to their knees through devastating bombing campaigns. At the same time, the United States supplied much of the matériel necessary to sustain the sprawling ground wars in the USSR and—to a lesser extent, given transportation difficulties—in China.[7] Only in the closing stages of the war would Washington deploy substantial ground forces in Europe, and it avoided the wartime commitment of American land armies to East Asia entirely.

Planning for Hegemony

The air-sea war, with its necessary ground-based components and its supply of war matériel to key allies, was the military-strategic form taken by Washington's bid for global hegemony during the Second World War. The military campaigns that constituted this war and the vast logistical operations that supported them were orchestrated by a small army of military planners working for the new (and informally constituted) Joint Chiefs of Staff and for the combined structures of the Anglo-American alliance. The sustained application of military force that they orchestrated was the spearhead of a broader, more complex, and often more nebulous growth of

---

[6]See Norman S. Naimark, *Stalin and the Fate of Europe: The Postwar Struggle for Sovereignty* (Cambridge, MA: Harvard University Press, 2019), 5.
[7]Phillips Payson O'Brien, *How the War Was Won* (Cambridge: Cambridge University Press, 2015), esp. 1–16, 479–88.

American power. This expansion unfolded across interlocking spheres of economic, political, diplomatic, cultural, and ideological affairs that were themselves constituted by the long preparatory development of American agricultural, industrial, and financial capitalism. From this grand strategic viewpoint, the establishment of global predominance was not something that could be scripted—or planned—beforehand: it was too complex, took place over too long a time, and was too dependent on responding to the actions of others and to the unpredictable outcomes of military conflict. British historian Sir John Seeley had these considerations in mind in 1883 when he famously suggested that the British Empire had been "conquered [...] in a fit of absence of mind."[8]

Seely's witticism captures something of the chaotic and unplanned expansion of Britain's empire, but it does not tell the whole story. Regional or global hegemony is necessarily underpinned by the long-term and largely unplanned development of economic forces, but at the level of politics and military affairs imperial systems are constructed by the conscious actions of human beings. The formulation of grand strategy, which demands a politico-military capacity to act "beyond the demands of the present," is thus located in the *interplay* between large impersonal historical forces and conscious human action.[9] President Franklin D. Roosevelt embraced this dialectical relationship with gusto, managing minute details of wartime leadership while keeping the goal of global predominance—"Americanism," as historian Warren Kimball describes it—firmly in view.[10] As journalist and presidential confidant Anne O'Hare McCormick noted, the key to Roosevelt's policies lay in his ability to "ride the currents of time in the direction in which they are going."[11]

During the war, Roosevelt positioned himself at the center of webs of formal, semi-formal, and informal agencies, military planning bodies, State Department committees, think-tanks, and informed individuals, whose blurry jurisdictions often overlapped and who all recognized the president himself as the ultimate arbiter of policy. Key decisions, as top diplomat and presidential representative in the Mediterranean Robert Murphy noted, always reflected the "president's personal policy."[12] Beyond simply reflecting Roosevelt's style of leadership, these methods stemmed from the fact that due to its late emergence as a world power, the central state apparatus of the

---

[8]Sir J. R. Seeley, *Expansion of England* (Boston: Little, Brown, 1905 (1883)), available via Hathi Trust, 10.
[9]Williamson Murray, "Thoughts on Grand Strategy," in Williamson Murray, Richard Hat Sinnreich and James Lacy (eds.), *The Shaping of Grand Strategy: Policy, Diplomacy, and War* (Cambridge: Cambridge University Press, 2011), 2.
[10]Warren F. Kimball, *The Juggler: Franklin Roosevelt as Wartime Statesman* (Princeton: Princeton University Press, 1991), ch. IX, "This Persistent Evangel of Americanism," 185–200.
[11]Anne O'Hare McCormick, "At 60 He Is Still a Happy Warrior," *New York Times*, January 25, 1942, SM3.
[12]Robert Murphy, *Diplomat Among Warriors* (New York: Doubleday, 1964), 68.

United States lacked the formal bodies within which broad grand strategic leadership might have taken place. At the same time, Roosevelt's free-flowing decision-making process was well suited to working through the broad range of challenges and opportunities that presented themselves in the early 1940s. As historian Steven Wertheim shows, the goal of establishing American global hegemony by military means only came into sharp focus for foreign policy elites in the months following the fall of France in June 1940. Faced with the imminent danger of a German-dominated Europe—a development that would have posed long-term economic and military challenges for the United States—senior figures in the Roosevelt administration, participants in prestigious academic seminars and think tanks like the Council on Foreign Relations, and influential commentators like Walter Lippmann, pivoted away from a focus on hemispheric predominance in the Americas and towards the establishment of global hegemony.

Initially, many of these foreign policy elites imagined postwar predominance being structured through some form of American-British condominium, and the Anglo-American alliance remained central to Washington's strategic planning throughout the war. Nevertheless, within this transatlantic framework the power relationship between the two states shifted slowly but inexorably in favor of the United States. This shift reflected an accelerating hegemonic transition from a British-led world order to a new American-led system assembled during the course of the fighting, and Washington pursued this goal with measured determination rooted in its rapidly expanding economic and military power. Economic largesse and the establishment—against London's wishes—of a liberal government in June 1944 secured American predominance within the Allied occupation of Italy, while Washington clearly called the shots in the 1944 invasions of France. Meanwhile, the Pacific had always been an American-run theater of operations, and by 1944 even the Australian troops who had initially played a critical role in the fighting in New Guinea had been largely sidelined. British-Imperial forces did lead the reconquest of the former British colony of Burma, but after deciding against opening an American-led land campaign in China, Washington essentially viewed this as a sideshow.

America's growing military predominance within the Atlantic alliance reflected broader shifts in the relationship between the two countries. From the desperate months in the summer of 1940 when London turned to the United States following the fall of France, Washington had placed Britain on rations, supplying an increasing proportion of its military needs along with food, fuel, and finance while exercising an ever-stronger voice in the conduct of the war. Despite Roosevelt's homey imagery of Lend-Lease as a means of offering unconditional help for a neighbor in need, the vast quantity of material flowing across the Atlantic necessarily changed the political relationship between the two states. Early signs of this shift came in September 1940 when the 'destroyers for bases' agreement saw Washington exchanging fifty aging warships for long-term leases on key

British military bases in the Caribbean and Newfoundland. Subsequent Lend-Lease transfers were less overtly transactional, but the reduction of Britain to junior partner status was increasingly evident. British leaders were not unaware of the disparity between the two states—indeed, the rise of American power had also been a cause for concern during the First World War—but they believed that their political sophistication and long experience of global hegemony would enable them to manage their powerful but naive ally. The shock felt by Winston Churchill and other British leaders as these arrogant assumptions were shattered was muffled by the necessity of maintaining the wartime alliance, but it was both real and deep.

Washington's capacity to fight the kind of war that it wanted to fight also depended on its marriage of convenience with the Soviet Union. After the German invasion in June 1941, most American leaders assumed that the Soviets would collapse as quickly as France had done, or—better still, some thought—that the two 'totalitarian' states would grind each other into oblivion. Roosevelt, however, grasped the grand strategic significance of a Eurasian ally capable of carrying the bulk of the ground war against Germany, and he moved quickly to extend Lend-Lease to the USSR. This massive supply effort did not contribute directly to the survival of the Soviet Union—that was secured at the Battle of Moscow in 1941/1942 and at Stalingrad the following winter—but it did smooth the road to final victory. The staggering scale of the bloodletting on the Soviet front effectively broke the back of the German military and greatly reduced the burden of ground combat borne by the Allies in Western Europe from summer 1943. As this strategic prospect of sub-contracting most ground combat to the USSR come into focus in late 1942, American planners scaled back their own initial plans for a massive 213-division land army in favor of a more modest ninety-division force.[13]

America's Wartime Economy

The '90-division gamble' enabled the United States to fight a war for global predominance while simultaneously releasing millions of potential soldiers for war work. Their labor, along with that of the millions of other workers—including African American migrants from the rural South and six million Black and Caucasian women—who flooded into the war plants after long years of high unemployment enabled the massive expansion of the wartime economy while laying the basis for capitalism's long postwar boom. War production began well before the United States' formal entry into the war. Passed by Congress after the German conquest of France, the

---

[13]Maurice Matloff, "The 90-Division Gamble," in *Command Decisions* (Washington, DC: U.S. Army Center of Military History, 1990), 365–6, 374.

Two-Ocean Navy (or Vinson-Walsh) Act began a sustained drive to expand US military capacity by doubling US naval strength in order to maintain powerful fleets in both the Atlantic and Pacific oceans. This projected expansion would soon be surpassed by actual wartime production, and by 1945 Vinson-Walsh's goal of building eighteen new aircraft carriers had been exceeded five-fold.

The sheer magnitude of America's wartime arms output is astonishing: by 1945 US factories and shipyards had churned out 5,777 merchant ships, 1,556 warships, nearly 300,000 aircraft, over 88,000 tanks, and 6.5 million rifles.[14] American arms production surpassed Britain's by summer 1942, and by 1944 it exceeded it six-fold. By this time, over 60 percent of *all* allied arms production was pouring out of American plants, and while the Red Army halted the German invasion without American aid, it rolled westwards into Germany riding in Jeeps and Studebaker trucks while eating spam and communicating with American-made radios. American engineers applied the assembly line production techniques pioneered by the Ford Motor Company to other branches of industry, including the production of giant four-engine bomber aircraft. In a pre-computer age, the technical difficulties were enormous, prompting critics of Ford's new B-24 bomber plant at Willow Run, Michigan, to ask will it run? Once the teething troubles were ironed out, however, 'The Run' was cranking out a finished bomber every hour. Shipbuilding was similarly transformed, with the Kaiser Corporation's giant Richmond, California shipyard pioneering the technique of assembling vessels from pre-built modules. By 1943, the Richmond yard was taking just forty-one days to build a Liberty ship from keel-laying to splash, and it was working on several ships simultaneously.

It is hard to grasp the sheer physical scale of wartime production. From the airplane factories of Los Angeles and Seattle to the tank and truck works of Detroit, massive new assembly plants and the dense networks of sub-contractors that kept them supplied with parts transformed entire regions of the country. New airplane assembly plants sprang from green fields from New Orleans, Louisiana to Wichita, Kansas and Marietta, Georgia, accelerating the industrialization and urbanization of the South. Shipyards studded the coastline from the Pascagoula River in Mississippi to the Kennebec in Maine and from San Diego, California to Tacoma, Washington, while 'cornfield shipyards' around the Great Lakes turned out landing craft and other small vessels. Textile and shoe factories expanded to meet the demand for uniforms, boots, and backpacks, while electronics plants scrambled to fill military orders for everything from light bulbs and radar sets to proximity fuses and aircraft wiring harnesses. On top of all

---

[14] On war production, see David M. Kennedy, *The American People in World War II* (Oxford: Oxford University Press, 1999), esp. 230.

FIGURE 1.2 *Women welders at the Ingalls shipyard in Pascagoula, Mississippi, 1943. (Photo: Spencer Beebe, Department of Labor, Image 86-WWT-85-35.)*

this, the development of nuclear weapons required the construction of giant reactors and production facilities at Hanaford, Washington and at the Clinton Engineering Works in rural east Tennessee, where 82,000 workers lived in the newly built—and racially segregated—town of Oak Ridge.

Wartime production accelerated the transformation of rural America, promoting the concentration of farmland into ever-larger spreads that relied on tractors, chemical fertilizers, and insecticides to sustain high crop yields. Meat and produce flowed into massive processing plants, where industrial-scale canning, freezing, and dehydration preserved it for shipment around the world. These developments necessitated the development of extensive supply chains, some snaking across the United States—oilfields in Texas and Oklahoma were producing flat-out—while others connected American factories to raw materials imported from Africa and Latin America. Bauxite (alumina ore) was mined in the British colonies of Jamaica and Guyana and in Dutch-ruled Surinam, shipped to Quebec, where it was smelted using massive inputs of hydroelectric power, and then moved by train into the United States for use in aircraft production. As Jeffrey Fear notes, wartime demand for aluminum fundamentally "rerouted trade connections between the Caribbean, Canada, and the United States."[15] It also rerouted politics: after the German occupation of Holland in 1940, Surinam was occupied by US troops, while the giant aluminum company Alcan opened a bauxite trading post inside a newly acquired American military base in Jamaica.

America's wartime economy and the mechanized military machine it served were both heavily dependent on oil, and US control of much of the world's reserves quickly became critical both to its own war effort and to its postwar predominance. In 1940, American domestic production still accounted for over two-thirds of world output, and major American oil corporations—which along with Anglo-Iranian (later British Petroleum) and Royal Dutch Shell comprised the Seven Sisters—operated important concessions in Venezuela and Saudi Arabia. During the war, American planners recognized that the Middle East was going to become the long-term center of world oil production, and with Washington's backing US oil companies began a determined campaign to secure a lock on the region's reserves. American corporations often resented government intervention in their business affairs, but they were happy to benefit from Washington's close wartime ties to the Saudi and Iranian monarchies. By 1945 they were poised to dominate not only domestic and Latin American production but also the Middle Eastern output critical to rebuilding war-damaged economies in Europe and Japan. At the same time, and driven by hopes that new underwater drilling techniques would give access to vast new oil fields in the Gulf of Mexico, Washington unilaterally annexed nearly a million square miles of "submerged lands" on the continental shelf.[16] With this stunning submarine land grab, an area four times the size of Texas became sovereign US territory.

Boosted by long hours of overtime, workers' incomes rose during the war. For the first time in their lives, many women workers secured a degree of economic self-sufficiency that enabled a broader challenge to perceptions of their second-class status. Significant though they were, however, advances in working-class living standards were far outstripped by expanding corporate revenues as industrialists and financiers raked in enormous profits. Military managers incentivized wartime production by issuing lucrative cost-plus contracts that guaranteed high profits. Factories idled during the Depression were brought back into production, and Washington funded new plant and machinery that private companies then ran on a 'government owned, contractor operated' basis. The government financed two-thirds of all new plant built during the war, and it owned over

---

[15] Jeffrey Fear, "War of the Factories," in Michael Geyer and Adam Tooze (eds.), *The Cambridge History of the Second World War*, Vol. III (New York: Cambridge University Press, 2015), 119.
[16] Daniel Margolies, "Jurisdiction in Offshore Submerged Lands and the Significance of the Truman Proclamation in Postwar U.S. Foreign Policy," *Diplomatic History*, Vol. 44, No. 3 (2020), 447.

25 percent of all capital assets in manufacturing. After the fighting was over, $17 billion worth of buildings and equipment was sold off to private industry at bargain-basement prices.

At the beginning of the war, the Navy, Army, and Army Air Force all raced to place contracts with individual suppliers, and market competition for scarce resources constantly threatened to disrupt broader priorities and plans. A range of government agencies battled to establish some semblance of centralized control, finally leading to the establishment of the Office of War Mobilization in May 1943. By this time, however, the enormously profitable channels through which military orders were placed and filled were already well established, and efforts at planning relied primarily on rationing access to scarce raw materials. Despite these limitations, state intervention worked to normalize the networks of intimate interconnection between government, the military, and private industry that would later be referred to as the military-industrial complex. Top-level corporate executives flocked to Washington, staffing government planning agencies and exercising considerable control over the procurement policies of the military departments. The ubiquitous presence of bankers, financiers, corporate directors, and high-powered lawyers blurred the lines between government and business, so that former president of General Motors William Knudsen could be made an 'instant general' and given oversight of Army procurement.[17] Eased by a relaxation of anti-trust laws and regulations, wartime production accelerated the concentration of capital, and amid a wave of mergers over 70 percent of all war contracts went to 100 big companies, with over one-third going to just ten.[18] Buttressed by advancing monopolization and eased by a small army of lobbyists, these deep interconnections became emblematic of postwar American capitalism as—in contrast to the rapid demobilization that had followed earlier wars—high levels of defense spending continued during the long postwar economic upswing.

The massive expansion of Washington's military spending drove ballooning levels of national debt, which by 1945 had climbed to over $250 billion, or 112 percent of annual gross national product.[19] The debt was funded primarily through bonds purchased by big investors and finance houses, allowing bankers and speculators to join the wartime profits bonanza: commercial banks alone increased their holdings of Treasury Bonds from $1 billion in 1941 to $24 billion in 1945. At the same time, fully 45 percent of government spending was paid for directly out of tax income: the top rate of personal income tax was raised to 94 percent (it is 37 percent today!) and—more importantly for most people—lower personal

---

[17]Joe R. Feagin and Kelly Riddell, "The State, Capitalism, and World War II: The U.S. Case," *Armed Forces and Society*, Vol. 17, No. 1 (Fall 1990), 69.
[18]Ibid., 72.
[19]Kennedy, *The American People in World War II*, 201.

exemptions brought millions of middle-class Americans onto the tax rolls for the first time since income tax was first levied in 1913. By the end of the war, nearly one-third of Americans were paying income tax deducted at source by their employers, and although billed as a temporary wartime measure, that number continued to rise after 1945, fundamentally changing the relationship between millions of middle-class individuals and the state.

Wartime production also tied many manual workers into a new relationship with government, not as individuals but as members of their trade unions. In exchange for the participation of union leaders in various national planning boards, along with an important War Labor Board ruling that workers hired into a union shop would be automatically enrolled in the union, labor officials pledged that there would be no strikes for the duration of the war. The labor board's 'maintenance-of-membership' rule helped to boost union membership from ten to fifteen million during the war, but while no-strike pledges kept war production moving and allowed union leaders to appear as patriotic statesmen, they had surrendered labor's most effective weapon. Indeed, in many large plants, the unions effectively took responsibility for labor discipline. The long-term consequences of this devil's bargain were not immediately obvious, but the integration of union leaders into management at both national and company levels helped to transform American trade unions from the militant and socially conscious organizations forged in the great labor battles of the 1930s into associations narrowly focused on the wages and conditions of their own members. This shift did not go unchallenged, with half a million members of the United Mine Workers of America striking successfully for higher pay in 1943 and millions more joining a great wave of strikes in 1946, but—as we will discuss in Chapter Eight—it did set the framework for the integration of labor into the long postwar expansion of American capitalism.

The United States Reorganizes the World Economy

Many Americans feared that the end of wartime production would lead to the return of high unemployment. Instead, after a short wave of layoffs as factories converted to the production of consumer goods, the wartime economy—which had seen gross domestic product double in just four years—morphed into a long postwar boom. This protracted period of capitalist expansion shaped both the United States and the world for the next quarter century. The boom was fueled in part by pent-up domestic demand for consumer goods as workers finally got to spend saved-up wartime earnings and the financial reward for their military service offered by the 1944 Servicemen's Readjustment Act, commonly known as the GI Bill. More fundamentally, the postwar boom was constituted by the United States' new place in the world as American investment, capital goods, and consumer products flowed out to markets around the globe. Today, it takes a leap of imagination to envisage the United States as the productive heart of world capitalism, but after 1945 American factories and farms flooded domestic and world markets with vast quantities of manufactured goods from machine tools, aircraft, and automobiles, to radios and washing machines, along with millions of tons of wheat, corn, pork, and beef. Until its gradual exhaustion in the late 1960s and early 1970s, this productive dynamism—both a key constituent element and a product of American global predominance—underpinned the entire postwar order.

In economics, as in military affairs, the fundamental structures of postwar predominance were established during the war. In addition to supplying food and war matériel to Britain, China, and the Soviet Union, over thirty other countries were declared eligible for wartime aid, and Lend-Lease supplies poured into places from Iran and Saudi Arabia to Ethiopia, Cuba, and Yugoslavia. As they organized the delivery of aid, American planners, administrators, and shippers established new networks of connectivity, gaining knowledge of local markets and distribution networks, and building relationships with officials and businessmen. These experiences and the knowledge they generated proved critical when the wartime agencies like the Middle East Supply Centre were wrapped up in favor of a return to free trade. Since the long years of Britain's global predominance in the nineteenth century, free trade—with its promise of unrestricted access to markets worldwide—had been the favored trade policy of the world's leading economic power. Now, as American economic power expanded, Washington moved beyond its own Depression-era protectionism and enthusiastically embraced free trade, enshrining it as the central principle of the new world economic order outlined at the United Nations Monetary and Financial Conference held in the New Hampshire resort of Bretton Woods in July 1944.

Meeting just weeks after the Allied landings in France and as American troops were invading the Marianas Islands, the Bretton Woods Conference highlighted the emergence of a new world order even as the fighting raged on. Over 700 delegates from 44 countries participated. Major delegations represented the Allied combatants including China and the Soviet Union, as well as the governments-in-exile of countries still under Axis occupation in Europe and the Philippines. Delegates came from countries across Central and South America, but Argentina, then facing Washington's hostility for its refusal to abandon its own claims to regional leadership, was not invited. Britain's 'White Dominions' (Australia, Canada, New Zealand, and South Africa) were present, as were representatives from British-ruled India, but with sub-Saharan Africa largely under European colonial rule, only Ethiopia and Liberia sent their own delegates. As nominally independent states, Egypt, Iran, Iraq, and Syria had their own delegates. Given the range of participants, the conference was bound to be a complex affair, marking both a key step in the hegemonic transition from Britain to the United States and an opportunity for delegates from the global south—and from Latin America in particular—to help shape a world order in which the industrialization and 'modernization' of their 'underdeveloped' economies was presented as a central concern.

Washington's insistence on worldwide free trade challenged long-standing British and French policies that privileged trade with their own colonies and dominions. France's resistance to the new order was weakened by the fact that it was still largely under German occupation at the time of the conference and had no officially recognized pro-allied government, but Washington had to beat down British opposition by threatening to withhold key loans for postwar reconstruction. Even so, while the letter of the Bretton Woods system demanded the removal of tariff barriers and the adoption fully convertible currencies, it took time to overcome the still-strong legacy of the British Empire. Britain's predominance within the sterling area—a loose bloc of former colonies and bilateral trading partners whose business was conducted in British pounds—continued into the early 1960s, while in the immediate postwar between 36 and 49 percent of world trade was still denominated in sterling.[20] Rather than immediately establishing worldwide free trade, Bretton Woods thus initiated a long American-led push toward open markets that led in 1947 to the ratification of the General Agreement on Tariffs and Trade and to a gradual worldwide reduction of protective tariffs.

This march toward lower tariffs and free trade was intertwined with the re-establishment of the fixed currency exchange rates held to be critical to restoring the market stability that had collapsed during the Great Depression. But there was an important modification. Under the old gold standard, national currencies had been directly convertible to gold at a fixed rate, but under the new Bretton Woods system the US dollar, backed by America's enormous gold reserves and convertible at the fixed rate of $35 an ounce, would serve as the main medium of world trade and the fixed point to which other currencies were pegged. This system was reinforced by the new International Monetary Fund (IMF), an international consortium designed to mitigate market pressures that might otherwise having forced countries to devalue their currencies by loaning them money. The catch was that IMF loans could be made conditional on recipients reforming their domestic economic practices, often by cutting expenditure on social programs. Since representation on the IMF board was proportional to contributions to the fund, the United States had a controlling voice here, too.

---

[20]Wm. Roger Louis and Ronald Robinson, "The Imperialism of Decolonization," *Journal of Imperial and Commonwealth History*, Vol. 22, No. 3 (1994), 463.

Not surprisingly, measures to establish the dollar as the world's principal currency did not sit well with London, and British economist John Maynard Keynes worked to fend them off by proposing instead that a new international bank issue its own currency, or bancor. Unfortunately for the British, Keynes's sophisticated arguments stood no chance against the raw economic might of the United States, and London was forced to agree to the American plan. Nevertheless, rather than present these new measures and institutions as simply another American victory, Washington carefully framed the new world financial system as one that would be mutually beneficial to all. This liberal internationalism was given shape by measures designed to promote industrialization and economic development in the colonies, semi-colonies, and former colonies of the global south, including the establishment of the International Bank for Reconstruction and Development (IBRD)—later the World Bank. Designed to loan money for "development" projects, the IBRD built on existing ties between the United States and several Latin American states, and it was crafted in discussion with them and with delegates from India and the Middle East.

The establishment of the IBRD and the work of the delegates from the colonial and semi-colonial world that helped to craft it were central to the Bretton Woods system as a whole. Looking forward, development projects and the ideologies of modernization within which they were framed helped to structure Washington's relationships with countries of the newly named Third World. Nevertheless, while formulated in collaboration with local elites, this was hardly disinterested philanthropy on the part of the United States. From the early 1940s, when planners and policymakers had begun to talk openly about Washington's coming global predominance, economists had been linking America's own postwar prosperity to the promotion of robust new markets for capital investment and for consumer goods in the global south. Writing in the influential journal *Foreign Affairs* in April 1942, economists Alvin Hansen and Charles Kindleberger argued that while "increases in the productivity of the Balkan peasant, of the Hindu and Moslem in India and of the Chinese might seem of remote interest to many Americans," they were in fact vital to the "economic and political security of the United States."[21] The conclusion was clear: American-funded measures to boost economic activity worldwide would simultaneously strengthen the domestic economy, yoking American self-interest to the development of the global south while wrapping it in an uplifting vision of disinterested benevolence. In fact, the need to fund the economic reconstruction of Europe delayed the roll-out of development projects, and the IBRD's first mission to the global south left for Colombia in 1949. Overall funding for development was always relatively modest, but the modernizing agenda embedded in the

---

[21] Alvin Hansen and Charles Kindleberger, "The Economic Tasks of the Postwar World," *Foreign Affairs*, Vol. 20, No. 3 (April 1942), 474.

Bretton Woods conference was central to the new American-led economic order, brightening its ideological aura while structuring new relationships of domination and dependence.

Washington Structures Its Political Hegemony

Washington's push to create a new world economic order was intertwined with a drive to project worldwide political leadership structured through the new United Nations Organization. America's new global predominance was thus embedded within an organization that, by proclaiming the equality of all nation-states and the sanctity of human rights, created a powerful impression of universality and justice. Like the Bretton Woods system, this new political order emerged directly from the war and was constituted by it. By the time the United States joined the world war in December 1941, its leaders had already come to see global predominance as the desired outcome of the struggle, but it was far from clear how this coming hegemony would be organized. The perceived failure of the League of Nations led planners, politicians, and public opinion formers to be deeply skeptical of any new world organization. Initially, many turned instead to some form of Anglo-American condominium, but as US power grew, schemes for global dyarchy gave way to detailed planning for a new world organization that would both facilitate and legitimize Washington's emerging predominance.

The United Nations Organization was founded in San Francisco in spring 1945, but it had begun to take shape in August 1941—four months before the United States entered the war—when British and American leaders met to adopt common war aims. The Atlantic Charter they approved rejected territorial aggrandizement, supported national self-determination, advocated worldwide free trade, and envisaged a world in which "all men in all lands may live out their lives in freedom from fear and want."[22] The charter's implicit anti-colonialism sat uneasily with the British, but they swallowed it in the hope of drawing the United States into the war. When the United States finally joined the war in December 1941, however, it quickly incorporated the principles of the Atlantic Charter into a new Declaration by the United Nations. Signed in Washington on January 1, 1942, by Britain, China, the Soviet Union, and the United States, the 'big four' were joined the following day by a further twenty-two states including eight European governments-in-exile, Britain's white dominions, the government of colonial India, and nine Central American and Caribbean nations. This process modeled in embryo the two-tier structure later embodied in the 1945 U.N. Charter, which elevated a Security Council invested with executive powers and composed of the big four (plus France) over the other united nations.

---

[22]The Atlantic Charter, http://avalon.law.yale.edu/wwii/atlantic.asp.

With Britain, China, and France expected to emerge from the war beholden to the United States, American leaders anticipated that this set-up would give them a decisive say in matters brought before the United Nations, along with veto power over proposals that they disagreed with, thus entrenching and formalizing their own world leadership.

By design, the United Nations alliance created in January 1942 was a hybrid creature, worldwide in scope and aspiration but without organizational structure or obligation. As such, the United Nations worked primarily to frame America's war effort, and hence that of the allied combatants more broadly, as a struggle to create a new and universally beneficial world order. The United Nations also provided the ideological home for another key American initiative, the United Nations Relief and Rehabilitation Administration (UNRRA). Pledged to relieve civilian suffering in war-damaged countries by providing of food, shelter, medicine, and other basic necessities, UNRRA was established in November 1943 by representatives of forty-four governments. In practice, it was largely funded, administered, and controlled by Washington, which appointed its director-general—former New York governor Herbert Lehman—and housed its central administration. Initially intended to bring relief to countries freed from Axis occupation, Washington quickly pushed aside British objections and began UNRRA operations in formerly-Axis Italy. Between 1944 and 1947 UNRRA distributed nearly $4 billion worth of relief supplies and—increasingly—the tools, farm equipment, locomotives, and machine tools necessary for economic reconstruction.

UNRRA housed competing visions of internationalism, many of which would later be reprised within the new United Nations Organization as Washington's plans for a rapid return to social and political stability tugged against the hopes of aid workers and activists who saw disinterested aid as a first step to a more just and egalitarian world. UNRRA's relations with countries of Eastern Europe were further complicated by deepening tensions between the United States and the Soviet Union. These conflicts quickly overwhelmed UNRRA, which was dissolved in 1947, but the Cold War tensions that underpinned them were already evident at the founding of the United Nations in San Francisco in 1945. At that conference, Washington and Moscow clashed over the veto power assigned to countries on the security council, over questions of membership and representation—Moscow wanted all fifteen Soviet republics to be seated—and over the extent, pace, and character of decolonization. These divisions were temporarily resolved through long rounds of bargaining without ever being really settled. Instead, housed from 1952 in a soaring temple to modernity on New York's East River, the United Nations functioned both as a vehicle for the exercise of American world leadership *and* as a forum for multilateral collaboration in fields of health, development, and human rights. Washington's great trompe l'oeil was that the later functions enwrapped the former, investing its hegemony with an aura of universality.

There has been a long-running debate among historians over whether or not this new American-led world order constituted an empire. The most accurate answer might be both "yes" and "no." The new order was grounded on American economic might, backed by a world-spanning military of unprecedented strength, and structured through American-led organizations. By facilitating free flows of capital and access to markets and raw materials worldwide, the new set-up functioned primarily to benefit wealthy American elites. By these key definitions, this was truly an imperial system. At the same time, however, and with the important exceptions of Puerto Rico, Guam, and—under the banner of UN trusteeship—the Trust Territory of the Pacific Islands, it was not an empire of direct colonial rule, a reality underscored by the formal decolonization of the Philippines in July 1946. The structural relationships of power underpinning America's new global predominance were thus masked by organizations and alliances that pictured all nation-states as equals and their relationships as acts of sovereign free will. This new 'rules-based international order' thus served the interests of American elites while cloaking their hegemony in universalized claims to the promotion of justice and freedom, in developmental agendas packaged as disinterested aid, and in real processes of negotiation and collaboration with local leaders and non-state actors.

By the end of the world war, this new liberal internationalism—described by one historian as "missionary internationalism"—commanded broad popular support within the United States, where over 70 percent of those questioned by pollsters in July 1944 backed a postwar "union of nations" and 84 percent favored the acquisition of overseas military bases.[23] This support for global engagement reflected a remarkable turnaround in public opinion: in 1937, only 26 percent of those questioned had wanted the United States to participate in a "new League of Nations." This new sense of national mission nested within broader constructions of 'Judeo-Christian' culture and recharged notions of the United States as a 'city on the hill' willing and able to offer guidance and inspiration to the rest of humanity. While isolationism may never have been the dominant outlook of American elites bound to the broader world by myriad ties of trade and diplomacy, in the depths of the Depression large numbers of ordinary Americans had not envisaged their country as the world hegemon in waiting. Many had drawn negative conclusions from American participation in the First World War, and they did not want to fight in a new world war. Their ranks embraced everyone from nationalists organized by the America First Committee to internationalist socialists, but their opposition to war—and hence to an American-led postwar order—was a fact of American political life.

---

[23]Jessica Reinisch, "Internationalism in Relief: The Birth (and Death) of UNRRA," *Past and Present*, Supplement 6, (2011), 269; Andrew Buchanan, "Domesticating Hegemony: Creating a Globalist Public, 1941–1943," *Diplomatic History*, Vol. 45, No. 2 (2021), 317.

These attitudes were shifting even before America entered the war, thanks in part to the vigorous campaign waged by a cohort of influential ideologues including publisher Henry Luce, vice-president Henry Wallace, Republican presidential candidate Wendell Willkie, and commentators like Walter Lippmann and Dorothy Thompson. Luce's famous February 1941 "American Century" editorial set the tone, arguing forcefully for an interconnected and mutually beneficial postwar world order led by the United States. These ideas, which explicitly challenged ordinary Americans to embrace world leadership, gained currency as the war economy boomed and allied military advances multiplied. This was a thoroughly bipartisan effort, reinforced by the vision of humanity united under American leadership presented by Willkie in his 1943 book *One World*. Over the course of the war, liberal internationalist or globalist ideas became woven deeply into the fabric of American daily life. They were presented in newspapers and on the radio, discussed in schools, churches, trade unions, women's organizations, and professional associations, and argued over in public lectures and talks. Globalist ideas were particularly well received within the 'middle-brow' middle classes, but they were also influential among industrial workers, who anticipated that new export markets would boost production at home, and among African Americans, who hoped that Washington's stated commitment to national self-determination would advance anti-colonial struggles around the world while strengthening opposition to racism within the United States. As the end of the war approached, support for the ideas of American globalism created a powerful domestic bloc in support of liberal internationalism and the exercise of global hegemony.

As liberal internationalism recast American nationalism in global terms, Washington presented its coming leadership to a world audience as a benevolent, anti-colonial, and thoroughly modern force for good. Widely circulated in the colonial world, many interpreted the Atlantic Charter as a pledge of support for decolonization. American diplomats noted that in the Middle East, the United States was the only major power whose reputation was not tarnished by previous imperial ventures, and they leveraged this perception to forge relationships with national elites from Egypt and Iran to India. In Morocco, for example, Sultan Mohammed V believed that President Roosevelt had personally pledged to support postwar decolonization at a formal dinner in January 1943.[24] The weighty presence of American matériel underpinned its ideological attraction. The volume and quality of American military equipment impressed friends and foes alike, modeling modernity, efficiency, and mass production. Lend-Lease aid made many who would never see an actual American soldier aware of American largesse, as food aid pouring into countries from Italy and Greece to China was carefully

---

[24] Brian T. Edwards, *Morocco Bound: Disorienting America's Maghreb, from Casablanca to the Marrakech Express* (Chapel Hill, NC: University of North Carolina Press, 2005), 26.

emblazoned with the letters U.S.A. Meanwhile, well-fed and confident-looking American soldiers functioned as vectors of connectivity and as often unwitting conduits of Americanism, with every candy bar handed out, every tourist photo snapped, and every bit of gear that found its way onto a black market betokening American power and prestige. These impressions, created during and immediately after the fighting, were soon reinforced by a flood of consumer goods and cultural products—from movies to music—that advanced what has been referred to as the "coca-colonization" of big chunks of the world.[25]

The Apex of American Power

As economic, military, political, and ideological strength combined to deliver victory in the Second World War, the fall of 1945 saw the United States at the apex of its worldwide power. Much still needed to be done to organize and consolidate its new hegemony, and powerful challenges to American predominance were already present in the Soviet Union, in China, and in a world gripped by anticolonial revolt. But American leaders, acting with the confidence, energy, and can-do spirit of a class that feels that its time has come were sure of their ability and capacity. They sat atop a massive and dynamic economy. They alone possessed nuclear weapons, and they expected their monopoly control of them to continue for many years. They commanded fleets of long-range bombers, a worldwide network of bases from which to fly them, and a navy dominant in all the seas and oceans of the world.

Since 1922, cities across the United States had celebrated Navy Day on October 27, Theodore Roosevelt's birthday. Following the Japanese surrender and the end of the war, the 1945 celebrations were particularly significant. A powerful US flotilla visited Shanghai, while in Hawai'i Admiral Chester Nimitz asserted that the worldwide projection of seapower was America's "birthright."[26] In New York, a seven-mile line of warships lay at anchor in the Hudson River as squadrons of navy aircraft flew overhead, reprising the spectacle in Tokyo Bay for the five million New Yorkers who turned out to watch. President Truman visited the Brooklyn Navy Yard to commission the aircraft carrier *Franklin D. Roosevelt*, soon to be flagship of the new Sixth Fleet in the Mediterranean. The President went on to address a huge crowd in Central Park, his words broadcast nationwide by radio and, in another harbinger of modernity, beamed to an east-coast audience by television.

---

[25] See Reinhold Wagnleitner, *Coca-Colonization and the Cold War: The Cultural Mission of the United States and Austria after the Second World War* (Chapel Hill, NC: University of North Carolina Press, 2007).
[26] "Navy Acclaimed around the World," *New York Times*, October 28, 1945, 1.

Earlier in the week, Truman had announced to a joint session of Congress that a "just and lasting peace" required that the United States "preserve our superiority on land and sea and in the air."[27] His public comments on that blustery fall day in New York were less blunt, but the message was the same: even after demobilization, America would remain the "greatest naval power on earth."[28] The United States, the president continued, would maintain sole control over nuclear weapons, holding them in "sacred trust" for the "people of the world." Truman linked this assertion of muscular military predominance to a promise of "full support" for the United Nations and for a series of "just and righteous" principles that included worldwide free trade and freedom of the seas, international economic collaboration, and close cooperation with "good neighbors" in Latin America. Turning to the colonial world, he proclaimed—somewhat ambiguously—that "all people who are prepared for self-determination" should be free to exercise that right. The United States, the president concluded, would not recognize territorial or governmental changes imposed by force. Nevertheless, while President Truman's comments amounted to a policy manifesto for America's coming "century," his Central Park audience was noticeably "tense" and "in no holiday mood."[29] For many, perhaps, the threat of new wars already hung heavy in the fall air.

For Further Reading

Andrew Buchanan, "Domesticating Hegemony: Creating a Globalist Public, 1941–1943," *Diplomatic History*, Vol. 45, No. 2 (2021).

Eric Helleiner, *Forgotten Foundations of Bretton Woods: International Development and the Making of the Postwar Order* (Ithaca, NY: Cornell University Press, 2014).

David M. Kennedy, *The American People in World War II* (Oxford: Oxford University Press, 1999).

Mark M. Mazower, *No Enchanted Palace: The End of Empire and the Ideological Origins of the United Nations* (Princeton: Princeton University Press, 2013).

Phillips Payson O'Brien, *How the War Was Won* (Cambridge: Cambridge University Press, 2015).

Jessica Reinisch, "Internationalism in Relief: The Birth (and Death) of UNRRA," *Past and Present*, Supplement 6 (2011).

---

[27]Harry S. Truman, quoted in John Fousek, *To Lead the Free World: American Nationalism and the Cultural Roots of the Cold War* (Chapel Hill: University of North Carolina Press, 2000), 54.

[28]"Text of the President's Navy Day Speech in Central Park on the Aims of U.S. Foreign Policy," *New York Times*, October 28, 1945, 33.

[29]Will Lissner, "Park Throng Tense Hearing President," *New York Times*, October 28, 1945, 32.

CHAPTER TWO

Hegemony Qualified: The Soviet Union, Eastern Europe, and the Deepening Cold War

Advancing toward Torgau in central Germany on April 25, 1945, a US Army patrol spotted Red Army troops on the far bank of the River Elbe. When the Soviet soldiers started shooting, Lt. William Robertson urged an escaped Red Army prisoner of war to call on his comrades to cease fire. After the shooting stopped, Robertson's patrol inched across a wrecked bridge to join the Soviets for a "frontline banquet" of vodka, sardines, and chocolate.[1] The party grew. Americans crossed the river by paddling racing sculls with their rifle butts, while Soviet soldiers—both men and women—danced and sang patriotic songs. Soon, the riverbanks were crowded with soldiers from both armies who chatted, compared weapons, swapped insignia, and drank endless toasts to "lasting peace": for these frontline soldiers, the war was finally over.

Despite the joyful partying, however, the allies' crushing victory over Germany brought no "lasting peace." Instead, challenges to America's emerging global hegemony unfolded on three broad fronts, and each one precipitated new conflicts. First, occupation by the Red Army secured Moscow's predominance in Eastern Europe, gradually but effectively adding this substantial region to the Soviet territory already removed from the capitalist market. Second, the fragile wartime alliance between the Guomindang and the Chinese Communist Party soon collapsed into civil war and popular revolution. And third, across South and Southeast Asia, the Middle East, and later sub-Saharan Africa, the new American-led order was

---

[1] Harold Denny, "First Link Made Wednesday by Four Americans on Patrol," *New York Times*, April 28, 1945, 1.

destabilized by the waves of anti-colonial revolt. Powerfully rooted though it was, Washington's postwar hegemony was thus qualified from its inception, and across much of the world the end of the war literally brought no peace.

The Wartime Devastation of Eastern Europe and Moscow's Plans for the Postwar

From the battle at Kursk in July 1943 to the fall of Berlin in May 1945, the Red Army advanced westward in a series of giant offensive bounds that drove German forces out of the USSR, Poland, and the Baltic states, toppled Berlin's allies in Romania, Bulgaria, Hungary, and Slovakia, and pushed deep into Germany to join hands with the Western Allies, crushing Nazi resistance and ending the war. To the south, Soviet forces linked up with Communist-led insurgencies that were already driving Axis armies out of Albania and Yugoslavia. The Red Army's conquests imposed a degree of unity on a region stretching from the Baltic to the Black Sea, establishing 'Eastern Europe' in the postwar imagination as a homogeneous site of Soviet domination. This image obscures a great deal of complexity. Postwar Eastern Europe was forged in a series of complex interactions between Moscow's plans for a frontier zone of loyal buffer states, sharpening tensions—soon termed the Cold War—between the USSR and its former allies, and specific national histories and circumstances. In particular, the advance of the Red Army prompted popular uprisings across much of the region, some led by nationalists and some by Communists, through which people sought to stamp their own imprint on the emerging postwar world.

These processes unfolded amidst death, destruction, and social and economic dislocation on an almost unimaginable scale. The Soviet Union alone suffered more than twenty-seven million deaths—some 14 percent of the prewar population—and more than 1,700 towns and 31,000 factories were ruined.[2] While American industrial output doubled during the war, Soviet production declined to just 80 percent of its prewar level.[3] Poland lost around six million people, a staggering 17 percent of the prewar population, while countries from the Baltic to the Balkans and the Black Sea were fought over—some many times—and were the site of occupations, purges, pogroms, and ferocious guerrilla wars. The widespread disruption of agriculture produced severe food shortages and famines that spilled into the immediate postwar years. These bloodlands of Eastern Europe—

---

[2]Vladimir O. Pechatnov, "The Soviet Union and the World," in Melvyn P. Leffler and Ode Arne Westad (eds.), *The Cambridge History of the Cold War* (Cambridge: Cambridge University Press, 2010), Vol. 1, 90.
[3]Charles S. Maier, "The World Economy and the Cold War in the Middle of the Twentieth Century," in Leffler and Westad, *Cambridge History of the Cold War*, Vol. 1, 55.

particularly Poland and Ukraine—had also been the epicenter of the Nazi's genocidal drive to exterminate the Jewish people in a brutal holocaust that claimed over six million lives.

Numbers quantify the devastation, but journalist Edward Crankshaw's account of a journey to Moscow in fall 1945 describes what it looked and felt like. For hundreds of miles, Crankshaw reported,

> every town was flat, every city. There were no barns. There was no machinery. There were no stations, no water-towers. There was not a solitary telegraph pole left standing in all that vast landscape, and broad swaths of forest had been cut down all along the line as protection against ambush by partisans. [...] In the unkempt fields, nobody but women, children and very old men could be seen—and these worked only with hand tools.[4]

This devastation shaped Moscow's plans for the postwar, which aimed above all at preventing any future invasion of the USSR. Soviet strategists hoped to translate military victory into long-term security by establishing a glacis, or defensive frontier, between the USSR and Western Europe constructed from a chain of pro-Soviet buffer states. In addition, Moscow planned to use resources taken as reparations from Germany and its Axis allies to boost the economic reconstruction of the USSR. Naïve though it now seems, Moscow hoped to achieve these goals within the framework of a continuation of the wartime Grand Alliance with Britain and the United States. Soviet leaders believed that the critical role of the USSR in the defeat of Germany had won them the moral authority and mutual respect upon which ongoing postwar collaboration could be based, and they assumed that their willingness to respect American-British predominance in Western Europe and their active opposition to popular insurgency there would ensure reciprocal recognition for their hegemony in the east. At no time did Soviet leaders desire or promote revolutionary upheavals either in Europe; on the contrary, Moscow feared the democratizing energy of popular insurgency quite as much as did Washington.

The Russian Revolution and the Rise of Stalinism

It is useful here to step back and look at how the history of the USSR shaped the outlook of its leaders at the end of the war. After Lenin's death in 1924, a fierce struggle had broken out in the leadership of the Soviet Communist Party (CPSU). Faced with the post-First World War stabilization of world

---

[4]Edward Crankshaw, quoted in Ernest Mandel, *The Meaning of the Second World War* (London: Verso, 1986), 162.

capitalism and the economic and social dislocation of the Russian Civil War (1917–23), a faction of the CPSU led by Joseph Stalin and based largely on party bureaucrats and administrators, rejected the revolutionary internationalism of the 1917 Russian Revolution. Instead of promoting revolution worldwide, Stalin instead pledged to build 'socialism in one country' by driving rapid industrialization and the organization of large-scale collective farming. By the end of the 1920s, Stalin's faction had won the fight, and it consolidated its position by establishing a police state organized to crush all opposition, overturning the participatory soviet— or council—democracy of the early revolution in the process. During the 1930s, literally hundreds of thousands of Old Bolsheviks and others whose loyalty to the regime was questioned by those in power were killed, imprisoned in forced labor camps known as Gulags, or cowed into silence by bloody purges. Private capital had been brought under state control at the start of the revolution, and centralized five-year plans now advanced industrialization at breakneck speed, producing dramatic economic growth at the cost of enormous human suffering. Meanwhile, efforts to dragoon peasants into collective farms dislocated rural life. In Ukraine alone, at least 3.5 million people starved in the *Holodomor*, or Terror-Famine. At the same time, the substantial national autonomy enjoyed by Ukraine and the other constituent republics of the early Union of Soviet Socialist Republics was sharply curtailed as Stalin's Moscow imposed hierarchical centralization and greater Russian domination within the former Tsarist empire. More than a personal dictatorship, Stalinism was the political expression of a privileged bureaucratic elite that feared the self-activity of workers and peasants at home and abroad and whose nationalist and great-Russian chauvinist politics negated the revolutionary Marxism of the Russian Revolution. The trick, however, was that while pursuing this antirevolutionary course Soviet leaders continued to associate themselves with the worldwide popularity of the revolution by claiming that they were its true Communist continuators.

Much of the Soviet economy had been brought into state ownership in the early years of the revolution and, in contrast to capitalist economies where investment decisions are made by individuals acting in pursuit of private profit, resources were allocated according to priorities set by the government. The Second World War highlighted the great potential strengths of this socialized and planned economy, which organized the rapid relocation of plants threatened by German attacks and the large-scale production of military matériel. At the same time, in the hands of self-serving officials and without popular democratic control, the Soviet economy was plagued by mismanagement. The USSR's Stalinist leaders were embedded within this contradictory reality: as bureaucratic administrators rather than private capitalists, their privileged lifestyles rested on their political control of the planned economy rather than on inherited family wealth and the personal ownership of capital. This gave them a vested interest in defending the USSR and its socialized economy, since the re-establishment of capitalism would destroy the economic foundations of their own power and likely lead to their violent liquidation. At the same time, they could not defend the USSR by promoting socialist revolutions elsewhere—the course advocated by the Bolsheviks in 1917—because popular agency posed an existential challenge to their own bureaucratic and anti-democratic hold on power. As a result, Moscow's foreign policy as it emerged under Stalin in the 1930s was defensive, nationalistic, risk-adverse, and without overarching political principle.

Moscow's post-1945 desire for an ongoing alliance with the capitalist West was not new. Since the rise of Stalin, Moscow had sought to mitigate the fundamental conflict between its nationalized and state-planned system and the capitalist world by establishing mutually recognized spheres of influence. The division of the capitalist world into Axis and Allied blocs during the 1930s enabled Moscow to play one off against the other. Initially, Soviet leaders hoped to draw Britain and France—the so-called democratic imperialists—into an anti-German (or anti-fascist) alliance, but when this policy stalled due to the 'democrats' refusal to participate, Moscow turned instead to an alliance with Germany. The August 1939 Nazi-Soviet Pact opened the door to the Second World War in Europe, which began the following month with the joint German-Soviet invasions and partition of Poland. Paradoxically, however, the pact also paved the way for the German invasion of the USSR in June 1941. Now in a desperate fight for survival, Moscow turned back to the West, forging the tripartite Grand Alliance with London and Washington. With Britain already at war and American leaders fearful of a German-dominated Europe, an alliance with Moscow also conformed to their perceived short-term interests.

At the conference of allied leaders held in Tehran in November 1943, Washington signaled its readiness to divide Europe into American-led and Soviet spheres of influence, and in return the Soviets promised to use their influence over European Communist parties to tamp down potentially revolutionary uprisings such as those that had accompanied the end of the First World War. On this basis, Soviet leaders concluded that a stable and ongoing postwar relationship with the capitalist world was possible: as Stalin noted boastfully "Lenin did not think you could conclude an alliance with one wing of the bourgeoisie against the other, but we have done just that."[5] Moscow also expected divisions between London and Washington to deepen after the war, allowing it to play one set of imperialists off against

---

[5]Stalin to Croatian communist leader Andrija Hebrang, quoted in Norman S. Naimark, *Stalin and the Fate of Europe: The Postwar Struggle for Sovereignty* (Cambridge, MA: Harvard University Press, 2019), 12.

the other. Soviet leaders formulated their war aims within this framework. Reconquered territory within the USSR's 1941 borders—including the Baltic States, Ukraine, and Belorussia (Belarus)—would be reincorporated into the Soviet Union, while Poland, Czechoslovakia, Hungary, Romania, and Bulgaria would be marshaled into the new defensive buffer zone. At least in the short term, Moscow was willing to allow capitalist economic relations to continue in these countries, and while subordinate to the Soviet Union in matters of defense and foreign policy, they would be multi-party 'people's democracies' rather than one-party Communist states. At the center of Europe, Germany would be 'denazified' and set up as a unified, neutral, and demilitarized state. Soviet leaders also hoped to strengthen their southern borders by prolonging their wartime occupation of northern Iran and securing control over regional oil production. Moscow also believed that the Allies would permit them a degree of control over the Turkish Straits between the Black Sea and the Mediterranean, perhaps even agreeing to the construction of a Soviet military base there. Underscoring their misjudgment of Allied intentions, the Soviets even hoped to be given oversight of the former Italian colony of Libya, thus establishing their presence in the Mediterranean.

Moscow recognized that its socialized economy could not be integrated directly into the new world economic order proclaimed at Bretton Woods since free trade and currency convertibility would necessarily undermine the planned economy by opening it up to foreign capital. Nevertheless, Soviet leaders hoped to take advantage of revived financial markets to secure large American loans and dollar credits for postwar reconstruction. They also intended to participate in capitalist world markets in a controlled manner by exporting grain, oil, and raw materials in exchange for capital goods and technical know-how. In this context, the Eastern European buffer states were expected to serve as a bridge to the capitalist West, and Moscow permitted the continued operation of private capital while refraining from the large-scale nationalization of industry and the collectivization of agriculture. Socialism was presented as the long-term goal, but Soviet ideologues suggested that it could be attained by following nonrevolutionary 'national roads' tailored to specific countries: as Stalin told a surprised delegation of Yugoslav Communists in 1945, a "people's democracy, a parliamentary republic, or even a constitutional monarchy" could all eventually lead to socialism.[6]

---

[6]Stalin, quoted in Geoffrey Roberts, "Stalin's Wartime Vision of the Peace, 1939–1945," in Timothy Snyder and Ray Brandon (eds.), *Stalin and Europe: Imitation and Domination, 1928–1953* (Oxford: Oxford University Press, 2014), 248.

Truman, Trieste, and the Shaping of US Policy

Despite Moscow's hopes for ongoing collaboration, their former allies in the West turned quickly back into determined foes. Washington had been deeply hostile to the 1917 Russian Revolution, even dispatching troops to Archangelsk in the north and Vladivostok on the Pacific coast between 1918 and 1922 in support of efforts to topple the new Bolshevik regime. There was a clear ideological and anti-communist dimension to this enmity, but beneath that was the blunt and unavoidable fact that the establishment of a socialized and centrally planned economy in the Soviet Union removed a great chunk of territory from the capitalist world market. Washington's systemic hostility was temporarily suspended in 1941 as American leaders grasped the utility of allying with Moscow against the proximate threat of a German-dominated Europe. As the tides of war turned, however, old enmities resurfaced, now sharpened by the fact that Moscow's looming predominance in Eastern Europe placed even more of the world beyond the reach of American capital. In the context of America's emerging hegemony, such a qualification to its global predominance was intolerable. Writing from Moscow in September 1944, ambassador Averell Harriman warned that Soviet leaders had become "bloated with power," while Navy Secretary James Forrestal pointed to the USSR as the "emerging new enemy" against which "U.S. foreign and security policy should be directed."[7] While the war was still going on President Roosevelt tamped down any public expression of these sentiments, but among senior officials and military commanders talk of a looming conflict with the Soviet Union was very much in the air.

By the time allied leaders met in the Crimean resort of Yalta in February 1945, Red Army advances in the Balkans and Eastern Europe had deepened American fears, but until Germany was defeated the alliance remained central to Washington's plans. The conference reflected the military situation on the ground, and while the Soviets were buoyed by a string of victories, American forces were still reeling from Germany's final offensive in Belgium—the Battle of the Bulge—in December 1944. In this context, the Allies were in a weak position to resist Soviet demands, and the Yalta conference approved Moscow's plans for Eastern Europe, recognizing the Soviet-backed provisional government of Poland and moving the entire country westward by adding land taken from Germany and giving Polish territory in the east to the USSR. Some American commentators viewed these concessions to Moscow as a product of Roosevelt's naive trust in

---

[7] Averell Harriman and James Forrestal, quoted in Mark A. Stoler, *Allies and Adversaries: The Joint Chiefs of Staff, the Grand Alliance, and U.S. Strategy in World War II* (Chapel Hill: University of North Carolina Press, 2000), 211, 215.

Stalin, but in fact there was little the United States could have done to oppose them.

The military balance changed rapidly after Yalta, and politics changed with it. In March, US forces finally broke into Germany, and while some raced deep into the country, others turned south toward Austria and Czechoslovakia. When Germany surrendered on May 8, Soviet soldiers still comprised the bulk of the allied troops in Europe, but American, British, Canadian, and French forces were much more strongly established than they had been in February. This military shift coincided with the death of President Roosevelt on April 12. New president Harry S. Truman was strongly inclined to follow the advice of those like Averell Harriman who were pushing a hard line against Moscow. Had he lived longer, Roosevelt himself may well have moved in this direction—in an April 6 telegram to Churchill he argued for a "tougher" policy toward the USSR—but change at the top undoubtedly facilitated Washington's rapid policy shift.[8]

Washington's assertive new stance was showcased during the May 1945 Trieste Crisis. Control of Trieste, a strategically important port on the Adriatic, had been contested between Italy and Yugoslavia since the dissolution of the Hapsburg Empire in 1918. Yugoslavia's Communist-led Partisans, emerging triumphant from their long struggle against Axis occupation, demanded the inclusion of Trieste in their new federal republic, and on May 1 Partisan fighters entered the city in support of an anti-fascist uprising. At the same time, Allied commanders rushed New Zealand troops into the city, establishing an uneasy joint occupation. London and Washington had previously approved Trieste's inclusion in Yugoslavia, but both were now determined to hand it to Italy. When the Yugoslavs refused to back down, British general Harold Alexander prepared for a fight, explaining that Yugoslav leader—and recent ally—Josef Broz (better known as Tito) was "reminiscent of Hitler and Mussolini."[9] After a tense few days Tito backed down and accepted the formation of an Allied military government. As his angry public comments made clear, the Yugoslavs had been undercut by Stalin, who told Tito that he would not "begin World War Three" over Trieste.[10] By demonstrating that the Soviets would back down rather than risk conflict, the Trieste crisis seemed to vindicate the confrontational stance of Washington's hard-liners.

---

[8] Roosevelt To Churchill, Telegraph R-736, April 6, 1945, in Warren Kimball (ed.), *Churchill and Roosevelt: The Complete Correspondence* (London: Collins, 1984), Vol. III, 617.
[9] Harold Alexander, quoted in J. R. Whittan, "Drawing the Line: Britain and the Emergence of the Trieste Question, January 1941–May 1945," *The English Historical Review*, Vol. 106, No. 419 (April 1991), 369.
[10] Stalin, quoted in R. S. DiNardo, "Glimpse of an Old World Order? Reconsidering the Trieste Crisis of 1945," *Diplomatic History*, Vol. 21, No. 3 (Summer 1997), 378.

Eastern Europe in the Immediate Postwar

The final phases of the German-Soviet war are often presented in ways that seem to envisage the Red Army rolling westward into an undifferentiated space known as 'Eastern Europe.' Yet, while political developments in countries across this region were shaped by common factors—including the action of Soviet forces, popular uprisings and rebellions, and the response of local bourgeoisies—they unfolded in specific national contexts. Within the overarching framework of the rapidly deepening tensions between the Soviet Union and its former allies, local agency shaped distinct national trajectories. For clarity, it is useful to organize these national developments into several broad groupings. These include: the states that had been part of the prewar USSR (the Baltic States, Belorussia, and Ukraine), states that had been occupied and dismembered by Germany (Czechoslovakia and Poland), states that were Germany's wartime allies (Bulgaria, Hungary, and Romania), the countries of the southern Balkans (Albania and Yugoslavia), and, finally, Finland.

Within the borders of the prewar USSR (the Baltic States, Belorussia, and Ukraine) Soviet rule was quickly reimposed following the arrival of the Red Army as handpicked pro-Moscow governments were installed. Local capitalists had been dispossessed before the war, and industry was renationalized. Moscow presented these states as self-governing Socialist Republics, but actual political independence was ruthlessly suppressed. Guerrilla bands that included local workers and peasants, Jewish fighters, and escaped prisoners of war had actively supported the Soviet advance, but their rapid incorporation into the Red Army narrowed their capacity to shape postwar politics. At the same time, some Ukrainian and Baltic-state nationalists had attempted to collaborate with German occupation forces, and although often rebuffed as Slavic *Untermenschen*, their image as defenders of national sovereignty had won significant popular support. Denied legal representation in the postwar states, anti-Communist nationalists launched sporadic guerrilla campaigns against the Soviet authorities that continued into the early 1950s. Here, too, the end of the war brought no peace. In particular, resistance to forced collectivization continued: as imprisoned anti-Stalinist activist Brigitte Gerland reported after talking to Ukrainians in the Vorkuta prison camp in Siberia, the Soviet's "punitive expeditions, arrests of hostages [and] burning of villages" were hardly designed to convince peasants of the benefits of collective farming.[11] In 1945–46 alone, ruthless guerrilla attacks and brutal Soviet counterinsurgency operations in western Ukraine resulted in the deaths of 26,000 Soviet soldiers and officials and up

---

[11] Brigitte Gerland, "Vorkuta (1950–53): Oppositional Currents and the Mine Strikes," in George Saunders (ed.), *Samizdat: Voices of the Soviet Opposition* (New York: Pathfinder Press, (1974) 2022), 274.

to 100,000 insurgents.[12] Soviet officials also deported tens of thousands of "bandit accomplices" to Siberia, including 43,000 from Latvia alone.

In Poland, the advance of the Red Army prompted a major popular uprising in August 1944 after the London-based government-in-exile ordered its supporters in the Home Army (AK)—the main Polish resistance force—to drive German troops from Warsaw. Pro-Western exiles hoped that by liberating Warsaw they could create a counterweight to the Moscow-backed Provisional Government set up in Lublin in July 1944. Moscow viewed the Warsaw Uprising as a challenge to its predominance in Poland, and Red Army forces made no attempt to help beleaguered AK combatants. Getting Soviet troops into Warsaw would not have been easy, but Moscow was happy to sit back while the rebellion went down to bloody defeat at the hands of the Germans. By the time the fighting ended in October, 15,000 AK fighters and upwards of 100,000 civilians had been killed, and over 700,000 Poles had been forced to flee their burning city.

Moscow's hostility to the Warsaw Uprising reinforced anti-Russian sentiment in Poland, laying the basis for clashes between underground AK fighters and Soviet troops that continued into the 1950s. As the war ended, Moscow attempted to buttress the appeal of the Communist-led Provisional Government of National Unity by bringing Stanisław Mikołajczyk, the former prime minister of the government-in-exile, into the cabinet. Mikołajczyk's inclusion certainly broadened support for the new government, but the rapid growth of his Polish People's Party (PSL)—largely a result of the break-up of large estates and the distribution of land to small peasant farmers—quickly led to new clashes with the Soviets. The widespread intimidation of Mikołajczyk's supporters by Communist-controlled security forces and blatant vote-rigging led to the PSL's defeat in a June 1946 constitutional referendum and then to the overwhelming victory of the Communist-led Democratic Bloc in the January 1947 general elections. After just eighteen months, Poland's experiment in people's democracy was facing a deep crisis of legitimacy.

Revolts also greeted the Red Army's advance into both parts of German-divided Czechoslovakia. In Slovakia, army officers and leaders of the conservative Democratic Party joined Communists in an uprising against the pro-Nazi government of Josef Tiso, while in the German-occupied Czech lands the Communist Party (KSČ) led a National Council that included socialists and bourgeois nationalists in an armed insurrection. Soviet forces delayed their advance into Slovakia until the revolt there had been crushed, but they responded to the KSČ's leadership role in the Czech lands by speeding their advance on Prague, entering the city to a rapturous welcome on May 8, 1945. In an outpouring of grassroots democracy, local

---

[12]See Richard Overy, *Blood and Ruins: The Last Imperial War, 1931–1945* (New York: Viking, 2022), 873–5.

committees of the National Council were soon in control throughout the newly reunified country. The KSČ won 38 percent of the vote in a relatively free and fair national election in May 1946, and Communist leader Klement Gottwald became prime minister in a coalition government that included socialists and bourgeois liberals. Liberal democrat and prewar president Edvard Beneš was reelected with Communist support in June 1946. Here, at least, people's democracy seemed more firmly established.

In Romania, Bulgaria, and Hungary—all wartime allies of Germany—sections of the ruling elites responded to the Soviet advance by switching sides in an attempt to preserve their position. In Romania, King Michael I joined local Communists, socialists, and leaders of the Liberal and Peasant parties in a coup against pro-Nazi dictator Ion Antonescu. The new National Democratic Bloc government signed an armistice on September 12, 1944, and under the supervision of a Soviet-led Allied Control Commission Romanian troops joined the Red Army's advance into Hungary. Unlike Czechoslovakia, where Soviet troops soon moved out, Romania was subject to a protracted Red Army occupation that—with its attendant mistreatment of Romanian civilians—lasted into the late 1950s. Moscow soon moved to tighten its grip on Romanian politics, using Communist-led street protests to force King Michael to push the Liberal and Peasant parties out of the government before securing an overwhelming victory for pro-Communist forces in the November 1946 elections. Following King Michael's abdication, a people's republic was proclaimed in 1947. Meanwhile, a series of SovRoms—ostensibly equal Soviet-Romanian business partnerships—funneled coal, oil, and other Romanian resources to the USSR.

The Red Army's advance into Bulgaria in September 1944 also triggered a nationwide wave of insurrectionary strikes and street protests led by the Fatherland Front, an alliance of Communists and nationalist army officers in the Zveno movement. The pro-Axis regime was toppled and replaced by a Fatherland Front government under Zveno leader General Kimon Georgiev. With women voting for the first time, Fatherland Front candidates swept parliamentary elections in November 1945, and a plebiscite abolished the monarchy the following September. As the Communists moved to tighten their control, veteran party leader Gregori Dimitrov replaced Geogiev as prime minister of the new People's Republic of Bulgaria.

Sections of the Hungarian elite also attempted to switch sides at the last minute, but their efforts were blocked by a German invasion that installed a government led by local fascists of the Arrow Cross movement. The prolonged and bitter fighting that followed cost the Red Army half a million casualties, and embittered Soviet soldiers turned on Hungarian civilians in widespread acts of theft, rape, and violence. Even under these conditions, however, popular insurgencies flared. In the southeastern borderlands peasant farmers and agricultural workers seized land and established organs of local self-government, while urban workers formed factory committees to restart production and distribute food. The Hungarian

Communist Party (MKP) grew rapidly, and with Soviet backing it formed a Popular Front government with the conservative Independent Small Holders Party (FKgP). As in Poland, land redistribution boosted the peasant-based party, and the FKgP won a majority in the November 1945 parliamentary elections. Backed by Moscow, the MKP held onto the leadership of the Popular Front government and began using state security forces to crush some factions of the FKgP while co-opting others.

A very different pattern of events unfolded in the southern Balkans, where Tito's Communist-led Partisans waged a long, bloody, and ultimately successful struggle against the Axis occupation and dismemberment of Yugoslavia. Partisans also fought their nominal allies, the Serbian nationalist Chetniks, some of whom were collaborating with the Germans. Partisan military successes won Allied backing at the Tehran Conference, and from late 1943 Tito's embryonic state—now formally recognized as Democratic Federal Yugoslavia—received shipments of weapons and equipment along with medical aid and air support. Partisan operations were further reinforced when Soviet forces joined their advance on Belgrade in October 1944. While they welcomed allied support, however, the Partisan's victory was rooted in their own military strength, which was itself a product of their conscious intertwining of war and social revolution. In dramatic illustration of this process, the Antifascist Women's Front helped to recruit 100,000 female combatants while organizing two million more into the work of supporting the Partisan army and administering its liberated zones.[13] Women fighters joined up for a wide variety of reasons, but it was not lost on them or their male comrades-in-arms that their actions staked a claim on the kind of postwar society they hoped to live in.

As the guerrilla war in Yugoslavia intensified, many landlords and other elites either fled the country or collaborated with the Axis occupation. With the old order unraveling, the Communists encouraged peasants to take control of the land and to establish new organs of local government in areas freed, however temporarily, from Axis control. Factories owned by collaborators or by foreign capitalists were confiscated by the Partisan provisional government, laying the basis for the rapid postwar socialization of the economy. On a Yugoslav-wide level, the Partisans' advocacy of a multiethnic state promoted unity by cutting across the region's complex national and religious divides. The Yugoslavian Communists also displayed a stubborn independence. Despite their formal subordination to Moscow, Yugoslav leaders resisted allied plans for a postwar government based on sharing power with King Peter I's government-in-exile. Instead, the rapid socialization of capitalist property meant that the inclusion of pro-western ministers in the new government could only be a temporary

---

[13]Chiara Bonfiglioli, "Women's Social and Political Activism in the Early Cold War Era: The Case of Yugoslavia," *Aspasia*, Vol. 8 (2014), 5.

arrangement. After pro-Western ministers quit the government in October 1945, the Communist-led People's Front won 90 percent of the vote in the November federal elections, leading to the abolition of the monarchy and the proclamation of a socialist republic.

In Albania—an Italian colony since 1939—Enver Hoxha's Communist-led National Liberation Front organized an anti-Axis insurgency with support from the Yugoslav Partisans. In 1945 they blocked the return of the exiled King Zog and established a Communist-led provisional government. As in Yugoslavia, many local elites sided with the Axis, while the resistance promoted land redistribution and social reforms. Communist-backed candidates swept national elections held in December 1945, and while they were the only ones on the ballot there is no doubt that they enjoyed considerable popular support. Despite these victories, Moscow had little interest in a country it viewed as both economically worthless and peripheral to its defensive plans, and Soviet leaders approved the absorption of Albania into the Yugoslav Federation. An initial treaty between Belgrade and Tirana in February 1945 proposed to provide Albania with much-needed food in exchange for oil and coal.

Finally, Finland was different again. Formerly part of the Tsarist empire, Finland fought two wars with the Soviet Union during the long Second World War: the 1939–40 Winter War and the 1941–44 Continuation War. However, while Soviet forces crossed northern Finland to attack German forces in Norway in 1945, the Red Army did not invade and occupy Finland as a whole. Instead, a 1944 armistice, confirmed by the 1947 Paris Peace Treaty and a 1948 Treaty of Friendship, maintained Finland as a self-governing, capitalist, and neutral state while ceding Karelia, a naval base on the Gulf of Finland, and nickel-rich Pestamo to Moscow. Soviet hopes for growing Communist Party influence in Finnish politics were never fully realized, but Moscow was happy enough to deal with the military-conservative leadership of Marshal Carl Gustav Mannheim and Juho Paasikivi, particularly after they rejected American Marshall Plan aid in favor of economic ties with the USSR. Adjacent to neutral Sweden, a neutral Finland secured Moscow's northwestern frontier while avoiding the financial cost and potential political complexity of direct occupation. Although unrepeatable in more hotly contested parts of Eastern Europe, it was in many ways Moscow's ideal solution to the problems of the postwar.

*

Across much of Eastern Europe, these postwar political developments were accompanied by border changes and large-scale forced migrations that made the postwar states significantly more homogeneous than their prewar analogs. The new people's democracies expelled twelve million ethnic Germans (*Volksdeutsche*), driving them westwards into Germany, while over one million Poles were forced out of western Ukraine and Belorussia and 500,000 Ukrainians and Belorussians moved in the opposite direction. The *Volksdeutsche*, many of whom had lived in places like the Czechoslovak Sudetenland for generations, faced vengeance killings, sexual assault, and property confiscation at the hands of police and local militias. Justified by notions of ethnic homogenization and the exchange of populations approved after the post-First World War breakup of the Ottoman Empire, these Moscow-backed mass deportations were popularized by anti-German propaganda and Russo-centric Pan-Slavism.[14] In further confirmation of Stalinism's negation of working-class internationalism, the great Russian chauvinism long central to tsarism was now bizarrely repackaged as "Slavophile Leninism."[15]

Coming on top of the extermination of six million Jews in the Holocaust, these waves of postwar ethnic cleansing produced much more homogenous nation-states: in Poland, for example, ethnic Poles now comprised 90 percent of the population, up from just 69 percent in 1939, while the Jewish population fell from 8 percent to just 0.3 percent.[16] Jews who did return home often faced anti-Semitic attitudes that made it impossible to recover prewar property and businesses. Not surprisingly, many sought new lives in Palestine/Israel or in the West, even if it meant enduring years in Displaced Persons camps or braving the dangerous journey to British-ruled Palestine. In some places the authorities tried to retain skilled workers—like Silesian and German miners—and others seen to have particular economic importance, but death and dislocation also created possibilities for upwards mobility for those willing to take over the homes, jobs, and businesses left behind by the expelled. Particularly in cities where Jews and Germans had formed a large part of prewar the population, large-scale property seizures helped to create a new middle class that owed its status to the state, thus broadening the privileged layers upon which a caste of loyal administrators was constructed.

Germany: The Central Question

Soon after the Trieste crisis, the leaders of the Grand Alliance met in the Berlin suburb of Potsdam in July 1945 for the final summit conference of the war. Behind the carefully posed images of Big Three amity, the ground was already shifting rapidly. With Germany defeated, the western Allies were no longer reliant on the Red Army, and the successful test of

---

[14]Yasmin Khan, "Wars of Displacement: Exile and Uprooting in the 1940s," in Michael Geyer and Adam Tooze (eds.), *The Cambridge History of the Second World War*, Vol. III (New York: Cambridge University Press, 2015), 289.
[15]Stalin, quoted in Roberts, "Stalin's Wartime Vision of the Peace," 248.
[16]Holly Case, "Reconstruction in East-Central Europe: Clearing the Rubble of Cold War Politics," *Past and Present*, Special Supplement 6 (2011), 88.

the first atomic bomb created the prospect of forcing Japan's surrender without Soviet assistance. Moscow reaffirmed its commitment to joining the war against Japan, but Washington now hoped to keep the Soviets *out* of China. The Red Army's physical presence in the countries of Eastern Europe gave Washington no choice but to acknowledge Soviet domination of Poland—with a face-saving promise of early elections—and of the rest of the region, but with its own large military presence now firmly established in the West the United States was able to push back forcefully on other fronts. In this context, the postwar future of Germany quickly became the central question.

At the previous great power summit at Yalta in February 1945, the Big Three had agreed that Germany would be demilitarized and deindustrialized, producing—after a period of four-way military occupation and denazification—a unified and neutral nation-state in the heart of Europe. Soviet leaders envisioned neither a protracted military occupation of Germany nor its integration into the Soviet system, and Moscow's crude anti-German propaganda, the mass rapes and other violence inflicted on German civilians by its soldiers, and the large-scale looting of German plant and equipment all suggest that it had no interest in having any part of Germany as an ally. Three 'initiative groups' of exiled German Communists accompanied Soviet forces into Germany and worked to rebuild the German Communist Party (KPD), but the Soviet Occupation Zone (SBZ) remained firmly under Moscow's control. At the same time, harsh Nazi oppression, the social dislocation caused by Allied bombing, and the brutal behavior of the Red Army combined to ensure that the popular uprisings that greeted Soviet troops elsewhere in Eastern Europe were almost entirely absent in Germany.

By the time of Potsdam, the Western allies were already abandoning the idea of a neutral and demilitarized Germany. Writing from Moscow, American diplomat George Kennan advocated the permanent "dismemberment" of Germany and the creation of a west German state "so prosperous, so secure [and] so superior" that "the East" could not threaten it.[17] Kennan's views conformed to those of senior American leaders, and while the four-party occupation of Germany was reaffirmed at Potsdam, for Washington it now pointed toward permanent partition and the establishment of two new states. At the same time, the conference laid the economic foundations for partition by insisting that Moscow could only extract reparations from its occupation zone while receiving plant and equipment from the western zones in exchange for food and raw materials. As the Allies limited the reparations extracted from their zones,

---

[17]George Kennan, quoted in David S. McLellan, "Who Fathered Containment?: A Discussion," *International Studies Quarterly*, Vol. 17, No. 2 (June 1973), 206–7.

this effectively shielded Germany's industrial heartland in the Ruhr from Soviet pillage and reinforced the deepening pro-American orientation of German capitalism.

As the Allies pushed toward partition, the British and American occupation zones were merged into a 'bizone' in late 1946—expanded to a trizone by the inclusion of the French zone in early 1948—within which an embryonic West German government began functioning. In summer 1947 the United States launched the large-scale economic reconstruction of western Germany using massive cash infusions organized through the European Recovery Program, or Marshall Plan. As a result, the Soviets walked out of the Allied Control Council the following spring in protest over financial reforms that effectively established a new national currency in the western zone. As the last vestiges of joint Big Three oversight collapsed, Moscow tried to block the integration of West Berlin into the emerging West German state by preventing food and fuel entering the city, which was located deep within the eastern part of the country. The Soviet blockade of West Berlin proved to be a major blunder. Unwilling to risk a military confrontation, Moscow was forced to look on as a year-long airlift supplied the food and fuel necessary to sustain Berlin. This dramatic air bridge also built support for partition by forging a new West German identity and underscoring the new country's shift in the Western imagination from wartime enemy to postwar victim of Communism. The end of the blockade was thus quickly followed in May 1949 by the establishment of the Federal Republic of Germany or West Germany. After repeating its call for a neutral Germany, Moscow acknowledged the reality of partition by sponsoring the formation of the German Democratic Republic (East Germany) in October 1949.

Although it had been an integral part of Germany during the war, Austria was excluded from this partition. In November 1943, the allies announced that thanks to the *Anschluss*—the 1938 annexation by Germany—Austria would be regarded as a victim of Nazi aggression. Given that the *Anschluss* was widely welcomed and that over one million Austrians fought in the German army, this was a convenient fiction. When the war ended, Soviet troops occupied eastern Austria, while US troops controlled the west, and although technically 'liberated' Austria was subject to a German-style four-way occupation. Moscow hoped that the Austrian Communist Party (KPÖ) would lead the creation of a pro-Soviet people's democracy, but the party's unpopularity—hardly helped by the behavior of the Red Army—precluded that possibility. Instead, careful political maneuvering by Social Democratic Party leader and postwar president Karl Renner and inflows of Marshall Plan aid established the united, capitalist, and neutral country recognized by the 1955 State Treaty. Ironically, Moscow's preferred outcome for Germany was thus realized in smaller, economically weaker, and less strategically central Austria.

Washington Steps Up the Pressure

The partition of Germany took place amid heightened American military pressure on the Soviet Union. At the end of the war, virtually all senior American leaders, with the exception a few hotheads like General George Patton, understood that a hot war to roll back the Soviet domination of Eastern Europe was both militarily and politically impossible, opting instead for a 'cold' strategy based on the threatened use of force. Their hope was that unrelenting military-economic pressure backed by Washington's nuclear monopoly would weaken the Soviet economy and undermine Moscow's political legitimacy to such a degree that more direct intervention would become possible. This approach, packaged as the containment of Soviet expansionism, was given intellectual coherence in an extended analysis of Soviet foreign policy penned from Moscow by George Kennan in March 1946. Kennan argued that the Soviet leadership, like the imperial Russian state before it, was determined to expand its power and territorial sway, but noted that its unwillingness to "take unnecessary risks" meant that while "impervious to the logic of reason," it was "highly sensitive to the logic of force."[18] This stance, American planners believed, had already been vindicated during the face-off over Trieste.

The rapid development of Washington's policy of 'containment' was intertwined with an important diplomatic initiative that served to strengthen and legitimize America's nuclear monopoly. Presented to the newly established United Nations Atomic Energy Commission in March 1946 by American businessman and presidential advisor Bernard Baruch, the Baruch Plan called for a new Atomic Development Agency (ADA) to oversee the worldwide development of nuclear energy for peaceful purposes. The ADA would be authorized to impose armed sanctions on states that tried to produce nuclear weapons, and such actions would not be subject to veto by members of the UN Security Council. Until these measures were fully and verifiably established, America would maintain its nuclear monopoly, refusing, as President Truman put it, "to throw away our gun" until world disarmament was assured.[19] The Baruch Plan thus cloaked the hard-nosed interests of the emerging hegemon in a universalist appeal to peace, international collaboration, and nuclear disarmament.

Not surprisingly, Moscow quickly rejected the Baruch Plan, with Russian ambassador to the United Nations Andrei Gromyko calling instead for the outlawing the use of nuclear weapons and the destruction of existing

---

[18] George Kennan, quoted in Arnold A. Offner, *Another Such Victory: President Truman and the Cold War, 1945–1953* (Stanford, CA: Stanford University Press, 2002), 133.
[19] Larry G. Gerber, "The Baruch Plan and the Origins of the Cold War," *Diplomatic History*, Vol. 6, No. 1, (1982), 77.

stockpiles. Soviet opposition ensured that the plan could not win Security Council approval, and by the end of 1946 it was effectively dead. Meanwhile, in July 1946 Washington conducted a well-publicized nuclear test on Bikini Atoll in the central Pacific, and in August the passing of the Atomic Energy Act further restricted the dissemination of nuclear knowledge, even to America's closest allies. Nevertheless, while these measures demonstrated Washington's drive to develop and protect its nuclear monopoly, the failure of the Baruch Plan allowed it to present itself as the champion of unselfish internationalism while painting the Soviet Union as the main obstacle to world peace and nuclear disarmament.

The nuclear monopoly allowed American leaders to meet domestic demands for postwar demobilization while simultaneously stepping up military pressure on the USSR. This task was entrusted to the long-range bombers of the new Strategic Air Command—formed in March 1946— whose ability to penetrate Soviet airspace was strengthened by being able to operate from the world-circling chain of airbases acquired during the war. Planners recognized that an attack by vulnerable bombers was unlikely to be completely successful, and they anticipated that Moscow would respond by launching a massive invasion of Western Europe. By projecting a Soviet invasion as the logical military response to their own nuclear plans, American planners manufactured a Soviet threat that quickly became a central ideological and political axis of the Cold War. In fact, the Red Army had been largely demobilized at the end of the war in order to concentrate resources on reconstruction, and sober estimates suggest that Soviet forces fell far short of the numbers required for such an attack.[20] Moreover, given its defensive mindset and lack of interest in spreading Communism, Moscow had absolutely no desire to unleash the uncontrollable social and political turmoil that an attack would set in motion both in Western Europe and in its own Eastern European borderlands, and it never seriously contemplated launching such an offensive.

In the immediate postwar, American opinion-formers worked hard to replace popular wartime admiration for the Soviet war effort with their frightening new vision of an implacable, expansionist-minded and deeply evil foe. Former British prime minister Winston Churchill played a particularly important role, using a March 1946 speech in Fulton, Missouri, to present the graphic image of an "iron curtain" falling across Europe from the Baltic to the Adriatic.[21] In response, Churchill called for a "fraternal association" of Britain and the United States to resist the "infinite expansion" of Soviet "power and doctrines." A year later, President Truman widened the scope of what was now being widely

---

[20]See Matthew A. Evangelista, "Stalin's Postwar Army Reappraised," *International Security*, Vol. 7, No. 3 (Winter 1982–83), 118.
[21]Churchill, quoted in Offner, *Another Such Victory*, 136.

referred to as the Cold War with a March 1947 announcement that the United States would intervene in support of "free peoples" resisting "subjugation from armed minorities or outside forces" anywhere in the world.[22] This new Truman Doctrine led directly to America's intervention in the Greek Civil War, where a communist-led insurgency, long abandoned by Moscow, was crushed in 1949. The Truman Doctrine went hand in hand with the June 1947 announcement of the Marshall Plan. Aimed primarily at kickstarting the economies of Western Europe and at undercutting Communist influence in France and Italy, Washington also dangled the prospect of Marshall Plan aid before the East European people's democracies. Moscow quickly—and rightly—concluded that Washington aimed to use Marshall aid to weaken Soviet predominance by expanding the possibilities for capitalist trade, and it pressured Poland into rejecting US overtures. In Czechoslovakia, however, President Beneš and other non-Communist leaders were tempted to accept American aid, and the resulting crisis opened a new phase in the Cold War.

Moscow Tightens Its Grip

Moscow initially allowed the Eastern European people's democracies a degree of autonomy in their domestic affairs, but it permitted no independence in foreign policy. In July 1947, Czech foreign minister and leading non-Communist politician Jan Masaryk was summoned to Moscow and bullied into rejecting Washington's offer of Marshall aid: as Masaryk recalled bitterly, "I went to Moscow the foreign minister of a sovereign nation and returned the lackey of a foreign country."[23] These moves were part of a broader push to strengthen Soviet political control in Eastern Europe, launched in response to Washington's drive to partition Germany and its accelerating Cold War hostility more broadly. In September 1947, Moscow summoned leaders of the Eastern European, French, and Italian Communist parties to the founding meeting of the Information Bureau of Communist and Workers' Parties (Cominform). Pro-Moscow Communist parties had had no formal international organization since the dissolution of the Communist International or Comintern at the height of the Grand Alliance in 1943, and the formation of the Cominform signaled Moscow's recognition that the wartime alliance was definitively finished. Addressing the conference, Soviet leader Andrei Zhdanov announced that the world was divided into two antagonistic and irreconcilable 'camps,' and that specific national roads to socialism—encouraged by Moscow since 1945—were impermissible. This sharp political turn signaled the end

---

[22]Truman, quoted in Offner, *Another Such Victory*, 202.
[23]Jan Masaryk, quoted in Naimark, *Stalin and the Fate of Europe*, 19.

of the experiment in peoples' democracy and the beginning of more direct Soviet control over the nations of Eastern Europe.

International and national pressures broke with particular force over the National Front coalition government in Czechoslovakia. Following the new Cominform line, the Czech Communist Party (KSČ) launched a campaign for the ideological 'purification' of the National Front while consolidating its control over state security forces. When twelve non-Communist ministers resigned from the coalition government in protest in February 1948, the KSČ mobilized street demonstrations that forced President Beneš to appoint a new government composed entirely of leaders of the KSČ and Communist-led front organizations. This power grab was legitimized by a national election held in May 1948 in which candidates of the newly purged National Front were the only ones on the ballot. Of the leading non-Communist politicians, Jan Masaryk remained in office until his death in a mysterious fall from his apartment window in March 1948, while Edvard Beneš resigned the presidency in June 1948 before dying in September.

Within the Cominform, Moscow's drive for ideological conformity came particularly down hard on the Communist Party of Yugoslavia (KPJ). Moscow had long been wary of the Yugoslav's political independence—a product of having led a successful revolution—and it saw Belgrade's proposal for a Balkan Federation with Bulgaria and Albania as a challenge to its own authority. A ferocious campaign against 'Titoism' followed, leading to the KPJ's expulsion from the Cominform in June 1948. These events came as a profound shock to the many people who had been inspired by the Yugoslav Revolution, and they marked the first postwar crack in the facade of Communist unity. As Moscow's drive for ideological conformity gathered momentum, anti-Titoist purges and show trials rippled through Eastern Europe. In 1951, Moscow denounced Polish Communist leader Władysław Gomułka, whose appeal to nationalism was viewed as dangerously anti-Soviet. Gomułka was imprisoned, but others were not so lucky, and leaders of the Albanian, Bulgarian, Hungarian, and Romanian parties were executed for Titoism. Thousands of rank-and-file party members also suffered imprisonment and execution in the campaigns of terror that solidified Moscow's control of national Communist parties and, through them, of political and economic life in the buffer states. Moscow's campaign for conformity was laced with anti-Semitism, with Jewishness seen—as it had been in both the Soviet Union and Nazi Germany in the 1930s—as a marker of dangerous 'cosmopolitanism.' Within the USSR, an anti-Semitic campaign raged from 1951 to 1953, focused on a group of Jewish doctors accused of plotting to kill Stalin.

Moscow's campaign of purges, show trials, and executions overlapped with a drive to turn residual multiparty people's democracies into what were effectively one-party states. Across Eastern Europe, nominal coalition governments remained in office, but their constituent parties were now reduced to Communist controlled fronts. Parties not already under Communist control were subjected to campaigns of harassment and intimidation, and while some of their leaders—like Stanisław Mikołajczyk in Poland—fled into exile, others—like Bulgarian oppositionist Nikola Petkov—were framed and executed. Many more were coerced into silence. As non-Communist groups were shut down or reorganized under Communist leadership, social democratic organizations were merged with the Communists to form what were presented as united working-class parties.

Tightening Communist political control was accompanied by the accelerated liquidation of private capital as factories, financial institutions, and distribution networks were nationalized. Beginning in 1947 and organized with the help of Soviet experts, Two-, Three- and Five-Year Plans were set in motion across Eastern Europe and—as partition hardened—in East Germany. Socialized and planned economies soon accounted for the majority of economic activity, so that by 1952 almost all Hungary's industrial output and three-quarters of its retail turnover came from state-run enterprises.[24] On the land, the need to boost food production drove deeply unpopular campaigns to accelerate collectivization, reversing the distribution of land to individual peasant farmers typical of the immediate postwar years and using punitive taxes and food requisitions to eliminate so-called rich peasants.

As state planning advanced, Eastern European economies were structurally assimilated into the Soviet Union, a development signaled by the formation of the Council of Mutual Economic Assistance (Comecon) in 1949. Economic integration led to an expansion of trade between the USSR and its Eastern European clients, especially industrialized Czechoslovakia and the GDR. Despite western propaganda images of an exploitative Soviet empire, the USSR effectively subsidized its Eastern European "buffer" states.[25] Within the USSR itself, these measures were matched by the forceful reassertion of centralized control, reversing the limited toleration for local initiative that had been decisive to wartime survival and intensifying the repression of dissent voices. Cold War pressures ensured that the Soviet economy was increasingly militarized as programs to develop atomic weapons, missiles, and jet aircraft moved into high gear. Secretive industrial cities proliferated in the USSR's far east, often run on the forced labor of those incarcerated in the camps of the sprawling Gulag, including German prisoners of war, members of relocated national minorities, and political prisoners.

Spurred by competition with the United States, Soviet military spending doubled between 1948 and 1953, stimulating broader economic advances as annual growth rates exceeded 8 percent.[26] Comparative statistics

---

[24]Mark Pittaway, *Eastern Europe, 1939–2000* (London: Arnold Publishers, 2004), 55.
[25]See Oscar Sanchez-Sibony, *Red Globalization: The Political Economy of the Soviet Cold War from Stalin to Khrushchev* (Cambridge: Cambridge University Press, 2014), 69–70.
[26]Pechatnov, "The Soviet Union and the World," 110.

were often politically massaged, but in this period industrial growth in Czechoslovakia, Poland, and Yugoslavia clearly outstripped that in the weaker capitalist economies of Western European, including Italy and Spain.[27] High growth rates lent plausibility to Moscow's claim that the Soviet Union was on course to overtake the United States. In fact, strong growth was only achieved by utilizing plant looted from former Axis countries and by blunt measures to raise labor productivity by incentivizing 'shock' production campaigns. These efforts were unsustainable, particularly as high military expenditures resulted in the relative underdevelopment of the consumer goods sector. Moreover, top-down bureaucratic planning, political and cultural repression, and the denial of democratic working-class control over economic planning stifled initiative and collaborative action. Here, Moscow's profound fear of popular agency came home with devastating consequences: far from offering humanity a communist future, the Stalinist regimes in the Soviet Union and Eastern Europe were driving themselves into a historic dead end.

The consolidation of Stalinism in the USSR and the tightening of Soviet control across Eastern Europe fell particularly heavily on women. Over 800,000 women had served in the Red Army during the Second World War, many in combat roles as tank crew, fighter pilots, frontline medics, and snipers, while tens of thousands more fought with partisan forces.[28] For Moscow, the mobilization of women was prompted by military necessity rather than a commitment to women's equality. Nevertheless, women's wartime service and the generally positive response it elicited from male comrades undoubtedly pointed toward a more gender-equal society. Instead of realizing these possibilities, however, at the end of the war Soviet authorities moved quickly to reassert traditional gender norms. Women soldiers were rapidly demobilized, and their wartime service was either ignored or denigrated, while strident natalist campaigns promoted "motherhood" as the "primary duty" of former female combatants.[29] Instituted in 1944, the honorary title of "Mother Heroine" was awarded to women who bore ten or more children. In Yugoslavia, where women had participated in a social revolution, Antifascist Women's Front (AFŽ) members pushed back against this trend, running literacy classes aimed at peasant women and training them as midwives, nurses, and teachers. Nevertheless, the AFŽ was dissolved in 1953 amid a deepening "patriarchal backlash": as its leaders noted ruefully, male Communist Party members thought that "the revolutionary time in which [women] could be revolutionary workers has passed."[30]

---

[27]Case, "Reconstruction in East-Central Europe," 98.
[28]Reina Pennington, "Offensive Women: Women in Combat in the Red Army in the Second World War," *Journal of Military History*, Vol. 74 (July 2010), 785.
[29]Pennington, "Offensive Women," 817.
[30]Bonfiglioli, "Women's Social and Political Activism," 15, 9.

American Pressure Intensifies: H-Bombs and NSC 68

Aided by espionage in the United States and fueled by uranium mined in East Germany by thousands of forced laborers, Soviet scientists detonated their first atomic bomb in August 1949. The Soviet bomb abruptly ended Washington's cherished nuclear monopoly, and in conjunction with the advancing Chinese Revolution it created the impression that the 'free world' was rapidly losing ground. Washington had already begun to intensify anti-Soviet pressure, marshaling most of Western Europe, plus Canada and Iceland, into the North Atlantic Treaty Organization (NATO) in April 1949 while scrambling to develop new and immensely powerful nuclear weapons. In spring 1950, a new strategic masterplan known as NSC 68 was adopted by the National Security Council. NSC 68 reiterated the vision of a Soviet state determined to impose "absolute authority over the rest of the world," and it called for countering this threat with a massive military build-up that included covert, psychological, and economic warfare as well as expanded nuclear and conventional forces.[31] NSC 68 also promised increased military aid for America's NATO allies and outlined plans for rearming the new West German state. This broad-spectrum military escalation was designed to weaken Soviet predominance in Eastern Europe, block 'expansionism' elsewhere, and force the collapse of the Soviet system.

NSC 68's proposed tripling of defense spending to around 20 percent of American GNP was approved amid the rapid expansion of the military that followed the outbreak of war in Korea in June 1950 (see Chapter Three). In November 1952 the United States began testing powerful fusion (or "Hydrogen") bombs and, with policymakers drawing negative conclusions from Korea about the prospects for fighting and winning conventional wars, nuclear weapons became even more central to American strategy. The New Look strategic policy adopted by the incoming administration of President Dwight D. Eisenhower in early 1953 called for confronting Soviet expansionism with 'massive retaliation'—effectively all-out nuclear war. New delivery systems, including long-range B-52 jet bombers (1955), submarine-launched missiles (1959), and intercontinental missiles (1959) gave the threat of nuclear war greater credibility. Despite alarmist claims to the contrary by American politicians, however, Soviet nuclear stockpiles always lagged far behind those of the United States. Nevertheless, by the mid-1950s both superpowers had enough nuclear weapons to guarantee 'mutually assured destruction,' and with that the global military architecture of US-Soviet rivalry—the core of the later Cold War—was locked into place.

---

[31]NSC 68 quoted in Melvyn P. Leffler, *Preponderance of Power: National Security, the Truman Administration, and the Cold War* (Stanford, CA: Stanford University Press, 1992), 355.

Washington's heavy reliance on nuclear weapons gave the Air Force the lion's share of military spending, while the navy, a necessary instrument of global power projection, maintained a massive fleet capable of dominating the world's major waterways. The army, meanwhile, shrank from a wartime high of eight million soldiers to around one million.[32] Army commanders trained primarily to fight a threatened Red Army invasion of Western Europe—a threat that, as we have seen, existed primarily in Washington's imagination. Much of the army was based permanently in Germany, where from the early 1950s it formed the core of NATO's military capability. After a long and contentious diplomatic negotiation, these forces were augmented in 1955 by the formation of the *Bundeswehr*, a new West German army. German rearmament reinforced Moscow's fear of an aggressive imperial power on its western frontier, and after again proposing a unified, demilitarized, and neutral Germany, the Soviets formed the Warsaw Pact, an East European military alliance, in May 1955.

The Crisis of Stalinism

The Sovietization of Eastern Europe, produced by overturning capitalism 'from above' and without the active involvement of broad sections of the population, created unique social formations. As already-weakened capitalist classes were pushed aside, new governing elites were consolidated. These were scaled-down versions of the Soviet Union's own bureaucratic caste of managers, planners, administrators, educators, and military and internal security personnel, and as in the USSR they were bound together by membership of their national Communist parties. These bureaucratic elites enjoyed considerable power and they were entirely willing to use force to repress dissenting voices, but they lacked the deep organic resources of a capitalist ruling *class*: they did not own private property, they did not have the dense and flexible networks of social connectivity built up over long periods of time, and they lacked the legitimacy and broad social hegemony derived from long years of rule. As a result, while all-intrusive and heavily armed, these bureaucratic castes had a brittleness that reflected the absence of the kind of social buffers—including moderate socialist parties and trade unions—that absorb and defuse class conflicts in capitalist society. In particular, the expropriation of private capitalists and their replacement by bureaucratic planners and plant managers meant that even modest factory-level protests over wages and working conditions could quickly spill over into conflicts with the state and its security forces that posed point-blank questions of political legitimacy.

---

[32]Brian McAllister Linn, *The Echo of Battle: The Army's Way of War* (Cambridge, MA: Harvard University Press, 2007), 153, 165.

These structural realities meant that the nonstop efforts of government propagandists to legitimize and popularize the new 'socialist' states were constantly undercut by the workings of the regimes themselves. Central planning and rapid industrialization boosted short-term output, but the use of Soviet-style financial rewards to incentivize individual productivity—a method known as Stakhanovism after a Soviet miner who exceeded his production quota fourteen-fold—was deeply divisive. By the early 1950s, rising production quotas and declining wages were evident across Eastern Europe, with take-home pay in Hungary falling 16 percent between 1949 and 1953.[33] At the same time, Soviet-style efforts to collectivize agriculture provoked peasant resistance, disrupting production and making food shortages part of daily life in the cities. These issues, combined with endemic shortages of consumer goods, poor housing, economic breakdowns caused by mismanagement, and undemocratic constraints on political and cultural expression, produced deep resentments that generated episodes of explosive resistance.

In June 1953, protests over wages and conditions by workers at the Škoda auto plant in Plzeň, Czechoslovakia, escalated into a localized uprising as demonstrators took over city hall and erected street barricades. Worryingly for the regime, local KSČ members and police officers joined the protestors. Later the same month, protests against increased production quotas by construction workers in East Berlin triggered a nationwide wave of strikes and demonstrations involving over a million people. State security forces—backed in Germany by the Red Army—suppressed both uprisings, but plant-level protests rumbled on. In Germany, thousands of members of the Socialist Unity Party (formed through the merger of the Communist and Social Democratic parties) quit in protest. Rebellions by industrial workers—the key social group upon which Communists claimed to anchor their legitimacy—combined with peasant resistance to collectivization to highlight the precarity of Soviet predominance in Eastern Europe. Far from the solid defensive glacis envisioned by Moscow in 1945, the Eastern Europe buffer zone was fast becoming a fractious borderland whose destabilizing influence rippled back into the USSR itself. Here, in summer 1953 the news of Stalin's death and the removal of secret police chief Lavrentiy Beria sparked a strike by 30,000 prison-camp inmates in the Vorkuta Gulag.[34] Forced laborers in the Siberian coal mines, led by political opponents of the regime including Trotskyists, anarchists, and Ukrainian nationalists, struck for two weeks, and although finally driven back to work their action secured improvements in working conditions while accelerating the dissolution of the Gulag system.

---

[33]Pittaway, *Eastern Europe*, 59.
[34]Gerland, "Vorkuta," 289.

In response to this mounting pressure, a faction of Soviet leaders led by Nikita Khrushchev took advantage of Stalin's death in March 1953 to advance a New Course, instituting reforms that would have been unthinkable while the dictator was alive. It took the reformers three years to consolidate their position, but at the Soviet Communist Party's Twentieth Congress in 1956 Khrushchev delivered a shocking denunciation of Stalin's brutal dictatorship. Khrushchev's 'secret speech' initiated a process of de-Stalinization—or thaw—that allowed a degree of cultural and political expression while decentralizing economic planning, promoting local initiative, and expanding the availability of food, consumer goods, and housing. There were strict limits to this process, which was fundamentally aimed to secure the rule of the bureaucratic elite by making concessions to popular discontent: as artists and political dissidents quickly discovered, de-Stalinization relaxed controls on speech and expression but did not remove them, and there was no broadening of popular democratic participation in political or economic decision-making.

Moscow's New Course had far-reaching consequences throughout Eastern Europe. Eager to reverse what Soviet leaders now saw as a destructive blunder, Khrushchev traveled to Belgrade in May 1955 to heal the rift with Yugoslavia. The Soviet leader expressed regret for the split, but while Belgrade welcomed the normalization of relations, it did not wholeheartedly rejoin Moscow's camp. After the split in 1948 Belgrade had tacked toward the United States, receiving security guarantees and military equipment from NATO while carving out a 'third path' in world politics in conjunction with leaders from India, Indonesia, Egypt, and elsewhere in the global South. Yugoslav leaders appreciated renewed ties with Eastern Europe, but they had no intention of abandoning the benefits of 'non-alignment'; as a result, instead of moderating political tensions in Eastern Europe, Soviet-Yugoslav rapprochement worked to legitimize and popularize new and unorthodox national roads.

With Khrushchev's encouragement, Eastern European regimes paused unpopular farm collectivization and boosted the production of consumer goods, and in 1956 the Cominform—Moscow's instrument of ideological conformity—was dissolved. But there was no easy out. Khrushchev's denunciation of Stalin had cracked the facade of Communist orthodoxy, but the results were unpredictable and often uncontrollable. In response to a strike by manufacturing workers in Poznań, Poland, in June 1956, Moscow sanctioned Gomułka's release from prison and his reinstatement as leader of the United Workers' Party on a reformist program. This concession to popular discontent had consequences in Hungary, which was already gripped by political crisis as reform-minded Communists confronted the unreconstructed Stalinism of central party leaders. Workers throughout Hungary were inspired by the uprising in Poznań, and events spun out of control after the violent repression of a student demonstration triggered a popular insurrection in Budapest in October 1956. As the brittle Stalinist

FIGURE 2.1 *The 1956 Hungarian Revolution: Mass demonstration in central Budapest against Soviet control, October 25, 1956. (Photo: FOTO: FORTEPAN/ Nagy Gyula, CC BY-SA 3.0 via Wikimedia.)*

state fractured, political power passed into the hands of factory councils and neighborhood committees. While forces backed and encouraged by Washington urged the restoration of capitalism, many workers' councils made it clear that their goal was the establishment of democratic and participatory socialism, not a return to private capitalism. Meanwhile, the new Communist prime minister Imre Nagy, installed to head off a revolution, announced free elections and Hungary's withdrawal from the Warsaw Pact. This was too much even for Moscow's most reform-minded leaders, and in November Soviet troops entered Budapest, killing several thousand people, toppling Nagy, and crushing the revolution. Nevertheless, despite continued repression launched by new Moscow-backed premier János Kádár, strikes continued through 1957, underscoring the fact that a 'Communist' regime could not stabilize itself by force alone.

'Peaceful Coexistence'

The crisis of Stalinism in the early 1950s took place within the vise of the Cold War stand-off with the United States. Eager to escape this terrible pressure, Khrushchev hoped to lower tensions between the 'camps' by establishing 'peaceful coexistence' between them. This approach recycled Moscow's long-standing willingness to avoid confrontation with the United States and it included an implicit pledge to utilize Communist parties in Western Europe and elsewhere to tamp down explosive class struggles. Khrushchev brought new dynamism to the pursuit of détente, traveling to the first postwar summit in Geneva in July 1955 with a proposal to dissolve both NATO and the Warsaw Pact in favor of a new collective security agreement. This initiative was quickly rebuffed by Washington, but the conference clearly marked a lessening of tension as American leaders toned down the shrill campaign for liberation from Communism that had accompanied the early phases of the Cold War. In its place they adopted a more low-key drive to intensify military-economic pressure on the USSR through an accelerating nuclear arms race while avoiding both conventional hot wars and a mutually devastating nuclear conflict.[35] The Soviets responded in kind, testing their own H-bomb in late 1955 and then announcing that they were "turning out missiles like sausages."[36]

Despite Khrushchev's bravado, Soviet production of nuclear weapons trailed far behind that of the United States, with the USSR stockpiling 3,300 weapons between 1950 and 1962 to the Americans' 27,000.[37] Without overseas bases or (until 1956) a long-range bomber, Soviet delivery systems also lagged. Moreover, while Soviet technology could produce spectacular successes—including the 1957 launch of Sputnik, the world's first orbital satellite—the USSR lacked the industrial capacity to turn them to strategic advantage. Instead, the pressure to keep pace with the Americans deepened distortions in the Soviet economy as resources flowed into weapons production instead of toward rounded and comprehensive economic development.

This heavily armed nuclear stand-off was the form taken by peaceful coexistence for the remainder of the Cold War. The Communist regimes in the Soviet Union and Eastern Europe thus remained trapped between US military pressure on the one hand and the aspirations of workers and peasants on the other. By the end of the 1950s, modest economic growth, combined with limited post-Hungary concessions to the working classes and expanded participation in world markets, generated a degree of precarious political stability. But, while bureaucratic 'self-reform' and recharged economic growth could postpone an existential crisis, they could not resolve the underlying tensions: as the Hungarian Revolution demonstrated, deep-going democratic transformations involving the active participation of working people in running society would quickly sweep away the entire

---

[35]David Foglesong, *The American Mission and the "Evil Empire"* (Cambridge: Cambridge University Press, 2007), 127.
[36]Nikita Khrushchev, quoted in Sergey Radchenko, "The Soviet Union and the Cold War Arms Race," in Thomas Mahnken, Joseph Maiolo, and David Stevenson, *Arms Races in International Politics* (Oxford: Oxford University Press, 2016), 164.
[37]David Holloway, "Nuclear Weapons and the Escalation of the Cold War," in Leffler et al., *Cambridge History of the Cold War*, 387.

bureaucratic superstructure of Stalinism. As a result, there were strict limits to self-reform. Instead, Communist leaders hoped to head off discontent by promoting 'socialist consumerism,' an effort that could only fuel desire for the American-made real thing. In this sense, the *modus vivendi* established on both national and international levels following the crisis of Stalinism in the mid-1950s offered no fundamental resolution to the predicament facing the bureaucratic elites. And, as events in Czechoslovakia (1968), Poland (1980), and throughout the Soviet Union and Eastern Europe in 1989–91 would show, unresolved—and unresolvable—tensions in the buffer zone increasingly weakened Stalinism on its home ground in the USSR.

Despite the deep and ultimately irresolvable contradictions of the Stalinist regimes in the USSR and Eastern Europe, however, it is important to recognize that their non-capitalist economies necessarily qualified the global dimensions of America's postwar hegemony. Washington's ongoing Cold War against the Soviet Union flowed from this reality and from the associated fear that despite Moscow's anti-revolutionary politics, the USSR might be joined by additional non-capitalist states as rebellions in China and the colonial world deepened. From this point of view, a protracted cold war marked by long stretches of uneasy coexistence was not Washington's preferred course, but given the military and political impossibility of a hot war it was the least bad alternative, and it shaped Washington's outlook as it confronted challenges to its global predominance in China and in the colonial world.

For Further Reading

Chiara Bonfiglioli, "Women's Social and Political Activism in the Early Cold War Era: The Case of Yugoslavia," *Aspasia*, Vol. 8 (2014).
Holly Case, "Reconstruction in East-Central Europe: Clearing the Rubble of Cold War Politics," *Past and Present*, Special Supplement 6 (2011).
Norman S. Naimark, *Stalin and the Fate of Europe: The Postwar Struggle for Sovereignty* (Cambridge, MA: Harvard University Press, 2019),
Mark Pittaway, *Eastern Europe, 1939–2000* (London: Arnold Publishers, 2004).
Sergey Radchenko, "The Soviet Union and the Cold War Arms Race," in Thomas Mahnken, Joseph Maiolo, and David Stevenson (eds.), *Arms Races in International Politics* (Oxford: Oxford University Press, 2016).
Geoffrey Roberts, "Stalin's Wartime Vision of the Peace, 1939–1945," in Timothy Snyder and Ray Brandon (eds.), *Stalin and Europe: Imitation and Domination, 1928–1953* (Oxford: Oxford University Press, 2014).
Oscar Sanchez-Sibony, *Red Globalization: The Political Economy of the Soviet Cold War from Stalin to Khrushchev* (Cambridge: Cambridge University Press, 2014).
Vladislav M. Zubok, *A Failed Empire: The Soviet Union in the Cold War from Stalin to Gorbachev* (Chapel Hill: University of South Carolina Press, 2009).

CHAPTER THREE

Hegemony Qualified: The Chinese Revolution and the War in Korea

The Great American Mutiny

In late 1945, tens of thousands of American soldiers took part in one of the largest and most effective mutinies in history. From the Philippines to Western Europe and the continental United States, servicemen and women on military bases around the world joined meetings and demonstrations demanding their immediate demobilization. Five thousand protested in Frankfurt, 5000 in Calcutta, and 15,000 in Honolulu.[1] In Manila, 20,000 packed the burnt-out Hall of Congress, setting up a Soldiers' Committee representing military personnel of "all creeds and backgrounds."[2] In America's segregated military, African Americans broke down barriers of discrimination and exclusion to protest alongside their Caucasian comrades. Soldiers openly flouted military regulations by protesting in uniform, commandeering military vehicles and, at Camp Shelby, Mississippi, shouting down their commanding general. Army newspapers like *Stars and Stripes*, long seen by commanders as a useful wartime safety valve, were suddenly overwhelmed with letters of protest— around two hundred a day arrived at the *Daily Pacifican*—and transformed into vectors of transnational connectivity.[3] GIs encouraged friends and

---

[1] Mary-Alice Waters, "1945: When U.S. Troops Said 'No!': A Hidden Chapter in the Fight Against War," *New International*, No. 7 (1991), 284.
[2] "Manila GIs Draft Protest to Army," *New York Times*, January 11, 1946.
[3] Daniel Eugene Garcia, "Class and Brass: Demobilization, Working Class Politics, and American Foreign Policy between War and Cold War," *Diplomatic History*, Vol. 34, No. 4 (September 2010), 683, fn 9.

FIGURE 3.1 *American soldiers demanding rapid demobilization march on US headquarters in Manila, January 6, 1946. (Photo: Army Signal Corps, Image SC 248840, National Archives.)*

family members to bombard politicians with messages demanding their rapid demobilization, and Senator Elbert D. Thomas, chair of the powerful Military Affairs Committee, complained that congressmen were receiving tens of thousands of letters every day.

Many mutinous citizen-soldiers had come to appreciate the power of collective action during the great labor battles of the 1930s, and their leaders included experienced union organizers. Manila Soldiers' Committee leader Sergeant Emil Mazey, for example, had been president of the militant Briggs local 212 of the United Auto Workers Union in Detroit and was an outspoken critic of wartime 'no-strike' pledges. For many GIs the issue was simple: the war that they had been drafted to fight was over, the Axis powers had been defeated, and it was time to go home. But time and again their speeches, picket signs, and letters home evoked a broader political outlook. Recruited to fight in the name of freedom, many soldiers were leery of serving as occupiers or—worse still—as agents of the restoration of European colonial rule or of the suppression of popular insurgencies like the one waged in the Philippines by the People's Anti-Japanese Army, or

Hukbalahap. Writing from Manila to the *Daily Pacifican*, one private argued that the United States was now on the wrong side of history, noting that "in the Oriental surge toward freedom, we cling to imperialism."[4] Opposition to being sent to China in support of Chiang Kai-shek's Guomindang (Nationalist) government loomed particularly large: writing to the *Chicago Defender* from a base in Burma, African American soldiers of the 823rd Aviation Engineer Battalion made it clear that they wanted no part of efforts to "'unify' China with bayonets and bombing planes and American lives."[5]

As we shall see in later chapters, the great American mutiny of 1945–46 overlapped with other uprisings and rebellions, including strike-mutinies by sailors in the Royal Indian Navy, protests by soldiers in British-Imperial armies, and a mounting wave of anti-colonial insurgency from Burma and Malaya to Indonesia and Indochina. Meanwhile, in the United States millions of workers were taking striking for higher wages. In this context, the unprecedented transnational GI mutiny and the broad support it enjoyed back home forced the Truman administration to accelerate troop repatriation and demobilization. Twelve-million strong at the end of the war, by summer 1946 the US military was reduced to three million before falling to 1.5 million in 1947. Stunningly successful in just a few months, the great GI rebellion was then largely erased from history: for obvious reasons, it was not a story that the top brass or their political masters wanted to keep retelling. The success of the mutiny also contained another shocking truth, which is that at the very moment of their greatest triumph, American leaders discovered to their horror that their massively powerful military machine was no longer fully responsive to their commands. It had, they found, become politically impossible to carry out the extended deployments to China and Southeast Asia that were necessary to dominate the emerging postwar world and to shape American hegemony over it.

China in 1945

The China to which American planners wanted to send troops was a place of paradox: while Washington presented Chinese premier Chiang Kai-shek as one of the four main leaders of the victorious allied alliance, his Nationalist or Guomindang (GMD) government was barely master in its own house. During the war, the Roosevelt administration had insisted on presenting China as one of the 'four policemen' of the coming postwar world, the leading powers—along with Britain, the Soviet Union, and the United States itself—around which the new order would be organized. In January 1943, the United States had formally relinquished a series of

---

[4]Ibid., 691.
[5]Ibid., 695.

insults to China's national sovereignty that had been imposed by several 'unequal treaties' signed since the middle of the nineteenth century. These included extraterritoriality—the exemption of US citizens from prosecution under Chinese law—American control of China's oversea trade through the operation of treaty ports, and the maintenance of autonomous American settlements and legation districts. This long-delayed reaffirmation of Chinese sovereignty created the legal basis for more equal relations between the two states and allowed Washington to boost China's standing on the world stage. In November 1943, Chiang Kai-shek attended a top-level Anglo-American strategy conference in Cairo, and in June 1944 a large Chinese delegation participated in the establishment of the postwar economic order at Bretton Woods. China's status as a world power was further underscored in October 1945 through its membership of the five-member Security Council of the new United Nations. Guomindang leaders embraced their new world role, envisaging an independent China capable of offering leadership to the postcolonial states emerging from the crisis of empire in India and across Southeast Asia. At home, they sketched out an ambitious program of postwar reconstruction led by large-scale state-managed industries and accompanied by the construction of a welfare state modeled on that being created by Britain's postwar Labour government.

Unfortunately for the Guomindang, their new world status and their grand schemes for reconstruction bore little relationship to the real situation on the ground in China. As in Eastern Europe, the formal end of the war in China in August 1945 revealed a scene of widespread economic breakdown, social dislocation, and famine. Around ninety-five million people had become refugees in their own land as they fled the Japanese occupation of provinces in northern and eastern China: by the end of the war, 34.8 percent of the prewar population of Jiangsu had fled along with 42.7 percent of Hunan and 43.5 percent of Wuhan.[6] Moreover, in contrast to the Europe, where Germany's defeat was absolute and the continent was entirely occupied by the troops of one or another of the victorious allies, in China—as throughout Southeast Asia—the war came to a ragged end. The Guomindang only actually ruled in a relatively small part of the country centered on their wartime capital of Chongqing in south-central China. Japanese occupation forces, two million strong and undefeated in battle, still controlled most of the major cities, as they had done throughout the long war since 1937, but they exercised a much weaker hold on the vast Chinese countryside. Here, Guomindang rule had broken down entirely in the early years of the war, leaving local power vacuums to be filled by a kaleidoscopic succession of warlord militias, bandit gangs, and—especially

---

[6]See Richard Overy, *Blood and Ruins: The Last Imperial War, 1931–1945* (New York: Viking, 2022), 833; Jasmin Khan, "Wars of Displacement: Exile and Uprooting in the 1940s," in Michael Geyer and Adam Tooze (eds.), *The Cambridge History of the Second World War*, Vol. III, (New York: Cambridge University Press, 2015), 281.

in northern China—the well-organized forces of the Chinese Communist Party (CCP).

In sharp contrast to Europe, American troops were largely absent: indeed, their numbers had fallen from a mid-war height after Japan's 1944 *Ichi-gō* offensive—Tokyo's largest ground campaign of the war—forced the withdrawal of the long-range bombers of the US Twentieth Air Force. Many of the 60,000 US military personnel who remained in China were organized for logistical, communications, and training duties rather than for combat. Then in August 1945, a massive and long-promised Soviet offensive involving over 1.5 million troops routed Japanese forces in Tokyo's client state of Manchukuo, establishing a Soviet military presence in northeastern China/Manchuria. Moscow had promised Chiang Kai-shek that its forces would not move deeper into the country, the Red Army seemed disinterested in China's domestic politics, and Soviet troops were absorbed in looting industrial plant and equipment for shipment to the USSR; nevertheless, Washington hardly found the striking contrast between the United States and the Soviet military presence in China comforting.

In spring 1945, the overwhelming physical presence of allied military forces in Europe imposed a degree of political order—and later partition—on an otherwise chaotic scene: in China, on the other hand, the absence of any predominant military power opened the door to a period of intense instability in which ordinary Chinese people, many of them peasant farmers, had a chance to put their stamp on history. As the news of Japan's surrender rippled through China, the Guomindang scrambled to reassert its control over the country. At Washington's insistence, Japanese forces were instructed to surrender only to Guomindang officials and not to the Communists, and in Nanjing Japanese troops continued to police the city until GMD leaders arrived to accept their surrender. American officials also wanted the Guomindang to accept the surrender of Japanese forces in the former British colony of Hong Kong, but London, acting on a cabinet decision to "recover as much as possible of our former influence in China," rushed a Royal Navy squadron to the city.[7] Despite objections from both Washington and the Guomindang government now installed in Nanjing, British officers accepted the Japanese surrender on September 16, formally reestablishing London's colonial rule over the city. In other cities and along major transport routes, Japan's occupying armies remained under arms during the surrender, tasked by the Americans and the Guomindang with ensuring an orderly handover of power. In an effort to bolster Guomindang authority, Washington also dispatched two Marine divisions to China to secure ports and communication centers and to organize the repatriation of Japanese forces, while American air and naval units began moving Nationalist troops into northern China.

---

[7] The Cabinet's Far Eastern Committee, quoted in Overy, *Blood and Ruins*, 863.

With American assistance and aided by Japanese soldiers who remained under arms, the Guomindang quickly reestablished control over China's major cities. It also accelerated efforts to relieve the effects of famine and wartime destruction, particularly in rural areas. Since 1944, supplies of food and other emergency aid had been organized by the American-led United Nations Relief and Rehabilitation Agency (UNRRA), and between 1946 and 1947, $500 million of aid was distributed.[8] UNRRA's work in China highlighted new modes of cooperation between national governments and transnational relief agencies, but its effectiveness was undermined by tensions between UNRRA and the Guomindang, which American aid officials viewed as irredeemably corruption. These difficulties underscored the broader problem of reestablishing government control in the countryside. In many rural areas Guomindang officials had fled at the start of the war, and even where the government had retained a semblance of control its wartime policies—including forced conscription, taxation-in-kind, and the deliberate flooding of vast areas of farmland to deter Japanese advances—had made it deeply unpopular.

Where Guomindang authority had crumbled in northern China, wartime conditions facilitated the rapid growth of the Communist Party. After military setbacks early in the war, CCP leaders had abandoned large-scale military operations in favor of building 'base areas' in rural regions nominally under Japanese control. Protected by guerrilla forces, Communist cadres built popular support among peasant farmers by fostering literacy, basic healthcare, women's rights, and, most importantly, by promoting land reforms that reduced rents, broke the power of landlord elites, and distributed land to the tillers. As in Yugoslavia, war and social revolution were intertwined, with the flight of pro-Guomindang landowners and administrators—or their collaboration with the Japanese—opening space for popular political action. CCP base areas were fluid spaces, morphing amoeba-like in response to assaults by Japanese troops and forces of the pro-Tokyo Reorganized National Government, but the popular energy and enthusiasm that they generated are key to understanding this critical period.

From April to December 1944, Tokyo's *Ichi-gō* offensive dealt heavy blows to Guomindang and American forces in southern China, but the concentration of Japanese military resources into this one campaign relieved the pressure on Communist base areas in the north and facilitated the rapid expansion of CCP influence. In August 1944, the Communist-led Eighth Route Army crossed the Yangtze River, linking up with local fighters in Hunan province to begin rebuilding the party's influence in southern China. Communist forces grew rapidly, and by summer 1945 the party claimed 1.2 million members while leading over one million soldiers in the New

---

[8] Khan, "Wars of Displacement: Exile and Uprooting in the 1940s," 289.

Fourth and Eighth Route armies.⁹ The end of the world war in summer 1945 found CCP forces poised to advance on Beijing and on the great ports and Yangtze Valley cities of the south in a campaign that would have challenged the Guomindang for national predominance. As the world war ended, however, the Communist Party's advance faced opposition not only from the Guomindang, the United States, and the undefeated Japanese forces in China, but also from the Soviet Union. As in Europe, Moscow wanted to lower tensions with the United States with the aim of preserving the Grand Alliance, and in a sharply worded message to CCP leader Mao Zedong, Stalin insisted that China "must not have another civil war."¹⁰ What he meant, above all, was that it should not have a Yugoslav-style anti-capitalist revolution.

China in American and Soviet planning

In many ways, China—or rather control of the vast Chinese market—was the great prize of the Pacific War. It was a goal that had been on the minds of American business, military, and political elites since the end of the nineteenth century. Washington's Open Door notes, lodged with the other Great Powers in 1899, opposed European plans to partition China into rival spheres of influence and insisted instead on equal and unrestricted access to the Chinese market. Warily acknowledged by its rivals, Washington's Open Door policy reflected confidence in American economic competitiveness— free trade is always the policy of the strong—while facilitating imperial predominance without the costs and perils of direct colonial rule. Initially, Washington wanted to enlist the new capitalist nation-state of Japan as a junior partner in East Asia, but these hopes were dashed by Tokyo's own explosive overseas expansionism in response to the Great Depression of the 1930s. Following Japan's conquest of Manchuria in 1931 and its full-scale invasion of China in 1937, American policy settled on backing Chiang Kai-shek's Guomindang government by supplying it with war matériel. This was not as obvious a conclusion as it seems in hindsight. During the 1930s, the Guomindang had looked first to Germany and then to the Soviet Union for military backing, and while Washington finally approved plans to outfit thirty Chinese infantry divisions and sanctioned the operation of a small all-volunteer American air force, little actual aid was forthcoming prior to the Japanese attack on Pearl Harbor in December 1941.

America's formal entry into the war transformed the geopolitical situation, initiating a genuinely worldwide war while opening a struggle for naval

---

⁹Hans van de Ven, *China at War: Triumph and Tragedy in the Emergence of the New China* (Cambridge, MA: Harvard University Press, 2018), 198.
¹⁰Stalin, quoted in De Ven, *China at War*, 213.

supremacy in the Pacific. In relation to China, however, the United States faced some particular challenges. Beginning in 1937, Japan's invasion of China had secured control of all the major ports, and its conquest of British-ruled Burma in early 1942 cut land access to Nationalist China via the Burma Road. These developments made the supply of US aid to Guomindang forces headquartered in Chongqing much more difficult. Washington's grand-strategic preference for fighting an 'air-sea war' precluded the dispatch of a large land army to Asia and forced American planners to rely instead on efforts to modernize, equip, and train substantial Chinese armies. The lack of direct access to China made this effort dependent on supplies flown into China over the 'Hump,' an arduous air route from India across the Himalaya. Despite the commitment of substantial resources, this tenuous air bridge was entirely inadequate to the task of re-equipping the Chinese army, particularly from late 1943 to March 1944, when it was also used to support Operation *Matterhorn*, America's China-based strategic bombing campaign against Japan. Given these strategic and operational limitations, American policy was effectively reduced to simply trying to keep China in the war until a better situation opened up.

Until summer 1944, American leaders expected that the parallel advances of US forces across the central Pacific and through New Guinea to the Philippines would also allow the capture of Formosa (Taiwan), a move that would facilitate the reopening of direct routes into China. As it turned out, the success of Japan's *Ichi-gō* offensive, General Douglas MacArthur's insistence on the recapture of the Philippines, and the drive to establish bomber bases in the Marianas Islands to replace those lost in China, effectively derailed these plans. As a result, America's war with Japan ended *before* substantial US forces were established on the ground in China. Meanwhile, American relations with the Guomindang soured, due in no small part to Washington's inability to deliver on its promises of large-scale aid. In public American spokespeople continued to present China as a pillar of the coming postwar world, but officials on the ground in Chongqing, along with many of their superiors in Washington, were increasingly frustrated by the corruption of the Guomindang regime and by its apparent reluctance to fight the Japanese. Roosevelt managed to avoid an open rupture with Chiang Kai-shek, but relations remained strained, particularly after the July 1944 dispatch of an American military mission to the Communist capital of Yan'an. At least some State Department officials felt that the CCP offered the best prospect for long-term political stability and economic development in China, particularly if the party was viewed as an expression of peasant nationalism rather than communist revolution.

Like Washington, Moscow faced some difficult challenges in China. Following the Red Army's defeat of Japanese probes into Soviet Mongolia in 1939, Tokyo had signed a nonaggression pact with the USSR in April 1941. This pact held for the next four years, and it allowed Moscow to focus all its efforts on its struggle for survival against Germany on its western front. With Germany defeated, and in accordance with long-standing promises to the Allies reaffirmed at the Potsdam conference, Moscow finally joined the war against Japan in August 1945. Despite the scale of its dramatic two-week blitzkrieg in Manchuria, however, Moscow's war aims in China were strictly limited and, as in Europe, they had nothing to do with spreading communism. Instead, the USSR aimed to strengthen its own defensive position by annexing South Sakhalin and the Kuril Islands and by exploiting the resources of occupied Manchuria to boost its postwar economic recovery. In preparation for its drive into Manchuria, Moscow signed a treaty of Friendship and Alliance with Chongqing that formally recognized the Guomindang regime as the legitimate government of China. Soviet leaders assumed that these limited and explicitly non-revolutionary goals would avoid conflict with the United States, but they were not really a concession on Moscow's part; instead, Soviet leaders genuinely hoped that a Guomindang-Communist Party coalition government would establish China as a peaceful and capitalist nation-state neighbor while heading off both the prospect of a destabilizing and uncontrollable social revolution and the danger of an American-dominated China.

Moscow's actions conformed to these limited political goals. The Red Army's *August Storm* offensive smashed Japanese forces in Manchuria, overturned Tokyo's client states of Manchukuo and Mengjiang (Inner Mongolia) and helped force Japan's surrender. At the same time, Soviet troops kept the Chinese Communists at arm's length, pushing their fighters out of key cities in Manchuria and advocating that the CCP follow the "French way" by forming a coalition government with the Guomindang and merging its armed forces into a new national army.[11] As in Germany, the violent and anti-woman attacks inflicted by Red Army soldiers on people in Manchuria—including CCP supporters—were hardly calculated to win hearts and minds. In the industrial centers of Manchuria that had been developed under Japanese rule, Soviet troops began dismantling plant and equipment for shipment back to the USSR. At the same time, as Japanese colonial rule crumbled in Korea the Red Army expanded Moscow's Asian buffer zone by sweeping into the northern part of the country before halting on the 38th Parallel in accord with a hastily concluded agreement with the Americans.

The Chinese Revolution

In the months following the end of the war with Japan, both Moscow and Washington tried to cajole their recalcitrant Chinese protégées into a coalition government. Moscow approached this task from a position of strength.

---

[11]De Ven, *China at War*, 232.

In the context of its efforts to maintain the Grand Alliance, a coalition government was the Soviet's desired solution to the political crisis in China, and their crushing victory in Manchuria gave them the political leverage that came with a military presence on the ground. For the Americans, however, a coalition government was a poor substitute for the Guomindang-led client state they wanted, but they recognized that the strength of the Communist Party made this impossible short of victory in a renewed civil war waged with US military assistance. And, at least in the short term, that was effectively ruled out as the great GI mutiny undercut the ability to deploy large American ground forces to China. Instead of combat troops, Washington dispatched top wartime planner General George C. Marshall to China in December 1945 on what became a harrowing year-long mission to broker an accord between the Guomindang and the Communists that, it was hoped, would lead to the establishment of a stable coalition government.

Spurred on by Moscow—which saw a Communist-Guomindang administration as a kind of Chinese 'people's democracy'—the CCP signaled its willingness to join a coalition, which it hailed as a "great victory for China's democratic revolution."[12] Like Tito in Yugoslavia, Mao hated being ordered around by Moscow, but unlike the Yugoslavs, the Chinese Communists were far from taking power when the war ended, and they understood the danger of pursuing their revolution against *both* Moscow and Washington. For its part, the Guomindang was opposed to joining a coalition with the CCP. This, too, was a complex decision. A protracted period of peace and stability—along with substantial inflows of capital and aid—was needed to rebuild war-ravaged China, and Guomindang leaders recognized that a coalition with the CCP might create the political framework that would make this possible. At the same time, however, Chiang Kai-shek feared that a coalition would fatally weaken his position by embedding Communist forces in the administrative and military apparatus of the state while CCP-backed land reforms undermined the landed elites upon which the GMD was based. Guomindang leaders also recognized that their military advantage over the CCP—around four-to-one in 1945—would not last forever, and while promising Marshall that they were about to join a coalition, they resolved to crush the CCP.

The Sino-Soviet Treaty agreed between Moscow and the Guomindang in August 1945 allowed the Soviets to retain to key ports in Manchuria while recognizing Chinese sovereignty over the region as a whole. The CCP was not included in these deliberations. After delaying its withdrawal in order to allow it to finish looting local industry, the Red Army pulled out of Manchuria in spring 1946. As it did so, the US air and naval forces shipped in 228,000 Nationalist troops—70 percent of Chiang's army—who drove CCP forces out of southern Manchuria by the end of May. A confused political

---

[12] CCP statement, February 1, 1946, quoted in Arnold A. Offner, *Another Such Victory: President Truman and the Cold War, 1945–1953* (Stanford, CA: Stanford University Press, 2002), 322.

and military period followed during which General Marshall's unflagging efforts to establish a coalition government were punctuated by fresh bouts of fighting in Manchuria for which—as the Americans well understood—the Guomindang was largely responsible. Chiang's intransigence was underpinned by his belief that, in the context of sharpening Cold War tensions with the Soviet Union, the Americans would ultimately have no choice but to back the Guomindang to the hilt.

This turned out to be a major misjudgment. Frustrated by its inability to pull a stable coalition together and dismayed by mounting evidence that American-funded UNRRA aid was being stolen by Guomindang officials and sold on the black market, Washington wound up the Marshall Mission and completed the withdrawal of the bulk of the Marines from northern China in May 1947. The Guomindang responded to the American withdrawal by launching a ferocious anti-Communist offensive that registered sweeping gains in Manchuria and even captured the CCP's storied wartime capital of Yan'an in March 1947. Despite these advances, however, American observers concluded that without US support Guomindang forces would soon be overextended and exhausted, forcing Chiang back to the negotiating table. Unmoved by the deepening crisis, Truman—who likened supplying the Guomindang to "pouring sand down a rat hole"—refused to authorize new arms shipments.[13]

The renewed civil war that unfolded over the next two years saw Communist forces based in the Manchurian countryside launching punishing guerrilla attacks on the Guomindang's city-based garrisons before launching a counter-offensive in fall 1948 that involved a series of sweeping People's Liberation Army (PLA) advances. By this time, Moscow had finally given up on the wartime Grand Alliance, and the confrontational new course announced by the formation of the Cominform in October 1947 allowed Soviet weapons to begin flowing to CCP forces in Manchuria for the first time. During 1949, PLA forces led by General Lin Biao won control of much of northern China, capturing Beijing after a forty-day siege in late January and preparing to cross the Yangtze into the Guomindang's southern heartland in September. Lin Biao's inspired military leadership clearly played a part in these dramatic advances, as did Soviet-supplied weapons. But the key to CCP military successes remained fundamentally rooted in the advancing social revolution. In October 1947, the CCP accelerated the land reform program in its base areas by confiscating land from large landowners and distributing it to poor peasants and agricultural workers. These measures, combined with steps to expand literacy and healthcare, consolidated the party's popular support across much of rural north and northeastern China and helped to win new backing from urban students, workers, and intellectuals. At the same time, rampant inflation and plunging real wages provoked

---

[13]Truman, quoted Offner, *Another Such Victory*, 326.

a mounting wave of strikes in Shanghai and other industrial centers that further undermined support for the Guomindang. As the PLA advanced, the morale of the Guomindang army began to crumble as individuals, small groups, and then entire units—including the whole of the 60th Army—went over to the Communists, taking their American-supplied tanks and heavy weapons with them.

Despite backing the CCP's renewal of the civil war, Soviet leaders were concerned that a crushing and nation-wide Communist victory would destabilize world politics and provoke a sharp confrontation with the United States. Now, with Communist forces poised to cross the Yangtze into the south, Moscow made a final effort to contain the Chinese revolution. Since the resumption of full-scale fighting in 1947, Soviet leaders had been pressuring the CCP to revive talks with the Guomindang in the hope of resuscitating plans for a coalition government. As bitter fighting ended any hope of a coalition, Soviet leaders floated the idea of partitioning China on the line of the Yangtze, proposing—in a nod to Chinese imperial history—to set up "Northern [Communist] and Southern [Guomindang] Dynasties."[14]

FIGURE 3.2 *People's Liberation Army soldiers assemble for the assault on Shanghai during the closing phases of the Chinese Revolution, May 21, 1949. (Photo: Keystone/Hulton Archive/Getty Images.)*

---

[14]Mao Zedong, quoted in Donggil Kim, "Stalin and the Chinese Civil War," *Cold War History*, Vol. 10, No. 2 (May 2010), 186.

In Europe, the partition of Germany was being consolidated amidst sharpening Cold War tensions, and Moscow hoped that a parallel solution might stabilize politics in Asia. At the same time, Moscow's relationship with the CCP was complex, combining a patronizing underestimation of the party's military capacity with a reflexive hostility to social revolution. As Mao himself pointed out, Stalin feared that the Chinese leader would become a new "Asian Tito."[15] Moscow's proposal to partition China underscores the conservative and fundamentally anti-revolutionary character of its politics, but it cut little ice with a CCP leadership that was now riding a powerful wave of popular revolutionary enthusiasm.

Brushing aside Moscow's objections, PLA troops crossed the Yangtze in September 1949, reaching Guangzhou (Canton) in mid-October and then fanning out across the south. Meanwhile, back in Beijing Mao proclaimed the establishment of the People's Republic of China (PRC) on October 1, 1949. Defeated Guomindang forces retreated first to their old wartime capital in Chongqing and then, in early December, to the island of Taiwan. Guomindang forces had established their control over Taiwan after brutally suppressing an indigenous Taiwanese uprising in early 1947 with the loss of 35,000 lives. From here, Chiang Kai-shek continued to promote the fiction that this offshore Republic of China remained the legitimate government of the entire country.

Of China's major cities, only Hong Kong now remained outside Communist control. Here British colonial rule, given tenuous legal sanction by a ninety-nine-year lease on the New Territories of Kowloon signed with the Qing Dynasty in 1899, was reestablished in September 1945. Over the following years Hong Kong's population was tripled by the arrival of refugees fleeing China's civil war, while Chinese capitalists came from Shanghai and other cities to establish new manufacturing facilities under British protection. London was determined to hold onto this imperial outpost, which it viewed as a key entrepôt to China—where British investors still had very substantial investments—and as a vital business, military, and transportation center for operations across East and Southeast Asia. As People's Liberation Army advanced southward, the British moved substantial land and naval forces to Hong Kong and began digging in for a siege. Communist leaders demanded that the British withdraw, but they were unwilling to face the diplomatic crisis that would have been provoked by an armed assault. There is no doubt that a Chinese attack would have been successful, but London's willingness to fight stayed Beijing's hand. British Foreign Secretary Ernest Bevin referred to Hong Kong as the "Berlin of the East": in fact, it was more like an Asian Trieste.[16]

---

[15]Zhihua Shan and Yafeng Xia, "Leadership transfer in the Asian revolution: Mao Zedong and the Asian Cominform," *Cold War History*, Vol. 14, No. 2 (2014), 200.
[16]Ernest Bevin, quoted in Derek Leebaert, *Grand Improvisation: America Confronts the British Superpower, 1945–1957* (New York: Farrar, Straus and Giroux, 2018), 125.

The CCP Consolidates Control

By the end of 1949, most of mainland China was under at least the nominal control of the new Communist government in Beijing. The CCP now faced the daunting challenge of consolidating and securing its dramatic victory while reviving the war-shattered Chinese economy. In the long-standing CCP strongholds of north and northeast China—the so-called old liberated areas—sweeping land reform had already secured the firm peasant support critical to sustaining the revolutionary war, but in the rural expanses of south, central, and eastern China the party remained largely an unknown quantity.[17] Across much of this region armed bands loyal to the Guomindang, local warlord militias, and other 'bandit' groups continued to operate, and the old landlord elites remained firmly entrenched. As it faced these challenges, the CCP also had to work to rebuild popular support in the cities after years of functioning largely as a rural party. These were monumental tasks, but the party's credible claim to be the only force capable of restoring national unity, peace, and economic recovery quickly built its legitimacy, including among middle-class, intellectual, and administrative layers who were inspired by the CCPs vision of national revival. After long years of endemic corruption, this appeal exercised an energizing moral force as dishonest officials were turned out and rampant inflation tamed. Across the country, many people contrasted the disciplined and orderly behavior of Communist troops with that of the Guomindang.

Communist leaders trod carefully in this new situation. While the CCP clearly called the shots, the new government it set up contained numerous representatives—including eleven out of twenty-four ministers—drawn from several small middle-class parties that had long sought a third road between the Communists and the Guomindang. Likewise, large numbers of bureaucrats and administrators (including many former Guomindang members) remained in office, and while the new government nationalized large enterprises with close ties to the old regime, it worked closely with the members of the national bourgeoisie who continued to own and manage their businesses. In some factories CCP cadres curbed union militancy in order to boost production. Much of rural China outside of the old liberated areas remained under direct military rule as PLA forces tackled the remaining 'bandit' groups, and CCP-led land reform programs were soon underway. As in the old northern base areas, peasants confiscated and redistributed landlord property, and despite initial suspicion of newly arrived CCP cadres, land reform accelerated during 1950. It was not a

---

[17]Frederick C. Teiwes, "The Establishment and Consolidation of the New Regime, 1949–1957," in Roderick MacFarquhar (ed.), *The Politics of China: The Eras of Mao and Deng* (Cambridge: Cambridge University Press, 1997), 20–1.

peaceful revolution, with the upwelling of long-suppressed anger claiming the lives of many landlords and 'rich peasants.'[18]

Despite Moscow's disapproval of the CCP's relationship with China's national bourgeoisie—the people's democracy period was now definitively over in Europe—Chinese leaders believed that this United Front phase of their revolution might last for several years. As the party consolidated its new urban base and extended its geographical reach, membership grew from 2.8 million in 1948 to 5.8 million in 1950.[19] Despite this rapid growth, it took time to organize and train enthusiastic but inexperienced recruits, and in the meantime there was little choice but to rely on the closely supervised work of former city and government administrators. As CCP leaders recognized, centralized economic planning was beyond their capacity, and while Beijing issued slogans offering overall direction and guidance, local leaders enjoyed significant autonomy. Increasingly, however, CCP cadres were reinforced by the arrival of Soviet experts and by Chinese students returning from periods of study in the USSR. Nevertheless, while Chinese leaders welcomed Soviet aid and urged party cadres to study its economic model, they had neither forgotten nor forgiven Moscow's repeated attempts to force the Chinese Revolution to conform to its own narrow national interests.

Not surprisingly, Washington had little interest in the nuances of domestic politics in this 'New China.' For American political elites, the loss of China—as if it was theirs to lose!—was a stunning blow, all the more so because it had seemed to unfold in slow motion while they watched impotent on the sidelines. Washington had anticipated its postwar hegemony being temporarily qualified by the Soviet predominance in Eastern Europe, but American leaders had neither foreseen the coming Chinese Revolution nor been able to forestall it. Instead, after the end of the Marshall Mission in late 1946, American policy had essentially collapsed in confusion. In April 1947, Washington had lifted the arms embargo and instructed the departing Marines turn their weapons over to the Guomindang, and the 1948 China Aid Act opened the door to $463 million in economic and military aid. But American policymakers remained deeply concerned with what Marshall called the Guomindang's "corruption, inefficiency and impotence," and in early 1949 Truman delayed shipments of military supplies funded by the China Aid Act out of feared that they would simply end up in PLA hands.[20]

Tellingly, Washington never seriously contemplated direct American military intervention in China's civil war, despite occasional lurches in this direction by the Joint Chiefs of Staff: having missed its chance in fall 1945 due to the GI rebellion, the domestic and geopolitical dangers of getting

---

[18]Ibid., 36.
[19]Ibid., 22.
[20]George Marshall, Feb. 1948, quoted in Offner, *Another Such Victory*, 328.

embroiled in a major land war in Asia effectively kept this option off the table. Instead, Washington's response to the establishment of the People's Republic of China was to deny it diplomatic recognition and membership of the United Nations while pledging US military support for the defense of the new Guomindang regime in Taiwan. With American support, Chiang Kai-shek's Republic of China continued to occupy China's seat on the United Nations Security Council. For its part the British government was keen to establish a *modus vivendi* with China that would acknowledge its continued control of Hong Kong, and London granted diplomatic recognition to the PRC in January 1950. For Beijing, London, and Washington alike, continued British colonial rule in Hong Kong furnished an unexpected site of backdoor diplomatic contact and economic exchange.

War in Korea

On June 25, 1950, troops of the Korean People's Army crossed the 38th Parallel from the northern part of the partitioned country into the south. The involvement of American-led United Nations forces on one side of the war that followed, and that of the Chinese People's Volunteer Army on the other, have made it easy to picture this as a classic Cold War conflict. This Cold War framing has real importance. For Washington, the fighting in Korea offered the alluring prospect of reunifying Korean peninsula under American leadership and the establishment of a major client state—and a permanent US military outpost—in the Sino-Soviet borderlands. For Beijing and Moscow, America's intervention in Korea, along with its increased naval presence in the South China Sea and its moves to begin rebuilding Japan as a regional power, were seen as a major threat to the security of both the PRC and the USSR. At the same time, however, and like the events in Eastern Europe discussed in the previous chapter, the fighting in Korea was fundamentally driven by national and regional issues that unfolded within the framework of the wider Cold War: for most Koreans, the main issue was not the deepening world geopolitical divide, but rather the long denial of Korean sovereignty—first at the hands of Japanese imperialism and then as a result of the US and Soviet occupations—and the economic, social, and cultural oppression that accompanied it.

Beginning with the imposition of an unequal treaty in 1876 and consolidated with the establishment of direct colonial rule in 1910, Tokyo's domination of Korea was the cornerstone of wartime Japan's autarkic-imperial project in East and Southeast Asia. Substantial flows of Japanese capital promoted large-scale industrial development, and after Tokyo established the client state of Manchukuo in 1931, it joined with northern Korea to form a major center of industrial production geared to meet Japan's needs. Korea was also a major source of rice, grown by small peasant farmers for export to Japan. As in other colonies, colonial rule rested not only on structures of direct foreign rule but also on layers of locals—often landowners or businesspeople—who staffed the administrative bureaucracy, filled the ranks of the brutally effective Korean National Police, and volunteered for service in Japan's armed forces. Tokyo intensified its colonial exploitation during the Second World War, forcing two million Koreans to work in Japan—where tens of thousands were killed by American bombs—while millions more were dragooned into Japanese-owned factories and mines at home.[21] Beginning in 1943, Koreans were conscripted into Japanese military service, and as many as 200,000 women were forced into sexual slavery to serve Japanese soldiers as 'comfort women.'

Despite the severity of Japanese rule and its concerted campaign to extirpate Korean culture, anti-colonial resistance groups operated throughout the occupation, and their activities intensified during the Second World War. Northern Korea, with its geographical proximity to Communist base areas in northern China, was a center of anti-Japanese guerrilla activity, and many Korean resistance fighters—including future North Korean leader Kim Il Sung—trained and fought with the People's Liberations Army during the Chinese Revolution. Korean guerrilla forces had a broad transnational border region within which to operate, and their campaigns enjoyed substantial popular support: in 1945, US officers estimated that 95 percent of the two million Koreans in Manchuria were anti-Japanese, while only 5 percent were sympathetic to Tokyo.[22]

Most Koreans, whether living in Korea or in the enforced diaspora, viewed Japan's defeat in 1945 as a new dawn. Throughout the peninsula a broad social revolution took shape with astonishing speed, unfolding in step with the popular insurrections erupting across Japan's former Southeast Asian 'Co-Prosperity Sphere.' Acting under the overall umbrella of the Committee for the Preparation of Korean Independence (CPKI), local People's Committees composed of communists, trade unionists, Christian socialists, and social democrats as well as anti-Japanese landlords and businesspeople, assumed the functions of government as Japanese rule collapsed.[23] On September 12, CPKI activists met in Seoul to establish the Korean People's Republic (KPR), proclaiming the nationalization of banking, key industries, and transportation, along with a sweeping program of land reform, democratic rights, and women's equality. Meanwhile, workers seized control of Japanese-owned factories and those of their Korean collaborators, and by November 1945 over 700 plants were being run by workers' committees. In the countryside peasants took over land owned by collaborators and organized to impose reduced rents

---

[21] Bruce Cummings, *The Korean War: A History* (New York: The Modern Library, 2010), 103.
[22] Cumings, *The Korean War*, 50.
[23] Kornel Chang, "Independence Without Liberation: Democratization as Decolonization Management in U.S.-Occupied Korea, 1945–1948," *The Journal of American History*, June 2020, 81.

on land leased from 'patriotic' landlords. Members of the Communist Party of Korea (CPK) were part of this popular upsurge but, acting within the framework of Soviet policy and fearful of antagonizing the Americans, their cadres actively discouraged militant action by workers and peasants.

Even as the Korean People's Republic was being set up, however, Korea was already in the grip of new military occupations, with Soviet forces halting on the 38th Parallel while American troops advanced northwards to meet them. In the north, the Soviets had no firm plans: as in Eastern Europe, Moscow wanted to strengthen its geostrategic position rather than advance social revolution, but Soviet leaders were flexible enough to embrace local KPR leaders while gradually sidelining those resistant to the consolidation of Communist predominance. This was not an entirely smooth process, and while veteran nationalist Cho Man-sik was initially favored by Moscow, he disappeared in early 1946 after clashing with Soviet authorities. Nevertheless, violence in the north paled in comparison with the bloodbath unleashed in the southern part of the country. Here, under cover of plans for a five-year period of joint US-Soviet trusteeship that would prepare Korea for independence, American commander General John Hodge set out to overturn the KPR and the broad array of local People's Committees on which it rested. Working with Japanese officials and former Korean collaborators, American officers revived Tokyo's colonial bureaucracy—including the notorious Korean National Police (KNP)—and resuscitated the rightist Korean Democratic Party. In response, mass protests against the US-Soviet trusteeship plan took place across the country in late 1945. However, while the influential Communist Party of Korea CPK) initially supported the demonstrations, it quickly changed course and, taking its cue from Moscow's participation in the trusteeship scheme, began denouncing them. The CPK's pro-Moscow stance divided the popular movement at a critical moment, fatally undercutting the defense of the Korean People's Republic.

In October 1946 a further wave of strikes and peasant rebellions rippled across the south in the face of violent repression by the National Police and the American military. By this time, Washington had long abandoned plans for a demilitarized Korea under joint US-Soviet oversight and was preparing for the permanent partition of the peninsula and the establishment of a client state in the south. To advance this project, American officials worked closely with right-wing businessman Syngman Rhee, whose wartime residence in the United States meant that he was untainted by collaboration with the Japanese. Like Chiang Kai-shek, Rhee was distrusted by the American for his headstrong and unpredictable behavior, but he nevertheless made himself indispensable to their plans. His was also the first rightist dictator put in power by Washington in the postwar period. Rigged elections in 1946 and 1948—Moscow had no monopoly on this front—secured Rhee's position, and in August 1948 the Republic of Korea (ROK) was founded. American backing for the new regime was symbolized by General Douglas MacArthur's beaming presence at the inaugural ceremonies. Over the following months Washington reduced its military presence in Korea, but a strong Military Advisory Group stayed on to train South Korean forces and to lead their 'counterinsurgency' operations. In the north, Moscow sponsored the formation of the Democratic People's Republic of Korea in September 1948 in response to establishment of the ROK in the south.

Both the Republic of Korea and the Democratic People's Republic were the direct products of the violent overturn of the Korean People's Republic. In the south, Rhee's forces moved quickly to crush a peasant rebellion on the island of Cheju and to suppress an uprising led by mutinous soldiers in the port city of Yosu. By spring 1950, American advisors believed that the new regime was stable: over 100,000 Koreans had died in political violence since 1945, the vast majority of them at the hands of Korean rightists and their US backers.[24] While these events were unfolding south of the 38th Parallel, North Korean leader Kim Il Sung advocated invading the south in order to reunify the country, but he was restrained by Soviet leaders fearful of provoking a broader war with the United States. By spring 1950, however, Moscow was emboldened by the Chinese Revolution and by its own recent acquisition of nuclear weapons, and it saw an opportunity to push back against the United States while shifting attention away from Europe. In this context, Kim was authorized to proceed with an offensive against the ROK on the understanding that Moscow would provide no direct military support.

The ensuing war had four main phases. In the first, Korean People's Army (KPA) troops advanced rapidly southwards, capturing Seoul and driving American and ROK forces back into a tight perimeter around the port city of Pusan. Many Koreans in the south actively welcomed advancing northern soldiers who looked and acted "like brothers."[25] To them, the conflict was fundamentally part of an ongoing civil war—and a class struggle—between Koreans. In Washington, however, policymakers minimized the war's national dimensions and assumed instead that it had been launched on Moscow's orders as part of a greater Communist masterplan. With United Nations backing—secured in the absence of the Soviets, who used a protest over the exclusion of the People's Republic of China from the UN to cover their own unwillingness to confront Washington—the United States mobilized for war. In the second phase of the fighting, American forces, supported by British troops shipped in from Hong Kong, halted the KPA advance on Pusan and then used their overwhelming naval and air power to stage a landing behind North Korean lines at Incheon. As US troops moved north, American aircraft unleashed a strategic bombing campaign that dropped

---

[24]Dong Choon Kim, "Forgotten War, Forgotten Massacres—the Korean War (1950–1953) as Licensed Mass Killings," *Journal of Genocide Research*, Vol. 6, No. 4 (2004), 526.
[25]Masuda Hajimu, *Cold War Crucible: The Korean Conflict and the Postwar World* (Cambridge, MA: Harvard University Press, 2015), 58–59.

667,000 tons of bombs on Korea over the next three years, a number well in excess of the 503,000 tons dropped during the entire Pacific War.[26] American bombing razed most of North Korea's cities, wrecked factories in the country's industrial heartland, ripped up transport networks, and destroyed the country's electricity generating capacity in a series of attacks on hydro-electric dams. Tens of thousands of civilians died in the bombing.

The Incheon landings opened a new American (or United Nations) offensive as its forces drove into Seoul in pursuit of the retreating KPA. In late September, American troops were ordered across the 38th Parallel as Washington's war aims shifted from simply repulsing the northern attack to focus instead on reunifying the country under the ROK, a goal long advocated by Syngman Rhee. On the same day that commanders authorized the drive north, NSC-68 was formally approved, accelerating Washington's worldwide militarization drive (see Chapter Two). Chinese leaders had already concluded that the American advance, combined with the operations of the 7th Fleet in the Taiwan Strait, made Sino-American conflict inevitable, and as US troops moved north Beijing decided to intervene. The decision to send Chinese troops into Korea was driven primarily by a defensive interest in avoiding an American client state on China's border, but it was accompanied by a propaganda campaign to Resist America and Aid Korea that keyed into anti-American, anticolonial, and internationalist sentiments in China. Anti-American attitudes were fueled in part by memories of abuses suffered at the hands of American troops, including nationwide demonstrations against the rape of a young student by US marines in late 1946.[27] The Resist America and Aid Korea campaign, as Masuda Hajimu notes, produced a popular response in China that "often exceeded the Party line" and was accompanied by a surge in voluntary enlistment.[28] The 700,000 Chinese soldiers who fought in Korea did so as part of the Chinese People's Volunteer Army, and while the name was chosen to avoid the impression of a direct war between China and the United States, it also reflected genuine popular sentiment.

As American war aims expanded in the context of their rapid advance northwards, MacArthur ignored warnings of a coming Chinese intervention. Launched as American forces approached the Korea-China border on the Yalu River, the Chinese offensive opened the third phase of the war. Caught by surprise, American troops were soon in full retreat, and they were unable to stop and regroup until they were back at the 38th Parallel. A fourth phase of the war now opened as a war of rapid movement now settled down into two years of brutal trench warfare and First World War-style stalemate. Delayed by protracted negotiations over the repatriation of

---

[26]Cumings, *The Korean War*, 159–60.
[27]Zach Fredman, *The Tormented Alliance: American Servicemen and the Occupation of China, 1941–1946* (Chapel Hill: University of North Carolina Press, 2022), 19.
[28]Masuda, *Cold War Crucible*, 177.

prisoners of war, an armistice was finally signed on July 25, 1953. To this day the war—or the 'police action,' as Washington insisted on calling it—is still suspended rather than settled, and the demilitarized zone that snakes along the 38th Parallel remains one of the most highly militarized frontiers in the world. Often referred to as a draw, the fighting in Korea registered a clear and decisive check to Washington's hopes of using conventional military means to roll back the Korean and Chinese revolutions, let alone the power of the Soviet Union. As such, it was a defeat for the United States, even if it was far from a clear-cut victory for its opponents.

Throughout the war, military operations were intertwined with continuous and appalling violence against civilians on both sides of the 38th Parallel. Some attacks were undoubtedly committed by KPA soldiers, who lashed out against captured rightist militiamen as they retreated northwards after Incheon. At the same time, many observers noted the discipline and good behavior of North Korean troops who hoped and expected to win popular support in the south. The vast majority of the thousands of civilians who died were killed by ROK forces, while American troops were directly responsible for at least sixty massacres.[29] Such violence was particularly prevalent during the chaotic opening weeks of the war: in one terrible example in late July 1950, soldiers of the US 7th Cavalry massacred 400 civilians under a railroad bridge in the village of Nogun-ri. Many civilians were executed as "subversives," "bandits," or "Reds," including 100,000 people killed by ROK forces and rightist death squads shortly after the war began, and the tens of thousands of alleged Korean Worker's Party members rounded up as American troops marched north. The US Army's Tenth Corps issued explicit orders to "liquidate" Communists, and American counter-intelligence teams worked with Korean police units and rightist militias to implement them.[30] American troops and their allies dragooned young men from Pyongyang and other northern cities into a National Defense Corps, and over 50,000 of them died in ROK hands in the harsh winter of 1950–51. Racism undoubtedly contributed to the anti-civilian violence perpetrated by American troops, with Koreans being widely dehumanized as 'gooks.'

The War in Korea and the Transformation in China

In the short time between the victory of the Chinese Revolution and the outbreak of war in Korea (October 1949 to June 1950), Chinese Communists had anticipated an extended period during which a coalition government and a mixed economy with a large private sector would continue to operate.

---

[29]Kim, "Forgotten War, Forgotten Massacres," 524, 529.
[30]Cumings, *The Korean War*, 195–7.

While a socialized economy was the CCP's long-term goal, it was recognized that it would take time for the preconditions for effective state planning to be assembled. War upended these assumptions. Beijing feared—not unreasonably—that the war in Korea would open the door to heightened American and Guomindang attacks on China, and the scale of its counter-mobilization soon required a systematic and planned economic effort. At the same time, China's entry into the war released a new surge of popular revolutionary energy, manifest both in the Resist America and Aid Korea movement and in more unlikely places, such as a new willingness to pay taxes. Motivated by the desire to strengthen their position against American attack and pushed forward by popular enthusiasm, Beijing launched an accelerated drive to socialize the Chinese economy. Spearheaded by noisy campaigns against 'counterrevolutionaries,' corrupt officials, and profiteering capitalists, the fundamental goal was to shift the country's socio-economic center of gravity from the countryside to the cities and from agriculture to industry while at the same time building the administrative capacity necessary to begin country-wide economic planning.

Conducted under wartime conditions, this effort was remarkably successful. By the end of 1953, 70 percent of heavy industry and 40 percent of light industry were in state hands, and this economic base, combined with the establishment of joint state-private firms in other sectors, gave Beijing the leverage to begin centralized economic planning. An initial one-year plan was adopted in 1953, and it was followed in 1955 by a full Five-Year Plan. Particularly in Manchuria, where most of China's steel mills were located, the highly centralized corporate structures set up by the Japanese and the state ownership established by the Guomindang eased industrialization and state planning under the PRC, and in the early phases Communist officials drew on the help and advice of Japanese and Nationalists technicians.[31]

The advance of state control in industry was linked to a push toward the collectivization of peasant farming, a process that was largely complete by late 1956. In contrast to the disruption, bloodshed, and famine that accompanied forced collectivization in the Soviet Union, in China the process proceeded through carefully graduated steps. These began by organizing peasant families to pool tools and resources in Mutual Aid Teams before moving on to full collectivization within Agricultural Producers' Cooperatives (APCs). Unlike in the Soviet Union, where rich peasants (or kulaks) had been physically liquidated, in China they were admitted to the APCs after suffering economic penalties. This is not to say that there was no opposition to collectivization, and some peasants employed a variety of stratagems to avoid joining the new APCs, but the strength of local CCP organization and

---

[31] Koji Hirata, "Made in Manchuria: The Transnational Origins of Socialist Industrialization in Maoist China," *American Historical Review*, Vol. 126, No. 3 (September 2021), esp. 1101.

a range of economic incentives offered to encourage participation ensured that there were no rural rebellions and no famine. Moreover, in contrast to the USSR, where the agricultural sector was essentially plundered to support heavy industry, Beijing's planning also allowed for modest but real raises in rural living standards.

These socio-economic steps were combined with political measures designed to strengthen the CCP's presence in everyday life, including the establishment of mass organizations of women and youth, neighborhood block committees, and *danwei* (work units) that linked housing, healthcare, and recreational facilities to the workplace. Politically, the CCP led an increasingly centralized government, with a new constitution in 1954 dissolving regional administrations that were now viewed as obstacles to nationwide planning. Although unmentioned in the constitution, party hierarchies paralleled those of the state and were the ultimate locus of power. These moves further accelerated the growth of an administrative bureaucracy, which could now draw on large numbers of newly trained specialists whose middle-class lifestyles were increasingly divorced from those of workers and peasants. Similar developments were evident in the military, where new insignia, ranks, and highly articulated pay scales replaced the relatively egalitarian culture of the wartime People's Liberation Army. Boosted by the costly but successful intervention in Korea and by a modest rise in living standards, the regime retained considerable popular support throughout the 1950s. But as revolutionary enthusiasm cooled and discontent increased—there was a small wave of strikes in 1956—workers and peasants found that they had little direct say in political life. True to its Stalinist training and its practice in the old liberated areas, the CCP was hostile to the kind of participatory democracy that would have offered real control over decision-making. Instead, the Party relied on hyperbolic campaigns that substituted dramatic mass mobilizations and carefully orchestrated ritual events for the actual popular political participation.

Throughout the early 1950s, the social and economic transformation of China proceeded with Moscow's support and encouragement, codified in the February 1950 Sino-Soviet Treaty of Friendship and Alliance. As well as formally recognizing the PRC and returning the East China Railroad and the port of Dalian (Port Arthur) to Chinese control, Moscow also advanced a $300 million loan for economic reconstruction. Several thousand Soviet specialists worked with Chinese planners, and their expertise was particularly important in shaping China's first economic plans. Nevertheless, Chinese leaders were not star-struck by the Soviets. They remembered Stalin's attempts to derail their revolution and were quietly critical of Moscow's fixation on heavy industry and its policy of forced collectivization. Moreover, as China's own economic transformation advanced and its leaders gained experience and confidence, they became increasingly sensitive to Moscow's patronizing attitudes. Above all, Chinese leaders resented the fact that despite loans and technical assistance, Chinese economic development remained low on Moscow's list of priorities, a fact underscored by Khrushchev's determination to raise living standards in the USSR to western levels while much of rural China remained mired in poverty. The Soviet's refusal to pool the resources of the 'socialist' world made a mockery of its claims to internationalism and underscored the narrow nationalism animating the Stalinist leadership in Moscow.

The Chinese economy recovered quickly from the crises of war and revolution, but by the middle of the 1950s Beijing was forced to deal head-on with the challenge of economic development in an overwhelmingly rural country. Russia had been far more industrialized than China at the time of the 1917 revolution, and in the 1930s Stalinist planners had ransacked the agricultural sector for the resources with which to jump-start further industrial development. The peasant origins and base of the CCP effectively precluded this option in China, and given American hostility and Soviet parsimony, no other sources of capital were available. Instead, Beijing lurched out on an idiosyncratic plan designed to merge industry and agriculture in large communal organizations that would also assume responsibility for trade, education, entertainment, and numerous other aspects of everyday life. Beginning in 1958 and billed as the Great Leap Forward, these communes were expected to boost industrial output by tying village-level 'backyard' steel production directly to agriculture—in effect having people work double-time as both workers and farmers. Overlapping with a period of bad weather, the resulting dislocation of agriculture had utterly disastrous consequences, with famine claiming at least 16.5 million people as gain production plummeted.[32]

Mimicking Khrushchev's pledge to overtake the United States within fifteen years, in June 1958 Mao promised that the Great Leap Forward would allow China to "surpass Britain in two years."[33] Mao's goal was to stake a claim leadership of the international Communist movement—or at least its Asian component—and amid the hothouse atmosphere of the Great Leap Forward, Beijing underscored the point by launching attacks on Kinmen and Matsu, two island outposts of Guomindang Taiwan. Moscow was not consulted. The resulting Taiwan Straits Crisis subsided after a month, but not before Washington had dispatched substantial naval and air forces to the region and contemplated the use of nuclear weapons. The threat of war alarmed Soviet leaders, who were already deeply concerned by the 'putschism' of the Great Leap Forward and by Beijing's bid for influence within the world movement. These events highlighted the divergent courses of the two major national-Communist powers and tipped tensions between them into increasingly open hostility. The ensuing Sino-Soviet split took full

---

[32] Wei Li and Dennis Tao Yang, "The Great Leap Forward: Anatomy of a Central Planning Disaster," *Journal of Political Economy*, Vol. 113, No. 4 (2005), 841.
[33] Zhihua Shan and Yafeng Xia, "The Great Leap Forward, the People's Commune and the Sino-Soviet Split," *Journal of Contemporary China*, Vol. 20, No. 72 (November 2011), 863.

form in the early 1960s, reprising Moscow's 1947 rupture with Yugoslavia on a grand scale and demolishing the notion of a world divided neatly into two camps.

Throughout this period, British-ruled Hong Kong was both an undefendable imperial outpost under constant threat of Chinese attack *and* an indispensable capitalist bridgehead into mainland China. In moments of crisis, as when Chinese advances in Korea coincided with a renewed Vietminh offensive in Indochina in early 1951, London readied plans for the evacuation of Hong Kong. For the most part, however, both London—discretely backed by Washington—and Beijing were happy to exploit the ambiguities in Hong Hong's situation. For both sides, Hong Kong was a site of espionage and informal contact, while in the mid-1950s London's fear of antagonizing Beijing justified its refusal to join Washington's deepening involvement in Vietnam. The PRC never formally recognized the British colony, resuming control when the lease on Kowloon finally expired in 1997. Nevertheless, while a 1951 United Nations embargo on the sale of strategic materials to China disrupted Hong Kong's cross-border export trade, shipments from China—mostly destined for Western markets—were the island colony's single largest source of imports. The massive trade surplus that resulted from these transactions provided Beijing with its major source of sterling and US dollars, invaluable assets that militated against asserting Chinese sovereignty by force.[34]

By the 1970s, Hong Kong's liminal status allowed it to serve as a conduit for foreign direct investment in China, particularly from countries like Japan and Taiwan where mid-century history made more open relations difficult. Hong Kong's postwar story and its subsequent role in the transformation of China into a state-capitalist regional superpower underscore the bigger processes at work here. The conventional historiographical separation—a veritable Chinese Wall—between apparently discrete events known as World War II and the Cold War makes it impossible to see this clearly, but the Chinese Revolution, uncoiling directly out of the crisis of world war, qualified Washington's victory and limited its postwar hegemony. Irrespective of politics and ideology, China's socialized economy joined that of the Comecon countries in removing a huge swath of the world from the capitalist market and hence from the profit-making reach of American business. This fact alone earned, and in some ways continues to earn, Washington's undying enmity. Moreover, of course, politics and ideology *were* involved, particularly in the early 1950s when still-hot revolutionary enthusiasm enabled Chinese armies to fight the US-led forces to a halt in a campaign that, as we shall see in Chapter Eight, exploded within the United States in the form of the McCarthyite witch-hunt.

---

[34] Stella Chan, "Hong Kong's Economy, 1949–1959," unpublished MA thesis, University of Ottawa, 1961, 18.

For Further Reading

Kornel Chang, "Independence without Liberation: Democratization as Decolonization Management in U.S.-Occupied Korea, 1945–1948," *The Journal of American History*, June 2020.

Bruce Cummings, *The Korean War: A History* (New York: The Modern Library, 2010).

Daniel Eugene Garcia, "Class and Brass: Demobilization, Working Class Politics, and American Foreign Policy between War and Cold War," *Diplomatic History*, Vol. 34, No. 4 (September 2010).

Masuda Hajimu, *Cold War Crucible: The Korean Conflict and the Postwar World* (Cambridge, MA: Harvard University Press, 2015).

Chen Jian, *Mao's China and the Cold War* (Chapel Hill, NC: University of South Carolina Press, 2001).

Dong Choon Kim, "Forgotten War, Forgotten Massacres—the Korean War (1950–1953) as Licensed Mass Killings," *Journal of Genocide Research*, Vol. 6, No. 4 (2004).

Donggil Kim, "Stalin and the Chinese Civil War," *Cold War History*, Vol. 10, No. 2 (May 2010).

Daniel Kurtz-Phelan, *The China Mission: George Marshall's Unfinished War 1945–1947* (New York: Norton, 2018).

Wei Li and Dennis Tao Yang, "The Great Leap Forward: Anatomy of a Central Planning Disaster," *Journal of Political Economy*, Vol. 113, No. 4 (2005),

Zhihua Shan and Yafeng Xia, "The Great Leap Forward, the People's Commune and the Sino-Soviet Split," *Journal of Contemporary China*, Vol. 20, No. 72 (November 2011).

William Stueck, *Rethinking the Korean War: A New Diplomatic and Strategic History* (Princeton: Princeton University Press, 2004).

Frederick C. Teiwes, "The Establishment and Consolidation of the New Regime, 1949–1957," in Roderick MacFarquhar (ed.), *The Politics of China: The Eras of Mao and Deng* (Cambridge: Cambridge University Press, 1997).

Hans van de Ven, *China at War: Triumph and Tragedy in the Emergence of the New China* (Cambridge, MA: Harvard University Press, 2018).

Odd Arne Westad, *Decisive Encounters: The Chinese Civil War, 1946–1950* (Stanford, CA: Stanford University Press, 2003).

CHAPTER FOUR

Hegemony Qualified: Anti-Colonial Revolt in South and Southeast Asia

As President Truman was outlining his vision of a peaceful and American-led world order to the Navy Day crowds in New York in October 1945, on the other side of the world fierce fighting was raging in the Indonesian port city of Surabaya. In August, rebellious young nationalist fighters—or *pemuda*—had taken advantage of the collapse of Japan's wartime occupation to push Indonesian leaders Sukarno and Mohammad Hatta into proclaiming independence from Dutch colonial rule. That independence was now being tested. In October, war weary British-Imperial troops began arriving in Indonesia to reestablish Dutch rule. Fighting broke out in Surabaya when British-Imperial troops tried to recover weapons handed over to the Indonesians by surrendering Japanese soldiers. Efforts to calm the situation by flying Sukarno and Hatta into the city broke down, and British officers ordered Indian troops to launch an all-out assault backed by tanks, heavy artillery, and air strikes. Led by *pemuda* fighters, some armed only with bamboo spears, the people of Surabaya resisted fiercely. By the time British-Imperial forces finally secured control of the city in late November, between 10,000 and 15,000 Indonesians had been killed along with 600 British-Imperial soldiers, including their commanding general.[1] Many more civilians fled the devastated city. Surabaya was a military defeat for the newly proclaimed Republic of Indonesia, but the fighting spirit displayed by

---

[1] Christopher Bayly and Tim Harper, *Forgotten Wars: Freedom and Revolution in Southeast Asia* (Cambridge, MA: Harvard University Press, 2007), 180–1.

the 'Generation of '45' inspired the hard but ultimately successful struggle against Dutch colonialism that unfolded over the next five years.

The struggle for Indonesian independence was one of a series of popular revolts that erupted across South and Southeast Asia as Washington was bringing its Pacific War against Japan to a triumphant conclusion. The roots of these revolts lay in long years of colonial oppression and exploitation, but their outbreak was a direct product of the war. Here, as elsewhere, the passage from war to postwar was not a leap from one state to another but a process of transition that began before the formal end of the war and continued long after it. In Southeast Asia, these processes unfolded in a region where European and American colonial rule had been upended by Japan in the early 1940s, and where Japan's surrender in 1945 occurred *before* the arrival of Allied forces intent on reimposing imperial predominance. In the ragged spaces opened by this disjunction, popular new futures emerged.

FIGURE 4.1 *Indonesian anticolonial revolutionaries armed with sharpened bamboo spears and Japanese rifles rally in Java, 1946. (Collection Nationaal Museum van Wereldculturen Coll.nr. RV-1971-271.)*

The fighting in Surabaya showed that far from simply consolidating its postwar hegemony in a pacified world, the United States would face unexpected challenges that posed awkward questions of power, legitimacy, and the nature of the postwar order. The situation in Southeast Asia was particularly sensitive. During the war, Washington had pinned its moral claim to world leadership on the implicit anti-colonialism and explicit promise of national self-determination embedded in the Atlantic Charter. This was hardly altruism—policymakers expected that American business would be the primary beneficiary of the ending of the old systems of imperial protectionism—but it led many anticolonial activists to believe that that they enjoyed Washington's backing. Now, however, the perceived needs of political stability and European economic recovery, shaped by the deepening Cold War confrontation with the Soviet Union centered in Europe and buttressed by racially inflected notions of who was—and who was not—capable of self-government, inclined Washington to favor the re-establishment of colonial rule.

Given Washington's stated opposition to colonialism, American leaders could not simply proclaim this policy publicly, and in conflicts between colonizer and colonized their official position was generally one of disengaged neutrality. Behind the scenes, however, the real policy was clear: in the Dutch East Indies, a December 1944 agreement between United States and Dutch officials paved the way for the restoration of the "full sovereignty of the Netherlands government," while in Indochina President Roosevelt agreed in March 1945 that "France [should] retain these colonies."[2] The American press got the message, and the *New York Times* consistently described Indonesian nationalist fighters in Surabaya as "extremists," "Moslem fanatics," and "bandits," all of whom were by implication incapable of self-rule.[3] At the same time, however, American policymakers differentiated between 'moderate' nationalist leaders like Sukarno and rebellious young workers and peasants, making it clear that their problem was not necessarily with anti-colonial independence per se but with uncontrollable popular struggles that might overspill the boundaries of the capitalist nation-state and push toward a fundamental restructuring of society. In their ideal world, therefore, American officials hoped that the restored colonial powers would crush radical—and perhaps communist-inspired—movements before preparing their colonies for independence under responsible, moderate, and pro-capitalist leaders.

---

[2]Civil Affairs Agreement between General Douglas MacArthur and Hubertus van Mook, December 10, 1944, quoted in Robert J. McMahon, *Colonialism and Cold War: The United States and the Struggle for Indonesian Independence, 1945–49* (Ithaca: Cornell University Press, 1981), 72; Roosevelt, conversation with Charles Taussig quoted in Walter LaFeber, "Roosevelt, Churchill, and Indochina, 1942–1945," *The American Historical Review*, Vol. 80, No. 5 (December 1975), 1293.

[3]*New York Times*, October 24, 1945, 2; November 24, 1945, 2; November 3, 1945, 5; October 10, 1945, 2.

Japan's Great East Asia Co-Prosperity Sphere

The postwar crisis in Southeast Asia was framed by the collapse of Japan's wartime empire. This empire was itself the product of the rapid overturn in early 1942 of European and American colonial rule across a vast region that included British-ruled Burma and the Malay peninsula, the Dutch East Indies, French Indochina, and the American-ruled Philippines. The Japanese offensive, which brought long years of Western rule to an abrupt end, was launched in response to Tokyo's inability to bring its war in China to a successful conclusion, and its goal was to strengthen Japan's war effort by securing control of the region's vast resources of oil, tin, bauxite, rubber, rice, and other raw materials. For millions of toilers throughout the region, Japanese rule meant harsh exploitation, forced labor, hunger, and famine. But as Tokyo began to administer its new colonial territories, it—like all imperial powers—was forced to rely on the cooperation of local elites. In Burma and Indonesia, many welcomed Japan's victory over their old colonial rulers, but others—like the Filipinos who had already been promised independence by Washington—were more reluctant. Nevertheless, Japan increasingly framed its imperial project as a site of Pan-Asian and anti-Western collaboration, a Greater East Asian Co-Prosperity Sphere rather than an exploitative empire.

As the war in the Pacific began to turn against Japan, Tokyo reinforced the ostensibly anti-colonial aspects of its imperial project by granting Burma and the Philippines independence in 1943. At the same time, Tokyo established a Provisional Government of Free India under former Indian National Congress leader Subhas Chandra Bose on the Andaman Islands in the Bay of Bengal, and it began preparing independent governments in Malaya and Indonesia. Independence was qualified by continued Japanese occupation, but in Burma and the Philippines 'patriotic collaborators' gained experience of government and of foreign relations long denied them by their former colonial masters. In Indonesia, Japanese officials worked with Sukarno and Hatta to organize nationalist forces, even assisting in the formation of the 'home guard' militias that later formed the basis of an independent Indonesian army. To pull these various initiatives together, Tokyo convened a Greater East Asia Conference in November 1943 at which leaders of seven countries—Japan, Manchukuo, the Reorganized National Government of China, Burma, the Philippines, Thailand, and Free India—presented a vision of pan-Asian unity. Mirroring the emancipatory anti-colonial rhetoric of the Anglo-American Atlantic Charter, the conference adopted its own Pacific Charter.

In contrast to its explosive arrival, the Co-Prosperity Sphere's departure was a protracted affair. By summer 1945, Japan—like Germany—had been utterly defeated, but unlike the Nazi regime in Berlin, Tokyo surrendered *before* its military forces had been liquidated and its extensive territorial empire occupied. Across the Japanese empire, at least three million undefeated soldiers—including 630,000 in Southeast Asia—surrendered to Allied forces as they fanned out across the region in early September.[4] Allied forces quickly began repatriating surrendered Japanese soldiers, along with another three million civilian Japanese settlers, businesspeople, and administrators, but with shipping in short supply, this was a slow process. Many Japanese civilians had their possessions confiscated by Allied authorities in the course of repatriation, with one official US report noting that items including "kimonos, obis, lacquer, in-laid pearl boxes, vases, and pearls" were stolen and sold to American soldiers as souvenirs.[5]

Most Japanese soldiers were home by summer 1946, but many remained overseas, some of them under arms and deployed by the British in combat operations against Communist and nationalist forces in Indonesia, Indochina, and Malaya. London categorized these soldiers as Japanese Surrendered Personnel (JSP), a legal nicety that allowed them to sidestep the Geneva Convention's restrictions on the use of prisoners of war for military purposes. Even after most Japanese soldiers had been repatriated, at least 105,000 JSPs were retained by the British for use in military operations and civilian reconstruction projects, and some were even hired out to private businesses.[6] The last of them did not return home until late 1947. Thousands of former Japanese soldiers also remained under arms in China, some of them organized into the combat units and logistical forces of both sides in the deepening civil war.

Wars of Indonesian Independence, 1945–50

In contrast to the complete control exercised by the allied armies who filled Europe in spring 1945, the ragged and protracting endings of the war in Asia opened windows of opportunity for nationalists, communists, and other radical forces as power vacuums gave them—and workers and peasant farmers more broadly—a chance to put their stamp on history. A study of developments in Indonesia offers a useful starting point for a review of this process. Sukarno's proclamation of independence on August 17, 1945, triggered a popular uprising across the Indonesian heartlands of Java and Sumatra. From remote villages to populous cities, millions embraced the exhilarating prospect of liberation embodied in veteran revolutionary Tan

---

[4]Bayly and Harper, *Forgotten Wars*, 5, 270.
[5]See Susan L. Carruthers, *The Good Occupation: American Soldiers and the Hazards of Peace*, (Cambridge, MA: Harvard University Press, 2016), 185.
[6]Stephen Connor, "Side-Stepping Geneva: Japanese Troops under British Control. 1945–7," *Journal of Contemporary History*, Vol. 45, No. 2 (2010), 402.

Malaka's call for "one-hundred-percent *Merdeka* (freedom)!" It was, as peasants in the Karo plateau of northern Sumatra recalled, a "delicious" time that marked an end to "feeling colonized."[7] After hundreds of years of colonial rule, the belief that a better future was at hand inspired the young *pemuda* fighters in Surabaya and then sustained a broad insurgency through the turbulent *bersiap*—or "Get Ready!"—time that followed.[8] Popular militias and new political organizations proliferated, some originally formed by the Japanese, some political—including those organized by Nationalists, and various groups of communists—and some religious. Many rebel organizations were based in specific villages and urban barrios, and while they were loosely linked into a nationwide movement, many home-grown rebellions were 'village wars' centered on righting local injustices through land redistribution, rent reduction, and attacks on landlords and other wealthy elites.

Historians often shoehorn this sprawling popular insurgency—and others like it across Southeast Asia—into the framework of nationalist revolt against colonial rule. This framing implies both more and less than the lived reality of *bersiap* time. The vast archipelago of the Dutch East Indies had only been given political coherence by its colonial rulers, and many of its inhabitants had little notion of 'Indonesia.' Their "nationalism" developed in response to the injustices of colonialism manifest at local level, and they only began to enter the imagined community of the nation-state over time and through participatory experience. At the same time, the achievement of national independence did not limit the possibilities of this explosive moment: Tan Malaka's radical call for "one-hundred-percent" *Merdeka* combined anticolonialism with popular democracy, land reform, and anti-capitalist measures aimed at ending the power of Indonesia's own landlord elites. In this sense, *bersiap* time was not simply the prelude to an independent capitalist Indonesian nation-state, but a fluid and contingent period of popular revolt during which competing futures were in play.

Even the Dutch government in Den Haag recognized that there could be no simple return to the prewar world and—in line with similar projects being mooted in London and Paris—it proposed to secure control of the region's resources by reforming the empire into a Dutch-led Union that would include both self-administered states—including Java and Sumatra—and directly ruled colonies. First, however, the Dutch needed to reassert control, and with British-Imperial forces leading the way they launched a protracted and bloody drive to bring the population to heel. This effort failed, despite two ferocious military campaigns (Operations *Product* in

---

[7]Mary Margaret Steedly, *Rifle Reports: A Story of Indonesian Independence* (Berkley: University of California Press, 2013), 117.
[8]Bayly and Harper, *Forgotten Wars*, 181.

July 1947 and *Crow* in November 1948) and two compromise agreements (Linggajati in November 1946 and Renville in January 1948). In fast-moving offensives, 120,000 Dutch troops supplied with American weapons and equipment established nominal control over much of Java and Sumatra but, as the Japanese discovered in China and the French and then the Americans would learn in Indochina, extensive territorial control simply overextended imperial forces and opened them up to guerrilla attacks on isolated bases and supply lines.[9] In common with other counter-insurgency efforts, Dutch military campaigns were also characterized by episodes of shocking violence against Indonesian civilians: in one particularly brutal case, pro-Dutch forces led by Captain Raymond Westerling imposed a reign of terror on the island of Sulawesi that killed over 3,000 people. Overall, four years of fighting left 200,000 Indonesians and 6,000 Dutch dead, while seven million more were uprooted and displaced.[10]

Indonesian resistance to Dutch recolonization inspired international solidarity. In Sydney, Australia, wharfies—dock workers—blocked the loading of American-supplied arms being shipped to Dutch forces in Indonesia, while Indian *lascars*—sailors—refused to crew Dutch troopships sailing from Australian ports. In one particularly dramatic incident, *lascars* on the troopship *General Vespijck* stopped the ship's engines and took to the lifeboats while Australian wharfies cheered them on, effectively blocking an arms shipment intended for use against their "Indonesian brothers."[11] Soldiers in the imperialist armies were also inspired by the anti-colonial struggle, with several hundred Japanese soldiers joining the Indonesian rebels, and when the British Army's Seaforth Highlanders were shipping out of Jakarta in late 1946 they greeted arriving Dutch troops with clenched fist salutes and shouts of "*Merdeka!*"[12] Opposition was particularly strong among soldiers in Britain's India Army, a force long critical to London's imperial rule throughout the region. India's own mounting struggle for independence now made many Indian soldiers leery of enforcing British rule elsewhere. Meanwhile, and as other imperial powers would later discover, protracted counterinsurgency started to collapse imperial forces from the inside, and protests by Dutch conscript soldiers against their deployment to Indonesia in September 1946 were supported by strikes and mass demonstrations in Amsterdam.

---

[9]Leopold Scholtz, "The Dutch Strategic and Operational Approach in the Indonesian War of Independence, 1945–1949," *South African Journal of Military Studies*, Vol. 46, No. 2 (2018), 17.
[10]Scholtz, "The Dutch Strategic and Operational Approach," 21.
[11]Heather Goodall, "Port Politics: Indian Seamen, Australian Unions and Indonesian Independence, 1945–47," *Labour History*, No. 94 (May 2008), 57–8.
[12]Bayly and Harper, *Forgotten Wars*, 189.

Formed under the twin pressures of popular rebellion and colonial reconquest, Indonesian politics were shaped by a complex kaleidoscope of class, religious, and regional forces. At the center of this process, Sukarno and Hatta—an architect and an economist who were both members of Indonesia's narrow educated elite—sought to balance conflicting forces as they battled to create a unitary capitalist nation-state. With their fiery anti-colonial rhetoric, and backed by military forces assembled under Japanese rule, they brokered shifting coalitions of Communist, Socialist, Nationalist, and Islamic parties. Emerging from underground and exile at the end of the war, the pro-Moscow Indonesian Communist Party (PKI) advocated an anti-colonial alliance with the 'national bourgeois' forces represented by Sukarno and his colleagues. The PKI advanced this policy by both overt and covert means, and undercover party leader Amir Sjarifuddin served as minister of information in Sukarno's first independent cabinet and then as prime minister of the short-lived 1947–48 coalition government.

In line with Moscow's efforts to perpetuate the wartime Grand Alliance, the PKI hesitated to advocate a complete break with Den Haag, endorsing compromise agreements within the framework of a new Dutch 'Union' instead. In this context, a key goal of Sukarno's alliance with the PKI was to blunt the radical challenge advanced by Tan Malaka's newly formed Struggle Front. Often referred to as a Trotskyist, Tan Malaka had rejected Moscow's Stalinist politics in 1927 and his call for "one-hundred-percent *Merdeka*" envisioned national independence as the start of a process of social revolution, not its endpoint. In the intense heat of *bersiap* time the Struggle Front quickly won a mass following, and in spring 1946 it seemed poised to assume leadership of the anticolonial movement. Despite its impressive popular support, however, the Struggle Front was a loose alliance rather than a disciplined party with a clear program and policies, and the movement stalled after Sukarno had Tan Malaka arrested and imprisoned without trail in March 1946. Released in 1948, Tan Malaka founded the Proletarian Party, but with the tide of popular radicalism now ebbing it could not repeat the early successes of the Struggle Front. Isolated and on the run, Tan Malaka was captured and executed by Sukarno's Republican troops in February 1949. With PKI backing, the national bourgeoisie was both willing and ready to clamp down hard on popular radicalism.

The PKI's strategy of alliance with the Indonesian bourgeoisie was itself thrown into crisis following the sharp turn in Soviet policy announced at the October 1947 founding conference of the Cominform (see Chapter Two). In August 1948, PKI leader Muso was sent back to Indonesia from Moscow with orders to implement the confrontational new 'two camp' policy. A former friend and collaborator of Sukarno's, Muso now denounced the PKI's policy of support for the Nationalist leader and reoriented the party toward an immediate challenge for power.[13] In September 1948 the PKI launched an armed coup in Madiun, Indonesia's third largest city, with the aim of sparking a popular uprising that would topple Sukarno. Given the party's abrupt change of course, the attempted insurrection lacked both popular support and effective preparation, and it succeeded only in provoking a bloody battle with Indonesian army. Eight thousand PKI supporters were killed in the fighting that followed and thousands more were imprisoned, while Muso and other party leaders were captured and executed.[14]

The failed putsch in Madiun neutralized the PKI as a major force in Indonesian politics for the next several years. It also paved the way for a major shift in American policy. Concerned by Den Haag's continued inability to reimpose stable colonial rule and discomforted by Indian-led criticism of Dutch colonialism in the United Nations, Washington saw Madiun as evidence of the Nationalist regime's ability to serve as a viable bulwark against Communism. Seeing Sukarno in this new light, Washington pressured Den Haag to recognize Indonesian independence. This pragmatic policy shift did not imply generalized American support for anti-colonial struggles, but it did produce a round-table conference in Den Haag that prepared the formal transfer of sovereignty to Indonesia in December 1949. Indonesian leaders agreed to remain within a loose imperial Union, but these ties were further weakened after the defeat of a pro-Dutch coup prompted Sukarno to proclaim the unitary Republic of Indonesia on August 17, 1950. Fresh violence followed as Indonesian troops crushed autonomous local states and separatist movements in Sumatra and on Ambon and other islands east of Java.

Independence finally brought Indonesia's long Second World War to a close, but with American and other foreign capital dominating the economy and with much of the population facing poverty, high unemployment, and a grinding crisis on the land, it was a long way from Tan Malaka's "one-hundred-percent *Merdeka*." Moreover, the new state was directly shaped by the brutal foreclosure of the radical vision of Tan Malaka and others by military forces loyal to Sukarno, a process facilitated by the PKI's Madiun putsch. The increasingly dictatorial Sukarno regime—self-described after 1957 as a 'guided democracy'—continued to lean heavily on the army and on a massively expanded (and massively corrupt) administration. Ironically, with the Soviet policy of peaceful coexistence that emerged following the death of Stalin in 1953, Sukarno was again able to draw on popular support mobilized by a rebuilt and newly moderate PKI.

---

[13] Harry A. Poeze, "The Cold War in Indonesia, 1948," *Journal of Southeast Asian Studies*, Vol. 40, No. 3 (2009), 506.
[14] M. C. Ricklefs, *A History of Modern Indonesia since 1200*, 4th Edition (Stanford, CA: Stanford University Press, 2008), 266.

Popular Revolt and Postwar Crisis in Southeast Asia

Although they combined in unique ways in different places, many of the main features of the Indonesian Revolution were repeated across Southeast Asia as it emerged from the turmoil of the Second World War. The first and most decisive common feature was that the summer of 1945 saw the eruption of a "connected arc" of popular anti-colonial uprisings stretching across the region.[15] These rebellions were triggered by the economic breakdown and social dislocation produced by the rapid collapse of Japan's wartime empire. As the war ended, hunger tipped into outright famine in northern Vietnam, while total output in the Philippines stood at only 20 percent of 1941 levels, and rubber plantations and tin mines in Malaya were idled.[16] This economic and social breakdown was intertwined with the anger generated by centuries of colonial exploitation and oppression, fueling uprisings that erupted as the straitjacket of Japanese rule was loosened. In French Indochina and the Malay peninsula, rebellion was interwoven with wartime resistance to Japanese rule, while in Burma it was led by forces that had collaborated with the Japanese before changing sides in the last months of the war. As in Indonesia, local village wars were often led by young people driven by a fierce desire to settle scores with old elites and to push for radical social change, and in particular for far-reaching land reforms. Across the region, women joined the revolts, often taking leadership positions and challenging traditional social and gender norms in the process. Shaped by local conditions, rebellions were given broader national coherence as news and inspiration pulsed along lines of wartime connectivity and vectors of shipping, supply, and troop deployment. Soldiers in the imperial armies were impacted by what they saw, with hundreds of Japanese soldiers joining the insurgents while the thousands of the GI's marching in Manila to protest delayed demobilization chanted "we don't want to fight Filipinos!"[17]

The second commonality was that the collapse of Japanese rule *before* the arrival of American, British-Imperial, and European troops created a series of power vacuums within which anticolonial and nationalist forces could stake their claim to popular leadership and political legitimacy. In Indonesia and Vietnam, independent governments were quickly established, with enthusiastic young fighters forcing Sukarno's declaration of independence on August 17, 1945, while Ho Chi Minh, Communist leader of the nationalist Viet Minh, announced the establishment of the Democratic Republic of

---

[15]Bayly and Harper, *Forgotten Wars*, 190.
[16]Ode Arne Westad, *The Cold War: A World History* (New York: Basic Books, 2017), 66.
[17]Colleen Woods, *Freedom Incorporated: Anti-Communism and Philippine Independence in the Age of Decolonization* (Ithaca: Cornell University Press, 2020), 84.

Vietnam (DRV) before a massive crowd in Hanoi on September 2. The Viet Minh had already taken advantage of Tokyo's belated overthrow of French rule in Indochina in March 1945 to strengthen its village-level organization in the north and to rebuild its forces in the south: as one American agent reported from the northern province of Tonkin, "every village flew the Viet Minh flag" and was protected by a well-organized local militia that included women and children.[18] In both Indonesia and Vietnam, the establishment of anticolonial governments opened protracted periods of dual power in which new centers of state authority contested French and Dutch efforts to reestablish colonial rule.

A power vacuum also opened in the Malay peninsula, but here the Communist-led Malayan People's Anti-Japanese Army (MPAJA), which had waged a long guerrilla war against the Japanese, balked at proclaiming independence. Their reticence stemmed in part from the fact that the party's main base of support lay among Chinese workers and squatters rather than the ethnic Malay majority, but it also reflected a policy of collaboration with London advanced by Moscow and reflected in the Communists' own wartime cooperation with British forces. Here, then, the power vacuum was filled by the shaky reestablishment of British rule. In Burma, granted independence by Tokyo in 1943, Aung San's Burmese National Army switched sides in May 1945 and played a key role in the southward advance of British-Imperial forces. After the capture of Yangon (Rangoon) in May 1945, Aung San insisted that his Anti-Fascist People's Freedom League be treated as the leadership of a new independent nation. In this case, radical nationalists triumphed because the British viewed them as preferable to the Communists and baulked at using military force against them.

The third common feature was the former colonial masters' region-wide drive to reestablish their control. Like the Dutch in Indonesia, London and Paris viewed their Southeast Asian colonies as critical both to their postwar economic recovery and their global status. This was no idle claim: Malaya alone accounted for 10 percent of Britain's overseas trade and 35 percent of its net dollar earnings.[19] At the same time, however, the reassertion of colonial rule had somehow to be squared with the promise of national self-determination that was central to the ideological packaging of the Allied war effort, and colonial reconquest was prettified by the formation of new imperial unions, commonwealths, and other semi-colonial arrangements.

The United States played a critical, if largely backstage, role in this process. During the war, Washington had floated the general idea of

---

[18] OSS political report, October 17, 1945, reprinted as an appendix to *Causes, Origins and Lessons of the Vietnam War* (Washington: USGPO, 1973), 319.
[19] Bayly and Harper, *Forgotten Wars*, 408–9.

placing colonial territories under a system of international trusteeship administered by the new United Nations. This vague notion was focused with particular force on French Indochina, where American officials believed that France's general failure as a great power—registered in its crushing defeat by Germany in 1940—combined with specific maladministration meant that Paris had forfeited its claim to the postwar restoration of its colonies. In its place, Roosevelt argued—with Stalin's approval—at the Tehran conference, China should be given trusteeship of the former French colonies with a view to preparing them for independence within "20 to 30 years."[20] In the last months of the war, however, Roosevelt and other senior administration figures dropped this proposal, arguing instead that France should exercise postwar trusteeship over its former colony with the proviso that "independence was the ultimate goal."[21] Under the pressure of the looming crisis of decolonization in Southeast Asia, it was, of course, essentially a proposal for continued colonial rule repackaged as trusteeship within a new French Union.

This shift to new semicolonial arrangements was accomplished most successfully in the United States' own colony in the Philippines. Here, and in contrast to the rest of the region, there was no postwar power vacuum. Instead, Washington translated military predominance on the ground—a product of General MacArthur's insistence on making the recapture of the Philippines central to American strategy in the Pacific—directly into political control by organizing the rapid return of Sergio Osmeña's pro-American government-in-exile. The numerous and powerful business and landlord elites who had collaborated with the Japanese during the war were quickly reintegrated into the newly restored Commonwealth. Washington recognized the importance of the archipelago for the regional projection of US power, but policymakers also understood that this did not necessarily require direct colonial rule, and since the 1935 Tydings-McDuffie Act they had been grooming Filipino elites for self-government. Interrupted by the war and the short period of independence under Japanese oversight, this process of transition from colony to postcolonial nation-state culminated in July 1946 with the establishment of the Republic of the Philippines under newly elected president Manuel Roxas. Despite "voluntarily relinquish[ing] its sovereignty," as one State Department official put it, Washington ensured its continued use of key naval and air bases at Subic Bay and Clark Field and its domination of the Philippine economy through the 1946 Bell Trade Act.[22]

---

[20]LaFeber, "Roosevelt, Churchill, and Indochina, 1942–1945," 1284.
[21]Roosevelt memorandum, March 15, 1945, in LaFeber, "Roosevelt, Churchill, and Indochina, 1942–1945," 1293.
[22]Edward Mill, "The Philippines Prepare for Independence," *Department of State Bulletin*, 1946, quoted in Woods, *Freedom Incorporated*, 80.

At the opposite extreme, French efforts to reestablish colonial rule in Indochina ended in disaster. By rebranding its empire as a 'Union,' France hoped to integrate the constituent regions of Indochina as five nominally independent 'associate states.' Led by an advance guard of British-Imperial forces, supported by American logistics and Lend-Lease aid, and helped by Japanese Surrendered Personnel, French troops began reestablishing their rule in Saigon and the southern part of the country. Unfortunately for Paris, Ho Chi Minh's proclamation of the Democratic Republic of Vietnam (DRV) in August 1945 had already created a rival center of governmental authority, based in the northern city of Hanoi. Here, and by agreement of the allies at the Potsdam conference, 150,000 Guomindang troops led by regional warlord Lu Han arrived in early September to accept the Japanese surrender in areas north of the sixteenth parallel. Lu's forces were openly hostile to the French, but they quickly established an uneasy cohabitation with the Viet Minh-led DRV. Had this situation prevailed across the entire country, historian Fredrik Logevall observes wryly, the "long and bloody struggle" that followed might have been "over before it began."[23] It was not to be. Instead, as French troops took over from the British in the south and Lu Han's troops pulled out of the north in March 1946, Paris plunged into a protracted war to topple the DRV. Moscow had no interest in defending the DRV and was suspicious of Ho Chi Minh's independence, while Ho himself repeatedly stated his willingness to see Vietnam locked into long-term association with France: none of this mattered to Paris, which was determined to reassert direct colonial rule. As in Indonesia, anticolonial fighters were strengthened by acts of international solidarity as dockworkers in Ceylon, Malaya, and Singapore refused to load ships carrying French troops and military supplies to Indochina, and newly independent India and Burma limited French flights through their airspace.[24]

Facing an increasingly difficult and unpopular struggle to reimpose colonial rule, Paris changed tack and began working to establish a nominally independent state under former Emperor Bao Đai in the southern part of the country. Installed in 1949, Bao Đai's State of Vietnam provided the framework for continued neocolonial domination of Vietnam within a reformed French Empire. The new and nominally independent state helped overcome American reluctance to give open backing to a colonial war, and in February 1950 Washington recognized the new regime and supplied it with an initial $15 million in military aid.[25] In the aftermath of the Communist victory in China in 1949, the United States assumed increasing responsibility

---

[23]Fredrik Logevall, *Embers of War: The Fall of an Empire and the Making of America's Vietnam* (New York: Random House, 2013), 110.
[24]Mark Atwood Lawrence, "Transnational Coalition-Building and the Making of the Cold War in Indochina, 1947–1949," *Diplomatic History*, Vol. 26, No. 3 (2002), 463.
[25]Ibid., 479.

for supplying the French war in Vietnam. Meanwhile, the DRV established close ties with the new Communist regime in China, which in a major diplomatic breakthrough in 1950 recognized the Viet Minh-led regime, effectively forcing Moscow to follow suit. The dispatch of a Chinese Military Advisory Group soon followed to help the People's Army transition from a guerrilla force into a regular army capable of sustained operations.[26] As in the Chinese Revolution, Viet Minh military efforts were sustained above all by popular support rooted in a deepening socio-economic transformation on the land, and in May 1954 the People's Army won a decisive victory over the French at the battle of Điên Biên Phủ.

In the aftermath of the French defeat, an international conference met in Geneva to impose a solution on the crisis in French Indochina. Under tremendous pressure from the Chinese delegation, who—with Moscow's backing—pointed to the danger of American intervention, the leaders of the Democratic Republic were forced to accept the partitioning of Vietnam on the seventeenth parallel. This forceful denial of national self-determination was sweetened by promises that partition would be temporary and that nationwide elections slated for 1956 would prepare for peaceful reunification. The conference also recognized the newly independent kingdoms of Laos and Cambodia, paving the way for the withdrawal of French troops by April 1956. Southern Vietnam moved firmly into Washington's orbit, with strongman Ngo Dinh Diem establishing himself as prime minister of the Republic of Vietnam in 1955. The nationwide elections promised in Geneva—which would have almost certainly produced a Viet Minh victory—never took place, and with American backing Diem consolidated his rule through a ferocious campaign of political repression and ballot rigging that targeted religious groups and criminal gangs as well as Communists. Meanwhile, despite its role in enforcing the partition of Vietnam, Beijing viewed the Geneva conference as a major success: China had established itself on the world stage and had secured the creation of a North Vietnamese buffer state between it and capitalist Southeast Asia.[27]

Britain's postwar efforts to reestablish its Southeast Asian colonies fell between these extremes. In Burma, London quickly recognized that the reestablishment of colonial rule in the face of rising popular protests was beyond its means' and granted independence in January 1948. British officials hoped that Aung San and his successor Thakin Nu would preside over a "stable and friendly" country hospitable to British investments.[28] In its rush to get out, London effectively abandoned the Karen, Shan, and

---

[26]See Xiaohe Cheng, "The Chinese Advisory Groups in the First Indochina War: Their Formation, Evolution, and Disbandment," *Cold War History*, Vol. 22, No. 2 (2022).
[27]Chen Jian, *Mao's China and the Cold War* (Chapel Hill, NC: University of South Carolina Press, 2001), 143.
[28]Bayly and Harper, *Forgotten Wars*, 380.

other minority groups that it had long favored over Burma's Buddhist majority.

London faced a more complex challenge in Malaya. Beyond the strategic port of Singapore, British rule in the Malay peninsula had traditionally been exercised through local sultans who, as London quickly found out when it tried to establish a Malayan Union in 1946, resisted incorporation into a unified colonial state. Nevertheless, the Communist-led MPAJA's refusal to challenge British rule despite a postwar wave of strikes and peasant uprisings gave London a breathing space within which it could recover political control, and by 1948 it had restored relations with traditional Malay rulers by establishing the Federation of Malaya. As a result, by the time Malay Communists followed Moscow's new course and launched an anti-British insurgency in 1948, the postwar power vacuum had been already closed. British forces respond forcefully to the 'emergency,' interning thousands of alleged Communists and building prison-like 'new villages' to separate peasant farmers from guerrilla fighters. Presented as an effort to win 'hearts and minds,' this counterinsurgency campaign established a harsh police state wrapped in a paternalist veneer. Yet despite its apparent success—the campaign is often presented as a model counterinsurgency effort—Britain's defeat of the MCP simply strengthened Malay elites' own desire for independence, and in 1957 the Federation became an independent state within the Commonwealth.

The fourth and final region-wide commonality was the complex interplay between nationalists, Communists, and other political forces in the formation of new nation-states. Anticolonial nationalism was itself a fluid concept, shaped in different places by ethnic and religious sentiment, regionalism, and the inevitable indeterminacy of borders bequeathed by imperial rule. How, and under what conditions would the Karen, Kachin, Shan, and Chin minorities be integrated into Burma? Could a new Malayan nationality include both Malay and Chinese, or should part of the peninsula—along with British-ruled Borneo—be included in Greater Indonesia, as Sukarno claimed? How would nationalists respond to the breakup of French Indochina into four states, including two in Vietnam? These questions, posed with particular intensity in the turbulent years following the Second World War, were not answered by blueprints and schemas but were worked out by the concrete unfolding of contingent events. There was no simple teleological path from colony to nation-state.

Pro-Moscow Communist parties played a particularly important role in this process. During the war, Communists throughout Southeast Asia had operated within the framework of the worldwide 'anti-fascist' alliance championed by Moscow, an approach that required them to drop anticolonial campaigns against the USSR's 'democratic imperialist' allies. This policy left them flat-footed in the face of the popular rebellions that erupted from below in summer 1945. In Malaya, for example, uprisings by peasant farmers and landless Chinese squatters brought 70 percent of the country under the control of the Communist-led Malayan Peoples' Anti-Japanese Army, but party leaders decided against proclaiming a Malayan Democratic Republic and instead welcomed the return of British rule.[29] A Communist-led bid for independence would undoubtedly have provoked resistance from princely elites and from some ethnic Malays, but the MCP also rejected a proposal from Malay nationalist—and wartime Japanese collaborator—Ibrahim Yaacob for a joint fight against the reimposition of British rule. Likewise, the Communist-led Hukbalahap (People's Anti-Japanese Army) in the Philippines was politically disarmed at the end of the war. The largest Filipino force fighting the Japanese, the 'Huks'—like the Yugoslav Partisans and the Chinese Communists—combined guerrilla warfare with a radical land reform program directed against landlord elites who were collaborating with the Japanese. This approach, combined with measures to promote healthcare, education, and women's rights, gave the Huks control of a broad swath of central Luzon by the time of the American invasion in late 1944. Nevertheless, despite welcoming American troops as liberators, the Huks soon found themselves on the receiving end of a brutal US-led counterinsurgency campaign that involved massacres of Huk fighters and their civilian supporters, the assassination of key leaders, and purges of elected officials.

In Vietnam, Communists were likewise propelled toward a protracted struggle with the returning French by their involvement in a popular peasant uprising, but even so, top Communist leaders were temporarily sidelined by the youthful local cadres who spearheaded the August Revolution. Elsewhere in Southeast Asia adherence to Moscow's efforts to perpetuate the wartime Grand Alliance ensured that the power vacuums opened by the collapse of Japanese rule were filled by pro-capitalist nationalists. The essentially nonrevolutionary stance of many official Communist parties also fueled a series of sharp clashes with forces to their left. In Saigon, Vietnamese Communists launched a bloody purge of local Trotskyists in September 1945, while in Burma Red Flag communists split from the pro-Moscow party in early 1946 to launch a guerrilla war against British rule. Only in Indonesia, however, did radical forces pose a sustained challenge to the official pro-Moscow line, and here Tan Malaka's Struggle Front was effectively contained by the Sukarno's Nationalist regime with the support of both the Dutch and the Communists. In Indonesia, as elsewhere in the region, the integration of new postcolonial capitalist nation-states into the emerging American-led world order did not proceed smoothly, but it did foreclose on the more radical futures posed by the postwar uprisings.

---

[29]Bayly and Harper, *Forgotten Wars*, 39.

The Bloody End of British India

The British colony of India, commonly referred to as the Raj, was connected to Southeast Asia by geographical proximity and by long-standing imperial networks of war, administration, and trade. At the height of Japan's explosive expansion in early 1942, warships of the Imperial Japanese Navy prowled the Indian Ocean, while Tokyo's armies seemed poised to invade India from occupied Burma. The dire military situation, combined with the stunningly rapid disintegration of British rule in Malaya and Burma, triggered a political crisis in India, where a popular rebellion demanding that Britain 'Quit India' erupted in summer 1942. This powerful wave of strikes, demonstrations, and peasant rebellions prefigured the popular uprisings that swept Southeast Asia at the end of the Second World War. The Indian National Congress (INC) launched the Quit India campaign after the breakdown of talks with London aimed at securing a promise of postwar independence in exchange for INC support for the war effort, but the rebellion quickly escaped its control. Across northern India protests spilled over into armed attacks on police stations and other sites of imperial control, and British officials reckoned that they faced the most serious challenge to their rule since the Great Rebellion of 1857. Prompted by London, the British government in Delhi responded with harsh military repression, and hundreds of Indians were killed as troops crushed the rebellion. Thousands more were imprisoned—including the entire INC leadership—before imperial order was restored.

The Quit India movement was the largest outpouring of popular protest anywhere in the world in the early years of the war, and its brutal suppression did nothing to sooth popular opposition to British rule. Anti-British sentiments were further inflamed by London's indifference to the terrible Bengal Famine, itself a product of wartime economic dislocation, that claimed three million lives in 1943. Hostility to British rule burst into the open again at the end of the war, this time in the form of a new wave of strikes and peasant protests focused on the fate of Indian National Army (INA) soldiers held in British captivity. Recruited to Subhas Chandra Bose's Free India movement from the ranks of Indian Army prisoners of war, INA soldiers had joined a renewed Japanese advance into India in 1944. Captured by the British after the defeat of the Japanese offensive, INA prisoners were slated for trial as traitors to their 'king-emperor.' Many Indians, however, viewed the INA combatants—including a battalion of women soldiers—as national heroes, and huge protests centered in Delhi and in industrial Kolkata (Calcutta) forced the British to drop the prosecutions and release most of the INA prisoners. Former INA soldiers—Hindus, Moslems, and Sikhs alike—often received a rapturous public welcome when they returned to their hometowns and villages.

This victory over India's British rulers overlapped with a new round of protest as virtually the entire Royal Indian Navy (RIN) joined a strike—regarded by British commanders as a mutiny—against poor conditions, including inedible food and poor pay. The strike-mutiny quickly took on broader political dimensions. Many RIN sailors had been inspired by the revolutionaries and militant nationalists that had met in ports across the greater Indian Ocean, and they now demanded the withdrawal of Indian troops from Indonesia and Indochina. Like the protests in support of the INA soldiers, the strike-mutiny cut across caste and religious divisions, with communist banners, Congress tricolors, and Muslim flags all flying from the mastheads of RIN ships. In the industrial port city of Mumbai (Bombay), the strike-mutiny prompted an outpouring of popular solidarity in the form of a city-wide general strike. British fears that they were losing control were heightened by a wave of protests demanding immediate demobilization the involved 50,000 Royal Air Force and British Army personnel, including members of the elite Parachute Regiment.[30]

These popular uprisings, like their counterparts across Southeast Asia, shaped the politics of the immediate postwar period. In India, however, they unfolded in a political space that already had many of the features of a modern capitalist nation-state. India had a small but significant native

FIGURE 4.2 *Royal Indian Navy sailors from HMIS* Talwar *march in central Mumbai, February 19, 1946. (Credit: The Times of India Group.)*

---

[30]Bayly and Harper, *Forgotten Wars*, 217–23.

capitalist class of bankers and industrialists, and Indians staffed much of the administrative bureaucracy that ensured the smooth running of the Raj. Founded in 1885, the leadership of the Indian National Congress (INC) was drawn from these social classes, and by 1937 an astute combination of parliamentarianism and well-organized mass protests had enabled it to win regional elections in eight of the eleven provinces of British India. These advances toward a self-ruled India within the British empire (effectively the 'dominion status' enjoyed by Canada and Australia) did not sit well with die-hard imperialists like Churchill, who took advantage of the war crisis to push back against the INC.

In the aftermath of the Quit India crisis, India was fully mobilized in support of the British war effort. Indian industry churned out war matériel, relieving the pressure on British manufacturing and growing India's economy by a remarkable 12 percent in 1943–44.[31] Massive profits flowed in the pockets of Indian capitalists, while Britain ran up a historically unprecedented debt to its Indian colony. Meanwhile, the British-led Indian Army grew to a 2.5-million-strong force that played a crucial role in British-Imperial campaigns from Burma to North Africa and Italy. Most Indians did not join up out of a deep commitment to the Empire, but military service gave many a basic education, new skills, and exposure to new experiences and political perspectives. As a result, and as the army's British commander Claude Auchinleck explained, by 1945 every "Indian officer worth his salt [was] a Nationalist."[32]

By the end of the war, British leaders recognized that they could not simple continue to govern India as they had before the war. The challenge facing the newly elected Labour Party government was to negotiate formal decolonization while maintaining what it could of Britain's former economic and strategic predominance in South Asia. This goal, British politicians and administrators came to believe, could be achieved by partitioning the subcontinent into a Muslim-majority state of Pakistan and an INC-led and Hindu-majority India. Prepared during the war by London's careful promotion of the Muslim League, partition took shape with bewildering speed during 1946–47, even as the RIN 'mutiny' and other popular mobilizations clearly pointed to a very different—and more socially radical—postcolonial India. For its part, INC opposition to partition quickly crumbled, and in multiethnic Bengal Congress leaders became ardent proponents of division. Partition unfolded in the context of deepening communal violence that began with riots that left 4,000 people dead in Kolkata in August 1946.

---

[31] Srinath Raghavan, *India's War: World War II and the Making of Modern South Asia* (New York: Basic Books, 2016), 326–7.
[32] Sir Claude Auchinleck, quoted in Jonathan Fennel, *Fighting the People's War: The British and Commonwealth Armies in the Second World War* (Cambridge: Cambridge University Press, 2019), 242.

Ethnic and religious violence on this scale was quite new to modern India, and while leaders on both sides deliberately inflamed popular opinion, most of the killing was carried out by gangs of thugs. Violence intensified over the summer of 1947 as twenty million Indians were displaced, many forcibly: Hindus and Sikhs abandoned homes in Punjab and East Bengal—the two core regions of the new Pakistan—while Muslims fled Indian territory. As many as one million people were killed across the subcontinent as British-led troops averted their gaze.[33]

The bloody processes of partition can be viewed simply as the product of British divide and rule tactics designed to maximize London's continued influence in the subcontinent. There is some truth to this view, but no partition would have been possible without the complicity of both Muslim League *and* Indian National Congress leaders: as historian Sumit Sakar argues, partition enabled elites on both sides of the new India-Pakistan border to "detach the attainment of political independence from radical social change" through the establishment of two new capitalist nation-states.[34] Along the way, the political radicalism and communal unity so vividly displayed during the RIN 'mutiny' and on the streets and in the factories of Mumbai and Kolkata was shattered.

World war also shook British rule in Ceylon. Located south of India, this island colony produced rubber and other raw materials vital for the British war effort while providing a key strategic base for controlling the Indian Ocean and projecting power into Southeast Asia. With the outbreak of war, colonial authorities imposed a virtual military dictatorship and used draconian measures to break the momentum of a prewar strike wave of plantation and factory workers. With many strike leaders—including members of the Trotskyist Lanka Sama Samajist Party (LSSP)—in prison, pro-Moscow Communists came to the fore in Colombo, effectively stilling mass protests for the rest of the war.[35] Building on its close relationship with local elites, London moved to establish a new neocolonial relationship in the immediate postwar, granting Ceylon conditional independence as a British Dominion in 1948 while maintaining major air and naval bases on the island. This arrangement was buttressed by the deliberate deepening of differences between the Sinhala-speaking majority and the Tamil-speaking minority, many of who were effectively disenfranchised. Despite these difficulties, popular resistance flared after the war, culminating in a 1953 *hartal* (or general strike) led by the LSSP that united Tamil plantation workers and Sinhalese factory workers in protests against rising rice

---

[33]Martin Thomas, *Fight or Flight: Britain, France, and Their Roads from Empire* (Oxford: Oxford University Press, 2014), 105.
[34]Sumit Sakar, "Popular Movements and National Leadership, 1945–47," *Economic and Political Weekly*, Vol. 17, Nos. 14–16 (1982), 686.
[35]Ashley Jackson, *The British Empire at War* (London: Hambledon Continuum, 2006), 324.

prices. As postwar militancy receded, however, Ceylon's national elites strengthened their hand, in particular by combining limited social reform with discriminatory measures like the 1956 Sinhala Only Act; as in India, the stabilization of the new nation-state went hand in hand rested on a deliberate deepening of communal, religious, and ethnic divisions.

New Nation-States and Alternative Solidarities: The 1955 Bandung Conference

As the experiences discussed here demonstrate, the transition from colony to postcolonial nation-state was far from straightforward, even at the basic level of geographical space. In 1947, two new nation-states emerged from the British Raj, and the two sides of the newly divided army were soon at war over the contested province of Kashmir. Further division would follow in 1971, when Bengal-based East Pakistan, separated by over one thousand miles from Punjab-based West Pakistan, became the independent nation of Bangladesh after a bloody war of independence. Meanwhile, in the years following independence the new government in Delhi campaigned to integrate India's 500-plus 'princely states' into the new nation. Many Indian princes, whose territories covered around 40 percent of the subcontinent and who had enjoyed nominal independence under the Raj, were won to integration with promises that their traditional prerogatives would be respected. Nevertheless, in 1948 Delhi sent the army into the recalcitrant state of Hyderabad to force its accession. During the fighting that followed at least 40,000 Muslims were slaughtered in army-initiated pogroms. In 1961, India's territory was rounded out by the military seizure of the Portuguese colonies of Goa, Diu, and Daman, but the conflict with Pakistan over Kashmir continues today.

As in the Indian subcontinent, nationalists across Southeast Asia engaged with the territorial legacies bequeathed by colonial states that, driven by their own imperial logic, had sprawled across pre-existing geographical, ethnic, and religious space. In this context, anticolonial nationalists were driven by seemingly contradictory impulses, often fighting to expand and consolidate their own new capitalist nation-states while joining with others to proclaim anti-imperial solidarity and transnational unity. Many postcolonial states thus combined practices of territorial expansionism—like that of Indonesia into West Papua/Irian Jaya—and the forced integration of 'domestic' minorities—like the Karen and Shan in Burma and the Naga in India—with ringing declarations of anti-colonial solidarity.[36]

---

[36] See Lydia Walker, "Decolonization in the 1960s: On Legitimate and Illegitimate Nationalist Claims Making," *Past & Present*, No. 242 (Feb. 2019).

Given India's relatively high level of industrial development, the development of a prestigious nuclear program—the first in a former colony—was intertwined with the struggle to establish an independent nation-state. Passed just months after independence, the 1948 Atomic Energy Act gave the new government control of all potential nuclear resources, including the monazite—a source of radioactive thorium and beryllium—produced in the princely state of Travancore. New Delhi hoped to break the cycle of neocolonial dependency by imposing a ban on monazite exports with the aim of encouraging overseas investment in a processing plant sited in India. Until Travancore joined India in 1949, however, both Britain and America sought to exploit the princely state's ambiguous status to subvert the export ban, prompting India to develop a collaborative nuclear relationship with France instead. In a 1951 agreement, French and Indian scientists agreed to collaborate on a number of nuclear projects, including the development of an advanced beryllium-moderated reactor. While the British fumed that they were "running a bad third to the French and Americans" in their former colony, Washington resorted to bribery, making a $190 million loan for the purchase of desperately needed food conditional on the resumption of monazite exports and on a promise not to sell nuclear materials to China. The terms of the American loan provoked deep resentment in New Delhi, which voiced its appreciation for an unencumbered shipment of Soviet grain and expressed a willingness to sell monazite to the Communist world. Again, Washington discovered that the task of organizing its new world order was much more complex than it had initially anticipated.

Given the regional weight of their new countries, India's prime minister Jawaharlal Nehru and Indonesia's president Sukarno projected themselves as leaders of new pan-Asia solidarities. India had begun to play an international role while still under British rule, with the colonial government—at Roosevelt's insistence—being recognized as a signatory to the 1942 Declaration of the United Nations and then participating in both the Bretton Woods conference and the founding of the United Nations. Both Nehru and Sukarno contemplated forging transnational associations, in Delhi's case an expansive "south Asian federation of India, Iraq, Iran, Afghanistan and Burma" and in Jakarta's a "Greater Indonesia" embracing Malaya, Borneo, and Portuguese Timor as well as the former Dutch East Indies.[37] Moreover, even before the formal decolonization of India was concluded, Nehru began projecting regional leadership by inviting over 200 delegates and thousands of observers to Delhi for the 1947 Asian Relations Conference. Despite denunciations of imperialism and expressions of

---

[37]Nehru, quoted in Lorenz M. Lüthi, *Cold Wars: Asia, The Middle East, Europe* (Cambridge: Cambridge University Press, 2020), 164.

anticolonial solidarity, however, the conference was short on practical steps to aid those resisting the violent campaigns of colonial reconquest then underway in Indonesia and Indochina. Given their economic precarity and fundamentally pro-capitalist outlook, few leaders wanted to risk a decisive rupture with Washington.

Many of these features were reprised at the Asian-African Conference held in the Indonesian city of Bandung in 1955. Assembling leaders of twenty-nine countries that represented half the world's population for a meeting held without any of the Western powers being formally present was a major achievement in itself, but the much-vaunted 'Bandung spirit' promised more than it delivered. Representing China, a conciliatory Zhou Enlai sought "common ground" and peaceful coexistence, while Washington worked through its clients in the Philippines, Pakistan, and Thailand to urge opposition to "Communist colonialism."[38] The conference concluded with a policy statement that was so modest in its criticism of colonialism that the *New York Times* believed that the "free world [could] subscribe wholeheartedly."[39] Described by historians Su Lin Lewis and Carolien Stolte as a "theatrical performance" designed to capture the "zeitgeist of the postcolonial moment," Bandung marked the highpoint of an attempt by national elites, along with activists, artists, journalists, and other non-state actors, to forge networks of postcolonial solidarity independent of both the American-led West and the Soviet bloc.[40] The hope, as expressed by the 1953 Asian Socialist Conference in Yangon, was to create a "third way" that was independent and "non-aligned."[41] Given American predominance within the capitalist world and Moscow's disinterest in advancing anticolonial revolution, there was never any real prospect of finding such a 'way,' and increasingly such meetings and conferences became venues for political posturing, bilateral deal-making, and artistic performances sponsored by the CIA-backed Congress for Cultural Freedom.

Communism in South and Southeast Asia

Exploding into the power vacuums that opened in the interregnum between the collapse of Japan's Co-Prosperity Sphere and the reassertion of European and American colonialism, popular uprisings created potentially revolutionary situations across South and Southeast Asia. As in Europe and China, however, Moscow had no interest in advancing socialist revolution,

---

[38]Ibid., 126.
[39]Editorial, "After Bandung," *New York Times*, April 25, 1955, 22.
[40]Su Lin Lewis and Carolien Stolte, "Other Bandungs: Afro-Asian Internationalisms in the Early Cold War," *Journal of World History*, Vol. 30, Nos. 1–2 (June 2019), 1–2.
[41]Ibid., 7.

and beyond buttressing its own security and economic recovery, the region was of peripheral interest to a Soviet leadership focused primarily on Europe and on avoiding conflict with the United States. Moreover, since the rise of Stalinism in the 1920s Moscow had viewed the achievement of postcolonial national independence as an end in itself and not—as the revolutionary internationalists of the early Russian Revolution had proposed—as a critical step that would strengthen the capacity of the toilers to push toward the overthrow of capitalism. As a result, pro-Moscow Communist parties had often given 'popular front' support to pro-capitalist nationalists, even going so far as to dissolve their own parties into nationalist organizations like the Guomindang and the Indian National Congress. This approach led directly to the 1927 massacre of Communist forces by Chiang Kai-shek's Guomindang, but it remained central to Moscow's strategy in the colonial world. The picture was further complicated during the war, when Moscow instructed Communist parties in the colonial world to support the 'People's War' against fascism. In India the Communist Party dropped calls for independence, denounced Congress' Quit India campaign, and mobilized support for the British war effort, while their comrades across Southeast Asia organized anti-Japanese guerrilla armies with American and British support.

In the postwar crisis, these policies led Communists to function as supporters—or even, as in Indonesia, disguised leaders—of nationalist forces, who they encouraged to seek accommodation with the imperialist governments that Moscow wanted to keep on good terms with. Only in Vietnam did Communists lead a protracted struggle against colonialism, and even here they did so while embedded within a broad nationalist coalition. Then in late 1947, and in the context of the deepening Cold War in Europe, Moscow lurched to the left. The confrontational new 'two camp' policy announced by Andrei Zhdanov at the founding conference of the Cominform had major implications for Communist policy in South and Southeast Asia. Translated into the region through Communist-led meetings of youth, women, and trade unionists, this new line led to the overturn of 'collaborationist' party leaderships in India and Indonesia. Support for bourgeois nationalism was out, and it was replaced by a turn to armed struggle, pursued irrespective of the specific political situation in any given country.[42]

Communists across South and Southeast Asia responded to Moscow's new line, which seemed to reflect the experience of the advancing Chinese Revolution. In Malaya, the Communist-led National Liberation Army launched an armed insurgency, while the Indian Communists removed the old party leadership, denounced Nehru as a servant of British imperialism, and

---

[42]R. Palme Dutt, quoted in Milton Sacks, "The Strategy of Communism in Southeast Asia," *Pacific Affairs*, Vol. 23, No. 3 (September 1950), 231.

launched a peasant-based rebellion in the Telangana region of Hyderabad. In Indonesia, as we have seen, Muso's return from Moscow in August 1948 precipitated the PKI-led putsch in Madiun in September. Except in Vietnam, where Communist-led forces enjoyed broad popular support rooted in substantial Chinese-style base areas, these guerilla insurgencies all ended in disastrous defeats. In Burma, for example, British military supplies and financial aid flowed to Thakin Nu's government, strengthening the role of the army in domestic politics in the process. Moreover, armed insurgencies convinced American policymakers that they faced a coordinated worldwide challenge—a conclusion that was reinforced by the victory of the Chinese Revolution and by the outbreak of war in Korea in 1950.

Moscow's encouragement of armed insurgency in Asia was short-lived, thanks both to the crushing defeats suffered in Burma, Malaya, and Indonesia, and to the Soviet leadership's own turn toward peaceful coexistence with the West in the early 1950s. This new turn emphasized inter-government relations, and it was registered in a series of trade and aid agreements between Moscow and various postcolonial governments. The initiative for such agreements often came from nationalist leaders like Nehru and Sukarno, who understood that political independence did not guarantee economic independence and that their new nation-states remained embedded in a world capitalist market whose terms of trade—the relative value of exported raw materials and imported capital and consumer goods—were stacked against them. Even basic access to export markets was often mediated by companies based in the old colonial metropoles. At the same time, many new nationalist regimes inherited highly centralized states from their old colonial rulers that were staffed by well-trained administrators with experience of wartime economic planning. Informed by this powerful statism, and often despite their own repression of domestic Communism, many nationalist leaders turned to Moscow for economic aid. These ties were particularly attractive because Moscow was willing to accept barter—Burma, for example, paid for the services of Soviet architects, planners, and technicians with rice—and to offer low—or no-interest credit and loans. Nationalist leaders also hoped that the display of political independence implicit in these arrangements would give them the leverage to secure better terms from the West.

Under Nikita Khrushchev's leadership in the mid-1950s, Moscow established collaborative relationships with Afghanistan, Burma, India, and Indonesia, with the Soviets agreeing to supply technical expertise, communications equipment, and capital goods—including equipment for the Bhilai steel mill in India—in exchange for food and raw materials. Moscow's own economic planners viewed the establishment of large state sectors based on heavy industry as offering the high road to postcolonial economic development, but they explicitly rejected the wholesale overturn of capitalist economic relations and argued instead for forms of mixed economy and 'state capitalism.' In a striking parallel to the modernization efforts then being championed by Washington, Moscow's approach reduced development simply to economic growth, effectively dismissing any connection to the emergence of new and more egalitarian social relations. Soviet leaders naturally hoped that trade, planning, economic aid, and military hardware would tilt political relations in their favor. These efforts to curry favor were buttressed by national Communist parties that—after abandoning the disastrous turn to guerrilla warfare in the late 1940s—were reorganized in support of Moscow's diplomatic and economic initiatives and often became, as in Indonesia, key organizers of grassroots support for nationalist regimes.

At the same time, the relative stability of the later 1950s—itself a product on a global scale of the consolidation of American hegemony—masked deepening divisions between Communist forces. In the late 1940s and early 1950s, Communists across Southeast Asia had been deeply inspired by the Chinese Revolution, and they naturally turned toward the Chinese Communist Party for advice and aid. The CCP's prestige was reinforced by Moscow's short-lived endorsement of armed struggle following the establishment of the Cominform in 1947, and in 1949 it won Soviet backing for the organization of a Beijing-based "Asian Cominform."[43] This project, which included the establishment of a training school based on the writings of Mao Zedong and the dispatch of military and political advisors to regional Communist parties, allowed the CCP to present itself as the leader of the "Asian revolution." Inevitably, the CCP's self-promotion did not sit well with Moscow: as John Leighton Stuart, American ambassador to Nationalist China noted perceptively in 1949, Mao's move to "set himself up as an Asian Lenin" was likely to provoke a split—and possibly a war—between the two major Communist states.[44] Their common pursuit of peaceful coexistence—reflected in Zhou Enlai's conciliatory speech to the 1955 conference in Bandung—muffled these tensions for much of the 1950s, but these transnational dimensions reinforced the rapid deterioration in Sino-Soviet relation at the end of the decade.

Organizing American Hegemony in South and Southeast Asia

Postwar developments in South and Southeast Asia unfolded within the world created by America's victory in the Second World War, but while American leaders certainly anticipated exercising global hegemony, its

---

[43]Zhihua Shan and Yafeng Xia, "Leadership Transfer in the Asian Revolution: Mao Zedong and the Asian Cominform," *Cold War History*, Vol. 14, No. 2 (2014), 201.
[44]Ibid., 205.

wartime planners had had no clear blueprint for structuring their coming predominance. Moreover, with its efforts focused on defeating Japan and then on 'winning' China, Washington's wartime engagement with South and Southeast Asia was limited. By 1945 American policymakers had largely dropped earlier plans for rapid decolonization, assuming instead that European colonial rule would be reestablished after the war. Allied military operations in the region were conducted under the British-led Southeast Asia Command (SEAC), and many joked that the command's acronym stood for 'Save England's Asian Colonies.' Washington hoped that the Europeans could be encouraged to begin preparing their colonies for independence at some unspecified time in the future, thereby fulfilling the promise of national self-determination enshrined in the Atlantic Charter while simultaneously opening the door to American economic predominance. In particular, Washington recognized that the economic and political development of British India had already laid the basis for a strong and independent capitalist nation-state, and from early in the war American leaders leaned on the British to move in this direction. At the same time, President Roosevelt and other top leaders also intended that Guomindang-led China would be one of the 'four policemen' of the postwar world with particular responsibility for maintaining order in Southeast Asia. This was a self-serving vision: Washington expected that China would function as a junior partner of the United States, thus guaranteeing its privileged access to Asian markets and raw materials without the necessity of maintaining a large US military presence.

By 1945, these vague schemes had been shattered by the deepening crisis of the Guomindang, the rising power of the Chinese revolution, and the region-wide popular uprisings and political instability that accompanied the formal end of the war. Fearing that anticolonial revolts might spill over into anticapitalist revolutions, American policymakers dialed back their already-tepid support for national self-determination and instead gave full backing to the reestablishment of European rule. To facilitate this process, in August 1945 General Douglas MacArthur, the top Allied commander in the Pacific, expanded the British-led Southeast Asia Command's operational area to include all of Southeast Asia. This organizational shift was justified by the need to concentrate American forces in Japan, but it had the additional advantage of ensuring that the initial responsibility for reestablishing colonial rule throughout Southeast Asia would fall to British-Imperial forces. The only fig leaf covering Washington's retreat from its wartime anticolonial rhetoric was the pious hope that over time the returning imperialist rulers would prepare their colonies for self-government. In this context, the Philippines assumed new importance. Washington hoped that its commitment to Filipino independence would create a "deep impression throughout Asia," boosting America's standing in nationalist eyes while modeling the sort of neo-colonial relationship that would encourage the

European powers to set their own colonies on the road toward eventual independence.[45]

Washington feared the radical potential of the postwar uprisings across Southeast Asia and, in the context of the crisis in China and sharpening Cold War confrontation with the Soviet Union in Europe, it tended to see them as part of a Communist master plan for world domination. In this sense, while social conflicts in Southeast Asia were indigenous products of the region's specific histories of colonialism and war, in the eyes of the new hegemon they became part of a worldwide challenge to order and stability. This discourse also dovetailed neatly with long-standing racialized fears of the so-called "yellow peril," a "dread blur"—as commentator Harold Isaacs described it—of "vast numbers, barbarism, and disease" that threatened to overwhelm "Western civilization."[46] The wreck of American hopes for a pro-Western China—"a grievous political defeat" according to the State Department—sharpened psycho-political fears of an advancing Asian-Communist tsunami that were further reinforced by the outbreak of war in Korea in June 1950.[47]

In this context, in the late 1940s Washington turned toward more direct engagement with Southeast Asia, reconfiguring the region as a critical Cold War battleground whose loss would menace key allies in Japan and Australia and threaten to upset the entire world order. A series of new top-level plans that culminated with NSC-68 in 1950 advocated distancing the United States from beleaguered colonial regimes while strengthening Washington's own military position in the region and using carefully targeted aid to advance its standing with emerging nationalist governments. Washington's turn in the late 1940s overlapped with Moscow's own lurch toward guerrilla warfare—a move that was itself driven by Cold War pressures in Europe. As a result, Communist insurgencies that challenged nationalist leaders unwittingly created new openings for American diplomacy. In particular, Sukarno's crushing of the PKI coup in Madiun in late 1948 prompted Washington to strong-arm the Dutch into granting Indonesian independence while arranging to supply the new postcolonial national government with American military and economic aid. At the same time, Paris's move to establish Bao Đai's nominally independent State of Vietnam enabled Washington to funnel resources to the French war against

---

[45]Mill, "The Philippines Prepare for Independence," quoted in Woods, *Freedom Incorporated*, 80.
[46]Harold Isaacs, quoted in Matthew Jones, "A 'Segregated' Asia?: Race, the Bandung Conference, and Pan-Asia Fears in American Thought and Policy, 1954–1955," *Diplomatic History*, Vol. 29, No. 5 (November 2005), 844.
[47]PPS 51, March 29, 1949, quoted in Gary R. Hess, *The United States' Emergence as a Southeast Asian Power, 1940–1950* (New York: Columbia University Press, 1987), 335.

the Democratic Republic of Vietnam without having to give open support to recolonization.

On the economic front, this policy shift was announced in President Truman's January 1949 inaugural address with a pledge to use American technicians and know-how to promote economic development in emerging postcolonial states. This Point Four initiative—named after its place in Truman's speech—took the New Deal-era Tennessee Valley Authority and wartime aid projects in Latin America as models for projects that combined modest government funding with private investment and the work of universities, churches, and other non-government agencies. The goal was to create development projects designed to build infrastructure and promote healthcare, education, and improved agricultural technique in ways that would, planners hoped, lead to sustained growth. This was not philanthropy: for very modest outlays in comparison with the Marshall Plan funds then flowing into Europe, planners aimed to secure outsize political influence while opening new markets to American business. Point Four modeled the use of American aid to promote economic growth in 'underdeveloped' countries—the term itself was a discursive product of the program—in order to raise living standards, strengthen governments aligned with the United States, and blunt the appeal of communism. Moreover, Point Four projects often led 'underdeveloped' countries to seek additional loans from the World Bank, America's own Import-Export Bank, and other state and private institutions, all of which served to tie the recipients ever more tightly into the circuits of debt and dependency within the capitalist world market. Packaged as modernization, this approach became central to both the practice and the ideology of American foreign policy.

Top-level American missions charged with preparing plans for economic and military aid fanned out across Southeast Asia in 1950 and, speeded by the war in Korea, technical assistance agreements were quickly concluded with governments in Afghanistan, Burma, Ceylon, Indonesia, Formosa/Taiwan, Nepal, Pakistan, the Philippines, and Thailand. Similar agreements were also negotiated with several Middle Eastern governments. In every case, as Washington's 1950 Griffith Mission to Southeast Asia reported, aid agreements were crafted with an eye to promoting "psychological patterns" conducive to a "pro-western orientation."[48] Jawaharlal Nehru welcomed US technical aid but deplored its linkages to the capitalist market and to Washington's political objectives. Nevertheless, despite the tensions in Indian-American relations that reflected Washington's concern over Nehru's "neutralism" in world politics, American experts oversaw the construction of a penicillin plant along with medical research facilities and a dam

---

[48]Report of 1950 Griffith Mission, quoted in Stephen Macekura, "The Point Four Program and US International Development Policy," *Political Science Quarterly*, Vol. 128, No. 1 (2013), 150.

construction program promoting rural electrification. In exchange, India pledged to uphold "individual liberty, free institutions, and independence" while maintaining "sound economic conditions and stable international relationships."[49]

In the late 1940s, American planners had become increasingly concerned by the strength of the Huk insurgency in the Philippines and by the evident corruption and inefficiency of the US-sponsored government. Here, Point Four assistance was combined with the imposition—on an ostensibly sovereign state—of sweeping political and financial reforms. With American advisors leading the way, the Philippine military now launched offensive operations that finally subdued the Huk rebellion in 1954. American diplomats armed with Point Four funds and military aid also steered the Thai government of Plaek Phibunsongkhram—a wartime ally of Japan—into Washington's orbit, and Bangkok joined Manila in sending a small but symbolic force to fight in Korea. More broadly, the crisis in Korea prompted the 1950 Melby-Erskine military mission, which recommended stepping up US military aid to Burma, French Indochina, and Indonesia, while cheering on British counterinsurgency efforts in Malaya.

Washington's moves to strengthen potential allies in Southeast Asia took place in the context of a reorganization of American military forces following the 'loss' of China. Ejected from the East Asian mainland, American planners now conceived of a line of containment stretching across the Western Pacific from the Aleutian Islands to Japan and on through Okinawa and the Philippines to India. Korea was excluded from Secretary of State Dean Acheson's initial public presentation of this line of containment in January 1950, only to become within months the site of the first major deployment of American combat troops since the Second World War. Nevertheless, American planners were not eager to repeat the experience of fighting a major ground war in Asia, and the new Pacific frontier was essentially an exercise in sea and air power centered on the US Navy's Seventh Fleet, based at Subic Bay in the Philippines and anchored by the maintenance of substantial ground forces in South Korea. The line of containment was backed by bases in Hawai'i, Guam, and on the Pacific islands seized from Japan during the war. Here, in a blatantly neocolonial arrangement that gave the US military airbases, nuclear test sites, and other key facilities, the Marshall and Marianas islands were organized in 1945 into the Trust Territory of the Pacific Islands and administered by Washington under nominal United Nations oversight.

US military power in Southeast Asia was arrayed under Washington's nuclear umbrella and this strategic reliance on atomic weapons deepened

---

[49]General Agreement for Technical Cooperation, January 1952, quoted in Macekura, "The Point Four Program," 149.

during the 1950s under President Eisenhower's New Look doctrine. There were top-level discussions about using nuclear weapons during the war in Korea, US planners pondered nuclear strikes in support of the French in Indochina, and Eisenhower pledged to use them in defense of Chiang Kai-shek's Republic of China in Taiwan. A lack of suitable targets helped to stay Washington's hand, but American planners were also aware that the perception that nuclear weapons were racist devices designed only for use against Asians meant that any military gains from their use would come at a heavy political price. Regional hostility to American nuclear weapons was further heightened in 1954 when the crew of the Japanese fishing boat *Lucky Dragon* was contaminated by deadly fallout from a nuclear test at Bikini Atoll in the Marshall Islands.

As in Europe, Washington sought to structure its regional predominance through multilateral alliances, signing the tripartite ANZUS treaty with Australia and New Zealand in 1951 and forming the eight-country Southeast Asia Treaty Organization (SEATO) in 1954. ANZUS was a mutual defense pact aimed ostensibly at the perceived threat of Chinese expansionism and Japanese revanchism, but it also registered the repositioning of Britain's former antipodean dominions in the new American dominated order. More significant in Southeast Asian politics, SEATO aimed to deter Chinese 'aggression' and provide mutual assistance against domestic 'subversion,' including by boosting economic growth and raising living standards. In practice, however, it was a strangely lopsided organization, with the alliance's three major participants—the United States, Britain, and France—located wholly outside the region, while two more—Australian and New Zealand—stood on the periphery, leaving only Pakistan, the Philippines and Thailand in Southeast Asia. As the State Department noted, its composition gave SEATO the look of a "white man's party."[50] This impression was reinforced by the fact that other Southeast Asian countries, including regional powerhouses India and Indonesia, had rejected invitations to join the new alliance despite their generally pro-Western leanings. Both Nehru and Sukarno preferred the room to maneuver granted by the non-aligned stance showcased at Bandung the following year, and the Indian leader explicitly denied that China had expansionist intentions. For its part, Pakistan joined the alliance in the hope of cultivating ties with Washington that would counterbalance India, an approach that led to a 1955 mutual defense treaty with the United States, American military use of the Peshawar airbase, and—at the end of the decade—US support for Ayub Khan's military dictatorship.

Given its structure and composition, SEATO was never able to play a role even remotely analogous to that of NATO in Europe. This obvious weakness in the structure of American hegemony was not the result of

---

[50] State Department memorandum, May 7, 1954, quoted in Jones, "A 'Segregated' Asia?" 849.

diplomatic misjudgment or of military incapacity, but instead reflected the realities of a vast region in which the ragged endings of the Second World War, the massive anticolonial revolts that followed it, and the incapacity of new capitalist nation-states to meet the basic needs of a large swaths of the population combined to drive political turmoil and social instability. Nevertheless, by the mid-1950s South and Southeast Asia had begun to resemble something like the orderly and non-revolutionary spaces that Washington had been seeking since 1945. That did not imply an end to gross economic inequality or a resolution of the class divisions, but as the great wave of postwar uprisings ebbed—aided by the Communist's disastrous turn to guerrilla warfare—relatively stable nationalist regimes oriented toward the United States were consolidated. Across the region, Washington strengthened its ties to nationalist strongmen, including Thakin Nu in Burma, Plaek Phibunsongkhram, in Thailand, and Ramon Magsaysay in the Philippines. Even the new Republic of Vietnam entered a short period of relative calm as Diem's American-backed regime strengthened its grip. Nevertheless, this was hardly the stuff of long-term stability, and by the end of the decade the unresolved national question in Vietnam led to a resumption of fighting and—eventually—to the full-scale involvement of the United States in another ground war in Asia.

For Further Reading

Christopher Bayly and Tim Harper, *Forgotten Wars: Freedom and Revolution in Southeast Asia* (Cambridge, MA: Harvard University Press, 2007).
Ang Cheng Guan, *The Southeast Asia Treaty Organization* (New York: Routledge, 2021).
Gary R. Hess, *The United States' Emergence as a Southeast Asian Power, 1940–1950* (New York: Columbia University Press, 1987).
Chen Jian, *Mao's China and the Cold War* (Chapel Hill, NC: University of South Carolina Press, 2001).
Matthew Jones, "A 'Segregated' Asia?: Race, the Bandung Conference, and Pan-Asia Fears in American Thought and Policy, 1954–1955," *Diplomatic History*, Vol. 29, No. 5 (November 2005).
Walter LaFeber, "Roosevelt, Churchill, and Indochina, 1942–1945," *The American Historical Review*, Vol. 80, No. 5 (December 1975).
Vina A. Lanzona, *Amazons of the Huk Rebellion: Gender, Sex, and Revolution in the Philippines* (Madison, WI: University of Wisconsin Press, 2009).
Frederik Logevall, *Embers of War: The Fall of an Empire and the Making of America's Vietnam* (New York: Random House, 2013).
Stephen Macekura, "The Point Four Program and US International Development Policy," *Political Science Quarterly*, Vol. 128, No. 1 (2013).
Robert J. McMahon, *Colonialism and Cold War: The United States and the Struggle for Indonesian Independence, 1945–49* (Ithaca: Cornell University Press, 1981).

Harry A. Poeze, "The Cold War in Indonesia, 1948," *Journal of Southeast Asian Studies*, Vol. 40, No. 3 (2009).

Srinath Raghavan, *India's War: World War II and the Making of Modern South Asia* (New York: Basic Books, 2016).

Sumit Sakar, "Popular Movements and National Leadership, 1945–47," *Economic and Political Weekly*, Vol. 17, Nos. 14–16 (1982).

Mary Margaret Steedly, *Rifle Reports: A Story of Indonesian Independence* (Berkley: University of California Press, 2013).

Martin Thomas, *Fight or Flight: Britain, France, and Their Roads from Empire* (Oxford: Oxford University Press, 2014).

Colleen Woods, *Freedom Incorporated: Anti-Communism and Philippine Independence in the Age of Decolonization* (Ithaca: Cornell University Press, 2020).

CHAPTER FIVE

Hegemony Transferred and Hierarchy Reorganized: Western Europe, Japan, and the British Dominions

War, Revolution, and Political Restabilization in Italy

Italy's postwar began early. After Allied troops landed in Sicily in July 1943, Fascist leaders recognized that they had lost the war and quickly deposed dictator Benito Mussolini, allowing King Victor Emmanuel III to appoint a new government led by former army chief of staff Pietro Badoglio. Badoglio began secret talks with the Allies, and by the time American and British troops began landing in mainland Italy in September, he was ready to change sides. Under the armistice agreement between Badoglio and the Allies, territory freed from German occupation would initially be administered by an Allied Military Government of Occupied Territories (AMGOT), but as Anglo-American troops advanced north they would turn regions behind the lines over to the Italian government, whose work would be supervised by an Allied Control Commission. This scheme quickly ran into difficulties as the Italian people demanded a say in the reconstruction of their country, a desire graphically expressed in the four-day uprising that expelled German troops from Naples in October 1943 and in the wave of peasant rebellions and land seizures that rolled across the rural south. As in Southeast Asia, the liminal time between the departure of the Germans and the arrival of the Allies opened ragged windows in which ordinary people could assert their independence, agency, and collective self-government in revolts that often appeared as "carnivals" of the oppressed.[1]

After Naples, American leaders recognized that their support for the unpopular Badoglio government would put them on a collision course with the Italian people. Such a clash would have had far-reaching consequences for the process of postwar political stabilization across Europe, and Washington decided to accommodate popular sentiment by pushing for the establishment of a more liberal Italian government. This course was endorsed by Soviet leaders, but the British were determined to keep the conservative Badoglio in power. As a result, the formation of a more liberal government was delayed until June 1944, when American troops got into Rome ahead of their British allies, ousted Badoglio, and facilitated the formation of a broad coalition under the leadership of socialist Ivanoe Bonomi.

Bonomi's coalition government included a broad range of anti-Fascist forces including Alcide Gasperi's newly formed Christian Democrats (DC) and the Communists Party of Italy (PCI), led by Palmiro Togliatti. Communist participation in the new government—critical to securing the support of Italy's radical working class—was the product of the agreement between allied leaders reached at the summit conference held in Tehran in November 1943. At this conference it was agreed to divide postwar Europe into an Anglo-American—and increasingly simply American—dominated sphere in the west and a Soviet sphere in the east. In line with this understanding, Soviet leaders pledged that national Communist parties in the West would work to tamp down popular uprisings, corralling enthusiasm for radical social change into nonrevolutionary and liberal-democratic channels. In March 1944, Togliatti returned to Italy from exile in Moscow with explicit orders from Stalin to control rank-and-file militancy. The veteran Communist carried out his mission to the letter, convening a special PCI congress that, in the so-called Salerno Switch, dropped calls for revolution, ended agitation for a referendum on the future of the monarchy, and cleared the way for the party to join the Italian government.

The participation of the PCI and other left-wing parties in the new coalition government gave it the authority to negotiate an agreement with the National Liberation Committee for Northern Italy (CLNAI) that prepared the political ground for the advance of Allied armies into northern Italy in spring 1945. The CLNAI claimed leadership over all Communist-led and other anti-fascist partisans operating in the north. British and American commanders were concerned that any time lag between the collapse of the German occupation and the arrival of Allied troops would be filled by Communist-led insurrections, but under the new agreement,

---

[1] Rosario Forlenza, "Europe's Forgotten Unfinished Revolution: Peasant Power, Social Mobilization, and Communism in the South Italian Countryside, 1943–1945," *American Historical Review*, Vol. 126, No. 2 (2021), 517.

known as the Protocols of Rome, the CLNAI pledged that partisan forces in the north would work with Allied troops to establish political stability. Allied concerns were not misplaced: as in much of Southeast Asia, a broad popular insurrection did indeed erupt across northern Italy in the untidy spaces between the end of the German occupation and the consolidation of the Allied military government. As Allied troops advanced into the Po Valley in spring 1945, local partisans launched attacks on German army units and on the fascist paramilitaries of Benito Mussolini's Italian Social Republic. Some partisans had no party affiliation, and some were organized by the Communist, Socialist, and Action parties, and while all owed allegiance to the Rome-based CLNAI, the chaotic conditions of the German collapse often gave them a great deal of local autonomy. In villages, small towns, and major cities across the north, guerrilla forces suddenly found themselves in complete political control.

As working people across the region began to take government into their own hands, provincial CLNAI leaders struggled to organize a bewildering array of popular committees at city, neighborhood, and even street level. In workplaces from the Fiat's giant Lingotto auto plant in Turin to small workshops and factories, committees of workers asserted control over

FIGURE 5.1 *Young Italian partisans prepare to combat German snipers during the liberation of Pistoia, northern Tuscany, December 9, 1944. (Photo: Keystone/Getty Images.)*

production, while in rural areas peasant farmers ousted fascist officials, attacked unpopular landlords, and staked claim to the land. As both fighters and political organizers, women played a major role in these events as popular democracy, driven by a deep desire for radical social change, flooded into the power vacuums opened by the collapse of the German occupation. For a brief moment, new futures—and a more egalitarian society—seemed within reach. For many these were, as one participant recalled, "weeks of joy," made bright by the belief that a "substantial measure of social justice" was coming.[2]

This sprawling popular insurrection alarmed British and American commanders, but while local partisans established new organs of popular government, they made no bid for political power at a regional or national level. Instead, as Allied troops arrived in 'auto-liberated' communities, partisan leaders handed governmental authority over to the representatives of the Allied Military Government. In many places, partisan fighters turned their arms over to Allied troops in carefully orchestrated and highly symbolic ceremonies: "In almost every instance," one relieved British officer reported, "the CLN has proved to be sensible and cooperative."[3] These peaceful transitions were carried out within the framework of the Protocols of Rome, which were rigorously enforced by local PCI leaders. It is impossible to know what would have happened if the PCI had adopted the revolutionary course many of its rank-and-file members desired, but any attempt to reorganize the national government on the basis of the mass participatory democracy that flowered at local level during the auto-liberation would surely have led to conflict with Allied troops. Whatever the outcome, the postwar settlement in Western Europe would have been quite different. As it was, the Soviets and the PCI ensured that the radical energy of the Italian Revolution ebbed away, allowing for the rapid reestablishment—under the oversight of the Allied Military Government—of bourgeois democracy and an increasingly stable capitalist nation-state.

The restoration of political stability in Italy was strengthened by large-scale inflows of American aid, with $50 million coming through the US-led United Nations Relief and Rehabilitation Administration (UNRRA) while another $37 million came from private charities like the newly established American Relief for Italy Inc.[4] Working through the Allied Control Commission that was tasked with overseeing all the work of the Italian government, Washington also dispatched civil engineers, technicians, and industrial experts to advance the work of reconstructing war-damaged infrastructure and boosting economic recovery. American corporations

---

[2]Quoted in David W. Ellwood, *Italy, 1943–1945* (New York: Holmes and Maier, 1985), 188.
[3]Ibid., 188–9.
[4]Andrew Buchanan, *American Grand Strategy in the Mediterranean during World War II* (Cambridge: Cambridge University Press, 2014), 200–1.

were also quick to spot the possibilities of closer economic ties, and as wartime constraints were lifted, they began to move into the Italian market. These steps, along with a series of other measures promoted by Washington to ease wartime economic dislocation and boost the supply of food and medicine, helped to soften the devastating aftermath of war and buffer popular discontent. At the same time, British influence in Italy, already damaged by London's unwavering support for Badoglio, declined significantly as the American presence increased. Moreover, with American aid and American money helping to stave off disease and starvation, the liberal democracy Washington was promoting became deeply associated with material well-being as the outlines of a new American-led order started to become evident.

Democracy, Disarmament, and the Restoration of Political Equilibrium

The political crisis in Italy in spring 1945 reveals with particular clarity the challenge facing the Allies as the war came to an end. In all the major capitalist nation-states—from the ruins of Europe and Japan to Britain, Canada, and Australia—millions of working people were deeply dissatisfied with the existing social set-up, and in some places their anger was sharpened by wartime hunger, physical destruction, and economic collapse. These sentiments drove waves of strikes for better wages and conditions in many countries, and—in a moderate British way—they led to the unceremonious dumping of storied wartime leader Winston Churchill and his fellow Conservatives in the May 1945 general election. Where war, occupation, and military defeat had combined to dislocate the old order and its state structure, as they had done in Italy, France, Greece, and—to some degree—Japan, popular protests could take an insurrectionary turn.

These political developments took place amid the war's shocking legacy of destruction and dislocation. In Japan, sixty-six cities had been bombed to rubble, and over 30 percent of the population was homeless. One-quarter of the country's productive capacity had been obliterated, and urban living standards had fallen to about 35 percent of prewar levels.[5] German cities, also, had been the targets of relentless Allied bombing, and in many well over 50 percent of habitable premises had been destroyed: from Hamburg, one British officer gazed at the appalling vista of "square mile after square mile of empty shells of buildings," a sight that was "incomprehensible unless seen

---

[5] John Dower, *Embracing Defeat: Japan in the Wake of World War II* (New York: Norton, 1999), 45–6.

[firsthand]."⁶ Physical destruction was concentrated in the Axis countries, but the allies did not escape unscathed: sprawling 'bomb sites' scarred many British cities, while Belgian, Dutch, and French towns and villages caught up in the ground fighting in 1940—and then again in 1944—were literally flattened. In France alone, Allied bombs killed over 53,000 civilians.⁷

The human suffering caused by the war did not end when the guns fell silent. Across Europe, thirteen million children had lost one or both parents.⁸ In Italy, Germany, and Japan, millions had fled their homes to escape Allied bombs, and they joined many more—including Jews fleeing the Shoah, over seven million Eastern European workers forced to work in Nazi Germany, and former prisoners of war of all countries—who were displaced and often homeless at war's end.⁹ Many were also stateless, unable or unwilling to return to their prewar homes. In Europe, Allied authorities established makeshift camps for some of the continent's eleven million Displaced Persons, often further dehumanized to just "DPs," and 850,000 were still living there three years later.¹⁰ Survival was no guarantee of good treatment, even for Holocaust survivors: American General George Patton, head of the Allied Military Government in Bavaria, noted in his diary that the appalling conditions under which Jewish refugees were living reflected the fact that they were "lower than animals."¹¹ These refugees and displaced persons were joined by around twelve million *Volksdeutsche*, ethnic Germans who had been living in Eastern Europe and who had either fled the advancing Red Army or else had been expelled from their homelands by the new pro-Soviet regimes.

These intertwined social crises underscored the urgency of re-establishing political stability. In contrast to the ongoing armed violence in East and Southeast Asia and in parts of Eastern Europe, the shooting wars in Germany and Japan ended quickly in summer 1945. This simple fact, enforced by the massive presence of Allied occupation forces and overseen by the establishment of military governments, facilitated the rapid reestablishment of political order. This process, beginning in Italy in summer 1943 and concluding with the establishment of the Federal Republic of Germany in October 1949, can be divided into two broad phases. During

---

⁶Keith Lowe, *Savage Continent: Europe in the Aftermath of World War II* (New York: Picador, 2012), 78.
⁷Richard Overy, *The Bombing War: Europe 1939–1945* (London: Penguin Books, 2014), 581.
⁸Martin Conway, *Western Europe's Democratic Age, 1945–1968* (Princeton: Princeton University Press, 2020), 49.
⁹Yasmin Khan, "Wars of Displacement: Exile and Uprooting in the 1940s," in Michael Geyer and Adam Tooze (eds.), *The Cambridge History of the Second World War*, Vol. III (New York: Cambridge University Press, 2015), 282.
¹⁰Ibid., 278, 282.
¹¹George Patton, quoted in Susan L. Carruthers, *The Good Occupation: American Soldiers and the Hazards of Peace* (Cambridge, MA: Harvard University Press, 2016), 174.

the first, extensive American aid helped to buffer popular discontent, while collaboration with local Communists and the enactment of a range of far-reaching democratic and social reforms helped to rebuild the legitimacy of the state. As Cold War tensions between Washington and Moscow deepened, a second phase opened in 1947. Communists now resigned or were expelled from governments in Belgium, Italy, and France, while American occupation forces in Japan adopted more overtly pro-business and anti-labor policies and the Marshall Plan kick-started European economic recovery. By the early 1950s, the restoration of political stability opened the way for a sustained period of capitalist expansion in both Western Europe and Japan while simultaneously facilitating the consolidation of American predominance. In this context, Allied military governments were wound up, ending in Italy after the signing of the Treaty of Paris between Rome and the allied powers in February 1947, in Germany in 1949, and in Japan in April 1952 as the 1951 Treaty of San Francisco came into effect.

These phases of postwar stabilization were not discrete events but overlapping processes that unfolded at different tempos in different places. It is instructive, however, to view them in comparison to events following the First World War. At the end of that war, capitalist political stability across Europe was profoundly shaken by popular insurrections led by forces inspired by the 1917 Russian Revolution. Many, like the German Spartacus League, were new and inexperienced parties, but all sought to overthrow capitalism; moreover, their revolutionary efforts were encouraged by the new communist government in Russia and by the new Communist International—or Comintern—it founded in 1919. As a result, the restoration of political equilibrium in Europe was a protracted and difficult process that was not concluded until 1923 as popular revolts continued to roil Germany and Italy. These contested processes of political stabilization made for a slow and relatively weak postwar economic recovery. After the Second World War, political equilibrium in the major capitalist countries was reestablished much more quickly, and the subsequent worldwide expansion of capitalism was both more powerful and more sustained. Two key differences help to explain these divergent outcomes: first, the post-1945 period was marked by a complete absence of the revolutionary political impulses that emanated from Moscow in 1917–23; and second, Washington's economic strength, political will, and massive military presence in both Europe and Japan, organized in the former Axis powers through regimes of military governance, facilitated the rapid emergence of stable capitalist states.

In both Japan and Western Europe, the post-Second World War restoration of political stability took place under the banner of democracy—a concept that, as a vague generality, had been central to America's self-proclaimed war aims. As a result, the reformed nation-states that emerged in the late 1940s shared broadly similar features, including parliamentary government and regular elections, centralized state bureaucracies run by meritocratic experts, and broad arrays of social welfare provision in the fields of healthcare, education, housing, and social security. In postwar Belgium, France, Italy, and Japan, new constitutions enfranchised women for the first time, and while economic and political life remained overwhelmingly male-dominated, formal political equality allowed democracy to be plausibly linked to visions of civic universalism or the 'right to have rights.' This democracy was fundamentally nonparticipatory, involving most people only by way of occasional voting, and it was largely non-ideological, with political processes characterized by negotiation and compromise between moderate parties—some slightly to the left, some slightly to the right—producing solid but uninspiring centrism.

Today, this mode of political functioning appears normal and natural in the capitalist countries of the global North, but in 1945 democracy did not enjoy such standing. Instead, the perceived weaknesses of prewar liberal democracy—including parliamentary deadlock and governmental instability—were frequently blamed both for the rise of Fascism, Nazism, and Japanese militarism *and* for the stunning collapse of France in 1940. At the end of the war, democracy was essentially an Anglo-American product that arrived in Western Europe and Japan with the victorious Allied armies, and even in France, where General Charles de Gaulle's Free French quickly established political control, the overthrow of the Vichy regime and the construction of the Fourth Republic unfolded in space created by Anglo-American arms.

Even before Washington's formal entry into the war, ideologues like publishing tycoon Henry Luce had envisioned the worldwide spread of American-style democracy as a central component of the coming "American Century." In practice, and contrary to Luce's imagining, postwar democracy did not involve the transposition of the American political system to Europe and Japan. Instead, the great affective force of American democracy was its intimate association with material prosperity, a connection showcased by the extensive and resource-rich logistical networks established by the US military, by the massive inflows of American aid channeled through UNRRA and the work of private charities, and by the freewheeling spending of American soldiers. American soft power, embodied in commodities from Coca-Cola, cigarettes, and nylons to automobiles and refrigerators, and woven into the popular culture of music and movies, became deeply associated with ideas of political democracy and personal freedom.

As they recovered their balance, political elites in Europe and Japan quickly grasped the utility of nonparticipatory democracy for casting—in Martin Conway's vivid description—a "cloak of national unity" over the deep divisions engendered by fascism, wartime collaboration, popular insurgency, and the class-divided experiences of economic depression and war.[12] Democracy enabled the war to slide quickly into the past as modest but

---

[12]Conway, *Western Europe's Democratic Age*, 48.

real social reforms buffered the desire for more radical change and ensured that there would be no root-and-branch transformation of society and no generalized settling of accounts with fascism and militarism. Instead, there were limited but high-profile trials of leading figures in the Axis regimes, the performative purging of local and national administrations, and—in Germany—a brief campaign of public 're-education.' Senior Nazis tried before an international tribunal at Nuremberg and top Japanese leaders charged with 'Class A' offenses faced execution for newly defined 'crimes against humanity,' but many other former officials were quietly reintegrated into the bureaucracies of newly refounded nation-states at local, regional, and finally national levels. By thinking about the end of the fighting as a fresh start—in Germany, *Stunde null* or Zero Hour—the experience of war could be reconfigured as one of shared suffering in ways that promoted national unity even while resting on denial and avoidance.

These processes went hand-in-hand with drives to restore both the legitimacy of the state and its monopoly of armed force by rounding up the massive quantities of guns, grenades, and other weapons of war that had found their way into civilian hands. In all the Axis countries, the task of disarming and demilitarizing civil society was begun by Allied occupation forces that often did not hesitate to assert their monopoly right to use lethal force. In Italy, partisan fighters handed over more than 185,000 guns to Allied troops at special ceremonies in April and May 1945. Meanwhile, Allied authorities in Germany imposed a complete ban— punishable by death—on civilian-held weapons, and in Japan the American military government netted 750,000 guns and one million swords in six rounds of collection.[13] Despite these official round-ups, large numbers of weapons remained in civilian hands, particularly in Italy, where many were stockpiled by former partisans and their erstwhile fascist opponents, by criminal gangs, and by individuals interested in sport—grenade fishing was popular—or in settling scores. Gun violence, some of it perpetrated by bandit gangs and some just the armed expression of everyday arguments, was a major feature of the transition from war to postwar, and the sense of insecurity it promoted undoubtedly contributed to a popular desire for the restoration of order. Prompted by wholly unwarranted fears of Communist insurgency, and with their eyes on the rebuilding of state legitimacy, the Allies made the full restoration of Italian political authority conditional on the progress of civilian disarmament. Enacted with the backing of the PCI, Italian gun-control laws led to police sweeps that garnered enormous numbers of weapons: as the state restored its own organization, legitimacy,

---

[13]Marco Maris Aterrano, "Civilian Disarmament: Public Order and the Restoration of State Authority in Italy's Postwar Transition, 1944–6," *Journal of Contemporary History*, Vol. 56, No. 2 (2021), 399.

and monopoly of armed force, authorities reported collecting 173 heavy artillery pieces, 798 mortars, and nearly 300,000 guns of all kinds in the decade after 1945.[14]

Communist parties in Western Europe and Japan played a particularly important role in the establishment of democratic and capitalist nation-states. At the start of Operation *Barbarossa* in June 1941, Moscow ordered Communists in the 'democratic imperialist' countries to throw their weight behind official government war efforts, while in Germany, Italy, and occupied Western Europe they were instructed to participate in anti-fascist resistance movements. In France, the Communist Party (PCF) played a leading role in the developing resistance movement, and in June 1943 it joined General de Gaulle's Committee for National Liberation. Only in Japan, where Communists faced harsh government persecution, was the party instructed *not* to act lest it provoke a breakdown of the April 1941 nonaggression pact between Tokyo and Moscow. As the 1945 Italian Revolution demonstrates, Moscow's injunction to pursue national unity with anti-Fascist sections of the bourgeoisie did not preclude participation in radical political and military actions, but it did provide the framework for channeling revolutionary enthusiasm into political spaces favorable to the reconstruction of capitalist nation-states.

In Western Europe and Japan, Communist parties welcomed the arrival of Allied troops and endorsed the bourgeois-democratic governments that they began constructing: as Stalin explained to German Communist leaders, the goal was to participate in the creation of "anti-fascist parliamentary democratic regimes."[15] In Europe, Palmiro Togliatti's PCI led the way, closely followed by the French Communists, whose leader Maurice Thorez returned from exile in Moscow in November 1944 to participate in De Gaulle's new provisional government. Released from eighteen years of prison, veteran Japanese Communist Tokuda Kyūichi expressed his "deepest gratitude" for the American occupation and the "democratic revolution" it brought with it.[16] Here, as in Europe, Communist leaders openly and explicitly rejected the idea of a revolutionary struggle against capitalism, calling instead for social and political reforms enacted within the framework of the American occupation. The impetus for these 'peaceful roads' flowed from Moscow's diplomatic needs, but it also conformed to the desire of many party leaders to enjoy the status and legitimacy bestowed by participation in governments of national reconstruction. For them, too, democracy—packaged and prefixed by 'popular' or 'people's'—offered a way to wrap themselves in the "cloak" of national unity. The

---

[14]Aterrano, "Civilian Disarmament," 407.
[15]Stalin, quoted in Silvio Pons, "Stalin and the European Communists after World War Two (1943–1948)," *Past and Present*, Supplement 6 (2011), 128.
[16]Tokuda Kyūichi, quoted in Dower, *Embracing Defeat*, 69.

rejection of revolution at the very moment that fascist and militarist regimes were disintegrating did not sit well with many rank-and-file Communists, most of whom had been isolated from the twists and turns of Soviet policy by police repression and German occupation. Nevertheless, while many Communists continued to yearn for the 'long awaited moment' of revolution, the enormous prestige enjoyed by the Soviet Union—and by the Red Army in particular—at the end of the war ensured that they accepted Moscow's dictates without serious dissention.

Variations on a Theme: Postwar Political Stabilization Japan, France, and Belgium

In Japan, as in Europe, American occupation authorities feared that the end of the war would be followed by an outpouring of popular radicalism. Under the negotiated terms of surrender—not quite the unconditional surrender promised by Allied leaders—American and Japanese officials agreed that Emperor Hirohito would remain in place as the nominal head of state. Hirohito was required to deny his divinity but, unlike other top Japanese leaders, he avoided prosecution for war crimes. The maintenance of the monarchy was intended to stress the continuity between prewar (that is pre-1931) and postwar Japan, thus providing a rallying point around which the state could be reconstructed. At the same time, real political power remained firmly in the hands of the American military government and its proconsular leader General Douglas MacArthur, now retitled Supreme Commander for the Allied Powers (SCAP).

Governing through a flurry of 'SCAP directives,' the military government purged some 200,000 alleged militarists from public life, initiated a land reform program, began dismantling the *zaibatsu* (giant family owned financial-industrial corporations), and legalized labor unions and the right to strike. These reforms were capped in early 1947 by the adoption of a new constitution—written by the occupation authorities—that established a parliamentary democracy, asserted women's equality, and renounced war. Often pictured as a "revolution from above" and as a benevolent effort to demilitarize and democratize Japanese society, SCAP's campaign to restructure Japanese society also registered the unbridled force of American predominance as Washington asserted its right to remake the world as it saw fit.[17] Unsurprisingly, many Japanese people viewed the occupation and its reform project from this point of view, their perception sharpened by uncountable daily interactions with American military personnel

---

[17]Dower, *Embracing Defeat*, esp. Chapter 2, 65–84.

whose boorish, sexually demanding, and often violent behaviors reflected the vastly unequal power relations embedded in the daily operation of military government. New research is revealing the considerable number of incidents—eighty or more in 1946 alone—in which army sentries and military policemen opened fire on Japanese civilians for alleged offenses including trespassing or theft.[18]

In this first phase of postwar political stabilization, American officials worked closely with the Japanese Socialist Party, brokering a JSP-led coalition government after the party won a plurality in the April 1947 general election. American collaboration with the JSP helped to blunt the sharp edges of the occupation and make its sweeping reorganization of Japanese society more broadly palatable. The American reform program was also embraced by Communist Party (JCP) leaders who returned from exile in China at the end of the war. Although relatively small, the party was influential within a trade union movement that was experiencing rapid growth—from 380,000 union members in 1945 to nearly seven million in 1952—as workers fought to improve their wages and conditions and pushed for broader social reforms.[19] During this period, over 19 million workers took part in nearly 6,500 strikes, and in this context JCP endorsement of the American occupation and its reformist agenda—dubbed a "bourgeoise democratic revolution" by Communist leaders—played a critical role in channeling insurgent energy into bourgeois-democratic channels. As JCP leader Nosaka Sanzō put it, "we Communists are the true patriots and the true service brigade for democracy."[20]

The rapid and relatively smooth consolidation of liberal-democratic state in Japan was the product of several specific conditions. First, while devastated by American blockade and bombing, Japan did not suffer the deep political divisions within the ruling classes evident in Italy and France. As a result, once they finally recognized that they had lost the war, Japanese elites pivoted toward cooperation with the Americans in a rapid and unified fashion. Second, the 'Allied' military government of Japan grew directly out of the Pacific war and was therefore fundamentally an American affair. This fact gave Washington and its military proconsul in Japan a free hand defining the liberal-democratic contours of the new state. Third, while political decision-making in the early stages of reconstruction remained firmly in American hands, acceptance of SCAP's reformist agenda was smoothed by the JSP, and its programs were implemented by a professional Japanese state bureaucracy that had survived the postwar purges largely intact. Finally, although the postwar labor upsurge was both

---

[18]Connor M. Mills, *Garrison Work: Everyday Life and Militarization in Japan at the Dawn of the Postwar American Empire*, forthcoming.
[19]Dower, *Embracing Defeat*, 257.
[20]Ibid., 256.

deep and powerful, it unfolded *after* the establishment of American military occupation and not—as in Italy—before it. This fact gave the American authorities, Japanese elites, and their Communist and Socialist allies in the labor movement tremendous leverage in their efforts to canalize radicalism into safe constitutional channels.

*

The establishment of political order in France presented a somewhat different set of challenges. Here the ruling classes had been deeply divided by the experience of military defeat and German occupation, with a substantial majority supporting the collaborationist Vichy regime established in summer 1940. The formation of the French Committee of National Liberation (CFLN) under Charles de Gaulle's leadership in summer 1943 brought together a modest number of elite figures from France and the French Empire along with representatives of the Communist and Socialist parties. The CFLN offered a clear political alternative to Vichy, but the Allies— and especially the Americans—remained hostile to De Gaulle's project of rebuilding France as a great power. As a result, they refused to recognize the CFLN as a legitimate government-in-exile and hence as the force that would form the government of France after the defeat of the German occupation. Roosevelt's hostility to the CFLN is often attributed to De Gaulle's notoriously difficult personality, but the real roots of this antipathy were more deep-seated and more political, stemming from Washington's plans for the postwar order and its stated desire to break up the French Empire.

As a result of these political difficulties, the Allies launched the D-Day invasion of France in June 1944 without having a clear political plan in place; indeed, some American leaders still hoped that that Vichy leader Marshal Philippe Pétain might switch sides at the last minute. American leaders also toyed with the idea of setting up a military government in France, but they concluded that taking such a step in an allied country—as opposed to a defeated enemy—would create more problems than it would solve. Anglo-American confusion gave De Gaulle and his numerous supporters within France the space in which to begin establishing a provisional government from the bottom up. As in Italy, Allied advances triggered a series of popular insurgencies in Paris, in the key ports of Toulon and Marseilles, and in towns and villages across the rural South. Communists played a leading role in these uprisings, and the perceived threat of revolution prompted Allied commanders to rush Free French troops into Paris and—finally—to back the establishment of a provisional government under De Gaulle.

De Gaulle's 'national unity' government, which included key Socialist and Communist leaders, acted quickly to blunt the burgeoning popular insurgency. Local groups of resistance fighters were brought under the discipline of a new national army, and the provisional government enacted a series of reforms designed to head off pressure for radical change. A national election in October 1945 set up the adoption of a new constitution—a parliamentary Fourth Republic—and opened a period of 'tripartism' in which power was shared uneasily between the Christian-democratic *Mouvement Républicain Populaire* (MRP), the Socialist SFIO, and the Communist PCF. De Gaulle himself retired briefly from politics in early 1946 after his proposal for a presidential system effectively centered on himself was rejected, and the strident nationalism of his *Rassemblement du Peuple Francais* (RPF) blocked the emergence of the kind of centrist Christian Democratic party that functioned as a vehicle for democratic stabilization in Italy and Germany.

*

Hubert Pierlot, Catholic Party leader and prime minister of the Belgian government-in-exile, returned to Brussels after British troops entered the city in early September 1944. Unlike De Gaulle, who enjoyed close ties to the resistance movement within France, Pierlot was widely viewed as indifferent to the suffering of German-occupied Belgium, and his return prompted no national rejoicing. Pierlot included three members of the Belgian Communist Party (PCB-KPB) in his cabinet, but as workers demonstrated for pay rises and sweeping social reforms, the Communist-led resistance movement refused to disarm. The PCB-KPB had no intention of defying Moscow's insistence on securing the peaceful transition to postwar capitalist stability, but amid baseless rumors of a Communist coup its efforts to strengthen the party's bargaining position led to violent confrontation with British troops deployed to defend the Pierlot government. As one British journalist put it, the Communists had "badly overplayed their hand," but the chief beneficiary of their misstep was not Pierlot, but Socialist Party leader Achille van Acker, who stepped up to establish a new coalition government in February 1945.[21] Van Acker's government, and those that followed it, gave Belgian expression to political developments unfolding across Europe and in Japan, establishing the pragmatic political centrism—in this case a Socialist-Catholic duopoly—and welfare state reformism that could buffer pressures for more radical social change while laying the basis for capitalist economic expansion. As Martin Conway notes, in Belgium, as in many other parts of the Global North, the seemingly unaltered outward appearance of the state masked far-reaching changes in "political culture, the social relations of power, and the interaction between state and society."[22]

---

[21] Martin Conway, *The Sorrows of Belgium: Liberation and Political Reconstruction, 1944–1947* (Oxford: Oxford University Press, 2012), 108.
[22] Conway, *The Sorrows of Belgium*, 367.

The Key to Europe: Partition and Political Stabilization in Germany

In Germany, the destruction and social dislocation caused by military defeat, the bombing of major cities, and the overwhelming presence of allied troops—including the Red Army in the eastern part of the country—combined to smother the kind of popular uprisings seen in France and Italy. At the same time, and in contrast to Italy and Japan, there was no section of the ruling class that was able to negotiate with the Allies *prior* to the defeat: the brutal suppression of the attempted military coup that followed the assassination bid against Hitler in July 1944 foreclosed that possibility. As a result, Germany's surrender was genuinely unconditional, and four-way Allied military rule was imposed without the collaboration of any national-level political forces. At local level, however, members of the Social Democratic Party (SPD) were soon working with Allied authorities to maintain order, clear rubble, and distribute food. The SPD had weathered long years of Nazi repression surprisingly well, and although political parties remained formally banned until late 1945, British and American military authorities relied on the knowledge, political experience, and deep working-class roots of local socialist leaders to smooth the postwar political stabilization. In this way, the Socialists reprised—albeit in a much less dramatic manner—the role that they had played in restoring the political stability of German capitalism during the revolutionary upsurge that followed the First World War. The reestablishment of political legitimacy also rested on the continuity of the bureaucratic apparatus of the German state, where the short and limited purge of former Nazis soon allowed many low-level party members to return to work in local government.

The German Communist Party (KPD) was hamstrung by Moscow's attitude toward Germany. Moscow's wartime hostility to 'Hitlerites'—a synonym for 'all Germans'—undercut the possibilities of solidarity between German workers and Soviet soldiers, and the shocking violence perpetrated by the Red Army against German civilians further militated against viewing the Soviets as liberators. At the same time, Soviet demands for economic reparations in the form of factory equipment angered German workers whose livelihoods depended on getting back to work. Unlike in Italy, where the Allies worked with the PCI to restore stability, occupation forces in western Germany avoided contact with the KPD and sought to marginalize it. Relieved of the need to buffer the kind of popular militancy seen in Italy and France, the postwar political stabilization in Germany thus unfolded comparatively quickly and smoothly in the context of the deepening partition of the country discussed in Chapter Two.

As party politics resumed in the winter of 1945–46, Konrad Adenauer's newly formed Christian Democratic Union (CDU) made rapid gains. The party's cautious conservatism and ardent anti-Communism struck a chord, as did its vision of a revived Germany living in harmony with its

Western European neighbors under American protection. In 1949, the party edged ahead of the SPD in the first national election in the new Federal Republic of Germany. Framed by deepening Cold War tensions, this victory set up fifteen years of CDU dominance at national level. Adenauer's 'social market' policies blunted class conflict as rapid economic growth—boosted by inflows of American aid—laid the foundations for a far-reaching welfare state that insisted on giving trade union leaders a voice in corporate boardrooms. Adenauer also established a substantial compensation fund that eased the integration of refugees from the east—*Vertriebene*—into West German society. At the same time, while the CDU dominated national politics, the SPD remained influential at local and regional levels, creating an effective dyarchy—two-party rule—that channeled political discourse toward a moderate and reform-minded center.

The Greek Civil War

The Greek Civil War (1944–49) presented a violent counterpoint to the relatively peaceful patterns of transition from war to postwar in Western Europe. The British had long viewed Greece as critical to their strategic predominance in the eastern Mediterranean and insisted that it should lie within their postwar sphere of influence. After the Axis invasion of Greece in 1941, London had sheltered the royal government-in-exile, and as Germany's grip weakened in 1944, they readied it for return to the country. This move was approved at an October 1944 meeting between Stalin and Churchill in Moscow, with the Soviet leader sanctioning British predominance in Greece in exchange for Soviet control of Bulgaria and Rumania. Again, Soviet leaders displayed their complete disinterest in spreading Communism. While Moscow was happy to cede Greece to the British, however, the Greek Communist Party (KKE) was already deeply involved in a national resistance movement that had succeeded in establishing a broadly based 'mountain government' in the northern highlands. Most KKE leaders reluctantly accepted Moscow's dictate, but the dispatch of British paratroopers—backed by American transport and logistics—to secure the return of the monarchy still provoked fierce fighting with Communist-led forces in Athens in late 1944. Faithful to its agreement with the Allies, Moscow offered no support to the insurgents, barely complaining when the KKE continued to face brutal repression even after it had agreed to a ceasefire. Moscow essentially blamed the crisis on the KKE—Stalin claimed that they would have to pay the price for acting "foolishly"—and with the Soviets looking the other way, a bloody counterrevolution facilitated by British arms and American logistics secured the return of the Greek monarchy.[23]

---

[23]Geoffrey Roberts, "Moscow's Cold War on the Periphery: Soviet Policy in Greece, Iran, and Turkey, 1943–8," *Journal of Contemporary History*, Vol. 46, No. 1 (2011), 61.

Open civil war broke out soon after the formal end of the war. Encouraged by Tito and the Yugoslav Communist Party, the KKE defied Moscow and boycotted both the 1946 general election and a referendum on the monarchy. As a result, majority votes lent legitimacy to the new regime. In response, radicals within the KKE had pushed for a resumption of armed resistance, and by spring 1948 the new Democratic Army of Greece (DSE) had won control of around half the country. As these events were unfolding, the British government, its limited resources stretched by a concurrent series of imperial crises, announced that it could no longer provide military backing for the royal government in Athens. In response, the proclamation of the Truman Doctrine in March 1947 signaled Washington's intention to step in in London's place. Justified by its stated commitment to support 'free peoples' anywhere in the world, American aid, weapons, and military advisors were soon pouring into Greece. Initially, the Soviet leadership's turn to more a confrontational stance toward the West, signaled by the formation of the Cominform in September 1947, allowed Soviet weapons to flow to the DSE, but the widening split between Moscow and Belgrade soon choked these supplies off. At the same time, Yugoslavia's expulsion from the Cominform prompted Tito to turn to the West for aid, a move that necessitated curtailing Yugoslav support for the Greek rebels. By summer 1949, these developments resulted in the crushing defeat of the DSE, ending a civil war that had claimed 250,000 lives. This brutal struggle offers a glimpse of the way events in Italy and France might have unfolded had the local Communists not welcomed Allied troops, turned power over to them, and smoothed the transition to postwar democracy. Clearly, sustained Greek-style combat between insurgent fighters and Allied troops in a major European country would have profoundly destabilized the entire transition from war to postwar.

The Second Phase of Postwar Stabilization, 1947–50

Framed on a world scale by the sharpening Cold War, the deepening revolution in China, and the explosive anticolonial struggles unfolding in South and Southeast Asia, 1947 saw the opening of a new phase in the postwar reorganization of Western Europe and Japan. Here, with the containment of popular insurgency, the establishment of bourgeois democracy and political stability, and the restoration of basic state functioning all accomplished, Washington could now begin to create the conditions for sustained economic growth.

In Japan, the second phase of postwar reconstruction—often described as the 'reverse course'—began as America policymakers, alarmed by the deepening crisis in China, began to reimagine Japan as the regional lynchpin in the containment of Communism. Within Japan, this shift led to the promotion of more conservative politicians and to the establishment of policies favorable to rapid economic expansion. A key turning point came in February 1947, when American occupation authorities derailed a mounting wave of labor militancy by banning a nationwide general strike for higher wages. This action sharply reversed SCAP's seemingly pro-labor stance and marked the moment when it became clear to many that, as trade union leader Ii Yashirō put it, the Americans were "deceiving the Japanese people with democracy only at the tip of their tongues."[24]

The cancellation of the planned general strike in the face of American threats undercut working-class militancy, and while a Socialist-led coalition was elected in April 1947, its subsequent disintegration paved the way for the January 1949 electoral victory of Shigeru Yoshida's Democratic Liberal Party. The new government quickly 'depurged' wartime militarists, halted the dismantling of the *zaibatsu* corporations, and launched a 'Red Purge' that led to the firing of 22,000 alleged radicals, many of them trade union activists.[25] Further regroupments of conservative forces in 1950 and 1955 created the Liberal Democratic Party, which would dominate Japanese politics for nearly forty years. In 1952, the Treaty of San Francisco ended the American military occupation and—despite opposition from the Soviet Union and China—began the reintegration of Japan into world politics. At the same time, and prompted by the war in Korea, Washington oversaw limited Japanese rearmament in the form of a new Self-Defense Force, while beefing up its own military presence in Japan and in Okinawa, which remained under American occupation.

Western Europe experienced its own versions of the reverse course. In Italy, the Communist (PCI)-Christian Democrat (DC) coalition central to postwar stabilization was reconfirmed in the 1946 general election, while a referendum secured the abolition of the monarchy. In February 1947, the Treaty of Paris formally ended wartime hostilities and concluded the Allied occupation. In addition, Italy was stripped of its colonies—with the exception of Somaliland, which it administered as a United Nations Trust Territory—and the region around Trieste was established as a Free Territory before being divided between Italy and Yugoslavia in 1954. With political stability achieved, and with Cold War pressures mounting, American officials encouraged Christian Democrat leader Alcide De Gasperi to purge the Communists from his government in May 1947. They also considered banning the PCI—or even partitioning the country—but feared

---

[24]Dower, *Embracing Defeat*, 270.
[25]Yong Wook Lee, "The Origin of One-Party Domination: America's Reverse Course and the Emergence of the Liberal Democratic Party in Japan," *Journal of East Asian Affairs*, Vol. 18, No. 2 (Fall/Winter 2004), 383.

that such a move might provoke open working-class resistance.[26] Instead, ambassador James Dunn channeled American aid, some of it open, some covert, to De Gasperi's Christian Democrats, helping them to secure a critical victory over the PCI in the April 1948 general election. In Washington, policymakers viewed De Gasperi's success as stunning confirmation of the efficacy of their 'political warfare' program, which they quickly came to see as a model for subsequent covert interventions. At the same time, the emergence of the Christian Democrats as Washington's key collaborators in Italy strengthened De Gasperi's ability to secure a good deal from the Americans in negotiations over aid and the siting of US military bases. The exercise of hegemony, Washington was learning, required building sustained relationships with local actors based on meeting at least some of their needs.

In France, too, the initial period of tripartite (MRP-SFIO-PCF) government unraveled as the Communists responded to working-class criticism that they were simply propping up a pro-American government by offering vocal support to striking Renault autoworkers. In response, and with American encouragement, the PCF's coalition partners threw it out of the government in May 1947. Stung by harsh criticism of their collaboration with the French bourgeoisie at the October 1947 conference of the Cominform, the Communist-led trade CGT (*Confédération Général du Travail*) union federation launched a further wave of strikes in fall 1947. These strikes ran into determined government opposition led by the Socialist interior minister, and the following year American agents worked to weaken the CGT by encouraging the breakaway of a moderate union federation, *Force Ouvrièr*. After the PCF's expulsion from government, France was led by a succession of centrist coalitions whose members—including the MRP, the Radicals, and (until 1951) the Socialists—were arrayed against the Communists on the left and the Gaullist RPF on the right. This arrangement precluded grounding bourgeois political stability on a single strong Christian Democrat party as was the case in Italy and Germany. Instead, the Fourth Republic was governed by a succession of twenty-one separate coalition governments between 1946 and 1958, when the entire set-up collapsed in the face of the deepening crisis of French colonial rule in Algeria and De Gaulle returned to office in a soft coup.

Despite their differences, these successive postwar governments were all broadly committed to De Gaulle's vision of restoring France to 'great power' status. This goal, given urgency by the humiliating defeat in 1940 and shrouded in mystic notions of French 'grandeur,' rested on the defense of empire, but it was also expressed in the pursuit of a high-prestige nuclear program. Despite pioneering work by French scientists, American hostility

---

[26]Kaetan Mistry, *The United States, Italy, and the Origins of the Cold War: Waging Political Warfare, 1945–1950* (Cambridge: Cambridge University Press, 2014), 123–4.

ensured that De Gaulle's French Committee for National Liberation was excluded from wartime development of nuclear weapons. In response, French scientists—including some affiliated with the Communist Party—pushed for the rapid postwar establishment of an independent nuclear program. The French Atomic Energy Commission (CEA) was set up in October 1945, and Zoé, the country's first nuclear pile, achieved criticality three years later.[27] Other steps quickly followed, including bilateral collaboration with nuclear programs in India (1951) and Israel (1957), and in 1954 prime minister Pierre Mendès-France launched an atomic weapons program designed to make France independent of the American nuclear shield. These developments were viewed with alarm by an American government keen to maintain its own nuclear predominance by restricting the proliferation of nuclear technology.

*

Like the first phase of postwar stabilization in Western Europe, the second also unfolded under American oversight. In particular, American predominance was strengthened by the operation of the Marshall Plan, first announced by Secretary of State George C. Marshall in June 1947, and then adopted by Congress as the European Recovery Program (ERP) in April 1948. Over the next four years, the ERP pumped over thirteen billion dollars (equivalent to over $130 billion today) into the economies of Western Europe in the form of direct aid and 'counterpart' or matching funds. This was not the first infusion of American funds—the initial political stabilization of Western Europe had been buttressed by American loans and UNRRA aid—but the ERP now built on these initial accomplishments to lay the foundations for sustained capitalist expansion.

The European Recovery Program had several interlinked objectives. First, it aimed to stimulate economic recovery in individual European nation-states. Second, American planners recognized that the revitalization of both intra-European and world trade could best be realized by the creation of an integrated Western European market, and the ERP worked to promote this goal. Third, Washington judged that its offer to include Poland and Czechoslovakia in the ERP—an offer that Moscow was calculated to reject—would deepen the partition of Europe and secure its predominance in the West while generating conflict between Moscow and its East European clients. Finally, Washington recognized that the success of these interlinked economic and political goals hinged on the creation

---

[27]Jayita Sakar, "'Wean Them away from French Tutelage': Franco-Indian Nuclear Relations and Anglo-American Anxieties during the Early Cold War, 1948–1952," *Cold War History*, Vol. 15, No. 3 (2015), 383.

of a strong nation-state in western Germany that could lead sustained Western Europe-wide growth.

With the support of Marshall Plan funds, industrial output in western Germany jumped over 200 percent between 1947 and 1952.[28] ERP aid also helped to repair widespread infrastructural damage by funding reconstruction projects beyond the financial reach of national governments, and it underwrote current account deficits created by importing much-needed capital goods, fuel, and food from the United States. It is often—and not wrongly—pointed out that ERP funding benefited American exporters by creating new markets for their goods. But as the emerging global hegemon, Washington was primarily interested in the expansion of capitalism as a *worldwide* system, and policymakers now recognized that the global free trade announced at Bretton Woods in June 1944 had to be grounded on strong national economies. In this light, Washington used the ERP to promote free trade and European economic integration. With French support, Washington encouraged the formation of the Organization of European Economic Cooperation (OEEC) in April 1948 to oversee the distribution of ERP funds while working to lower tariff barriers within Europe. Two years later, Washington prompted—and funded—OEEC's transformation into the European Payments Union, a multilateral trade organization designed to cut tariffs and boost intra-European commerce. These developments overlapped with the formation in April 1951 of the European Coal and Steel Community, another American-backed French initiative that drew Belgium, France, Italy, Luxembourg, the Netherlands, and the new Federal Republic of Germany into a supranational common market for coal and steel.

Western European growth and the associated steps toward economic integration were intertwined with the political reorganization of Germany and, after the founding of the Federal Republic in May 1949, with its assumption of a leadership role with Europe. Washington further stimulated German economic growth in 1952 by slashing Bonn's post-1945 debt and halving its outstanding Weimar-era obligations.[29] These measures, combined with the Christian Democrats' own pro-business policies, operated within the framework of advancing economic integration to open a new economic conjuncture in Europe. By the early 1950s, Germany had begun to reassert its pre-1914 role as the economic powerhouse of Europe, becoming the major regional exporter of both capital and consumer goods. At the same time, the establishment in 1947 of the Bank of German States (after 1957 the Bundesbank) reestablished Germany as the key European financial

---

[28]Benn Steil, *The Marshall Plan: Dawn of the Cold War* (New York: Simon and Schuster, 2018), 341.
[29]Adam Tooze, "Reassessing the Moral Economy of Post-War Reconstruction: The Terms of the West German Settlement in 1952," *Past and Present*, Supplement 6 (2011), 60.

center, and by the mid-1950s other European nations were becoming reliant on German credits. Economic heft brought political authority, and as the French Fourth Republic slipped into crisis, Germany stepped forward to anchor European integration.

Washington's Remilitarization Drive

As we have seen, Washington's postwar demobilization—speeded by pressure from mutinous GIs—was quickly followed by an accelerating remilitarization drive. This effort was already well underway by the time it was codified by the National Security Council in policy statement NSC 68 on the eve of the war in Korea. While an expansion of nuclear capacity was central to these plans, they also called for the increased worldwide deployment of ground, naval, and air forces. In Asia, Washington established a new Far East Command in early 1947 to oversee a large and permanent naval presence, centered from 1950 on the Seventh Fleet and backed by substantial Marine ground and air forces. Anchored at enlarged home ports at Subic Bay in the Philippines and at Yokosuka in Japan, US forces expanded bases, airfields, and other facilities in Okinawa, Guam, and on its virtual colonies throughout the western Pacific. After the occupation of Japan ended in 1952, America's military was augmented in 1954 by the establishment of Japan's own 'self-defense' forces, while its own bases in Japan were organized through status of force agreements (SOFAs) that embodied the power disparity between the two countries and shielded US troops from prosecution in local courts. While American diplomats argued that Japan's ability to negotiate status of force agreements offered confirmation of its sovereign right to "enter collective security arrangements," in the early 1950s inevitable tensions between US military personnel and "host" communities prompted the emergence of a nationwide anti-base protest movement.[30] By the end of the decade, ongoing anti-base protests seemed to threaten Japan's reliability as a military staging post, and over 40 percent of all US forces, including all ground troops were withdrawn from Japan—but not from Okinawa—by 1959. Again, Washington was learning that the exercise of hegemony involved maintaining complex dialectical relationships with powerful local actors.

The situation in Europe was equally complex, but after the 1948–49 Berlin crisis highlighted Washington's military weakness on the ground in Europe, collaboration with its European allies led to the formation of the North Atlantic Treaty Organization (NATO) in April 1949. Hastings

---

[30]Jennifer M. Miller, "Fractured Alliance: Anti-Base Protests and Postwar U.S.-Japanese Relations," *Diplomatic History*, Vol. 38, No. 5 (2015), 958.

Ismay, the senior British officer who was appointed NATO's first secretary general, famously quipped that the organization was designed to "keep the Russians out, the Americans in, and the Germans down," but his often-quoted comment was wide of the mark.[31] In fact, the "Russians" had no intention of advancing into Western Europe, the Americans had no plans to get out, and the process of economic restoration and alliance building was inevitably leading to the revival of German military power. The outbreak of the Korean War gave Washington the opportunity to press for the integration of a rearmed Germany into NATO, and after overcoming dogged French resistance, this was finally accomplished in May 1955. The consolidation of an American-led military alliance also required the repeated rejection of Soviet proposals for a united, neutral, and demilitarized Germany, a stand in which Washington received the unwavering support of the Adenauer government in Bonn.

American support for German rearmament was justified by wildly exaggerated claims that NATO forces were heavily outnumbered, with just twelve divisions facing nearly two hundred equivalent Red Army units. These alarming numbers enabled President Truman to brush aside Congressional objections to the deployment of more American ground troops to Europe, bringing their total number to 180,000 by early 1951.[32] To support this expanded deployment, the US military began a large-scale construction program that rooted American land, air, and naval forces on a series of sprawling military bases across the continent: in Italy alone, seventeen major bases were established, including the complex of airfields around Aviano, homeport facilities for the new Sixth Fleet in Naples, and other radar, communications, and logistical sites. Repeated across Europe, this base-building integrated the United States military into the 'defense' architecture of the continent and into the social and economic fabric of its daily life. After 1951, these relationships were governed by standard NATO Status of Force Agreements under which local authorities waived claims to jurisdiction over US military personnel, thus embedding the bases in legal regimes of hierarchy and inequality. As in Japan, military bases often became sites of popular protest, but they also served as nodes of connectivity and as points for the dissemination of American soft power. They were also centers of economic activity, pumping millions of dollars into local economies, both through the employment of tens of thousands of local people and through the money spent by soldiers on everything from housing and tourist trinkets to the sexual services of prostitutes.

---

[31]General Hastings Ismay, quoted in Lorenz M. Lüthi *Cold Wars: Asia, the Middle East, Europe* (Cambridge: Cambridge University Press, 2020), 365.
[32]Offner, *Another Such Victory*, 428, 435.

FIGURE 5.2 *Led by the aircraft carriers* Randolph *and* Midway *and the cruiser* Salem, *warships of the US Sixth Fleet at sea in the Mediterranean during the Suez Crisis, August 6, 1956. Headquartered in Naples, the Sixth Fleet gave the United States a large and permanent military presence in the Mediterranean. (Photo: Bettmann/Getty.)*

The expansion of America's network of military bases, including the establishment of forward sites for the storage and deployment of air and submarine-launched nuclear weapons, was intertwined with efforts to broaden the NATO alliance. In the early postwar, Washington maintained public hostility toward Spanish dictator Francisco Franco, a stance that it had adopted in 1944 after the successful completion of its early-war use of trade and diplomatic blandishments to keep Madrid out of the war. Many people in America and around the world viewed Franco's regime as a fascist dictatorship, but despite shows of public hostility that included backing a 1946 U.N. resolution critical of Madrid, Washington avoided calling for his overthrow. Instead, American leaders began working quietly toward a rapprochement with Madrid. In 1951, the Truman administration resumed ambassadorial relations with the appointment of former Hollywood executive Stanton Griffis. While the main accomplishment of Griffis' short tenure was the negotiation of a film distribution agreement, he worked hard to develop friendly relations with Madrid. With Franco emphasizing his anti-Communist credentials, Washington used its new relationship with

Madrid to explore ways of bringing Spain into the emerging architecture of Western European defense. The crisis in Korea accelerated this effort, and long negotiations finally produced the September 1953 Spanish-American Agreement, or Pact of Madrid. While Washington continued to voice criticisms of Franco, American aid—offered in exchange for the establishment of three key airfields and a naval base at Rota—helped to keep his regime afloat. Spain was not formally invited to join NATO until after Franco's death in 1975, but over the preceding decades the country was gradually assimilated into the 'West,' a process registered in Madrid's admittance to the United Nations in 1955.

Britain: Relative Decline and Hegemonic Transition

In Britain, as elsewhere, the experience of war generated a deep-going desire among working people for radical social change. This was particularly true for soldiers. Frontline comradeship, as historian Jonathan Fennel argues, encouraged "concepts of fairness and egalitarianism," with one official report on the morale of British soldiers serving in India noting that many had become deeply hostile to traditional "vested interests" back home.[33] These ideas took shape in countless informal discussions held in barracks, ships messes, and battlefield bivouacs, but they also flourished in army educational classes and in the politicized atmosphere of newly formed 'soldier's parliaments' and other discussion circles. In late 1945 and 1946, thousands of British soldiers took part in protests demanding their immediate demobilization and, like their American comrades, many also expressed solidarity with anticolonial struggles in India and elsewhere. Soldiers' enthusiasm for social change was part of a broader wave of working-class radicalism that found expression in the Labour Party's dramatic landslide victory over Churchill's Conservatives in the July 1945 general election.

The Labour Party was the political voice of Britain's powerful trade union movement, and its leaders had played a key role in Churchill's wartime coalition government. Contrary to patriotic mythology, however, popular support for the British war effort rested not on unquestioning nationalism but on an explicit social contract promising that wartime sacrifice would be rewarded by the creation of a postwar society marked by social justice, greater equality, and sweeping advances in healthcare, housing, and education. This vision, codified in the 1942 Beveridge Plan,

---

[33] Jonathan Fennel, *Fighting the People's War: The British and Commonwealth Armies and the Second World War* (Cambridge: Cambridge University Press, 2019), 631.

underpinned working-class support for the wartime coalition government, but as the war came to an end, many felt that only Labour could be relied on to realize these promises in the postwar world. In fact, Labour had no desire to challenge any fundamental aspects of capitalism at home or to begin to dismantle the Empire worldwide. Instead, Labour's program of extensive social welfare and the nationalization of ailing but essential industries like coal mining and steel production was intended to buffer working-class discontent while revitalizing the economy. Moreover, working-class support for Labour enabled the new government to continue rationing and other wartime austerity measures well into the 1950s, effectively holding down wages in the interests of restoring capitalist profitability. In common with the Communist parties in Europe, Labour thus played a decisive role in managing the critical initial stages of the transition from war to postwar.

Britain's industrial economy grew by around 15 percent between 1938 and 1945 despite German bombing and wartime dislocation, and while some sectors of industry—like cotton textiles—were badly in need of new machinery, others—like aerospace and chemicals—were modern, dynamic, and innovative.[34] At the same time, the wartime collapse of British exports left an acute shortage of dollars with which to pay for vital imports of food, raw materials, and oil. London's gold reserves had been exhausted early in the war, and the resulting "dollar shortage" was met by $31 billion worth of American Lend-Lease supplies that were effectively given to Britain, along with an additional three billion pounds in "sterling balances" earned by exports from Britain's colonies and held in London for use by the British government.[35] During the war, these open and hidden subsidies enabled Britain to import far more than it could pay for from its export earnings, allowing it to out-produce Germany in key classes of weapons while simultaneously providing the personpower to sustain a large military.

The real economic relationships underpinning Britain's wartime production were harshly exposed in August 1945 when Washington abruptly terminated Lend-Lease. London was now faced with a sudden and shocking inability to pay for its imports, and in July 1946 it negotiated a $3.75 billion American loan that was topped up—in another illustration of shifting economic power—by an additional $1.19 billion from Canada. Washington intended that this massive loan would force London into full compliance with the worldwide free trade proclaimed at Bretton Woods, and the cash infusion was conditional on the ending of preferential trade within the British Empire and on making the pound fully convertible on world currency markets. In fact, the bulk of the loan

---

[34]Mark Harrison, "Resource Mobilization for World War II: The U.S.A., U.K., U.S.S.R, and Germany, 1938–1945," *The Economic History Review*, New Series, Vol. 41, No. 2 (1988), 185.
[35]David Edgerton, *Britain's War Machine: Weapons, Resources, and Experts in the Second World War* (Oxford: Oxford University Press, 2011), esp. 281–2.

was spent on food and other necessities rather than on capacity-building investment, and when currency convertibility was implemented in August 1947 the result was a dramatic flight from sterling as the value of the pound collapsed. Convertibility was quickly suspended, new American loans were arranged, and the implementation of the Bretton Woods system was postponed.

American loans helped to stave off Britain's financial meltdown, but in 1949 renewed pressure on the pound forced the government to implement a deep cut in its value relative to the US dollar. These financial troubles gave acute expression to Britain's loss of global leadership—hegemony—to the United States. With Britain's still-strong industrial sector and its worldwide networks of trade and empire, this was not an absolute decline, but rather a profound and irreversible shift in Britain's position *relative* to the rising power of the United States. Prepared by the economic and financial growth of the United States over the previous half-century, war accelerated a process of hegemonic transition whose military and political dimensions unfolded within the framework of the wartime alliance with Britain. The post-1945 transition did not, therefore, involve a direct military clash between the old hegemon and the new. This did not mean that the transition was peaceful, but it did ensure that violence was displaced to the destruction of America's rivals in Germany and Japan and the shattering of major elements of the old world order embedded in colonial rule. At the same time, the specific way in which America's emerging hegemony was qualified by the expansion of the Soviet system into Eastern Europe, by the Chinese Revolution, and by the rising tide of anti-colonialism meant that in the early postwar Washington continued to draw on Britain's expertise and experience—and on its empire—as it struggled to reorganize the world. For their part, Britain's rulers—including their willing helpers in the Labour Party—hoped that they could leverage their wartime alliance with the United States to carve out a special and privileged place for themselves in the new world order.

In this framework, the Labour government was deeply committed both to the continuation of the 'Atlantic' alliance with the United States and to the preservation of as much of British Empire as possible. Unlike Churchill, however, Labour leaders recognized that surging anti-colonial sentiment necessitated the abandonment of direct colonial rule in India and Burma and—as we shall see in the next chapter—its overhaul in Africa. Labour's course—continued after 1952 by Conservative governments—aimed to position Britain as Washington's indispensable junior partner while reinforcing its own continued Great Power status by reenergizing the Empire and maintaining armed forces capable of worldwide power projection. London recognized that its own worldwide hegemony was passing, but it still hoped to maintain a sort of global dyarchy, or two-state hegemony. From this standpoint, London backed Washington's promotion of European economic integration but, with trade within the empire outstripping that with Europe by three-to-one, it balked at moves toward greater political union.[36] The underlying tension between maintaining a world role in conjunction with the United States and developing an orientation to the emerging European market remained—and remains—central to British politics, but in the early postwar Labour's choice was clear: as key ruling-class figure and former American ambassador to the USSR Averell Harriman announced, "Britain's socialists are our best friends in Europe."[37]

The 'Dedominionization' of Australia, Canada, and New Zealand

Soldiers in the armies of Britain's 'white dominions' were also swept up in the postwar radicalization. In New Zealand, soldier's votes secured the 1943 reelection of a Labour government pledged to extensive social reforms, and many voted for the more radical Democratic Labour Party. Canada's Co-operative Commonwealth Federation (CCF), a newly formed socialist party whose program included opposition to "imperialist wars," secured 14 percent of overall the vote in 1945 federal elections, but it won fully 39 percent of ballots cast by Canadian soldiers serving in Europe.[38] This electoral radicalism overlapped with strikes and protests demanding rapid demobilization and with an upsurge in labor militancy as union workers rebelled against wartime wage controls. In Canada, union membership jumped from 356,000 in 1939 to 724,000 in 1945, and a powerful wave of strikes in auto and other key industries began even before the war ended. Shopfloor radicalism was reflected in union endorsement for the CCF, and in Francophone Quebec—long subject to discrimination by Anglophone elites—it intersected with popular opposition to the conscription of soldiers for service overseas. In Australia, a wave of postwar strikes—including dockworker protests in solidarity with the Indonesian revolution—culminated in 1949 in a bitter coalminer's strike that was only defeated after the ostensibly pro-union Labour government sent in the army.

For all their combativity, however, these postwar strikes and soldier protests did not pose a direct challenge to postwar political stability. Instead, working-class radicalism in the dominions was absorbed by rapid economic expansion and the rising living standards it brought with it. Distant from combat—although Darwin in northern Australia was bombed

---

[36]Lüthi, *Cold Wars*, 373.
[37]Derek Leebaert, *Grand Improvisation: America Confronts the British Superpower, 1945–1957* (New York: Farrar, Straus and Giroux, 2018), 107.
[38]Fennel, *Fighting the People's War*, 647–8, 633.

by the Japanese in 1942—the dominions experienced substantial wartime growth. Canada's gross domestic product doubled, and both here and in Australia new manufacturing industries accelerated the development of diversified industrial economies. Cut off from trade with Britain, John Curtin's Labour government in Australia promoted the domestic manufacture of goods that had previously been imported. In Canada, new shipyards churned out merchant vessels and warships for Britain while building the Canadian navy into the world's fourth-largest fleet. These developments necessarily transformed the dominions' relations with both Britain and the United States.

Early in the war the Curtin government recognized that Britain did not have the military resources to defend Australia, and Canberra turned instead to the United States. After the loss of the Philippines in early 1942, Australia became the main forward base for American forces in the southwestern Pacific, and when Douglas MacArthur began a major counter-offensive in New Guinea in 1943, Australian troops bore the brunt of the initial fighting. Wartime Australia pitched itself as Washington's junior partner in the Pacific, but this orientation was not without problems as American commanders, intent on establishing their own regional predominance, sidelined Australian forces in later stages of the war. After the war an increasingly independent Australia balanced between the old and the new hegemon, reknitting its military relations with Britain while joining the United States and New Zealand in the 1951 ANZUS agreement and the 1955 South East Asia Treaty Organization (SEATO). Domestically, the defeat of the 1949 coal strike was quickly followed by the electoral victory a center-right coalition of the Liberal and Country parties. Mirroring developments in Japan and Western Europe, this alliance consolidated itself through a ferocious anti-Communist witch-hunt in the early 1950s before going on to dominate Australian politics until 1972.

In Canada, Mackenzie King's Liberal government also carved out an independent path that enabled it to benefit from close ties to the United States while at the same time using its longstanding links to Britain to resist being overwhelmed by its powerful southern neighbor. Under the 1940 Ogdensburg Agreement, Canada and the United States agreed to coordinate the defense of North America, but Ottawa refused to place its troops under direct American control. Washington also agreed to alleviate Canada's shortage of US dollars by expanding the importation of Canadian goods, raw materials, and power. Codified in the 1941 Hyde Park Agreement, this arrangement led to the Shipshaw Project, under which Washington funded a massive hydroelectric plant on Quebec's Saguenay River. The electricity powered the nearby Alcan aluminum smelting plant, and surplus energy was channeled to the United States along with the aluminum ingots critical to airplane production. This collaboration, as Canadian leader Herbert Symington put it, made it seem "as though there were no boundary" between the two countries.[39] In fact, of course, there *was* a border, and Ottawa made skillful use of it to secure economic benefit from its proximity to the United States while avoiding complete American domination.

In Australia, Canada, and New Zealand, the Second World War accelerated 'dedominionization,' an ungainly word for the evolution of formerly integral parts of the British Empire into fully independent imperialist nation-states. The Union of South Africa followed a similar path but given its critical relationship to broader developments in Africa, it will be discussed in the next chapter. Australia, Canada, and New Zealand all remained part of the British Commonwealth, and many of their people continued to see themselves as part of a British cultural world, a sensibility that was reinforced by large-scale postwar immigration from the old imperial metropole. Nevertheless, while new nationality laws (1946 in Canada, 1948 in Australia and New Zealand) continued to define people as subjects of the British monarchy, they also became *citizens* of their own countries for the first time. This latter usage, which defined people's direct relationship to the state, quickly became decisive, particularly as the term "dominion" dropped out of use. After two referendums the British colony of Newfoundland joined Canada in 1948, and the new Nationality Act also worked to promote a common national identity that was also designed to incorporate the discriminated-against French-speaking nationality in Quebec.

Organizing the Postwar World

By the early 1950s the transition from war to postwar in the advanced capitalist countries of Western Europe, Japan, and Britain's former dominions was largely complete. In countries that had experienced the direct and violent impact of war, vivid reminders of the war were ever-present, from the ruined bomb sites in many cities to the still-fresh memories of death and destruction. But these memorials to war were increasingly subsumed within the framework of dynamic economic growth as the postwar boom got into full swing. The popular uprisings, insurgencies, and other less dramatic but deeply felt yearnings for radical social change had ebbed away, some buffered by the social reforms enacted by new welfare states and some simply absorbed by the capitalist prosperity that flowed down into sections of the working class. By the mid-1950s, many Europeans could feel that they were finally leaving the devastating material legacies of the war behind. In their place, a growing middle class, much of it

---

[39]Herbert Symington, quoted in David Massell, "'As Though There Was No Boundary': The Shipshaw Project and Continental Integration," *American Review of Canadian Studies*, Vol. 34, No. 2 (2004), 207.

connected to sprawling state bureaucracies, expanding university systems, and expansive socialized healthcare, enjoyed rising lifestyles furnished with consumer goods like cars and television sets that doubled as aspirational symbols of success. Amid the ideological promotion of home, family, and motherhood, many women exercised their new political rights by voting for moderate conservative champions of "womanhood."[40] In reality, there was no generalized 'affluence,' and many in the working class—particularly women and the expanding layers of immigrant workers—continued to struggle to make ends meet. As organized class struggle receded, however, images of moderation and modest prosperity set the tone.

The advanced capitalist economies in Europe and Japan remained central to the world capitalist order, but the war had fundamentally reorganized the circuitry of the system. Western Europe and Japan remained critical—even indispensable—components, but the system's center of economic, military, and political gravity now lay in the United States. From this point of view, and despite the clear qualifications to its reach posed by the Soviet Union and Soviet-dominated Eastern Europe, by the Chinese Revolution, and by waves of anticolonial insurgency, the postwar reconstruction of Western Europe, Britain, Japan, and the former dominions was inevitably intertwined with the assertion of American predominance. As the postwar began to emerge, American planning still exhibited a certain naivete, and it took time to internalize the understanding that new world orders are not 'things' that can be proclaimed into existence but sets of relationships that take time to assemble and organize.

Some key aspects of the new order, like the economic system envisioned at Bretton Woods, would take a decade or more to be fully realized. Nevertheless, when that new system was finally consolidated in the context of accelerating economic growth, it took the form of a workable set of practices, not simply agreed-upon principles. Between 1947 and 1950, the first three rounds of the General Agreement on Tariffs and Trade cut or eliminated over 50,000 individual trade tariffs. At the same time, Washington revived the push toward dollar-based currency convertibility at the heart of the Bretton Woods' system, but it now recognized the benefits of trading with the sterling area in ways that eased its gradual dissolution rather than simply seeking its immediate end. Acting along these lines, by the mid-1950s the United States had succeeded—if within a more limited compass than initially envisaged—in creating the basis for a sustained and worldwide expansion of capitalism founded on the rebuilding of the advanced capitalist economies and on the reorganization of the relationships between them. In doing so, however, Washington had ensured that the United States would soon face stiff competition both from an integrated and German-led Europe and from Japan.

---

[40]Conway, *Western Europe's Democratic Age*, 244.

For Further Reading

Marco Maris Aterrano, "Civilian Disarmament: Public Order and the Restoration of State Authority in Italy's Postwar Transition, 1944–6," *Journal of Contemporary History*, Vol. 56, No. 2 (2021).

Susan L. Carruthers, *The Good Occupation: American Soldiers and the Hazards of Peace* (Cambridge, MA: Harvard University Press, 2016).

Martin Conway, *Western Europe's Democratic Age, 1945–1968* (Princeton: Princeton University Press, 2020).

John Dower, *Embracing Defeat: Japan in the Wake of World War II* (New York: Norton, 1999).

David Edgerton, *Britain's War Machine: Weapons, Resources, and Experts in the Second World War* (Oxford: Oxford University Press, 2011).

David W. Ellwood, *Italy, 1943–1945* (New York: Holmes and Maier, 1985).

Yong Wook Lee, "The Origin of One-Party Domination: America's Reverse Course and the Emergence of the Liberal Democratic Party in Japan," *Journal of East Asian Affairs*, Vol. 18, No. 2 (Fall/Winter 2004).

Derek Leebaert, *Grand Improvisation: America Confronts the British Superpower, 1945–1957* (New York: Farrar, Straus and Giroux, 2018).

Keith Lowe, *Savage Continent: Europe in the Aftermath of World War II* (New York: Picador, 2012).

Arnold A. Offner, *Another Such Victory: President Truman and the Cold War, 1945–1953* (Stanford, CA: Stanford University Press, 2002).

Silvio Pons, "Stalin and the European Communists after World War Two (1943–1948)," *Past and Present*, Supplement 6 (2011).

Benn Steil, *The Marshall Plan: Dawn of the Cold War* (New York: Simon and Schuster, 2018).

CHAPTER SIX

Hegemony Expanded: The Middle East and Africa

War and the Crisis of Colonial Rule in North Africa and the Middle East

As in South and Southeast Asia, the war between the Allied and Axis powers opened space in North Africa and the Middle East for local actors—including popular movements and elite nationalists—to advance their own claims. In May 1941, a revolt led by nationalist army officers in Iraq upended British control of their nominally independent state, and although their National Defense Government was quickly toppled by British-Imperial counterattacks, anti-imperialist revolts soon flared in other parts of the region. As an Axis army advanced on Egypt in spring 1942, tens of thousands of students, workers, and peasant farmers took to the streets of Cairo to cheer it on. Fearful of losing control over their client state, British authorities surrounded the royal palace with troops and forced King Farouk to appoint a pro-British government led by the Wafd (Delegate) Party. This action secured London's control of Egypt at a critical point in the war, but—as in Iraq—its high-handed actions deepened anti-British sentiments that would reemerge with full force after the war.

Inter-imperial war and anti-colonial revolt also intersected in the French-ruled Levant (Lebanon and Syria). After the First World War, this part of the former Ottoman Empire had been awarded to Paris as a League of Nations mandate, enabling France to exercise effective colonial rule while leaving promises of independence unfulfilled. In June 1941, a British-Imperial force—Australians and Indians did most of the fighting—invaded Syria, ejecting the pro-Vichy French administration and replacing it with one loyal to General Charles de Gaulle's Free French. With French rule shaken, however, parliamentary assemblies in both countries proclaimed national independence in November 1943. French efforts to regain control met resistance from London, which increasingly styled itself as the leader of a loose postwar coalition of client states in the Middle East. With popular protests in support of Syrian independence building, French forces bombarded Damascus in May 1945 to cow president Shuri al-Quwatli's National Bloc government. Hundreds were killed before British-Imperial forces—still the major military power in the area—imposed martial law and confined the French troops to their barracks. From Paris, De Gaulle denounced London's "policy of intimidation" against the French Empire, but he could not risk an open confrontation with the British.[1]

French colonial control was also shaken in North Africa, where its colony of Algeria and the protectorates of Morocco and Tunisia had been occupied by Anglo-American armies after the November 1942 *Torch* landings. Here, too, popular protests driven by the wartime economic hardship intersected with the nationalism of elite figures who—particularly in Morocco—were buoyed by hints of American support for their cause. Paris pushed back hard, attacking mass nationalist demonstrations and imprisoning leaders of the Istiqlal (Independence) Party in Morocco, while banning the Néo-Destour (New Constitution) Party and imposing direct colonial rule in Tunisia. America's half-promise of support Moroccan for independence was quickly walked back as Washington backed the repression of Istiqal and then negotiated the postwar establishment of Strategic Air Command bases directly with Paris. Nevertheless, when a renewed nationalist upsurge forced the French to grant Moroccan independence in 1956, the continuing power of the "Roosevelt Myth" among the country's elites ensured that they remained firmly within the American-led world.[2]

French wartime repression also stifled anticolonial voices in Algeria, France's oldest African colony. Algeria was home to one million French settlers—the *pieds noir*—out of a total population of nine million. Anticolonial protest flared here at the end of the war, driven in part by the poor treatment of the Arab and Berber soldiers who had been critical to the establishment of De Gaulle's authority in France. In May 1945, a march in the Algerian city of Sétif to celebrate the end of the war and call for the release of imprisoned nationalist leaders led to running battles with the French military and settler vigilantes that left at least 7000 dead.[3]

---

[1] Meir Zamir, "The 'Missing Dimension': Britain's Secret War against France in Syria and Lebanon, 1942–45," *Middle Eastern Studies*, Vol. 46, No. 6 (2010), 811.
[2] David Stenner, "Did *Amrika* Promise Morocco's Independence? The Nationalist Movement, the Sultan, and the Making of the "Roosevelt Myth," *The Journal of North African Studies*, Vol. 19, No. 4 (2014).
[3] Martin Thomas, *Fight or Flight: Britain, France, and Their Roads from Empire* (Oxford: Oxford University Press, 2014), 1, 196.

Harsh repression forced Algerian nationalism underground, where the new National Liberation Front (FLN)—a nationalist coalition uniting broad sections of the population—began to take shape. The FLN's membership was strengthened by the involvement of former soldiers in France's colonial armies, some of whom had drawn radical conclusions from the losing effort to restore French rule in Indochina. The FLN's long struggle against French rule, launched in 1955, finally provoked the political crisis that toppled the Fourth Republic, returned Charles de Gaulle to power, and ultimately secured Algerian independence in 1962.

While Paris was battling to reestablish control over the Maghreb, London was working to consolidate its leadership in the eastern Mediterranean and Middle East. British elites, led by the newly elected Labour Party, viewed the region's vast oil reserves and strategic location as critical to rebuilding Britain's economy and to its world standing more broadly. After the fighting in North Africa turned in its favor in late 1942, London had worked to strengthen alliances with local clients throughout the region, including King Farouk in Egypt and the Hashemite monarchies in Transjordan (now Jordan) and Iraq; the princely rulers of the Persian Gulf kingdoms of Qatar, Bahrain, Kuwait, Aden, and the Trucial States (now the United Arab Emirates); and the new republican governments in the Levant. During the war, the British had attempted to manage regional economic affairs through the Cairo-based Middle East Supply Center (MESC), and this transnational approach underpinned the formation of the Arab League in March 1945. Initiated by London but formally convened by the Egyptian government in Cairo, the League cloaked Britain's continuing regional predominance—including its control of the Suez Canal and the unfettered operation of its oil companies—in a veneer of pan-Arab solidarity. London's regional hegemony was buttressed by its military power, which included substantial garrisons in the mandate of Palestine—effectively a British colony—and the Suez Canal Zone, air bases in Egypt and on the island colony of Cyprus, and military missions to friendly Arab governments.

In contrast to Southeast Asia, where the early-war overturning of European colonial rule by Japan meant that its postwar reimposition was always going to be an uphill struggle, the British could survey their postwar prospects in the Middle East with some confidence. Across the region, anti-imperial uprisings seemed to have been contained and loyal clients were networked into a transnational alliance that helped to disguise London's imperial ambitions. British leaders expected that their ongoing regional predominance in the Middle East would help fuel Britain's economic recovery, but they also hoped to leverage it to strengthen their relationship with the United States. Washington's own diplomatic, economic, and military presence in the region had expanded significantly during the war, in part through their participation in the Middle East Supply Center, but Washington still lacked both the long-standing political relationships and the depth of military implantation that underpinned Britain's regional predominance. Moreover, as Washington grappled with major challenges in both Europe and Asia in the years after 1945, the Middle East was far from the top of their agenda, and American leaders were happy to rely on Britain to maintain order there. From this point of view, London's hopes for a global dyarchy did not seem so far-fetched.

Revolutionary Crises in Postwar Iran, 1945–53

Developments in postwar Iran highlight some of the ways in which these conflicting pressures began to work themselves out. Here the tide of popular radicalism that shaped the transition from war to postwar across much of the colonial world flowed with particular vigor. In Iran's northern province of Azerbaijan, a revolutionary government led by the newly formed Democratic Party (DPA) and buoyed by a wave of mass demonstrations took power in November 1945. The Azeris, a Turkic people who also lived in Soviet Azerbaijan, faced oppression and discrimination at the hands of the government in Tehran. The new government, led by radical teacher Ja'far Pishevari, aimed to reverse this long-standing oppression either by establishing regional autonomy within Iran or by separating from the Iranian state and joining Soviet Azerbaijan instead. This popular uprising was followed in January 1946 by the establishment of a second revolutionary government as Qazi Muhammad's Kurdish Democratic Party formed the Republic of Mahabad in the Kurdish-majority region of northern Iran. In both Azerbaijan and Mahabad, the new governments promised sweeping land reform, the use of local languages in education and government, and self-government within the Iranian state, and these radical policies generated broad popular support registered in the creation of local councils and militias.

These developments took place in parts of Iran that had been under Soviet occupation since 1941, when the Red Army moved into northern part of the country while British-Imperial forces occupied the south. Anglo-Soviet occupation forces removed the pro-Axis Reza Shah Pahlavi from the throne and replaced him with his more pliant son, Mohammad Reza Pahlavi. The occupation also secured British control of Iran's southern oilfields and established a critical transportation corridor for the movement of Lend-Lease supplies from newly expanded ports on the Persian Gulf northward into the Soviet Union. Since the Azerbaijani People's Government and the Mahabad Republic emerged in areas under Soviet control, they are often dismissed as mere puppets of Moscow. In fact, while Communist officials played a role in setting up the new governments, the rebel regimes tapped into deep hostility to local landlord elites and gave voice to the oppressed national minorities within the Iranian state. Contemporary observers confirmed this assessment, with the British consul in Tabriz noting that the Soviets were "exploiting a genuinely revolutionary situation" while his American counterpart reported that the People's Government enjoyed "substantial popular sympathy" among people who had "real grievances against central government."[4]

Moscow's backing for the rebel governments in Iranian Azerbaijan and Mahabad did not stem from a desire to extend socialist revolution or to defend the rights of national minorities. As ever, Soviet leaders had their own interests in mind, and they hoped to use the new revolutionary governments as levers to push Tehran into granting Moscow access to the oilfields of northern Iran like that enjoyed by the British-owned Anglo-Iranian Oil Company (AIOC)—later British Petroleum—in the south. To strengthen Moscow's hand, Red Army forces remained in northern Iran after the March 1946 deadline for withdrawal agreed in 1941. In early 1946, however, Moscow was still hoping to maintain the wartime Grand Alliance, and Soviet leaders responded to American criticism of their continued occupation—expressed through the United Nations—by withdrawing their troops in May 1946. By this time, Moscow had secured a promise from Iranian prime minister Ahmad Qavam to create a joint Soviet-Iranian oil company to develop production in the northern oilfields. As the Red Army pulled out, Stalin informed Pishevari that the "revolutionary demands of Azerbaijan" were being sidelined in order to maintain good relations with the British and Americans, adding that, in any case, there was no possibility of revolution in Iran.[5]

Even as Moscow was dismissing the prospect of revolution, popular protests began shaking southern Iran, culminating in a strike of 65,000 oil workers in summer 1946. Striking workers linked demands for better wages to calls for an end to the Anglo-Iranian Oil Company's interference in Iranian politics.[6] With popular governments already in power in Iranian Azerbaijan and Kurdistan, these working-class protests—the largest yet seen in the Middle East—posed a serious threat to the pro-Western regime in Tehran. In desperation, Qavam and the Shah turned to the pro-Moscow Tudeh (People's Party) to help them regain control, and with Soviet agreement the party acted to moderate working-class protests. In exchange, Tudeh was awarded three seats in Qavam's cabinet in August 1946. Moscow's seeming success was short-lived. With Washington's approval, Qavam waited until working-class militancy had subsided and then cracked down on the Tudeh, ejecting the party from government in October before declaring martial law in Tehran and sending troops to crush the revolutionary governments in Azerbaijan and Mahabad.

---

[4]Ervand Abrahamian, *Iran between Two Revolutions* (Princeton: Princeton University Press, 1982), 218.
[5]Geoffrey Roberts, "Moscow's Cold War on the Periphery: Soviet Policy in Greece, Iran, and Turkey, 1943–8," *Journal of Contemporary History*, Vol. 46, No. 1 (2011), 68.
[6]Abrahamian, *Iran between Two Revolutions*, 302–3.

With the Red Army gone, the rebel governments were quickly overthrown by Iranian troops and paramilitary gendarmes. In Azerbaijan, peoples' militias responded to calls from their government to resist Tehran's troops, but their efforts were undercut when local Communists endorsed Moscow's insistence on a peaceful settlement and laid down their arms. Eager to protect the oil deal, Stalin informed Pishevari that Qavam was "entitled to send troops to all parts of the country, including Azerbaijan."[7] Even so, bands of Azeri *fedayeen* guerillas waged a hit-and-run campaign against the Iranian army until summer 1947. In Mahabad, Kurdish *peshmerga* fighters led by Mustafa Barzani—the veteran commander of a wartime uprising in Iraqi-ruled Kurdistan—scored initial victories against Iranian forces before being forced to conduct a fighting retreat into the Soviet Union. Hundreds of Azeris and Kurds died in the fighting, and many more—including some 30,000 supporters of the DPA, were killed as Tehran reestablished control.[8] Meanwhile, in a stunning act of cynicism Moscow informed Tudeh leaders facing repression in the south not to expect any support from a Soviet government pledged to avoid "interference" in foreign countries.[9] Even as the Azeris and Kurds were being crushed, however, Qavam informed Moscow that the oil concession was no longer on the table, and at the same time Tehran signed a military pact with the United States. Soviet maneuvers had failed to secure access to oil while ensuring the bloody defeat of two popular revolutions; from Moscow's point of view, however, this was not a wholly negative outcome as it effectively sealed its southern border against potentially destabilizing struggles for national independence.

Despite these defeats, postwar militancy in Iran was not extinguished, and in 1950 oil workers and others launched a new wave of strikes and demonstrations calling on the Iranian government to take over Anglo-Iranian Oil. These protests opened a new crisis that led in September 1951 to the nationalization of Anglo-Iranian by Prime Minister Mohammad Mosaddeq's National Front government. Wildly popular in Iran, this step prompted a fierce reaction from London, which tried to starve Tehran of income by blocking the sale of Iranian oil on the world market. Under British pressure, the Shah dumped the liberal-nationalist Mosaddeq in favor of the reliable Qavam. These moves were quickly answered by a cascading series of nationwide protests that culminated in a massive march on Tehran in July 1952. Despite violent state repression, these strikes and demonstrations forced Mosaddeq's reinstatement.

With popular revolution in Iran looming once again, London and Washington activated their extensive—and in the CIA's case

---

[7] Roberts, "Moscow's Cold War on the Periphery," 69.
[8] Ibid., 70.
[9] Vladislav M. Zubok, "Stalin, Soviet Intelligence and the Struggle for Iran, 1945–53," *Diplomatic History*, Vol. 44, No. 1 (January 2020), 28.

FIGURE 6.1 *Iranian prime minister Mohammad Mosaddeq addresses a crowd of supporters shortly after the nationalization of the oil industry and the ejection of Anglo-Iranian Oil Company personnel from the Abadan refinery, October 19, 1951. (Photo: Keystone-France.)*

well-funded—networks of agents and began preparing a military coup. Meanwhile, the Tudeh party followed Moscow's lead and abstained from the mass movement to nationalize the oil industry. Guided by the pseudo-radicalism of the Cominform's two camp policy, Tudeh viewed both the National Front and the mass movement it led as 'bourgeois nationalist,' and hence unworthy of Communist support. Soviet leaders also harbored a grudge against Mosaddeq, who had blocked an oil concession to Moscow in 1944 and who they now portrayed as an American agent. With Tudeh standing on the sidelines, Mosaddeq was toppled in a CIA-led military coup in August 1953. Harsh state repression against the trade union movement followed as the Shah consolidated his dictatorship with American backing. The oil industry was denationalized, but in recognition of Washington's increasing prominence in Iranian affairs, Anglo-Iranian was denied its old monopoly. Instead, Iran's oil was divided up between various Western powers, with 40 percent going to AIOC, 20 percent to Dutch and French corporations, and the rest to American companies.[10] By the end of 1953,

---

[10] Wm. Roger Louis and Ronald Robinson, "The Imperialism of Decolonization," *Journal of Imperial and Commonwealth History*, Vol. 22, No. 3 (1994), 475.

the waves of popular revolt that had rolled across the country since the end of the world war were finally broken by the extensive police and prison apparatus of the Shah's dictatorship. Moreover, and in a shift that would soon have consequences throughout the region, the United States was beginning to assert its own leadership in Middle Eastern affairs.

Oil, the Cold War, and the United States in the Middle East

As we have seen, Moscow's vision of the postwar world was fundamentally shaped by its own national security interests, and in the Middle East that led it to seek a major role in the administration of the Turkish Straits connecting the Black Sea to the Mediterranean. These demands, which included plans for the construction of a military base close to the Straits, were justified by the need to secure the USSR's southern borders and its access to shipping routes into the Mediterranean. During the war, the Allies had indicated that they would be open to a revision of the 1936 Montreux Convention, the international agreement regulating control of the straits. As the war in Europe ended, however, Washington's forceful opposition to Soviet influence in the Straits—framed as resistance to military expansionism—quickly became a key component of its rapidly deepening postwar hostility to the USSR. In March 1946, a visit to Turkey by the battleship *Missouri* announced Washington's own accelerating military build-up in the region. American diplomats worked to draw Ankara into the framework of 'containment,' while military planners promised to strengthen the Turkish army and to build new ports and airbases. Confronted with this American pressure, most Soviet troops were quickly withdrawn from neighboring Bulgaria, while Moscow's demands on the Straits were limited to sharply worded diplomatic notes. As in Trieste—and as George Kennan argued in his February 1946 'Long Telegram'—Moscow again showed itself "highly sensitive to the logic of force" by backing down in the face of the threatened deployment of American naval forces to the eastern Mediterranean.[11]

After Moscow's retreat from both Iran and the Turkish Straits in 1946, Soviet intervention in the Middle East was largely restricted to attempts to disrupt Anglo-American predominance in the region by forging ties with nationalist forces. The specter of alleged Soviet expansionism nevertheless continued to provide powerful justificatory rhetoric for America's own rapidly expanding presence. America's own interest in the Middle East rested on two interlocking elements: the region's vast—and still largely

---

[11] George Kennan, quoted in Arnold A. Offner, *Another Such Victory: President Truman and the Cold War, 1945–1953* (Stanford, CA: Stanford University Press, 2002), 133–4.

untapped—oil reserves, and its critical strategic position. Oil was essential to the functioning of modern industrial economies, and the allied war effort had been largely powered by oil from America's own domestic oilfields and from the American-dominated Caribbean basin. By the end of the war, however, American planners were becoming concerned about the long-term viability of the US oil fields, and they were eager to secure a lock on reserves in other parts of the world. At the same time, American companies wanted to expand into the Middle East in order to place them in the best position to profit from the demand for oil generated by Europe's postwar recovery. Under these twin pressures, as one American expert explained in 1944, "the center of gravity of world oil production" shifted from "the Caribbean area to the Middle East."[12] American companies had begun moving into this British-dominated region before the war, striking oil in Saudi Arabia in 1938 and, with diplomatic backing from Washington, cracking the Anglo-Iranian Oil Company's monopoly in Kuwait. American diplomacy strengthened these positions during the war, cultivating ties with Saudi Arabia by supplying it with Lend-Lease aid—despite its nonbelligerent status—and then consolidating these arrangements in a February 1945 meeting between President Roosevelt and King Ibn Saud.

In the immediate postwar, the push to expand American control of Middle East oil quickly impinged on British interests, but with 51 percent of its shares in British government hands, Anglo-Iranian's ability to compete with the Americans was hobbled by politicians who needed to secure US loans and other favors. It was a losing battle. In March 1947, Washington approved the creation of ARAMCO, a cartel of four leading oil companies—Jersey Standard (Exxon), Socony Vacuum (Mobil), SoCal (Chevron), and Texaco—that was exempted from anti-trust legislation and given generous tax breaks as it worked with the government to gain a control of Middle Eastern oil. ARAMCO campaigned for the construction of a 754-mile Trans-Arabian pipeline—or Tapline—to connect the Saudi oilfields to the Mediterranean at Sidon in Lebanon, and when Shuri al-Quwatli's nationalist government refused to allow it to cross Syrian territory, American officials backed his ouster in a March 1949 military coup. Six weeks later, Syria approved the pipeline, which was soon carrying 300,000 barrels of Saudi crude to Sidon every day for onward shipment to energy-starved Europe.

ARAMCO, Gulf Oil, and nine independent American oil companies began pumping oil in Iran soon after the overthrow of Mosaddeq in 1953. Their presence in this former British-dominated oilfield was the price paid by London for Washington's involvement in the coup. By the end of the decade, American oil companies were also operating in newly independent

---

[12]Douglas Little, *American Orientalism: The United States and the Middle East since 1945* (Chapel Hill: University of North Carolina Press, 2002), 50.

Libya, courtesy of concessions granted by British-installed King Idris. Oil companies were the cutting edge of a broader expansion of America economic involvement throughout North Africa and the Middle East. During the war, American officials leveraged their participation in the Middle East Supply Center and other Anglo-American economic councils to introduce American goods—and American businessmen—to people throughout the region. In Egypt, collaboration between US diplomats and local elites ensured that by 1945 American companies—including Coca-Cola, Ford, Kodak, and Westinghouse—had secured key market footholds as British companies like English Electric and Imperial Chemical Industries were unceremoniously shouldered aside.[13] While London still hoped to maintain its predominance in the Middle East through its leadership of the Arab League, the economic foundations upon which long-term neocolonial relationships might have been built were passing into American hands.

The advance of American economic interests in the Middle East was intertwined with an expanding military presence. By the late 1940s, major US naval forces—including the aircraft carrier battlegroup at the heart of the new Sixth Fleet—were permanently based in the Mediterranean. They were backed by an array of logistical and communications facilities, airfields, radar sites, and repair bases that stretched from Morocco to Italy and, from 1948, to Wheelus Air Force Base in Libya. Adopted in stages from early 1946, American warplane *Pincher* and its regional derivatives envisaged launching nuclear bombing raids on the USSR from British bases in Egypt, and in 1950 these positions were reinforced by the construction of a massive new airfield at Incirlik in southern Turkey. Ankara's pro-Western course was registered by the commitment of Turkish troops to the war in Korea, and Turkish politicians used veiled threats of Cold War neutralism to secure full NATO membership in 1952. Despite Washington's expanding economic and military presence in the Middle East, however, it took time for the United States to grow into hegemony, and in the first postwar decade it continued to lean heavily on London's political leadership and military power: the postwar dyarchy was eroding, but it was not yet supplanted.

The Partition of Palestine

The matrix of forces that shaped postwar politics throughout the Middle East—the eruption of popular anticolonialism, the nationalism of local elites, the collaborative and competing imperial interests of the United States and Britain, and Moscow's maneuvering for influence—intersected

---

[13]Robert Vitalis, "The 'New Deal' in Egypt: The Rise of Anglo-American Commercial Competition in World War II and the Fall of Neocolonialism," *Diplomatic History*, Vol. 20, No. 1 (Spring 1996), esp. 226, 234.

with particular force in British-ruled Palestine. Granted to London as a League of Nations mandate in 1923, Palestine effectively became a British colony. As such, it was central to the post-First World War expansion of the British Empire in the Middle East, but it brought inbuilt problems for its new imperial masters. During the war, Britain encouraged an Arab revolt against Ottoman control of the region, but it also simultaneously recognized the right of the Jewish people to a 'national home' in Palestine. As Jewish immigration increased, long-standing and largely peaceful cohabitation between Palestinian Arabs and Jews began to fray as new arrivals competed for scarce farmland. In this context, and in contrast to the nominally independent Hashemite monarchies it established in Iraq and Transjordan, London decided to maintain direct control of Palestine. At the same time, Palestine's geopolitical significance was heightened by the completion of a pipeline connecting the Anglo-Iranian Oil Company's Iraqi oilfields to the Mediterranean coast at Haifa, where a major refinery was constructed.

In 1936, Palestinian Arabs launched a powerful revolt against British rule. Fueled in part by British support for Jewish immigration, the Great Revolt combined a general strike with guerrilla insurgency. The British responded with ferocious military repression that included the extensive use of airpower and the collective punishment of villages accused of harboring rebel fighters. In a classic example of imperial divide-and-rule, the British armed Jewish militias and incited them to join an orgy of anti-Arab violence. The revolt subsided in 1939, and with war looming London sought to rebuild its ties to Arab elites by banning 'illegal' Jewish immigration and prohibiting the sale of land to Jews. In response, Jewish terrorist organizations including Irgun (National Military Organization) and the more radical Fighters for the Freedom of Israel—sometimes known as the Stern Gang—began attacks on British personnel and infrastructure. Suspended at the start of the war, terrorist attacks resumed in 1944 when it became clear that the British were not going to organize Jewish military units, and in July 1946, ninety-one people were killed when Irgun bombed the headquarters British Mandatory Palestine in Jerusalem's King David Hotel. Adding to Britain's difficulties, the French government, incensed by London's push to evict it from the Levant, began supplying Irgun with weapons.

'Illegal' emigration to Palestine increased dramatically after 1945 as Jews fleeing the aftermath of the Holocaust—including continued anti-Semitism in their countries of origin—sought sanctuary in the promise of a Jewish state. By the end of the war, there were at least 250,000 Jews living in camps for Displaced Persons in Western Europe, some of them in conditions of extreme squalor, and many set out to brave the difficult and dangerous journey to Palestine.[14] It is impossible to understand the

---

[14] Yasmin Khan, "Wars of Displacement: Exile and Uprooting in the 1940s," in Michael Geyer and Adam Tooze (eds.), *The Cambridge History of the Second World War*, Vol. III (New York: Cambridge University Press, 2015), 281–2.

events that followed without grasping the simple and searing reality of the Holocaust and its aftermath. It does not mean that one terrible wrong—the systematic killing of six million Jews—justifies another, but in the context of the violent conflicts unfolding in the contested spaces of the Middle East and the efforts of various imperial powers to stoke them, it does help to understand what happened. The road to the establishment of the State of Israel in 1948 was convoluted, but its main outlines are clear. In the context of Britain's troubled postwar recovery and with Jewish-Arab conflict increasing, the Labour government abandoned its efforts to hold on to Palestine, announcing that its mandate would end in May 1948 and that it was turning the search for a solution over to the United Nations. In response, American diplomats pushed to secure a partition that would create separate Arab and Jewish states. With President Truman overriding the concerns of senior advisors who feared that support for partition would undercut Washington's standing in the Arab world, diplomats strongarmed America's allies into securing U.N. General Assembly backing for partition in November 1947. The Soviet Union, fishing for leverage in troubled waters, also endorsed partition.

Palestinian Arabs and regional Arab governments rejected partition, and civil war flared in late 1947 as well-organized Jewish forces battled Arab militias. Despite their anti-Zionist—often simply anti-Semitic—bluster, the leaders of neighboring Arab states were deeply divided and incapable of concerted action, and Arab League support for Palestinian Arabs was limited to the dispatch of a small and poorly trained Liberation Army. The civil war ended in devastating defeat for the Palestinian Arabs, and in the ensuing *Nakba* (Catastrophe) over 750,000 people were driven from their homes amidst violent assaults and terrorist bombings perpetrated by both sides.[15] Victory in the civil war allowed Jewish forces to expand the territory under their control, and the formal end of the British mandate in May 1948 coincided with the establishment of a much-enlarged State of Israel. The new state was soon subject to a series of uncoordinated invasions by the armies of Egypt, Iraq, Syria, and Transjordan, who were joined by Saudi, Lebanese, and Yemini volunteers. Initiated largely to head off deepening anti-imperialist and anti-government sentiment at home, the Arab invasions gave the newly formed Israeli Defense Force (IDF) the opportunity to spearhead further territorial expansion. Arab resistance was further undermined by a deal between Israel and King Abdullah of Jordan that gave Amman control of East Jerusalem and the West Bank of the River Jordan. By the time the fighting ended in early 1949, Israel controlled around 80 percent of the former British mandate.

Moscow quickly gave Israel diplomatic recognition and organized to supply it with the Czech weapons that underpinned the IDF's initial military

---

[15]Ibid., 286.

successes. Nevertheless, Tel Aviv had no interest in becoming a Soviet satellite in the Middle East, and after endorsing the American-led war in Korea in 1950 it turned sharply toward the United States. The Israel-US relationship developed slowly. Many in Washington remained wary of the new Jewish state, and despite backing it with a $100 million line of credit and supporting Israeli membership of the United Nations, they feared that Tel Aviv's refusal to grant territorial concessions or aid to Palestinian refugees would generate regional instability and facilitate Soviet 'penetration' of the Arab world. American fears were calmed by Saudi assurances that despite their heated verbal opposition to Israel, they had no interest in disrupting the work of American oil companies. In the early 1950s, Israel was gradually integrated federal into the broader framework of postwar consolidation, a development signaled in 1950 by being given diplomatic recognition by Washington's regional allies in Iran and Turkey. In 1952 Israeli diplomats—with American backing—secured Berlin's agreement to compensate the wartime suffering of the Jewish people, a deal that, however nominal, helped to normalize Israel's existence. The deal also allowed Washington to conclude the broader restructuring of debt that facilitated Germany's own economic 'miracle' (see Chapter Six). Tel Aviv never functioned simply as an American client, but by the late 1950s it was increasingly viewed as a stable pro-western bastion in a volatile region, and hence as a suitable recipient for major shipments of US arms.

Based on their mutual opposition to radical Arab nationalism, Israel also developed close ties with France. Paris began supplying weapons to Israel in 1953, and three years later agreed to provide the equipment and scientific know-how necessary for the development of an Israeli nuclear program.

The 'Tripartite Aggression' or Suez Crisis, 1956

The formation of the State of Israel and its ongoing conflict with its Arab neighbors increased the instability of the postwar Middle East. Tensions were further heightened by the 1952 overthrow of the Egyptian monarchy and its replacement by a military government headed (after 1954) by Colonel Gamal Abdel Nasser. Nasser was a radical bourgeois nationalist whose ability to confront imperialism—and British imperialism in particular—rested on his capacity to mobilize popular support through massive demonstrations of urban workers, students, and rural peasants or *fellah*. At the same time, however, this energized popular sentiment pushed Nasser toward confrontation with Britain and limited his room for maneuver. Nasser's government opposed Britain's continued military presence in Egypt, and its antipathy to London's Hashemite clients in Jordan and Iraq increasingly undercut even the show of Arab League unity.

Nasser was not inherently hostile to Washington, and he hoped to secure American weapons and patronage. Nevertheless, when a major arms deal collapsed in 1955 after the Egyptians refused to guarantee that the guns would not be used against Israel, Cairo turned to the Soviets instead. As ever, there was nothing ideological about Moscow's positive response, and Nasser continued persecuting Egyptian Communists even as he developed ties with the Soviets.

Nasser's turn to the USSR secured an agreement to supply Egypt with Czech weapons. The Egyptians hoped that this display of independence would force Washington to reconsider its own refusal to supply arms, but instead American officials viewed Cairo's burgeoning relationship with Moscow as a dangerous extension of Soviet influence in the Middle East. In the polarized light of the Cold War, American policymakers viewed Nasser's anticolonial nationalism as quasi-Communism, with President Eisenhower fretting that American leaders might suddenly discover that Egypt had "slipped behind the Iron Curtain."[16] In an effort to force Egypt to break with Moscow, Washington withdrew its funding for the Aswan High Dam, a massive irrigation and hydroelectric project that was central to Cairo's plans for modernization and industrial development. Nasser responded by announcing the nationalization of the Suez Canal—then in British hands—at a massive rally in Cairo on July 26, 1956. This move, Nasser explained, would restore Egyptian sovereignty over its own territory and secure funding for the Aswan dam out of the taxes levied on vessels transiting the canal. The complex interplay between bourgeois nationalism and popular protest thus set Egypt on a collision course with imperialism.

Cairo's actions prompted Nasser's enemies in Tel Aviv, Paris, and London to organize a coordinated military attack on Egypt. Each of the three had different reasons: Tel Aviv wanted to damage the Egyptian military before the Czech weapons arrived; Paris hoped that the Algerian insurgency would collapse without Egyptian support; and London wanted to regain control of the canal and reassert its status as a major world power. The implausible plan they cooked up involved an Israeli attack on the Sinai Peninsula to which the British and French would respond by dispatching 'peacekeeping' forces to the canal. On October 29, 1956, Israeli troops stormed into Sinai, breaking the Egyptian blockade of the Gulf of Aqaba and advancing to within ten miles of the canal. British and French airstrikes savaged the Egyptian airforce and after fierce fighting their paratroops secured control of the canal zone. Despite these military successes, however, it was a hollow victory. The Egyptians blocked the Suez Canal with sunken ships, causing massive disruption to world trade, while the Anglo-French invasion triggered a political crisis that quickly negated their military successes.

---

[16]Little, *American Orientalism*, 170.

FIGURE 6.2 *British troops on patrol in Port Said, Egypt, during the Suez Crisis, November 10, 1956. An oil refinery burns in the background. Despite rapid military success, the operation was a political disaster for the British and French governments. (Photo: Bettemann/Getty.)*

American officials would have been happy to see Nasser's ouster but, as Eisenhower put it, they feared that Anglo-French military action would unify "all of Asia and all of Africa [...] against the West."[17] Moreover, the

---

[17]Little, *American Orientalism*, 174.

Suez crisis coincided with the Soviet invasion of Hungary, and American leaders worried that any gesture of support for the Anglo-French invasion would demolish the moral high ground gifted to them by Moscow's brutal suppression of the Hungarian revolution. In this light, Washington called London and Paris to order, using economic leverage—including an unofficial oil embargo and an organized run on the pound—to force their withdrawal from Egypt. The invasion, organized in part to boost Britain's imperial prestige and shore up the 'sterling area,' thus ended up undermining the pound on world currency markets while unambiguously underscoring London's slide to the status of a second-rank power. Britain's ignominious retreat also weakened its political standing in the Middle East. The previous year, London had succeeded—with American encouragement—in bringing Iran, Iraq, Pakistan, and Turkey together in anti-Soviet Baghdad Pact, but this achievement was deeply compromised by the graphic exposure both of Britain's imperial intent and of its actual weakness. At the same time, Egypt's victory put wind in the sails of Nasser's demagogic appeals to pan-Arab unity, now focused on what turned out to be the short-lived fusion of Egypt and Syria into the 1958–61 United Arab Republic.

The Suez Crisis revealed the irreversible weakening of British imperial power that had *already* taken place. Britain's imperial decline was intertwined with the consolidation of American hegemony, and in December 1956 Vice President Richard Nixon recognized that Suez signaled the moment at which the United States assumed sole "leadership of the free world."[18] In the Middle East, as elsewhere, Washington would now stop—as Secretary of State John Foster Dulles put it—"walking a tightrope" between backing European colonialism and developing its own ties with postcolonial states.[19] With this turn in American policy, both Britain's continued imperial aspirations in the Middle East and the interim postwar dyarchy came to an end. When British prime minister Harold Macmillan and President Eisenhower met in Bermuda in 1957 to restore Anglo-American relations, the premier acknowledged that the British were now clearly "junior partners."[20]

There is another side to the story, however, and even as Suez showcased the consolidation of American hegemony it also showed its limits. Washington's inability to act (or to endorse action) against Nasser for fear of alienating 'Third World' opinion reveals the qualification of American power, not its absolute preponderance. Many American officials would have happily supported the use of force against Nasser—a "Moslem Mussolini," the British said—and just weeks after the crisis they assured London and

---

[18] Derek Leebaert, *Grand Improvisation: America Confronts the British Superpower, 1945–1957* (New York: Farrar, Straus and Giroux, 2018), 480–1.
[19] Louis and Robinson, "The Imperialism of Decolonization," 480.
[20] Ibid., 481.

Paris that they had simply chosen to act at a "bad time."[21] The following year, Vice President Richard Nixon lobbied Ethiopia to secure American use of a naval base at the Red Sea port of Massawa, quietly ratcheting up the pressure on Nasser while avoiding an open clash. Nevertheless, Washington was now being drawn more directly into the turmoil of the Middle East, dispatching Marines to Lebanon in 1958 to defend the presidency of Camille Chamoun from a pro-Nasser revolt while working to moderate General Abl al-Karim Qasim's nationalist revolt in Iraq. As Eisenhower feared, however, while overt intervention might bring short-term success, it tended to deepen popular radicalism: "we must adjust to the tide of Arab nationalism," the National Security Council warned in summer 1958, "before the hotheads get control in every country."[22]

War and Postwar in Sub-Saharan Africa

The waves of popular radicalism that shaped the postwar Middle East and North Africa also reached deeply into colonial Sub-Sahara Africa. Across this vast region, a new sense of confidence fueled resistance, inspiring innumerable local protests against the daily injustices of colonial rule and driving larger and more powerful struggles, including general strikes in British-ruled Nigeria (1945) and Kenya (1946), a walkout by South African gold miners in 1946, and a month-long strike by railway workers in French West African in 1947. Strikers appreciated the leverage enjoyed by industrial workers at a moment when colonial rulers in London and Paris needed to maximize output. Working-class struggles overlapped with widespread peasant protests driven by land hunger, resistance to forced labor, and opposition to rural 'modernization' projects that took little account traditional lifeways. In Madagascar (1947) and Kenya (1952) peasant-based insurgencies led by the MDRM (Democratic Movement for Malagasy Rejuvenation) and the Land and Freedom Army ('Mau Mau') shook colonial rule. In both places, imperial authorities responded with ferocious military repression, including the carpet-bombing of alleged terrorist bases and widespread use of detention without trial. At least 100,000 Malagasy were killed, while official estimates of 11,503 'terrorist' deaths in Kenya grossly underestimated the true number of Mau Mau casualties.[23]

These postwar revolts built on a wave of strikes that had rippled across the continent in the late 1930s, hitting—among other places—the Copperbelt of British-ruled Northern Rhodesia (Zambia), the railways

---

[21]Little, *American Orientalism*, 179, 181.
[22]Louis and Robinson, "The Imperialism of Decolonization," 482–3.
[23]Thomas, *Fight or Flight*, 193, 233.

of the Gold Coast (Ghana), and the textile mills of the Transvaal, South Africa. As the colonial powers prepared for war, trade union protests were temporarily stilled by strike bans and by the imprisonment of workers' leaders. Except for Ethiopia, where local insurgents and British-led forces combined to overturn Italian rule, and Madagascar, where a British-Imperial invasion toppled the pro-Vichy French administration in 1942, Africa avoided the direct military interventions that upended European colonial rule in Southeast Asia. Nevertheless, the world war still had profound and continent-wide effects, with African raw materials and African personpower making important contributions to British and French war efforts. For the Free French, control of France's colonies in Equatorial Africa provided a critical base of support, military personnel, and political credibility, while Britain's African colonies were a key supplier of essential raw materials, including rubber, tin, timber, and copper, and of foodstuffs like palm oil, corn, and groundnuts.

To meet wartime economic demands, British administrators strengthened colonial governance by establishing numerous organizations—like the West African Produce Control Board—to plan production and manage the bulk purchase and shipping of commodities. State-level planning was also evident in the infrastructure development projects that created new road and rail links and expanded port facilities. The development of transportation, mining, and industrial production accelerated urbanization and the creation of permanent working classes, and booming shantytowns full of footloose young people alarmed colonial administrators who viewed—not wrongly—them as seedbeds of trade union militancy and anticolonial politics. Colonial governments also increased the use of forced labor, leaning on traditional village leaders to conscript workers for large agricultural plantations and industrial operations like the tin mines on Nigeria's Jos Plateau. Here, 100,000 miners toiled for the British war effort, and at least 10,000 of them died in disease-ridden camps.[24] The expansion of transportation, mining, and the plantation production of rubber and other commodities disrupted traditional subsistence agriculture, advancing marketization and the prevalence of wage labor while accelerating the breakup of traditional social organization. These tendencies were exacerbated by rampant inflation and the collapse of rice imports, leading to intense rural hardship and outbreaks of famine. At the same time, white farmers benefitted disproportionately from wartime demand: in Kenya, the Agricultural Production and Settlement Board bought corn from settler farmers for twice the price it paid to Africans.[25]

---

[24]Karl Ittmann, *A Problem of Great Importance: Population, Race and Power in the British Empire, 1919–1973* (Berkley: University of California Press, 2013), 94.
[25]Judith A. Byfield, "Producing for the War," in Judith A. Byfield et al. (eds.), *Africa and World War II* (Cambridge: Cambridge University Press, 2015), 36–7.

Britain and France both mobilized substantial military forces from their colonies, with African troops helping to spearhead De Gaulle's reconquest of France in 1944 and fighting for the British in Burma. Tens of thousands more were recruited to perform military labor, building roads, ports, and airfields, and moving supplies. In the Union of South Africa, a self-governing dominion within the British Empire, the division between combatants and support troops was made along racial lines, with 200,000 white volunteers (around 25 percent of the male workforce) serving in frontline units while 120,000 Black, 'colored' (mixed race), and Indian soldiers labored unarmed in the Native Military Corps and the Cape Corps. During their service overseas, many Black Africans were exposed to new experiences and to radical political ideas, and officials fretted that when they returned home, they would no longer tolerate the daily injustices of colonial society. They had reason to be fearful: in French West Africa and in the British-ruled Gold Coast—as in Algeria—demonstrations by veterans were a key component of postwar protests, and former soldiers of the Kings African Rifles were prominent in the Mau Mau rebellion.

The 'Second Colonial Conquest': Planning for Postwar Empire

With their colonies in South and Southeast Asian facing powerful anticolonial rebellions in the immediate postwar, London and Paris viewed their African empires as vital both to their economic recovery and to their continued status as great powers. "Africa," one British official explained, was now the "only continental space from which we can still hope to draw reserves of economic and military strength."[26] At the same time, Africa's colonial rulers recognized that wartime changes, including the institution of centralized economic planning and the promotion of an African middle class to positions of leadership, meant that the *forms* of rule had to be overhauled if the colonies were to play their assigned role. British and French efforts to develop their African colonies have been described as a 'second colonial occupation,' but while this notion captures an important aspect of the process, it is important to recognize that these efforts unfolded at a time when wartime transformations had *already* pushed many colonies toward functioning as nation-states in-becoming. These were highly uneven processes, particularly at the level of economic relations. Here, while wartime planning, expanded raw material production, the marketization

---

[26]Frederick Cooper, "Reconstructing Empire in British and French Africa," *Past and Present*, Supplement 6 (2011), 199.

of agriculture, and the establishment of wage labor as a permanent feature of African life, all reflected the development of capitalist relations of production, the kind of rounded economies and strong manufacturing sectors on which independent nation-states might have been built were still largely absent.[27]

French colonial rule, organized into the large multi-territorial blocks of West and Equatorial Africa, was more centralized than Britain's empire and hence more open to top-down reform. In January 1944, General de Gaulle met leaders and administrators of France's African colonies in Brazzaville, Equatorial Africa, to announce the refounding of the empire as a transnational partnership. France's colonial subjects, De Gaulle argued, would become citizens of a new French Union, with the right to elect representatives to an imperial assembly in Paris. This project was embodied in the 1946 constitution of the Fourth Republic, which promised all inhabitants of the old empire the "qualities" of French citizenship.[28] Precisely what this meant was left deliberately vague, and it was unclear if former colonial subjects became citizens of the French Republic or just of a nebulous Union. Nevertheless, the new set-up gave African leaders like Léopold Senghor of Senegal a platform from which to press for the abolition of forced labor and other reforms. At the same time, Paris pushed the economic development—or modernization—of its colonies by channeling Marshall Aid funds and investment capital into Africa. The results were dramatic, with the economy of French West Africa growing by 14 percent annually between 1947 and 1951.[29] Not surprisingly, little of this new wealth trickled down to African workers and peasant farmers; instead, the disruption of traditional society by accelerating modernization only served to deepen popular anticolonial sentiment.

The reform of British colonial rule was a more complicated affair. Many leaders of the newly elected Labour government were ardent—if liberal—imperialists, and they viewed a reformed African empire as the key to Britain's postwar recovery. In this vision, Britain's African colonies would ship food and raw materials to the metropole and provide markets for its manufactured goods, while African exports to the United States would bring dollars into the sterling area, underpinning a continued world role for the pound. What shape political reform would take would be worked out in detail in individual colonies, and politicians and civil servants in London envisaged the Empire itself morphing slowly into a 'Commonwealth of Nations,' a loose association of self-governing states headed by the British monarchy and bound to Britain by ties of history, culture, and economics.

---

[27]Gareth Austin, "African Economic Development and Colonial Legacies," *International Development Policy/ Revue international de politique de développement*, No.1, 2010, 22.
[28]Cooper, "Reconstructing Empire," 200.
[29]Thomas, *Fight or Flight*, 240.

Given that most of Britain's African empire was far from self-governing in 1945 and that London intended to keep it that way for the foreseeable future, this was always a far-fetched notion. It was, however, accompanied by a new definition of imperial citizenship codified in Britain's 1948 Nationality Act. As the former dominions in Australia, Canada, and New Zealand moved to establish their own national citizenship after the war, this Act set up a new category of Citizen of the United Kingdom and Colonies for people born in Britain or its directly ruled colonies. Intended as a goodwill gesture, this provision had the unintended consequence of facilitating large-scale migration into Britain from its African, West Indian, and South Asian colonies.

Cold War Contexts: Washington Underwrites Colonial Empire

Britain and France's postwar efforts to reenergize their African empires took place in the context of steps to consolidate America's postwar hegemony amid the sharpening tensions of the early Cold War. For most of the immediate postwar period, however, neither the USSR nor the United States had much direct interest in, or engagement with, colonial Africa. Outside of South Africa, where members of a multi-racial Communist party helped to lead trade union struggles like the 1946 miners' strike and played a key role in organizing the African National Congress, Communists were thin on the ground in a continent where industrial working classes were just coming into existence. Moreover, from Moscow's point of view the continent was both too distant and too underdeveloped to play a major role in the security of the USSR and, as ever, this question effectively determined the level of Soviet interest.

During the war, Washington's stance toward colonial Africa was framed by a general, if vague and demagogic, critique of formal empire, but, as a result of limited prewar trade its actual wartime involvement was extremely limited. There were three significant exceptions to this lack of wartime engagement: one was America's own protectorate of Liberia, where rubber production by the Firestone Company expanded dramatically, the second was the importance of securing uranium from the Belgian Congo for use in the nuclear weapons program, and the third was in the independent state of Ethiopia. Here, a 1941 British-Imperial campaign had combined with a local insurgency to overturn Italian rule and return Emperor Haile Selassie to his throne. While London claimed to have restored Ethiopian independence, however, it retained a neocolonial grip on the country through its control of banking, foreign trade, and the main Addis Ababa railroad. Britain's hold was reinforced by its continued military occupation of the Ogaden region of eastern Ethiopia. London's denial of national sovereignty angered both popular opinion and the new Ethiopian government, and in 1944 strong American backing for Addis Ababa forced Britain to sign a renegotiated treaty that greatly expanded Ethiopian sovereignty. Britain still held onto Ogaden, which the 1945 Labour government hoped to merge with British-ruled Somalia, but under American pressure the United Nations rejected these plans. London finally turned Ogaden over to Ethiopia in 1948. Meanwhile, Washington had strengthened its own ties to Ethiopia, making it eligible to receive wartime Lend-Lease aid and organizing a 1945 meeting between Haile Selassie and President Roosevelt before signing a Treaty of Amity and Economic Relations in 1951. A further mutual defense treaty in 1953 gave Ethiopia access to US military equipment and training, while formalizing American operation of a key high-altitude radar base at Kagnew Station in Eritrea and then granting the US Navy access to the key Red Sea port of Massawa in 1957.

For Washington, this relationship with Addis Ababa modeled an ideal neocolonial setup, but the key condition that made it possible—Ethiopia's status as an independent nation-state—simply did not apply to the rest of colonial sub-Saharan Africa. As a result, American involvement in most of Africa was limited by colonial rule throughout the 1950s. In 1960, Africa accounted for only 5 percent of America's world trade, and while American private investment in the continent tripled during the 1950s, it still comprised just 2 percent of US overseas investment.[30] Despite its own limited engagement with Africa, however, Washington was deeply interested in the postwar recovery of Western European and in the overall stability of the capitalist world, and with these goals in mind policymakers dropped earlier critiques of empire and not only endorsed continued colonial rule in sub-Saharan Africa but also agreed to back it with direct and indirect aid. American strategists now saw Africa as a vast strategic reserve area in the event of war with Moscow, and Washington assured its NATO allies that it viewed their colonies as integral parts of their national territories and hence as eligible for defense by the United States. These concerns—advanced despite the lack of evidence for any significant Soviet interest in the region, let alone actual 'penetration'—anchored Washington's pro-colonial stance in the framework of Cold War politics.

Washington's support for ongoing colonial rule in Africa was at odds with the anticolonial proclamations and rhetorical invocations of freedom that were central to its wartime and postwar propaganda. By the early 1950s, some influential American commentators argued that this contradiction presented Washington an acute "dilemma," but policymakers escaped any embarrassment this might have caused them by the claiming that most colonized peoples were simple too "backward" to become self-governing in

---

[30] Vernon McKay, *Africa in World Politics* (New York: Harper & Row, 1963), 278.

the foreseeable future.³¹ "Premature" decolonization, policymakers argued, would simply open the door to Soviet influence, and they proposed that enlightened imperial administrators should continue to exercise "tutelage" over their colonial subjects while modernizing their economies and preparing them for independence in some unspecified future.³² This view, widely held by postwar policymakers and given academic legitimacy in the new area studies departments of American universities, rested on deep racial prejudice: as influential liberal commentator John Gunther explained, Black Africans were simply "too ignorant [...] too backward, childlike, and uneducated" to govern themselves.³³

Roads to Decolonization

Despite their grand postwar plans for imperial revival, by the early 1960s the British and French empires in Africa were in full retreat and the continent they had ruled was increasingly composed of independent nation-states. With hindsight, this continent-wide passage from colonies to nation-states appears natural and inevitable. It did not seem so at the time, not least because many anticolonial activists looked to a future based not on discrete individual nation-states but on expansive supra-national federations. Meeting in Manchester in 1945, many of the ninety delegates to the Fifth Pan-African Congress—including the future presidents of Ghana, Kenya, and Malawi—rejected the label 'nationalist' in favor of visions of freedom that were not delineated by the boundaries of existing colonies or nation-states in-becoming: it was, as conference president W. E. B. DuBois put it, an "idea of one Africa uniting the thought and ideals of all native peoples."³⁴ At the same time, other anticolonial activists doubted that a decisive and immediate break with the metropole was necessary, with Senegalese "African socialist" Léopold Senghor helping to draft the constitution of the new French Union in the hope that its claim of an equitable new relationship between France and its former colonies might actually be realized. With many so many competing futures, the roads that led from colony to nation-state were necessarily complicated.

---

³¹See Harold Isaacs, *Africa, New Crises in the Making* (New York: Foreign Policy Association, 1952), 46; Vernon McKay, "The Rise of Africa in World Politics," in Calvin W. Stillman (ed.), *Africa in the Modern World* (Chicago: University of Chicago Press, 1955), 313, 318; Gunnar Myrdal, *An American Dilemma* (New Brunswick, NJ: Transaction Publishers, 1996) (reprint of 1944 edition), lxix; Cornelius W. deKiewiet, "African Dilemmas," *Foreign Affairs*, Vol. 33, No. 3 (April 1955).
³²George McGhee, "United States Interests in Africa," *Department of State Bulletin*, Vol. 22 (1950), 1000–1.
³³John Gunther, *Inside Africa* (New York: Harper, 1953), 3.
³⁴Philip S. Foner (ed), *W. E. B DuBois Speaks* (New York: Pathfinder Press, (1972) 2021), 205.

In the immediate postwar, the *Rassemblement Démocratique Africain* (RDA), founded as an alliance of anticolonial parties by Ivory Coast coffee planter Félix Houphouët-Boigny, enjoyed significant electoral success across French Africa. In particular, Ahmed Sékou Touré, leader of the Democratic Party of Guinea—an RDA affiliate—led a seventy-one-day general strike that secured a labor code giving African workers the same rights as those in France. In the deepening Cold War, however, the RDA's association with the French Communist Party attracted fierce government repression— particularly in the Ivory Coast—that only eased after it broke its ties to the PCF in 1950. As the RDA became less radical, it also fragmented, with leaders concentrating on their own home territories as the alliance's original trans-territorial anticolonialism devolved into more narrowly focused nationalisms. This shift also reflected the ascendency of educated middle-class elites like Houphouët-Boigny and Senghor over the working-class and peasant radicalism that had driven the postwar wave of labor and anticolonial protest. At the same time, and amid a deepening crisis of its colonial rule in Algeria and in Indochina, Paris retreated from the Union project in favor of less formal neocolonial arrangements. Increasingly, substantial control over domestic affairs was turned over to individual colonial governments, advancing the 'territorialization' upon which discrete nation-states could be built.

In 1958, an empire-wide vote on the constitution of De Gaulle's new Fifth Republic opened the door to national independence within the framework of continued French economic predominance. This neocolonial relationship was structured by the common use of the CFA (African Financial Community) franc that was pegged to France's own currency. Most of France's African colonies voted to accept the new constitution and the continued French influence—or *Françafrique*—that it implied, becoming independent states in a wave of formal decolonization in 1960. In Sékou Touré's Guinea, however, a militant campaign of trade union and student protests secured rejection of the new French constitution in favor of immediate and unconditional independence. Paris responded by canceling aid, encouraging capital flight, and effectively crashing the Guinean economy, and French administrators trashed offices, hospitals, and military facilities on their way out of the country. These acts served notice that while formal colonialism was in retreat across French Africa, neocolonial dependency would be forcefully imposed.

A similar shift from Pan-Africanism to nation-centric visions of postcolonialism also occurred in the British Empire. In Gold Coast, Kwame Nkrumah's Convention People's Party led a wave of postwar anticolonial protests by urban workers, peasants, and ex-soldiers. Nkrumah, who had studied in Britain and the United States and collaborated with West Indian Marxists including George Padmore and C. L. R. James, was a committed Pan-Africanist and an advocate of a socialist United States of Africa. After returning to Gold Coast in 1947, however, Nkrumah concentrated on forging a movement that could lead the fight for national independence within a territorial entity that was already, thanks largely to wartime development, an embryonic nation-state. British officials quickly saw the advantage of working with Nkrumah—after releasing him from prison—to organize an orderly retreat from direct colonial rule. This process, they calculated, would enable Britain to maintain significant economic and political influence in the new nation-state of Ghana even after it became independent in 1957. As prime minister (and then president) of Ghana, Nkrumah continued to promote Pan-Africanism, drawing on the "inspiration of the thirteen American colonies" to buttress arguments for supranational federation and joining Mali and Guinea in a short-lived Union of African States.[35] Nevertheless, and despite offering George Padmore and other anticolonial radicals a home, Nkrumah's practical politics increasingly centered on building a strong nation-state, and an increasingly authoritarian one at that.

Variants of this process of negotiated decolonization—effectively a transfer of political power from colonial administrators to emerging national elites—occurred in Nigeria (independent in 1960) and, after the brutal suppression of the Mau Mau insurgency, in Kenya (1963). A different pattern unfolded in central Africa. Here, London sought to protract both colonial rule and control of the economically important Copperbelt by shackling Northern Rhodesia (Zambia) and Nyasaland (Malawi) to the self-governing colony of Southern Rhodesia (Zimbabwe) in a new Central African Federation (CAF). Formed in 1953, the CAF effectively placed power in the hands of Southern Rhodesia's powerful white minority (250,000 out of a total federal population of over six million). Black African resistance to this scheme was boosted by the militancy of the copper miners, and it produced powerful nationalist movements in Northern Rhodesia and Nyasaland. Resistance to the harsh state of emergency imposed on Nyasaland in 1959—described by an official British inquiry as a "police state"—underscored the impossibility of maintaining colonial rule by force, and squeezed between Black African resistance and the intransigent white minority in Southern Rhodesia, the Federation collapsed in 1963.[36] Britain relinquished control of Malawi and Zambia in 1964, and the following year the Unilateral Declaration of Independence proclaimed by leaders of Rhodesia's white minority established it as an independent nation-state.

As these varied paths demonstrate, there was no simple model for the transition from colony to nation-state. Nevertheless, by the end of the 1950s plans for reformed imperial unions and Pan-African federations, both so influential in 1945, had given way to postcolonial nation-states rooted within

---

[35]Quoted in Adom Getachew, *Worldmaking after Empire: The Rise and Fall of Self Determination* (Princeton: Princeton University Press, 2019), 116.
[36]Thomas, *Fight or Flight*, 216.

the territorial boundaries—and often the administrative structures—of the former colonies. Continued popular resistance had made even reformed versions of colonial rule untenable, but deepening divisions between plebeian radicals and more middle-class—and narrowly nationalist— leaders facilitated the emergence of the nation-state as the normative end point of decolonization. The talk of 'African socialism' that had been central to Pan-African visions in the late 1940s was effectively reduced to window dressing as capitalist nation-states, their economies distorted by the legacies of colonialism and by ongoing neocolonial dependency, structured new forms of exploitation.

Shifts in American Policy toward Africa

In the late 1950s, the accelerating shift from colonial to neocolonial dominance in Africa prompted a sharp turn in American policy. Where Washington had earlier cautioned London and Paris against moving too quickly toward decolonization, its diplomats—acting "in response to decolonization, rather than in support of it," as one historian explains— now scrambled to forge ties with the leaders of emerging African nation-states.[37] Returning from the independence ceremonies in Ghana in 1957, Vice-President Richard Nixon championed this new orientation to what he described as the "most rapidly changing area in the world today."[38] This new approach, codified by the National Security Council in August 1957, overlapped with an awareness that the emergence of new nation-states created new openings for American business as colonial restrictions on trade and capital flows crumbled.

Even as they embraced new independent governments, American policymakers fretted that decolonized nation-states might welcome trade links with the USSR and thus become open to Soviet political influence. Like Nasser, Nkrumah quickly saw the advantage of using economic ties with the USSR as a lever with which to secure more American funding for major infrastructure projects such as the construction of a hydroelectric plant and aluminum smelter on the Volta River. These maneuvers succeeded in winning Washington's support for World Bank funding, and Valco—a joint venture between major US corporations Kaiser Aluminum and ALCOA—took advantage of cheap electricity to build the smelter. Contrary to earlier plans,

---

[37]David N. Gibbs, "Political Parties and International Relation: The United States and the Decolonization of Sub-Saharan Africa," *The International History Review*, Vol. XVII, No. 2 (May 1995), 314.
[38]Richard M. Nixon, "Report to President Eisenhower by Vice President Nixon," *Department of State Bulletin*, April 22, 1957, 635.

however, Valco imported bauxite into Africa instead of using locally mined ore, short-circuiting the broader development of the Ghanian economy that had been the promised goal of the project.

Moscow was also keen to develop economic ties with newly independent states, but while Soviet leaders certainly planned to use trade to gain geopolitical leverage, they had no interest in spreading Communism. In Ghana, the Soviets hoped to secure large supplies of cocoa in exchange for shipments of manufactured goods and equipment, using barter to avoid spending precious dollars. This relationship was a reflection of Soviet weakness, and Nkrumah used it to secure a profitable market for Ghanaian cocoa during a long slump in global commodity prices in the early 1960s. Despite these ties, however, Ghana maintained—as Soviet diplomats noted grumpily—a "strikingly pronounced pro-West orientation."[39] Guinea followed a similar path. Desperate for aid and trade after its economy had been wrecked by France in 1958, Guinea developed trade ties to the USSR, but Moscow's domineering attitude derailed the prospect of building a long-term relationship, and Sékou Touré turned instead to joint ventures with American corporations.

South Africa: Anchor of Imperial Power

As Britain and France faced continent-wide anticolonial protests after the war, their position was reinforced by the development of a strong pro-Western bastion in the Union of South Africa. The Second World War was a boom time for the South African economy, with wartime demand propelling the development of state-owned steel production and boosting a manufacturing sector that far outstripped any other in Africa. War production required the creation of a large and stable working class, and with many white working-class men in the military, that necessitated the employment of women and of Black Africans. This process inevitably began to break down long-standing patterns of racial segregation and, as Black workers established permanent residency in sprawling urban shantytowns, it undercut the labor migration arrangements on which the super-exploitation of African workers was based. Racially mixed workforces also led to some multiracial labor protests, while black gold miners waged a successful strike for higher wages in 1946.

South Africa's rulers profited enormously from the booming wartime economy, but they were alarmed by the social consequences of wartime growth. Led by Afrikaner politicians—the descendants of South Africa's Dutch-speaking settlers—white elites responded by repressing labor unions

---

[39]Oscar Sanchez-Sibony, *Red Globalization: The Political Economy of the Soviet Cold War from Stalin to Khrushchev* (Cambridge: Cambridge University Press, 2014), 230.

and establishing a new system of deep-going racial segregation. Codified after the victory of Daniel Malan's Reunited National Party (HNP) in the 1948 general election, the apartheid system denied South African citizenship to black Africans and assigned them instead to Bantustans—nominally self-governing homelands—that were carved out of some the worst farmland in South Africa. These impoverished territories were in effect puppet statelets of Pretoria whose sole function was to supply migrant workers to South Africa's mines and factories. This drive to reinforce the employment of effectively rightless migrant labor was reinforced by a campaign to prevent Black African workers from establishing permanent residency in the industrial cities where they worked. Black and racially mixed districts and townships were bulldozed, and a strict system of pass laws imposed with the aim of controlling the movement of African workers. On this foundation, apartheid erected a dense thicket of legislation designed to enforce strict racial segregation in all areas of life, in effect imposing a kind of domestic partition that reserved citizenship to the white minority.

Soldiers played an important role in the emergence of apartheid. Voluntary military service in the Second World War had forged new bonds between English- and Afrikaans-speaking soldiers that helped to fashion a common sense of white South Africanness. At the same time, racial divisions within the military explicitly excluded Black Africans from this new national identity. Moreover, while many soldiers initially adopted left-wing views— to the alarm of military censors—they were increasingly drawn to visions of South Africa as a "white man's country" by National Party propaganda that played on fears of postwar competition from Black Africans for jobs and housing.[40] War radicalized South African soldiers as it did those of other armies, and many participated protests demanding rapid demobilization, but in racially polarized South Africa that radicalism—intensified by Pretoria's failure to provide work and homes for returning soldiers—turned in a deeply racist and reactionary direction.

The establishment of the apartheid regime presented American policymakers with a challenge. There was much for Washington to like in apartheid South Africa, including Pretoria's outspoken pro-Western and anti-Communist politics, its participation in the war in Korea, and its willingness to project economic, military, and political power into southern Africa. In 1950, Pretoria began supplying the United States with uranium critical to its nuclear weapons program, and in exchange American government loans and private investment began flowing into South Africa. At the same time, Pretoria's overt and uncompromising racism clashed with Washington's effort to present itself as the worldwide champion of freedom

---

[40]Jonathan Fennell, *Fighting the People's War: The British and Commonwealth Armies and the Second World War* (Cambridge: Cambridge University Press, 2019), 654.

and democracy, particularly at a time when Jim Crow segregation was facing a rising civil rights movement at home and intensified scrutiny abroad. The result, as the 1956 instructions for the new American ambassador to Pretoria made clear, was a tricky balancing act that involved fostering "friendly and harmonious" relations with South Africa without "giving the appearance of supporting apartheid."[41]

Despite these political difficulties, the apartheid regime quickly became a key link in the American-led world-system and one that also functioned as a junior imperialist power in its own right. Outflows of South African capital and inflows of migrant labor into apartheid's mines and mills worked to strengthen colonialism and neocolonialism across a broad swath of the continent, from the Portuguese colonies of Angola and Mozambique and Pretoria's own de facto colony of South West Africa (Namibia) to the more industrialized colonies of the Copperbelt—Northern Rhodesia and the Belgian Congo—and South Rhodesia (Zimbabwe). At the same time, the South African Defence Force, equipped with Western weapons as well as with those produced by its own booming armaments industry, played a major role in battling anticolonial forces across the region. The South African military also helped to organize mercenary forces, including those who defeated the supporters of murdered independence leader Patrice Lumumba in the former Belgian Congo in the early 1960s, paving the way for the establishment of a pro-American dictatorship under Mobutu Sese Seko.

The consolidation of apartheid in the early 1950s snuffed out the wartime flickering of inter-racial working-class unity by effectively wedding white workers to the apartheid state. Nevertheless, despite violent repression—including police attacks on peaceful protests, the long-term imprisonment of anti-apartheid activists, and the collective punishment of entire communities—popular resistance to apartheid by Black Africans, 'coloureds' (people of mixed race), and an increasing number of whites, continued throughout the 1950s. Campaigns of mass civil disobedience were organized by the youth wing of the African National Congress (ANC) under the leadership of young lawyer Nelson Mandela, and in 1955 a mass rally adopted the Freedom Charter as the program of the ANC. The Charter's call for a democratic and multi-racial South African nation-state, framed by its opening declaration that "South Africa belongs to all who live in it, white and black," shaped the mass movement that finally toppled apartheid in 1994.

*

---

[41] Letter, Fred Hadsel (Director of the Office of Southern Africa Affairs) to Henry Byroade, August 3, 1956, *Foreign Relations of the United States 1955–1957*, Vol. XVIII (Africa) (Washington: Government Printing Office, 1988), 786–90.

Speaking to the South African parliament in Cape Town in February 1960 during a month-long tour of Africa, British Prime Minister Harold Macmillan pointed to the "wind of change" that was blowing through the continent: "whether we like it or not," he concluded, "this growth of national consciousness is a political fact." Macmillan's speech, foreshadowing the wave of decolonization that swept British-ruled Africa in the 1960s, is often seen as a turning point in British imperial rule. In reality, the turning point had been passed much earlier. With the independence of the Gold Coast/Ghana already underway, London came to the realization that a broad tide of decolonization was now irresistible and, as a 1957 US-British policy paper put it, Europe's African colonies had to move rapidly toward "stable self-government or independence" in order that the newly emerging nation-states would be "willing and able to preserve their economic and political ties with the West."[42] This realization was fundamentally driven by the exhaustion of British and French hopes for the revitalization of their colonial empires in Africa in the face of rising nationalist pressure, and it registered the accelerating foreclosure of broader pan-African visions of post-coloniality. At the same time, and in the aftermath of the Suez Crisis, this course was also shaped by Washington's own rising interest in the continent. As Britain fell into line with American plans, this—as historians Wm. Roger Louis and Ronald Robinson point out—was truly the "imperialism of decolonization."[43]

For Further Reading

Ervand Abrahamian, *Iran between Two Revolutions* (Princeton: Princeton University Press, 1982).

Judith A. Byfield, "Producing for the War," in Judith A. Byfield et al. (eds.), *Africa and World War II* (Cambridge: Cambridge University Press, 2015).

Frederick Cooper, "Reconstructing Empire in British and French Africa," *Past and Present*, Supplement 6 (2011).

Adom Getachew, *Worldmaking after Empire: The Rise and Fall of Self Determination* (Princeton: Princeton University Press, 2019).

David N. Gibbs, "Political Parties and International Relation: The United States and the Decolonization of Sub-Saharan Africa," *The International History Review*, Vol. XVII, No. 2 (May 1995).

Douglas Little, *American Orientalism: The United States and the Middle East since 1945* (Chapel Hill: University of North Carolina Press, 2002).

---

[42]U.S.-U.K. joint paper, March 13, 1957, "Means of Combatting Communist Influence in Tropical Africa," *Foreign Relations of the United States, 1955–57*, Vol. XXVII, 759.

[43]Louis and Robinson, "The Imperialism of Decolonization," 495.

Wm. Roger Louis and Ronald Robinson, "The Imperialism of Decolonization," *Journal of Imperial and Commonwealth History*, Vol. 22, No. 3 (1994).

Oscar Sanchez-Sibony, *Red Globalization: The Political Economy of the Soviet Cold War from Stalin to Khrushchev* (Cambridge: Cambridge University Press, 2014).

Martin Thomas, *Fight or Flight: Britain, France, and Their Roads from Empire* (Oxford: Oxford University Press, 2014).

Vladislav M. Zubok, "Stalin, Soviet Intelligence and the Struggle for Iran, 1945–53," *Diplomatic History*, Vol. 44, No. 1 (January 2020).

CHAPTER SEVEN

Hemispheric Bedrock: Latin America and the Caribbean

The 1946 Haitian Revolt

In January 1946, a five-day general strike and a popular insurrection combined to topple the US-backed dictatorship of Élie Lescot in Haiti. Set in motion by radical students, some self-proclaimed Marxists and some Black nationalists, this turbulent movement of workers, peasant farmers, and agricultural laborers—many of them women—took control of the streets of Port-au-Prince before fanning out across the country. Radical leaders pictured themselves in the tradition of the great Haitian Revolution, proclaiming "1804 was a revolution [...] and now 1946!"[1] The uprising was a product of wartime hardships, including the failure of a US-backed scheme to create rubber plantations that had led to the forcible eviction of peasant families from 50,000 acres of farmland. Like other contemporary insurrections and rebellions, however, the Haitian uprising was also inspired by a profound sense that the end of the world war came pregnant with new opportunities to create a better society.

The 1946 revolt opened a decade of political instability in Haiti during which organized mass mobilizations of students, trade unionists, and peasant farmers were a constant feature of political life. In the weeks after the revolt anything seemed possible as new newspapers and political parties debated the road forward in a climate of unprecedented freedom. Nevertheless, in the absence of a radical force capable of establishing a new

---

[1] Matthew J. Smith, "Vive 1804!: The Haitian Revolution and the Revolutionary Generation of 1946," *Caribbean Quarterly*, Vol. 50, No. 4 (December 2004), 25.

government, political power quickly passed into the hands of a three-man military junta whose interim rule was approved by the American ambassador. The junta presided over the election of a new National Assembly, which in August 1946 nominated Dumarsais Estimé as president. A moderate Black nationalist who enjoyed the backing of the Haitian military, Estimé had served as minister of education before the war. He now walked a fine line, navigating between popular pressure for sweeping social reform on the one hand and American-backed elites fearful of radical change on the other. Estimé brought militant trade union leader Daniel Fignolé into the government along with pro-Moscow Communists from the Parti Socialiste Popularie (PSP), but he quickly broke with them when it became clear that their presence blocked closer economic ties to the United States. In reality, Moscow had little interest in Haiti, and the PSP, like other regional Communist parties, was more concerned with maneuvering for influence within the existing political setup than in leading a struggle to overthrow it. Moreover, radical forces in Haiti remained deeply divided between those who saw questions of social class—and US hegemony—as the decisive issues, and those Black nationalists who focused on long-standing divisions between the dark-skinned black majority and the lighter-skinned mulatto elite that dominated Haitian society.

The sometimes-violent divisions driven by these complex intersections of race and class helped to block the development of a unified popular movement in Haiti. In practice, Black nationalism often served as a convenient ideological tool to advance the interests of Black businessmen, administrators, and professionals who had long faced discrimination and exclusion at the hands of the mulatto elite favored by the United States. Moreover, Haitian politics played out under the watchful gaze of the United States, which had a long history of direct intervention—including a nineteen-year military occupation from 1915 to 1934—and which maintained close ties to the top echelons of the Haitian military. Under these competing pressures the postwar decade was marked by a dizzying kaleidoscope of governments and political alliances that culminated, after a rigged national election in 1957, in the presidency of François Duvalier. Duvalier's dictatorial regime, which cloaked itself in Black nationalism and claimed legitimacy from the 1946 revolt, used the brutal paramilitary *Tonton Makout* to crush its political opponents. Despite his outspoken anti-Communism, Duvalier's strident nationalism and sometimes unpredictable behavior meant that he was not Washington's ideal ally, but American policymakers recognized that his dictatorship brought stability after a decade of popular radicalism.

Like much of the Caribbean and Latin America, Haiti had little direct involvement in the Second World War. At Washington's bidding, Élie Lescot's government declared war on the Axis after the Japanese attack on Pearl Harbor, but beyond providing a base for a US Coast Guard squadron that conducted anti-submarine patrols in the Caribbean, Haiti played no part in the fighting. With the exceptions of a Brazilian Expeditionary Force that fought with the Allies in Italy and a Mexican fighter squadron that joined American forces in the Philippines, other Latin America and the Caribbean states made similarly modest military commitments to the war. Despite their lack of direct military involvement, however, the participation of Haiti and other Latin American and Caribbean states in the US-led United Nations signaled a broad reshaping of hemispheric politics as the United States utilized the war crisis to consolidate its regional predominance. Moreover, while weathering a wave of postwar radicalism that broke across the continent with particular force, Washington leveraged this regional predominance to underpin its efforts to construct a new global hegemony. Far from being a neglected backwater in a hegemonic project focused elsewhere, Latin America was the indispensable bedrock upon which the new American-led postwar order was constructed.

Good Neighbors

Washington's wartime engagement with Latin America built on the Roosevelt administration's Good Neighbor policy, first announced in December 1933. Framed by the assertion that the "democratically oriented nations of the Western Hemisphere" shared a common adherence to liberty and an "aversion to the use of force" as an instrument of national policy, the 'Good Neighbor' was more a general approach than a unified course of action.[2] Indeed, the policy is chiefly remembered for what it promised *not* to do: no longer, Roosevelt pledged, would the United States intervene militarily in the domestic affairs of its southern neighbors. While the promised abandonment of armed intervention turned out to be more of a temporary suspension, the new policy nevertheless signaled the end of the invasions and occupations that had dominated US relations with Central America and the Caribbean in the early twentieth century. The true heart of good neighborliness, however, lay in Washington's promotion of multinational and bilateral ties to the states of Latin America—including diplomatic alliances, military cooperation agreements, and trade pacts—that were designed to bind them to the United States in a tight hemispheric bloc.

Washington's new policy unfolded as the Depression-era collapse in world commodity prices slashed Latin American incomes from the export of agricultural goods and industrial raw materials, producing a continent-wide crisis of unemployment, inflation, and desperate poverty. In response, many Latin American governments hoped to use state power to promote

---

[2]State Department memorandum, September 12, 1939, quoted in Gerald K. Haines, "Under the Eagle's Wing: The Franklin Roosevelt Administration Forges an American Hemisphere," *Diplomatic History*, Vol. 1, No. 4 (1977), 373–4.

domestic industrial development, thereby reducing reliance on semi-colonial relationships based on the export of (cheap) raw materials and the import of (expensive) manufactured goods. In this context, the Good Neighbor policy emerged as the pan-American projection of the autarkic impulse towards self-reliance that was central to Roosevelt's domestic New Deal. Speaking at the inter-American conference in Buenos Aires in 1936, Roosevelt endorsed the development agendas advanced by several Latin American governments, linking the achievement of the "highest possible standard of living conditions for all our people" to regional cooperation, peace, and American leadership.[3] At the same time, the Roosevelt administration expected that the United States would benefit directly from economic development in Latin America as industrialization opened new markets for American investment, capital goods, and technical know-how while newly flourishing regional economies consumed American manufactured goods.

Given Washington's long history of armed intervention in the region, many in Latin America were inclined to take its new professions of neighborliness with a pinch of salt. Moreover, during the 1930s American business faced increasing competition in Latin America from Germany and the other Axis powers. Outspoken right-wing nationalism appealed to dictatorial strong men—or *caudillo*—like the Dominican Republic's Rafael Trujillo, and the 'corporative state' established in Mussolini's Fascist Italy was an influential model. Corporatism—which claimed to manage the economy through mutually beneficial collaboration between bosses, workers, and the state officials—was particularly influential in Brazil, where it inspired the *Estado Novo* (New State) set up by Getúlio Vargas following a military coup in 1937. Substantial Fascist-inspired parties operated in Brazil and several other countries. Backed by Berlin, German business interests also made headway across the continent, using export subsidies, barter, and guaranteed prices for Latin American goods to craft attractive trade agreements. Brazil, Costa Rica, the Dominican Republic, and Guatemala all signed bilateral agreements with Berlin, and German trade with Brazil doubled between 1933 and 1938.[4] German trade with Argentina and Mexico also soared, while Italian airlines established routes across the South Atlantic and German-funded national airlines operated throughout the continent. Not without reason, Washington feared that this booming trade would enable the Axis powers to advance their political and military position in Latin America, undermining the United States' influence in what it had long seen as its own backyard.

---

[3]Eric Helleiner, *Forgotten Foundations of Bretton Woods: International Development and the Making of the Postwar Order* (Ithaca, NY: Cornell University Press, 2014), 35.
[4]John F. Bratzel, Introduction to Thomas M. Leonard and John F. Bratzel (eds.), *Latin America during World War II* (Lanham, MD: Rowman and Littlefield, 2007), 7.

As war loomed in Europe, Washington moved to expand and secure its regional predominance, pushing—as senior diplomat Adolf Berle put it—to "intensify our South American policy to the limit."[5] Following Washington's lead, delegates to the 1939 Pan-American Conference in Panama proclaimed the neutrality of the western hemisphere and established a Pan-American Security Zone that extended up to one thousand miles into the Atlantic and Pacific oceans. The assembled foreign ministers declared that within this broad sea space, later unilaterally extended by President Roosevelt to include Iceland, belligerent acts like submarine attacks on merchant shipping would be met with armed force. A subsequent conference in Havana, Cuba, in July 1940 reaffirmed the maritime security zone and, in an agreement sweetened by promises of American aid, established a continent-wide mutual defense pact. These hemispheric agreements were buttressed by a dense thicket of bilateral military agreements, and by December 1941 teams of US advisers were based in every Latin American country except Argentina. Meanwhile, American troops secured critical bauxite (aluminum ore) mines by occupying the Dutch colony of Surinam after Germany occupied Holland in summer 1940, and in September Washington established military bases in Britain's Caribbean colonies in exchange for fifty aging US warships. In Washington, this intensified regional engagement was registered in July 1941 by the establishment of the Office of the Coordinator of Inter-American Affairs, an executive body headed by wealthy businessman Nelson Rockefeller. Charged with expanding economic and cultural ties with Latin America, the OCIAA promoted Hollywood movies, organized cultural exchanges, and spread pro-American propaganda throughout the continent. At the same time, more hard-edged OCIAA programs aimed to promote military cooperation and to provide FBI training for regional police forces.

These moves enabled Washington to marshal Costa Rica, Cuba, the Dominican Republic, El Salvador, Guatemala, Haiti, Honduras, Nicaragua, and Panama—ironically the states that had borne the brunt of US military intervention in the early twentieth century—into declarations of war against the Axis powers in December 1941. Despite the fact that they made no commitments to military action, formal entry into the world war qualified these states to participate in the January 1942 Declaration by the United Nations. This statement, modeled on the liberal war aims codified by Britain and the United States in the August 1941 Atlantic Charter, gave ideological shape to the wartime Grand Alliance and laid the initial framework for the postwar United Nations Organization. The inclusion of this initial group of Latin American countries—they would

---

[5]Helleiner, *Forgotten Foundations*, 44.

be joined by more in the coming years—simultaneously signaled their incorporation into America's coming world order as independent nation-states *and* the consolidation of a powerful hemispheric bloc under United States' leadership.

These transcontinental developments were underpinned by a thickening web of bilateral ties between the United States and individual Latin American nation-states. High-level delegations of American policymakers and bankers visited Cuba (1941–42) and Paraguay (1943–44) to work with local officials on wide-ranging monetary and financial 'reforms.' The mission to Paraguay was deemed particularly successful, with the establishment of a new central bank and a national currency being seen as key preconditions for accelerated industrialization. While liberal New Dealers like Harry Dexter White (Treasury) and Robert Triffin (Federal Reserve Board) presented these reforms as steps toward rounded economic development, the actual measures that they put in place effectively subordinated Paraguay's financial sector to its powerful counterparts in the United States. Subsequent missions achieved similar results in Bolivia, Costa Rica, the Dominican Republic, and Guatemala (all in 1945) and in Ecuador in 1947.

Washington's Wartime Relations with Brazil, Mexico, and Argentina

Washington's push to consolidate its hemispheric predominance hinged above all on its relations with Argentina, Brazil, and Mexico, the three most powerful Latin American states. Given its self-proclaimed affinity with fascism, Vargas' *Estado Novo* initially sought to maintain a position of "pragmatic equilibrium" between Germany, Britain, and the United States by cultivating good relations with all three.[6] The outbreak of war in Europe upended this approach, with British naval operations effectively blocking trade with Germany while the demands of Britain's own wartime economy curtailed loans and exports to Brazil. These developments opened the door to closer ties between Brazil and the United States. In May 1939, a visit by US Army chief of staff George Marshall paved the way for bilateral military cooperation, and the following year Roosevelt encouraged Pan American Airlines to begin work on a transatlantic air route to Africa via new airfields at Natal and Belém in northeast Brazil. Under Pan American's Airport Development Program, work began on twenty-nine Brazilian bases,

---

[6]Leslie Bethell, "Brazil," in Leslie Bethell and Ian Roxborough (eds.), *Latin America between the Second World War and the Cold War, 1944–1948* (Cambridge: Cambridge University Press, 1992), 33.

constructing a flyway that connected into Britain's 'Takoradi Route' across Africa.[7] This link soon proved critical for moving American supplies and reinforcements to embattled British-Imperial forces in Egypt, and it also established an air route across the Middle East and on to India.

After German submarines sank eighteen Brazilian merchant ships in early 1942, Rio declared war on the Axis in August, a decision that was followed by the signing of a bilateral defense agreement and the rapid expansion of military ties with the United States. Over the next three years Brazil received over 70 percent of all the Lend-Lease aid sent to Latin America, while Brazilian officers trained in the United States and a 25,000-person Brazilian Expeditionary Force, equipped and trained by the United States, joined Allied forces fighting in Italy in 1944. Leveraging its geographical and political position to maximum advantage, Rio used American aid to develop the strongest military in Latin America—surpassing Argentina—while staking a claim to regional leadership under US hegemony. Under American pressure, Brazilian airlines were 'de-Germanized,' and with US funding and equipment Varig developed a network of national, continental, and—in the 1950s—international routes. Meanwhile, US business interests took the opportunity of the enforced rupture of trade with Germany and Britain to move into Brazilian markets: in one striking case, the American Electrical Export Corporation pushed aside Manchester-based Metropolitan-Vickers' bid to electrify the Central Brazilian Railway despite London's energetic support for the British company. American trade and financial missions offered advice on Brazil's industrial development, and a massive Import-Export Bank loan funded the construction of the government-owned Volta Redonda steel mill. This plant, originally planned in collaboration with German capital, was the first major steel mill in Latin America and was a potent symbol both of Brazilian industrialization and of Washington's commitment to economic modernization.

After Washington formally entered the war in December 1941, Pan-American's airfields in northern Brazil came under US military control. Initially, relations between the US military personnel assigned to these new bases and Brazilian civilians, police, and legal systems were regulated by local agreements negotiated by American diplomats. When these ad hoc arrangements failed to resolve jurisdictional issues in cases involving American military personnel, Brazil's Supreme Court ruled in November 1944 that the country's courts were not competent to hear such cases. The US embassy lobbied hard to secure this ruling, which essentially secured extraterritorial rights for US military personnel based in Brazil. Since these soldiers often behaved with scant respect for local people and their laws and

---

[7]Rebecca Herman, *Cooperating with the Colossus: A Social and Political History of US Military Bases in World War II Latin America* (Oxford: Oxford University Press, 2022), 55–6.

customs, news of the Supreme Court ruling was kept secret lest news of this blatant abandonment of Brazilian sovereignty inflamed popular opposition to the American military presence.

War also reset relations between the United States and Mexico that had been strained during the presidency (1934–40) of leftist nationalist Lázaro Cárdenas. Claiming to stand on the radical legacy of the 1910 Mexican Revolution, the Cárdenas government had responded to the discriminatory treatment of Mexican workers by American oil companies by nationalizing their operations in Mexico with minimal compensation in 1938. As the approach of war boosted the demand for oil, however, Cárdenas' successor Manuel Ávila Camacho—elected in 1940—moved to restore relations with the United States. This rapprochement was eased by the fact that Cárdenas had been the only regional head of state to speak out against fascism, and it was sealed by Mexico's declaration of war on the Axis powers in May 1942. Unlike Brazil, Mexico refused to allow US bases on its soil, but its military eagerly accepted American equipment and training, and in 1944 a squadron of Mexican aircraft was dispatched to join US forces fighting in the Pacific. Mexico's booming wartime economy was firmly oriented toward the United States, with cross-border trade jumping from 56 percent of Mexican exports in 1937–8 to over ninety percent by 1940.[8] At the same time, over 300,000 Mexican workers went north to work on American farms under the 1942 Bracero Program. As Mexican migrant workers filled jobs vacated by Americans conscripted into the military, this bilateral agreement made a major contribution to the American war effort. Ávila Camacho used appeals to national unity to expand the corporate state established by Cárdenas, drawing representatives of industry, middle-class professionals, and the officer corps into what was effectively a one-party state led the Party of the Mexican Revolution (PRM).

Washington's wartime relations with Argentina headed in a very different direction. Argentina's long-standing ties to Britain—based on the export of beef and wheat—allowed it to accumulate substantial trade surpluses in the early part of the war, and industrial capitalists collaborated with sectors of the old landowning elite and the military to use state power to promote modest but real industrial development. Economic development reinforced Buenos Aires' long-standing self-image as the natural leader of Latin America and strengthened its resistance to Washington's drive to consolidate its own regional predominance. Opposition to the United States was reflected first in a determined refusal to break ties with the Axis powers and then in resistance to joining the war against them until the very last minute.

---

[8] Ian Roxborough, "Mexico," in Leslie Bethell and Ian Roxborough (eds.), *Latin America between the Second World War and the Cold War, 1944–1948* (Cambridge: Cambridge University Press, 1992), 194–5.

In 1943, a military coup strengthened Argentina's wartime neutralism as Colonel Juan Domingo Perón, a leading figure in the new government, built a base of support among Argentinian workers that acted as a counterweight to American pressure. Wage increases, state-funded pensions, and annual holiday bonuses combined with the sense of national pride generated by economic advance to solidify Perón's base of support within the country's powerful trade union movement. Wrapped in populist appeals to national unity and social justice, Perón's regime earned Washington's profound enmity. Throughout the war and well into the postwar, American policymakers routinely denounced Perón as a fascist even as they portrayed Vargas as a paragon of democracy. As punishment for its stubborn opposition to American hegemony, Washington excluded Argentina from the Bretton Woods conference in summer 1944 and blocked London's attempt to tie Argentina into its postwar sterling zone. This move had the additional benefit of undercutting British efforts to use trade with Argentina as a bridgehead for the postwar reestablishment of its own economic influence in Latin America.

The Consolidation of Washington's Regional Hegemony, 1944–48

Between 1944 and 1948, the strengthening of bilateral ties between Washington and countries across Latin America advanced hand in hand with the consolidation of its overarching regional hegemony. This complex process was based on the expansion of American economic influence and military might, reflected in the creation of over 200 US bases across Latin America and the Caribbean and in the development of bilateral ties with armed forces throughout the region.[9] At the same time, however, hegemony also required the negotiated development of political leadership on a continent-wide level. In this process, Latin American governments participated in a genuine dialogue with Washington, and while they certainly hoped to benefit from bilateral and multilateral ties to northern colossus, they also sought to use their collective influence to constrain unilateral action by the United States. In this way Latin American governments became active agents in the shaping of new regional relationships rather than simply being the objects of that process. Along this road, the United States' government and its regional collaborators built on a long history of state-level inter-American cooperation, effectively layering Washington's new push to consolidate regional predominance onto the pre-existing

---

[9]Herman, *Cooperating with the Colossus*, 1.

pattern of Pan-American conferences, meetings of foreign ministers, and other region-wide organizations.

This dynamic new relationship was showcased by the January 1942 declaration of the United Nations and reprised more fully at the Bretton Woods conference in July 1944. As we saw in Chapter One, Bretton Woods marked an important step toward establishing a new American-led world economic order based on free trade and the primacy of the gold-backed US dollar. In addition, however, the conference placed considerable emphasis on promoting the economic development of the global south through the creation of the International Bank for Reconstruction and Development (IBRD) and the International Monetary Fund. In advancing this developmental agenda, Washington drew on the experience of its own work with Latin American governments. Representatives from Latin American accounted for nineteen of the forty-four delegations participating in the Bretton Woods, and their collective weight was reflected in the choice of Mexican Finance Minister Eduardo Suárez to chair one of the conference's three major commissions. The forceful presence of Latin America did not sit well with London, with British delegation leader John Maynard Keynes grumbling that "the vote of Costa Rica is the same as that of the United Kingdom."[10] In the long run, Washington's promotion of development and modernization worked to tie the global south into US-dominated networks of trade and finance, but in a message effectively buttressed by the active participation of Latin American delegates, these relationships were presented as mutually beneficial and politically progressive.

The United States also wielded its leadership of this hemispheric bloc to great effect at the International Civil Aviation Conference held in Chicago in November 1944. Called to set rules for the worldwide operation of civilian airlines, this meeting of fifty-two nations was framed in effusively global language: as top American diplomat Adolf Berle proclaimed, the "air" was a "highway given by nature to all men."[11] Beyond the rhetoric, however, Washington had a hard-edged agenda that centered on promoting unregulated "open skies," a proposal that entrenched its own predominance in civil aviation while marginalizing London's effort to defend its prewar monopoly on air transportation within the British Empire. In a critical vote, eight Latin American governments—Brazil, Cuba, Ecuador, Mexico Nicaragua, Panama, Peru, and Venezuela—voted with Washington to ensure the defeat of the British position. In return, Washington dropped a proposal for the leadership of the new International Civil Aviation Organization that the Latin Americans saw as reducing them to a "riff-raff

---

[10]Helleiner, *Forgotten Foundations of Bretton Woods*, 159–60.
[11]Jenifer Van Vleck, *Empire of the Air: Aviation and the American Ascendancy* (Cambridge: Harvard University Press, 2013), 184.

of smaller nations," and endorsed a joint Cuban-Mexican plan instead.[12] This show of magnanimity secured Washington's victory on the main issue before the conference while burnishing its image as a hegemon that listened sympathetically to the "smaller nations" in its orbit.

In early 1945, the Inter-American Conference on Problems of War and Peace, meeting at Chapultepec, Mexico City, brought these relationships together at a pan-American level. Carefully prepared by Rockefeller's Office of the Coordinator of Inter-American Affairs, the Chapultepec meeting restated the Bretton Woods conference's insistence on lowering tariff barriers and promoting free market access to trade and raw materials. While American officials continued to talk about regional development, they also made clear their preference for limited government intervention and reliance on market forces.[13] The resulting 'Act of Chapultepec' also addressed concerns that pan-American cooperation would be marginalized in the new United Nations by laying the basis for a regional security pact that was formally adopted in Rio two years later. Reflecting their new regional standing, Brazilian leaders argued that the United Nations should recognize "regional understandings" like the Act of Chapultepec in order that Latin American states could help "safeguard the peace and security of the world."[14] After some heated discussion—and Argentina's declaration of war on the Axis on March 15, 1945—Washington also grudgingly bent to Latin American pressure and agreed that the Argentinians should be invited to the founding conference of the United Nations.

Washington used this success in consolidating its regional hegemony to reinforce its overall standing at the founding conference of the United Nations in San Francisco, held from April to June 1945. Here, American delegates argued that the Pan-American security system codified at Chapultepec complemented the United Nations rather than undermining it, and this interlocking system of global and regional commitments was embedded in Article 51 of the United Nations Charter, which recognized an "inherent right" to "collective self-defense" against "armed attack."[15] At the same time, Washington denied that regional blocs led by Britain and the Soviet Union could play a similar function because, as former secretary of state Cordell Hull put it, only the United States could demonstrate the "economic and other self-restraint" needed to play such a leadership role.[16] This approach gave Washington tremendous leverage at San Francisco,

---

[12]Van Vleck, *Empire of the Air*, 186.
[13]Herman, *Cooperating with the Colossus*, 181.
[14]Tom Long, "Historical Antecedents and Post-World War II Regionalism in the Americas," *World Politics*, Vol. 72, No. 2 (April 2020), 234.
[15]United Nations Charter, available at https://legal.un.org/repertory/art51.shtml
[16]Gabriel Kolko, *The Politics of War: The World and United States Foreign Policy, 1943–1945* (New York: Pantheon, (1968) 1990), 459.

where Latin American diplomats—carefully managed by Rockefeller and accounting for nearly half of the conference delegates—gave the United States' proposals their unwavering support.

After Chapultepec, the Truman administration initially planned to move quickly to formalize a regional defense agreement, but renewed tensions with Argentina forced the postponement of the Rio conference until September 1947. In the time between the two conferences, however, Washington was also forced to adjust to mounting popular opposition to the maintenance of permanent US military bases in Latin America. US troops were formally withdrawn from Brazil in March 1947, and at the end of the year widespread protests forced the abandonment of the Filós-Hines agreement that would have permitted the ongoing operation of US military bases in Panama. The loss of formal basing rights was mitigated by the fact that senior American commanders were confident that Latin America was securely in Washington's orbit, and consequently *access* to bases, structured through bilateral military agreements, was more important than the permanent control and the long-term basing of US troops. Moreover, as Rebecca Herman points out, despite "boisterous ceremonies" celebrating the return of US bases to sovereign control, American personnel often stayed behind—and out of uniform—to train the local military.[17]

These shifts were embodied in the September 1947 Inter-American Treaty of Mutual Assistance (the Rio Pact). The new treaty built on the mutual defense agreement initialed in Havana in 1940, and it was based on the idea that an attack on one American republic would be considered an attack on all. Framed by Article 51 of the UN Charter and based on formal principles of national equality, nonintervention, and common self-defense, American leaders made it clear that the new pact would expand the definition of "armed attack" to include domestic "subversion or political attack."[18] In the context of the rapidly deepening Cold War in Europe, Washington's Latin American allies were already framing even modest domestic political challenges as "subversion" and, urged on by the United States, opposition to Communism was made explicit in the discussions that led to the formation of the Organization of American States at Bogotá, Colombia, in 1948.

A Latin American Front in the Postwar Labor Insurgency

Despite its distance from the fighting fronts, the waves of popular militancy that accompanied the long transition from war to postwar elsewhere in the world also broke over Latin America. In Mexico, an upsurge in labor

---

[17]Herman, *Cooperating with the Colossus*, 197.
[18]Long, "Historical Antecedents," 241.

struggles peaked in 1944 with 887 strikes, while in Chile the number of strikes rose from just 19 in 1942 to 196 in 1946, and Brazil experienced two bursts of labor militancy, one in spring 1945 and the next in winter 1946.[19] This wave of strikes, many of them launched in the face of state repression, expressed a deep upwelling of working-class anger that was driven—as elsewhere—by wartime privation. Particularly in the more developed economies and those directly tied to the United States' war effort by the production of critical raw materials, wartime industrialization and the accompanying migration to urban centers had produced large new working classes. In Mexico, the number of manufacturing workers jumped from 568,000 in 1940 to 922,000 in 1945, while in Argentina it grew from 633,000 in 1941 to 938,000 in 1946 and Brazil's manufacturing workforce went from 995,000 in 1940 to 1,608,000 a decade later.[20] These growing industrial working classes resulted in rapidly increasing trade union membership, and by 1946 at least four million workers were unionized continent-wide, many of them in key sectors of industry and transportation.[21]

For many newly proletarianized workers arriving from the countryside, the "normal" difficulties of rapid urbanization like poor housing and minimal social services were compounded by wartime price inflation and by wages held down by social pacts and no-strike pledges justified by the needs of the Allied war effort. As the end of the war approached, these conditions drove workers to act, and their strikes formed a distinct Latin American front in the worldwide labor upsurge. As elsewhere in the world, labor militancy intersected with broader social and political struggles—such as those in Haiti—as wartime shocks created new openings and opportunities to press for greater political freedom. Moreover, in Brazil, Cuba, Ecuador, and Panama, labor militancy also fueled mounting popular opposition to American military bases. As a result, in a concentrated two-year window between 1944 and 1946 a series of popular uprisings and electoral overturns pushed back military dictatorships and opened new democratic space in countries across the continent.

Led by a coalition that included both Communists and conservatives, a popular rebellion in Ecuador in May 1944 prompted a military coup that toppled the dictatorship of Carlos Arroyo del Río, set up a constituent assembly, and installed populist demagogue José María Velasco Ibarra as president. At the start of the war, the United States

---

[19]Leslie Bethell and Ian Roxborough, "Introduction: The Postwar Conjuncture in Latin America: Democracy, Labor, and the Left," in Leslie Bethell and Ian Roxborough (eds.), *Latin America between the Second World War and the Cold War, 1944–1948* (Cambridge: Cambridge University Press, 1992), 14–15.
[20]Ibid., 13.
[21]Ibid., 13–14.

had established its own military presence in the country, and Arroyo's willingness to permit the construction of a US base in the Galapagos Islands now fueled opposition to his regime. Other popular revolts followed. In July 1944, the long Guatemalan dictatorship of Jorge Ubico was ended by an uprising that led to the election of 'spiritual socialist' Juan José Arévalo, while in Bolivia a bloody insurrection ousted the military government of Gualberto Villarroel in July 1946. This revolt, which included strikes by well-organized tin miners, schoolteachers, and students, was led by the *Frente Democrático Antifascista*, another broad coalition that included both Communists and conservative elites. Not all revolts were successful: in El Salvador, the dictatorship was toppled in spring 1944 only to be restored in the fall, while in Honduras protests initially led by women demanding the release of political prisoners shook the military government but did not bring it down. A split in the liberal camp in Colombia allowed a Conservative victory in 1946, and an intense revolt—the *Bogotazo*—launched in 1948 in response to the murder of liberal presidential candidate Jorge Eliécer Gaitán opened ten years of political violence.

This cluster of insurgencies—both successful and unsuccessful—was accompanied by a string of electoral victories by left-leaning parties and coalitions, many of them contesting the first free elections in many years. In Cuba, military dictator Fulgencio Batista's handpicked successor lost to Ramón Grau, leader of the nationalist *Auténtico* party, while the Renewal Party—a liberal coalition—won the May 1945 elections in Panama, and in June the leftist American Popular Revolutionary Alliance (APRA) carried José Luis Bustamante y Rivero to victory in Peru. In many countries, radical middle-class forces—advocates of democracy and of socially progressive measures like moderate land reform—came to the fore, reflecting the political interests of the national capitalist classes that had benefitted most from wartime economic development and from ties with the United States. Some, like the APRA, were capable of extremely radical rhetoric, which allowed them to develop ties with newly unionized working classes.

These developments were reflected—in distorted forms—in the region's three largest countries. In Mexico, Miguel Alemán, Ávila Camacho's chosen successor, won nearly the 80 percent of the vote in the July 1946 election: as the vote suggests, the PRM—newly renamed the Institutional Revolutionary Party (PRI)—maintained its tight grip on Mexican politics. In Brazil, military leaders tied to conservative landowning elites forced Vargas out of office in a soft coup in October 1945, but just two months later former minister of war General Eurico Dutra defeated a coalition of anti-Vargas forces in a relatively free election. In an electorate that included just 35 percent of the adult population—up from 10 percent in 1930—Vargas' appeal to the Brazilian working class on Dutra's behalf played a critical role

FIGURE 7.1 *General Juan Perón addresses a mass rally of his supporters, Buenos Aires, Argentina, January 1, 1955. (Photo: Keystone/Hulton Archive/Getty Images.)*

in his victory.[22] A similar pattern unfolded in Argentina. Here, senior officers concerned by Juan Perón's social radicalism purged him from the military junta in September 1945, only to see him sprung from prison by massive street protests organized by the General Confederation of Labor and led by his future wife Evita Duarte. Buoyed by these dramatic events, Perón defeated the candidate of a coalition that included both conservative elites and Communists to win the presidency in February 1946. Perón's victory, won despite the direct intervention of the American ambassador in favor of his opponent, rested in large part on his ability to connect with and mobilize working-class voters.

Populism, Communism, and the United States

In the immediate postwar period, liberal political forces that were tied to the emerging industrial bourgeoisie and that drew on nationalist rhetoric for their legitimacy and on working-class mobilizations for their strength

---

[22]Leslie Bethell, "Brazil," in Leslie Bethell and Ian Roxborough (eds.) *Latin America between the Second World War and the Cold War, 1944–1948* (Cambridge: Cambridge University Press, 1992), 55–6.

made the running across much of Latin America. The regimes they created are often referred to as populist, an overused term but one that works well enough in this context. Under different ideological guises, all embraced corporatist visions of the harmonious integration of capital, labor, and the military into a unified national project that was led by a benevolent leader or—as in Mexico—an all-powerful party. To be effective, populist regimes had to ensure that at least a modest sliver of the wealth generated by wartime industrialization flowed to the working class, and in particular to those organized in pro-government unions. Moreover, these material benefits were intertwined with a new sense of national pride: in Argentina, for example, many workers were inspired by the locally designed cars, trucks, and refrigerators produced by the State Aeronautical and Mechanical Industries, flagship of Perónist industrialization. Likewise, Vargas attempted to draw Afro-Brazilians into his nationalist project by criticizing long-standing structural racism and advocating a "racial democracy" and a "mixed" nation.[23]

Support for populism in Latin America was in part a reflection of the relative newness and political inexperience of the industrial working classes, but it was also a product of the political leadership offered by many regional Communist parties. When the first Communist parties were formed in Latin America in the 1920s, leaders like Peruvian José Carlos Mariátegui had sought to apply Marxism to local conditions. Mariátegui argued that despite Latin America's relative economic underdevelopment, its integration into the circuits of global capitalism meant that popular revolutions could move quickly toward anti-capitalism and socialism without having to pass through an extended stage of "bourgeois democracy."[24] With the rise of Stalinism in the Soviet Union, however, this revolutionary perspective was replaced by an insistence on a "two-stage" model—first liberal democracy, then socialism—that advocated strategic alliances with "progressive" wings of the local bourgeoisie against the old "feudal" landowning elites. This orientation was reinforced during the Second World War, when its policy of forging a global "antifascist" alliance led Moscow to instruct Latin American Communists to back regimes—including repressive dictatorships—that were supporting the Allied war effort.

This approach had contradictory consequences. On the one hand, rapid economic expansion, growing working classes, and periods of at least semi-legality led to the continent-wide growth of Communist parties, whose aggregate membership grew from 25,000 in 1935 to half a million in

---

[23]Alexandre Fortes, "World War II and Brazilian Workers: Populism at the Intersection between National and Global Histories," *International Review of Social History*, Vol. 62 (2017), Special Issue, 187.

[24]Tanya Harmer, "The Cold War in Latin America," in Artemy M. Kalinovsky and Craig Daigle (eds.), *The Routledge Handbook of the Cold War* (Abingdon, Oxford: Routledge, 2014), 138.

1947.[25] At the same time, Moscow's 'popular front' policy led many Latin American Communists to tie themselves into the framework of existing capitalist states. In Cuba, for example, the Communist Revolutionary Union (later renamed the Popular Socialist Party) backed Fulgencio Batista in the 1940 elections, attacking his liberal opponents as 'fascists' and being rewarded for their efforts by inclusion in government. Likewise, Brazilian Communist leader Luís Carlos Prestes, released from prison in May 1945, urged support for Vargas in the name of national unity and secured 500,000 votes for the BCP by campaigning on this line in the December 1945 election. Elected to the senate, Prestes participated in the writing of a new Brazilian constitution. The Mexican Communist Party (PCM) also operated entirely within the radical nationalist framework of the PRI, effectively abandoning efforts to build an alliance between workers and peasants—the true bearers of Mexico's revolutionary tradition—in favor of tying workers to national bourgeoisie and its main political party.[26] Pursuing similar policies, Communist parties across Latin America enjoyed significant electoral success in the narrow window between 1944 and 1947: in Chile, for example, Communist backing for the successful presidential campaign of Radical leader González Videla in September 1946 was rewarded with three seats in the cabinet. Only in Argentina did Communists follow a radically different course. Here, adherence to Moscow's hostility to Perón's wartime neutralism led the Communist Party to join conservative elites in opposition to his populist regime, a course that undercut working-class support for the party in the face of popular *peronismo*.

In this brief postwar window, Washington generally encouraged democratic reform in Latin America. For many years, US governments had formed close relationships with military dictators in Latin America when it suited their interests to do so, and in the early war years Washington's drive to secure strategic bases and access to critical raw materials ensured that Lend-Lease aid flowed to dictatorships in the Dominican Republic, Nicaragua, and—above all—Brazil. As both labor militancy and popular movements for democracy picked up steam, however, policymakers became increasingly concerned that alliances with undemocratic regimes in their own hemisphere threatened to discredit their criticism of Moscow's behavior in Eastern Europe. This produced a sharp change of course, signaled by the circulation of a November 1944 memorandum to US embassies in Latin America in which Assistant Secretary of State Adolf Berle expressed

---

[25]William A. Booth, "Historiographical Review: Rethinking Latin America's Cold War," *The Historical Journal*, Vol. 64, No. 4 (September 2021), 17.
[26]William A. Booth, "Hegemonic Nationalism, Subordinate Socialism: The Mexican Left, 1945–7," *Journal of Latin American Studies*, Vol. 50 (2017), 40.

Washington's preference for "governments established on the periodic and freely expressed consent of the governed."[27]

This turn deepened in 1945 as American diplomats made the rhetorical promotion of democratic principles a key aspect of their work at the Chapultepec conference. Practical consequences followed, registered in the suspension of arms shipments to the Dominican Republic and increasing diplomatic clamor urging reform of the Vargas dictatorship in Brazil. In Argentina, US pressure was more forceful, with ambassador Spruille Braden working to coordinate anti-government forces while supplying them with material exposing Perón's alleged ties to the Nazis. Washington also welcomed—and to some extent promoted—Bustamante's electoral victory in Peru in June 1945 and the popular revolt in Bolivia in July 1946, along with numerous other advances by pro-democracy forces. American diplomats cultivated close relations with 'progressive' nationalist forces led by middle-class radicals—like APRA in Peru—and, in the lingering glow of the wartime Grand Alliance and buoyed by Moscow's obvious lack of interest in the region, they appeared untroubled by Communist participation in pro-democracy movements. In this way, the wartime extension and consolidation of Washington's regional hegemony was concluded under the banner of democracy, even if free elections—as in Argentina and Brazil—did not necessarily produce the results American policymakers desired.

The Window of Democracy Closes

Almost as soon as it had opened, however, Latin America's democratic window began to slam shut. Beginning in 1946 and unfolding amid a continent-wide assault on organized labor, by 1948 a series of coups and dramatic shifts to the right by once-liberal coalitions had closed down most of the democratic space opened in the late war and early postwar. In these years, the conservative landed elites who had long controlled national politics through their interlocking control of government, military, and Catholic hierarchies pushed back against the fragile alliances of industrial capital, middle-class nationalism, and organized labor that had risen on the back of wartime economic development. These alliances, with their advocacy of industrialization, political democracy, limited social welfare, and state intervention in the economy, appeared deeply threatening to landed elites whose power rested on controlling peasant farmers through networks of clientage backed by violent repression. In countries across Latin America, these preexisting social realities ensured that the conservative

---

[27]Bethell and Roxborough, "Introduction," 8.

reaction had deep domestic roots, but it now unfolded within the broader framework of the United States' newly consolidated regional hegemony and at a time when the contours of Washington's global predominance were being delineated amid deepening Cold War tensions.

This complex nexus of class, national, hemispheric, and global pressures played out in specific ways in individual countries. Nevertheless, there were some broad commonalities. In particular, the counteroffensive against organized labor was as important in defining this second phase of postwar politics as the rise of labor militancy had been to the first. In some places, this effort was spearheaded by the introduction of new anti-union legislation: in Brazil, for example, Vargas' courtship of organized labor was sharply reversed in March 1946 when the newly elected Dutra government introduced laws to curb union militancy. Elsewhere, as with the defeat of the Chilean coalminers' strike in October 1947, the anti-labor offensive took the form of direct class battles against striking workers and their supporters. Everywhere, some combination of these methods worked to restrict the operation of independent unions, crush strikes, and imprison or silence union leaders. In Mexico, government interventions—*charrazo*—in the powerful unions of railroad, oil, and mine workers in the years 1948 to 1950 secured the installation of reliably pro-PRI leaderships while taming rank-and-file militancy and blocking labor support for the newly formed *Partido Popular*. Even in Argentina, where Perón's regime was deeply rooted in organized labor, the government tightened its control in ways that effectively prevented union actions outside of the narrow framework of *peronismo*.

This continent-wide drive against organized labor was accompanied by the outlawing of Communist parties and the exclusion of party members from leadership positions in the unions. In August 1947—and at almost the same time that Communists were being purged from governments in Italy and France—González Videla ejected the three Communist Party members of the Chilean government. These attacks, coming even as Communist leaders continued to advocate alliances with the 'progressive' national bourgeoisie, layered profound political disorientation on top of mounting state repression. As a result, pro-Moscow Communist parties had little purchase in much of Latin America. For their part, Soviet leaders had little interest in a distant region that was of peripheral importance to their own strategic defense and where challenges to American interests might trigger increased pressure on the USSR. Even in the late 1950s, the Soviet Union only had formal diplomatic ties with Argentina, Mexico, and Uruguay, and its trade relations with the region as a whole were, as contemporary observers noted, "small in magnitude" and centered on bartering capital goods for food and raw materials.[28] As in Africa, Moscow undoubtedly hoped to leverage trade

---

[28] Robert Loring Allen, *Soviet Influence in Latin America: The Role of Economic Relations* (Washington: Public Affairs Press, 1959), 86.

relations to gain expanded diplomatic recognition and political influence, but clear-eyed American analysts saw little reason to fear any expansion of Soviet influence in the region.

Across Latin America, moves to housebreak the trade unions and repress local Communist parties in the late 1940s led many of the left's former national bourgeois allies to adopt more conservative politics, often reknitting ties to landed elites through the consolidation of authoritarian and anti-democratic regimes in the process. In October 1948, Bustamante's APRA government in Peru—which had already been tacking sharply rightward—was ousted in a military coup, and the following month another military intervention initiated ten years of dictatorship in Venezuela. Similar developments rumbled on into the early 1950s, with Cuba's Fulgencio Batista ousting the corrupt and widely discredited *Auténticos* in a March 1952 coup. Elsewhere, authoritarian regimes were consolidated in more low-key ways, with Brazil's new 1946 constitution denying the vote to illiterate people—around half of the population—and skewing the geography of electoral representation so as to minimize the influence of workers in densely populated urban areas.

A parallel process took a somewhat different course in Mexico, where the one-party rule of the PRI continued to wrap itself in the aura of the Mexican Revolution and the *cárdenismo* of 1930s even as it cracked down on independent trade unions and peasant organizations. In 1952, the PRI faced an electoral challenge from former revolutionary general Miguel Henríquez Guzmán, who claimed to represent the true legacy of Cárdenas and promised the "recuperation of worker and peasant conquests."[29] After housebreaking the unions through the *charrazo*, the defeat of Guzmán's *henriquistas* in an election marked by widespread fraud and violence signaled the further solidification of PRI rule. In Argentina, meanwhile, Perón's regime ran into increasing difficulties despite steps to secure overseas investment in the domestic production of oil and cars—the country's two largest imports—and the promotion of social reforms including the legalization of divorce. These moves stirred the enmity of church leaders and the protracted period of instability that followed—including the bombing of a pro-government rally by airforce jets—culminated in Perón's ouster in a military coup in September 1955. Here, too, conservative landed elites were back in control.

The series of coups that closed Latin America's brief democratic window culminated in Guatemala in 1954. After the overturn of the dictatorship in 1944, 'spiritual socialist' Juan José Arévalo survived several attempted coups before his chosen successor, liberal nationalist Jacobo Árbenz, secured the presidency with a landslide electoral victory in November 1950. Árbenz

---

[29]Eric Zolov, *The Last Good Neighbor: Mexico in the Global Sixties* (Durham, NC: Duke University Press, 2020), 12.

led a political bloc that included the country's official Communist party, the newly formed Guatemalan Party of Labor (PGT). Taking its cue from Moscow, the PGT's stated aim was to collaborate with progressive sections of the bourgeoisie to create a modern capitalist nation-state, but the party's newness and inexperience nevertheless inclined it toward radicalism. With 80 percent of the population living on the land—many on vast estates owned by foreign companies like the American United Fruit Corporation— the PGT viewed far-reaching land reform as the first step in a struggle to break the political power of conservative landed elites. Árbenz shared this perspective, and he worked with PGT leaders to draft Decree 900, a land reform measure enacted in June 1952 that authorized the expropriation— with compensation—of uncultivated estates and distribution of their land to landless peasants. By summer 1954, 1.4 million acres had been expropriated, around 400,000 acres of it lying unused on two giant United Fruit plantations.[30]

The land reform program and an accompanying drive to promote literacy among peasant farmers generated considerable popular enthusiasm, and word spread quickly across Central America's porous borders. In Guatemala, the PGT grew rapidly, building broad peasant support and winning political office in three regional centers. These developments alarmed local landed elites, foreign estate owners, and the US government, which feared that peasant struggles might ripple outwards to threaten its allies in other countries. Árbenz had little contact with Moscow—a Soviet plan to barter machinery for bananas collapsed in farce—but a plan to purchase Czech weapons convinced Washington that this 'Communist' government had to be overthrown. Intense lobbying by United Fruit, a company with close ties to the US government, contributed to the decision to topple Árbenz. The resulting CIA-backed invasion ousted Árbenz in June 1954 and instituted a military dictatorship under Carlos Castillo Armas. The coup's success owed more to good fortune and to Árbenz's naive refusal to organize armed resistance than it did to brilliant CIA planning, but coming just a year after the overthrow of Mosaddeq in Iran it offered Washington seemingly convincing evidence of the efficacy of covert operations.

Bolivia followed a similar course by a longer and more circuitous route. Here, the *Frente Democrático Antifascista* leadership of the 1946 revolt fragmented in a series of shifts to the right before being toppled by a renewed popular upsurge in April 1952. Coming to power against the grain of continental politics, the new National Revolutionary Movement (MNR) government of Víctor Paz Estenssoro rested on the COB trade union federation and on its 60,000 well-organized, militant, and highly

---

[30]Piero Gleijeses, *Shattered Hope: The Guatemalan Revolution and the United States, 1944–1954* (Princeton: Princeton University Press, 1991), 155–6.

politicized tin miners in particular. The new government quickly enacted a series of radical reforms, including the introduction of universal suffrage, the nationalization of three large tin mining companies, and a land reform program designed to break up large estates in favor of landless peasants, who would receive government credits to purchase tools and seed. This land reform program was the most radical one enacted anywhere in Latin America in the postwar period, but its full implementation proved beyond the reach of the MNR's middle-class leadership. Instead, the government began to fragment as high inflation and a rapidly falling peso wreaked economic havoc and the COB threatened a general strike in response. By the late 1950s, Washington was working with conservative sections of the MNR to stabilize the economy and to equip and train a beefed-up national army, measures that culminated in the military coup that overthrew Estenssoro in 1964. Coming a decade after the overthrow of Árbenz, it was the last act in a long and continent-wide process.

From Development and Modernization to Intensified Neocolonialism

Despite their ostentatious wartime enthusiasm for promoting democracy, American officials generally had a low opinion of the prospects for democratic governance in Latin America. Many viewed Latin Americans as racially inferior and inherently childlike, a judgment offered with typical clarity by George Kennan, who reported after a tour of the continent in 1950 that "excessive intermarriage of all these elements (Spaniards, indigenous, and African slaves) [...] weighed heavily on the chances for human progress."[31] With views like this commonplace, it is not surprising that American policymakers gravitated easily toward local *caudillos* who promised to maintain order, safeguard supplies of critical raw materials, and provide suitable sites for US military bases. Moreover, in the supercharged atmosphere of the early Cold War the anti-labor and anti-Communist measures advanced by conservative elites in Latin America conformed closely to Washington's own outlook, making it easy for Americans to ignore—or even to embrace—their dictatorial tendencies. By mid-1947, supplies of US weapons, warplanes, and military advisors were again flowing to Trujillo in the Dominican Republic and to other dictatorial regimes throughout the region.

In key places—including the ejection of Communists from the Videla government in Chile in 1947 and the military coup in oil-rich Venezuela the following year—the United States was directly implicated in the

---

[31]Long, "Historical Antecedents," 221.

anti-democratic turn in Latin American politics. And, as Washington's role in the planning and execution of the 1954 coup in Guatemala demonstrates, its involvement deepened as the region-wide process gathered speed. At the continental level, Washington inserted anti-Communism—framed as the defense of democracy—into the Final Act of the founding conference of the Organization of American States in Bogotá in 1948. Official US government initiatives to promote anti-Communism were complemented by less formal but highly effective measures, including the backstage encouragement of American Federation of Labor (AFL) efforts to promote "free" unions at the expense of affiliates of the Communist-led World Federation of Trade Unions (WFTU). AFL representatives helped to initiate a series of heated factional struggles that led to national union federations across the continent cutting their ties to the WFTU, often weakening their own strength and combativity in the process.

The postwar turn in American policy rested on solid economic foundations. During the war, Washington's support for economic development in Latin America had played a key role in creating the hemispheric bloc that helped to carry its proposals at Bretton Woods and San Francisco. By late 1945, however, American enthusiasm for economic development in Latin America was already waning. Despite pressure from regional governments—including an impassioned speech from the Mexican secretary of state pointing out that underdevelopment condemned the people of Latin America to poverty and hunger—Washington sidelined discussion on economic development at the Chapultepec conference in 1945 and at subsequent gatherings in Rio (1947) and Bogotá (1948). At the same time, American supporters of regional economic development like Nelson Rockefeller were quietly shunted aside. Spruille Braden, Rockefeller's replacement as Assistant Secretary of State for the Americas, justified his refusal to approve development loans to Chile and other Latin American countries by denouncing the "virus of economic nationalism" alleged to be sweeping the continent.[32]

This turn away from wartime pledges of support for economic development based on state-funded industrialization reflected the renewed and assertive advocacy of free-market capitalism, with Braden noting that "free enterprise is the best and in most circumstances the only really sound means to develop the resources [...] of a new country."[33] This change of course was initially masked by the 1949 rollout of the Truman's Point Four program (see Chapter Four), but while providing technicians and advisors to work on development projects, this initiative offered little actual capital investment, and in 1950 less than 2 percent of American overseas aid went to Latin America.[34] As Washington again envisaged the Latin American states as

---

[32] Helleiner, *Forgotten Foundations*, 262–3.
[33] Ibid., 262–3.
[34] Bethell and Roxborough, "Introduction," 22.

exporters of food and raw materials and importers of American manufactured goods, it worked to reinforce dependency by curtailing government loans for economic development and by dropping price stabilization measures designed to guarantee income from raw material exports. When Carlos Ibañez del Campo, Videla's successor as Chilean president, tried to raise copper prices—and government tax income—he faced a sharp backlash from Washington and from Kennecott and Anaconda, the giant US copper producers that dominated the Chilean economy. Beating off Ibañez's threat to sell copper to the Soviet Union, Washington applied diplomatic pressure backed by manipulation of global markets to secure approval of the *Nuevo Trato* (New Deal) in 1955. Among other concessions, the Chilean government agreed to lower taxes on copper company profits, and with American backing Ibañez dropped the populist rhetoric typical of the first years of his administration and adopted a more openly reactionary and anti-labor stance: the "copper problem" was thus resolved in favor of Washington and the copper companies whose interests it defended.[35]

Washington's reassertion of semi-colonial dependency was not simply imposed on the countries of Latin America; instead, it meshed with the interests of landed elites that were tied into commodity exports and that also benefitted—through their leadership of the armed forces—from close ties with the US military. Anti-Communism served as an expression of this convergence and as a justification for brutal assaults on labor unions, peasant activists, and advocates of democracy throughout the region. This conjuncture, like the phase of democratization and developmentalism that preceded it, was shaped by the interplay between specific Latin American elites and the regional hegemon to their north; in this sense, while the shift in American policy unfolded in the context of the deepening Cold War and was conditioned by anti-Communist ideology, it did not represent an *extension* of the Cold War to Latin America. Moreover, these developments did not reflect any decline in Washington's interest in the region: on the contrary, they consolidated sets of relationships that ensured the United States enjoyed the profits of regional hegemony while securing the hemispheric bedrock upon which broader claims to global leadership could continue to rest. In the mid-1950s, Latin America's $3.5 billion annual market offered a larger outlet for US manufactured goods than either Europe or Asia, while direct private investment in US corporations operating in Latin America (or in their wholly owned regional subsidiaries) boomed. Meanwhile, relatively low commodity prices ensured a large 'dollar gap' that locked regional economies into permanent cycles of debt and underdevelopment.

---

[35] Glenn J. Dorn, "Chile, the United States, and the Korean War 'Copper Problem,'" *Diplomatic History*, Vol. 47, No. 2 (April 2023), 279, 302–3.

The Caribbean Colonies

Unlike the nation-states of Latin America which had been free of direct colonial rule since the early decades of the nineteenth century, most of the Caribbean islands and the coastal territories of British Guiana (Guyana), Dutch-ruled Surinam, and French Guiana, remained colonies of the European powers and the United States. Like the independent Caribbean states of Cuba, the Dominican Republic, and Haiti, these colonies were heavily dependent on the cultivation and export of food, especially sugar and bananas. Industrial development was extremely limited, with the important exceptions of oil production in Dutch-ruled Curaçao and Aruba and in British-rule Trinidad, and of bauxite mining in British Guiana and Dutch Surinam. Across the region as a whole, stable, and well-paid industrial work was a rarity. Instead, plantation sugar production created patterns of seasonal work and high unemployment or under-employment, and many peasant farmers, rural laborers, and urban workers lived in dire poverty. During the 1930s, waves of strikes and demonstrations led by oil workers, dockers, and sugar plantation workers swept the Caribbean as activists linked demands for better wages to calls for an end to colonial rule. Violent battles with imperial authorities followed: in Ponce, Puerto Rico, a sugar workers strike in 1937 overlapped with a campaign of bombings organized by Pedro Albizu Campos's Nationalist Party, and clashes between police and strikers in left eighteen dead.

War interrupted popular protest as tens of thousands of islanders were recruited into British and American military service. At the same time, major US military bases were established in Trinidad, Jamaica, and other British colonies, while American economic interest in the region, particularly in strategically critical bauxite mining, expanded dramatically. By the end of the war newly discovered reserves in Jamaica were being exploited, and the region as a whole supplied 86 percent of the aluminum ore smelted in the United States and Canada.[36] While underscoring the region's colonial status, American bases and businesses opened new opportunities for relatively lucrative employment, and American troops—including African Americans—modeled new images of modernity. The abrupt termination of this relative wartime prosperity in 1945 prompted a new wave of popular protest, opening a Caribbean front in the postwar labor upsurge. As strikes rippled through the British colonies, a new Caribbean Labour Congress was formed to extend solidarity to workers across the region. In Trinidad, protests led by the Oilfield Workers Trade Union, longshoremen, and public employees suffered violent attacks by colonial authorities in 1947,

---

[36] Gerald Horne, *Cold War in a Hot Zone: The United States Confronts Labor and Independence Struggles in the British West Indies* (Philadelphia: Temple University Press, 2007), 160.

while the following year participants in a massive strike by sugar workers on the Demerara Coast of British Guiana faced attacks by armed police. Anticolonial struggles also gained new momentum, with Albizu Campos returning from prison in 1947 to resume his campaign for Puerto Rican independence. These efforts were reinforced by popular opposition to the campaign of forced sterilization of Puerto Rican women launched by US medical authorities as a remedy for alleged overpopulation.

Against this background of popular protest, Puerto Rico and the Anglophone Caribbean moved in different directions. In Puerto Rico, senate president Luis Muñoz Marín—later the colony's first elected governor—worked with Washington to secure passage of the 1947 Industrial Incentive Act. This legislation aimed to transform the island's economy by offering cheap labor and generous tax incentives to American firms willing to set up manufacturing plants there. The results of these measures, known collectively as Operation Bootstrap, were dramatic, with nearly 450 new factories being built over the next ten years in a surge of industrial development unmatched anywhere in the Caribbean. This effort transformed Puerto Rico's traditional sugar-exporting economy into one based on manufacturing. At the same time, many Puerto Ricans took advantage of their American citizenship, established in 1917 in order to make Puerto Rican men eligible for the draft, and migrated to New York and other mainland cities. By 1950, one in seven Puerto Ricans lived in the continental United States, jumping to one-quarter just five years later. These measures, combined with a 1948 'Gag Law' that made it illegal to advocate anticolonialism—or even to fly the Puerto Rican flag—undercut support for independence and paved the way for the adoption of Commonwealth (or *Estado Libre Asociado*/Associated Free State) status in 1952. This new relationship tied Puerto Rico closely to the United States, simultaneously denying both independence *and* full statehood while securing UN recognition as a self-governed polity. For Washington, it was the ideal neocolonial solution.

The Anglophone Caribbean took a different path to neocolonial dependency. Here the Moyne Commission, set up by London to investigate the popular rebellions of the 1930s, recommended a series of government-funded welfare initiatives that signaled a major shift in British policy. Further codified at the 1947 Montego Bay Conference, this new course pointed toward ending direct colonial rule and replacing it with a West Indian Federation organized within the British Commonwealth. Like similar schemes for the reorganization of colonial rule in Africa, this plan was attractive to London as it offered a way to buffer popular demands for independence and reduce the costs of imperial administration while maintaining structured neocolonial dominance of regional economies. Unlike in Puerto Rico, however, this approach did not include plans for large-scale industrial development, envisaging instead that island economies would remain centered on the export of sugar, bananas, and other foods.

For rather different reasons, the idea of federation also appealed to anticolonial leaders, including Trinidadian Marxist scholar-turned-politician Eric Williams. Williams, like Kwame Nkrumah in Ghana, thought of transnational or regional federation as a means to strengthen the hand of small, fragmented, and economically underdeveloped states. Elected chief minister of Trinidad's colonial legislative council in 1956, Williams, along with other nationalists like Norman Manley in Jamaica, was carried to victory by a surge of anticolonial sentiment unleashed during the postwar wave of strikes and protests. As discussion on federation dragged on, however, popular enthusiasm dissipated. In part, this retreat was the product of repressive British policies that included the arrest and jailing of labor and political activists, raids on union offices, bans on international travel and even on movement between the islands of the West Indies, and an intense propaganda offensive that framed anticolonialism as Moscow-style Communism. With Washington's active support, the British worked to deepen divisions between anticolonial activists in the different islands and between different ethnic groups, setting descendants of enslaved Africans against those who had come to the West Indies from South Asia as indentured laborers. In the early 1950s, the Caribbean Labor Congress broke apart under these pressures. Given the climate of the early Cold War—and despite the fact that Moscow showed absolutely no interest in the region—British authorities justified their repressive actions as a response to alleged Communist influence. Stiffer measures faced those who actively sought a clear break with London and advocated greater control over national resources: elected chief minister of bauxite-rich British Guiana in May 1953, People's Progressive Party leader Cheddi Jagan was ousted by British troops just four months later on the pretext that he was cultivating ties to the Soviet Union.

As in Puerto Rico, popular militancy in the British-ruled Caribbean was also blunted by large-scale emigration. Between 1953 and 1960 over 150,000 people left the Anglophone Caribbean to seek work in Britain, with many taking advantage of official British recruitment schemes and of their new status as Citizens of the United Kingdom and Colonies established under the 1948 Nationality Act (see Chapter Five).[37] Many of the first migrants to arrive were ex-servicemen who had lived in Britain during the war, but they were soon joined by others seeking relatively well-paid year-round work. Their migrations—and the money they sent home to their families—helped to moderate the intense social pressures generated by permanent high unemployment. Often referred to as the 'Windrush' generation after the repurposed troopship ship that carried the first West Indian migrants

---

[37] Owen Jefferson, "The Economic Situation of the Commonwealth Caribbean," *Caribbean Quarterly*, Vol. 18, No. 1 (March 1972), 92.

to Britain in 1948, their arrival began to fundamentally remake the racial composition of the imperial metropole and of its working class in particular.

The West Indian Federation, formed within the British Commonwealth in 1958, was quickly torn apart by infighting between the leaders of the various island colonies. These battles pitted Williams's oil-rich Trinidad against chief minister Manley's Jamaica, whose government pinned its economic hopes on the massive new bauxite mines operated by the Canadian aluminum producer Alcan. In a further set of divisions, politicians from both Trinidad and Jamaica railed against the alleged costs of supporting the population of the 'small islands' in the Leeward and Windward groups of the Lesser Antilles, where industrial development was almost entirely absent. These divisions helped to turn public opinion against the Federation, and in a hotly contested referendum in September 1961, Jamaican voters narrowly rejected participation. With many West Indians coming to see the Federation as a means for London to manage decolonization rather than as a step toward genuine independence, the organization soon unraveled amid a bitter dispute over the location of the federal capital. After the collapse of

FIGURE 7.2 *A group of Jamaican men read a newspaper onboard the SS* Empire Windrush. *They were among the 800 West Indians who disembarked at London's Tilbury dock on June 22, 1948. (Image: Hulton Deutsch.)*

Federation, London began granting its West Indian colonies independence gradually and as separate nation states, starting with Jamaica and Trinidad in 1962. British Guiana, which had abstained from the Federation, became independent Guyana in 1964. In a process that paralleled the decolonization of French West Africa (see Chapter Six), dreams of broad postcolonial solidarity foundered on narrowly focused bourgeois nationalism, allowing London to manage the transition to neocolonial dependency with minimal disruption against a backdrop of anti-Communist scaremongering. As in Africa, some former anticolonial activists now emerged as increasingly authoritarian nationalists, with Trinidadian Eric Williams going so far as to ban his own earlier Marxist writings.[38]

The Cuban Revolution

Radical lawyer Fidel Castro's 1952 campaign to represent a working-class district of Havana was cut short when Fulgencio Batista's military coup canceled the election. Castro, then a leader of the youth wing of the nationalist *Partito Ortodoxo*, concluded that Batista's dictatorship blocked any possibility of achieving social reform through normal political channels, and he began campaigning for its armed overthrow. On July 26 of the following year, Castro led a band of young fighters in an attack on the Moncada barracks in Santiago de Cuba. Designed to spark a broader uprising, the attack was a complete failure. Fifty rebels faced summary execution, and others—including Castro—were tried and imprisoned. Nevertheless, Castro used the trial as a platform, with supporters outside the jail circulating his stirring speech from the dock—'History Will Absolve Me!'—to a broad audience. Released from prison in May 1955 after a nationwide campaign for amnesty, Castro organized supporters of his revolutionary course into the new July 26 Movement before heading to Mexico to prepare for guerrilla war.

Castro and a small band of July 26 Movement combatants returned to Cuba in late 1956, launching their revolutionary war amid army ambushes that reduced their numbers to a mere handful while violent police repression decimated the ranks of their urban supporters. Despite these difficulties, by early 1957 Castro had established the nucleus of a Rebel Army in the rugged mountains of the Sierra Maestra. Over the next two years the Rebel Army weathered ferocious army assaults on their mountainous base area before launching an advance on Havana, which they entered on New Year's Day in 1959. The rebel's westward march from the Sierra Maestra was accompanied by peasant uprisings, and July 26 Movement fighters were welcomed into

---

[38]Horne, *Cold War in a Hot Zone*, 206.

the capital by an insurrectionary general strike. Batista had already fled to Miami, leaving political power in the hands of the revolutionaries.

The military campaigns that produced this dramatic victory, moving from small-scale guerrilla ambushes to a mobile "war of columns," were intertwined with a deepening social revolution. In liberated zones under Rebel Army control, peasants and agricultural workers were given title to the land they worked, while popular political assemblies rallied support for the revolution and July 26 Movement activists promoted literacy and established rudimentary healthcare. In the cities, the movement worked with other liberal and left-wing forces, including the Popular Socialist Party (Cuba's official Communist party), to build support in the trade unions and working-class barrios. This emphasis on popular mobilization—rooted in the belief that Cuban working people were the makers of history—reflected Castro's own study of Marxism and that of his closest collaborators like Argentinian Ernesto "Che" Guevara. Castro and Guevara approached Marx directly, through their own reading, study, and political activity, rather than through the distorting lens of the doctrines and theories advanced by the Cuban PSP and other pro-Moscow Communist parties. Moreover, the PSP had been deeply compromised by its earlier support for Batista, and while its cadres helped build support for the revolution within the unions, the July 26 Movement effectively bypassed the pro-Moscow party's claim to leadership. The development of the Castro leadership registered a sharp break from pro-Moscow Stalinism as well as from radical bourgeois nationalism and from Perón-, Cárdenas-, and Vargas-style populism. In their different ways, all of these forces—like Nasser, Mosaddeq, Sukarno, or Nehru—viewed the mobilization of workers and peasants as key points of support for their political projects and not, as Castro and Guevara saw them, as the self-acting driving force of social transformation.

Throughout the revolutionary war, Castro organized alliances and blocs with other anti-Batista forces—including the *Ortodoxos*, *Auténticos*, and the pro-Moscow PSP—without allowing them to set the agenda, and the post-Batista government established in January 1959 included bourgeois politicians as well as leaders of the July 26 Movement. Divisions between these forces quickly deepened as Castro advanced a program of radical land reform and began arming the Cuban people. After just seven months in office, liberal Manuel Urrutia resigned the presidency in July 1959 and was succeeded by July 26 Movement leader Osvaldo Dorticós. The unfolding trajectory of the Cuban Revolution caused alarm in Washington, where it became apparent that it was going to be difficult to moderate the course of the Castro leadership either by buying it off or by overthrowing it, Guatemala-style. Instead, Washington responded to Havana's purchase of arms from the Soviet Union—itself a response to an American arms embargo—by cutting imports of Cuban sugar in summer 1960. Moscow stepped in to pick up the slack, and an American oil embargo soon followed. In an escalating spiral, Havana nationalized three American-owned refineries, Washington imposed a total trade embargo, and the Cubans accelerated the nationalization of US businesses and property.

Washington's attempt to overthrow the Cuban Revolution by launching a counter-revolutionary invasion at the Bay of Pigs in 1961 was neither an irrational impulse nor the product of lobbying by anti-Castro exiles. Instead, it flowed from Washington's recognition that the Cuban Revolution marked a real and dramatic break from previous patterns of Latin American politics, and one that threatened US predominance both in the region and more broadly. This is not the place to chart the effects of Washington's unceasing hostility to the Cuban Revolution, Havana's increasing economic reliance on the Soviet Union, or Castro's continued efforts to extend the revolution—and international solidarity more broadly—in the Americas, Africa, and Southeast Asia. It is, however, important to note that the long shift to the right in Latin American politics that followed the slamming shut of the democratic window in the late 1940s was finally broken by the triumph of a new kind of popular revolutionary movement. Unlike the 1946 Haitian revolt, the Cuban Revolution did not lose its way at the moment of victory but proceeded instead to overturn capitalist economic relations. Moreover, as Odd Arne Westad points out, the "international reach" of the Cuban Revolution focused the attention of friends and enemies alike on relations with "Third World" countries outside of Latin America, thus integrating the continent into new upsurges of popular radicalism.[39] Ironically, and on a global level, the final postwar consolidation of American hegemony in the late 1950s thus overlapped with the emergence of radical new challenges to that predominance.

For Further Reading

Leslie Bethell and Ian Roxborough (eds.), *Latin America between the Second World War and the Cold War, 1944–1948* (Cambridge: Cambridge University Press, 1992).
William A. Booth, "Hegemonic Nationalism, Subordinate Socialism: The Mexican Left, 1945–7," *Journal of Latin American Studies*, Vol. 50 (2017).
William A. Booth, "Historiographical Review: Rethinking Latin America's Cold War," *The Historical Journal*, Vol. 64, No. 4 (September 2021).
Thomas C. Field Jr. et al. (eds.), *Latin America and the Global Cold War* (Chapel Hill, NC: University of North Carolina Press, 2020).
Alexandre Fortes, "World War II and Brazilian Workers: Populism at the Intersection between National and Global Histories," *International Review of Social History*, Vol. 62 (2017), Special Issue, 187.

---

[39]Odd Arne Westad, "Conclusion: The Third World in Latin America," in Thomas C. Field et al. (eds.), *Latin America and the Global Cold War* (Chapel Hill, NC: University of North Carolina Press, 2020), 395; Harvey R. Neptune, *Caliban and the Yankees: Trinidad and the United States Occupation* (Chapel Hill, NC: University of North Carolina Press, 2007).

Piero Gleijeses, *Shattered Hope: The Guatemalan Revolution and the United States, 1944–1954* (Princeton: Princeton University Press, 1991).

Greg Grandin, *The Last Colonial Massacre: Latin America in the Cold War* (Chicago: University of Chicago Press, 2011).

Tanya Harmer, "The Cold War in Latin America," in Artemy M. Kalinovsky and Craig Daigle (eds), *The Routledge Handbook of the Cold War* (Abingdon, Oxford: Routledge, 2014).

Eric Helleiner, *Forgotten Foundations of Bretton Woods: International Development and the Making of the Postwar Order* (Ithaca, NY: Cornell University Press, 2014).

Rebecca Herman, *Cooperating with the Colossus: A Social and Political History of US Military Bases in World War II Latin America* (Oxford: Oxford University Press, 2022).

Daniel Immerwahr, *How to Hide an Empire: A History of the Greater United States* (New York: Farrar, Straus and Giroux, 2019.

Thomas M. Leonard and John F. Bratzel (eds.) *Latin America during World War II* (Lanham, MD: Rowman and Littlefield, 2007).

Harvey R. Neptune, *Caliban and the Yankees: Trinidad and the United States Occupation* (Chapel Hill, NC: University of North Carolina Press, 2007).

Matthew J. Smith, *Red & Black in Haiti: Radicalism, Conflict, and Political Change, 1934–1957* (Chapel Hill, NC: University of North Carolina Press, 2009).

Jenifer Van Vleck, *Empire of the Air: Aviation and the American Ascendancy* (Cambridge, MA: Harvard University Press, 2013).

CHAPTER EIGHT

Bringing It All Back Home

An American Front in the Postwar Labor Upsurge

Within weeks of the Japanese surrender in September 1945, members of the Oil Workers Union at sixteen major American oil companies walked out on strike. Striking workers demanded a 30 percent wage rise, which they needed to make up for the loss of overtime earnings as war-related production ramped down. The oil workers eventually went back to work in the face of intervention by the Truman administration, but other strikes soon followed. Building on a series of unofficial 'wildcat' strikes that had been rippling through the industry for the previous couple of years, over 225,000 members of the United Auto Workers (UAW) at General Motors plants across the country walked off the job in November 1945. Under the leadership of UAW president Walter Reuther, a veteran of the battles that had unionized the auto industry in the 1930s, GM workers picked up the oil workers' demand to maintain wartime incomes by fighting to reduce the workweek from fifty-two hours to forty with no loss of pay. After two months, striking autoworkers were joined by the members of other major unions, including electrical and packinghouse workers, and—most decisively—750,000 steel workers and 340,000 coalminers, and by the time the strikes finally ebbed in May 1946, over four million workers had been involved. As a result of the strike wave—the largest in American history—many unions workers secured substantial wage increases, with the autoworkers settling for a 17.5 percent hike.

This great postwar strike wave was driven by pent-up resistance to wartime wage controls combined with fear of a postwar economic slump. As war production ended, employers slashed overtime, and the take-home pay of a manufacturing worker plunged from an average of $46.35 a week in

FIGURE 8.1 *Striking members of United Auto Workers Local 15 on picket line duty outside General Motors' Fisher Body plant in Fleetwood, MI, November 24, 1945. Picket signs announce the union's demand for a 30 percent wage hike. (Photo: Bettmann/Getty.)*

June 1945 to just $35.60 in September.[1] On top of this, two million men and women were laid off, and many more were either reassigned to lower-paying jobs or forced to work shorter hours. This abrupt decline in working-class living standards took place in the context of dramatic wartime improvements in labor productivity that enabled employers to get more output from fewer workers, thus boosting already-inflated profits. These conditions were particularly galling for workers whose wages had been held down during the war by 'no-strike' agreements policed by their own union leaders as well as by the government's War Labor Board. When half a million members of the United Mine Workers of America had launched a successful strike for higher pay in 1943 in defiance of these restrictions, Congress responded with the Smith-Connally War Labor Disputes Act, a punitive measure designed to

---

[1] Congress of Industrial Organizations president Philip Murray, quoted in E. R. Frank, "The Great Strike Wave and Its Significance," *Fourth International*, May 1946, 135.

restrict trade union action while allowing the government to take over the running of struck plants by using soldiers to maintain production.

The postwar strike wave in the United States was intertwined with the worldwide wave of GI protests demanding rapid postwar demobilization (see Chapter Three). Many soldiers had taken part in the big union battles of the 1930s, and some of their leaders—like Emil Mazey, former president of the militant UAW Local 212—stressed the commonality of interest between soldiers and striking workers. These bonds of solidarity, embodied in official union messages of support for the soldier's protests, fed into discussions that had been going on in the UAW and other major unions for several years on the need to create a new party of labor, independent of both the Democrats and Republicans. Despite the strikers' militancy, however, the postwar strike wave remained largely focused on immediate issues of wages and conditions. To many workers, this essentially nonpolitical approach seemed to have been vindicated by the widespread achievement of significant wage hikes, and henceforth even militant labor leaders were hostile to the idea of creating a new working-class party, advocating closer ties to 'friends of labor' in the Democratic Party instead.

This apolitical approach left union members poorly prepared to face a ferocious counter-offensive by the employers and their bipartisan supporters in Congress that began as soon as the postwar strike wave began to subside. After the autoworkers, steelworkers, and other major unions had returned to work, railroad workers in two craft unions, the Brotherhoods of Railroad Trainmen and Locomotive Engineers, struck for higher wages in May 1946. Their strike quickly brought the railroads to an almost complete halt, with less than 400 trains running out of a scheduled 199,000.[2] Despite these dramatic initial successes, however, the rail workers had already been separated from other striking unions by President Truman's imposition of a sixty-day cooling off period under the Railway Labor Act, and the administration now took decisive action against them. Denouncing the strikers as unpatriotic, Truman threatened to mobilize the army to get the trains running. Under this pressure—augmented by a shrill anti-union and anti-communist campaign in the press—the Brotherhoods ordered their members back to work, settling for the modest pay raises imposed by the government.

The defeat of the 1946 railroad strike broke the momentum of the strike wave and opened the door to the legislative assault on the unions that culminated in the passage of the Labor-Management Relations Act—better known as the Taft-Hartley Act—in June 1947. Taft-Hartley built on the

---

[2] "Wages and Working Conditions: The Railroad Strike of 1946," National World War II Museum, https://www.nationalww2museum.org/war/articles/1946-railroad-strike, accessed April 16, 2022.

wartime Smith-Connally Act, and it outlawed many of the tactics central to the success of both the labor upsurge of the 1930s and the postwar strike wave, including wildcat or unofficial strikes, mass picketing to close struck plants, and various forms of solidarity action by which union members in work could extend support to those on strike. The new law also allowed states to outlaw union-only (or 'closed') shops and restricted the use of union funds for political purposes. This broad raft of measures reversed many of the legal rights and protections for trade unions that had been recognized in the 1935 National Labor Relations (Wagner) Act, making it more difficult to organize effective strikes. The new law took particular aim at multi-union general strikes that had flared during the strike wave, like the city-wide shutdown led by women store workers in Oakland, California. Keen to be seen as a friend of labor, President Truman refused to sign the bill, but a bipartisan congressional majority overrode his veto.

The Deepening Cold War, Loyalty Oaths, and the Defeat of the Progressive Party

The Taft-Hartley Act worked to reinforce the American trade union movement's focus on bread and butter issues of wages and conditions while deepening cooperation between union leaders, corporate management, and the government. Moreover, the long postwar expansion of the American economy that got underway as factories transitioned from war production back to the production of cars and other consumer goods soon enabled union leaders to negotiate significant pay raises without recourse to strike action. With employers keen to keep production moving and profits flowing, the threat of strike action was often enough to secure substantial pay hikes. As working-class living standards began to rise, it became possible for workers in well-paid union jobs—many of them male and Caucasian—to own homes and to purchase cars and other expensive consumer goods that had been beyond their reach before the war. For many working people, the material elements of what was increasingly being referred to as the 'American Dream' were starting to fall into place. This material reality also helped to create an ideological conviction that there was a causal relationship between American global hegemony—presented as the defense of freedom worldwide—and economic prosperity at home. This association was critical to the construction of broad domestic support for hegemony, and it was forcefully reinforced by Cold War anti-communism. Taft-Hartley was passed just three months after the proclamation of the Truman Doctrine and the establishment by presidential Executive Order 9835 of a loyalty oath for federal employees accused of supporting 'subversive' organizations. A special provision of the Taft-Hartley Act required union leaders to file affidavits declaring that they had no ties to the Communist

Party or other radical organizations, and 81,000 local and national officers quickly complied.

Truman's loyalty oath rode roughshod over constitutional rights to due process, with government employees accused of ties to 'subversive' organizations being denied the right to see the evidence against them, to confront their accusers, or to appeal decisions handed down by secretive loyalty boards. Millions of federal employees and applicants for government jobs were screened by the Federal Bureau of Investigation, and nearly 30,000 faced more intensive investigations. Less than 300 people were actually fired, but thousands quit rather than face intrusive FBI investigations into their private lives. Increasingly, a climate of intense anti-communism sought to place radical political beliefs and the organization of popular protests—including strikes—outside of the sphere of legitimate political discourse. Taft-Hartley's anti-communist clause was integral to its goal of restricting trade union activity in the aftermath of the great strike wave, and the willingness of union leaders to affirm their loyalty often undercut their ability to defend even normal trade union activity.

Henry Wallace, President Roosevelt's vice president from 1941 to 1945, was the only senior political figure to challenge this sharp rightward turn in American politics. A convinced New Dealer, since 1941 Wallace had advocated an American-led postwar order that would end colonialism and advance the worldwide interests of the 'common man.' Wallace's views had much in common with those advanced at the start of the war by publisher Henry Luce—author of the "American Century"—and by the 1940 Republican presidential candidate Wendell Willkie, and together they had helped to build domestic support for America's coming global predominance. After the war, Wallace was dismayed by the sharp anti-Soviet turn in US policy and the rapid plunge into Cold War, and he countered it with a vision of world peace based on continued US-Soviet cooperation. After an acrimonious break with the Truman administration in September 1946, Wallace contested the 1948 election as the presidential candidate of the newly formed Progressive Party. Although far from a radical himself, Wallace's opposition to the deepening Cold War led him to work with the Communist Party, which shared his hopes for a continuation of the wartime Grand Alliance and provided much of the organizational infrastructure of his new party.

Despite a barnstorming campaign that featured large and enthusiastic public rallies, Wallace's Progressives won just 2.4 percent of the popular vote. This relatively poor showing at the polls was due in part to a ferocious press campaign branding Wallace as a Soviet stooge, but it also reflected his failure to win the backing of any major trade union leaders. Instead, union tops—including some who had once flirted with the idea of an independent labor party—criticized Wallace's third party bid while strengthening their own ties to the Democrats. Convergence between Truman and the union leaders was helped along by the fact that Wallace's campaign pushed the Democrats so far to the left on domestic political questions—including forcing a pledge to address systemic racial discrimination against African Americans—that on these issues there was little to distinguish the Progressive Party from the incumbent Democrats. After the 1948 election, the Democrats' turn to the left made it seemed as if the New Deal coalition might be revived, as the re-elected Truman promised modest social reforms in the context of the deepening Cold War and accelerating war preparations. As it turned out, however, this prospect was cut short by developments in China.

The Chinese Revolution and the Rise of McCarthyism

On February 9, 1950, Wisconsin Senator Joseph McCarthy gave a speech to the Republican Women's Club of Wheeling, West Virginia, in which he made the startling claim that a large number of Communists had embedded themselves in the upper echelons of the State Department and were now steering the country toward disaster. Senior figures in the Truman administration, McCarty implied, were either part of this gigantic 'anti-American' conspiracy or else were knowingly covering up for it. McCarthy's allegations supercharged a political climate already defined by intense anti-communism. As historian Ellen Schrecker argues, there were actually "many McCarthyisms," each with its own agenda and mode of operation.[3] Independently of McCarthy, for example, the 1950 Internal Security Act (McCarran Act) required that the Communist Party and other radical organizations register with the attorney general and turn over details of their members and finances to a new Subversive Activities Control Board. Nevertheless, in the febrile atmosphere of the war in Korea, the crusade launched by McCarthy in Wheeling wove these various anti-communist efforts into a campaign that dominated American politics for the next four years. Moreover, while Communists and other radicals were McCarthy's immediate target, the 'witch-hunt' led by the powerful House Un-American Activities Committee (HUAC) and backed by the efforts of the Federal Bureau of Investigation aimed to narrow the space for political discussion more broadly by curtailing constitutional rights and legal norms. As McCarthy's campaign advanced, the waves of fear it generated pushed Republican and Democratic politicians and liberal elites—including college presidents, newspaper editors, and civil libertarians—to abandon seemingly deep-seated principles in the hope of avoiding the charge of being soft on Communism.

---

[3]Ellen Schrecker, "McCarthyism: Political Repression and the Fear of Communism," *Social Research*, Vol. 71, No. 4 (2004), 1043.

The McCarthyite witch-hunt unfolded in the immediate aftermath of the founding of the People's Republic of China in October 1949, and it was driven by a desire to explain and account for the unpalatable fact that just four years after America's overwhelming victory in the Second World War, China had been 'lost' to the Communists. Critics of the Truman administration, including the influential China Lobby in Congress, offered conspiratorial explanations for this deeply shocking reality. The administration's implausible claim that they had never favored a Communist-Guomindang coalition fueled McCarthy's attack, and in his pamphlet *America's Retreat from Victory* he charged General George Marshall—a senior architect of America's strategy in the Second World War—with personal responsibility for the loss of China, implying that his actions were deliberately treasonous. By taking aim at the highest levels of government, McCarthy and his supporters signaled that no one was safe from investigation. Academics like John King Fairbank, who argued that the Chinese Revolution was the product of "self-determination, not outside aggression," also became targets of intense public criticism, while State Department officials who had called attention to Guomindang corruption were accused of engineering the Communist victory.[4] Some lost their jobs, and many more were intimidated into silence by the fear of losing livelihoods and professional standing.

The climate of fear generated by the witch-hunt was intensified by the execution in 1953 of Ethel and Julius Rosenberg, former Communist Party members convicted of passing nuclear secrets to the Soviets. In this intense and fearful atmosphere, the Communist Party shied away from public defense of its members, responding to investigative probes with denials and evasions that served to embolden the witch-hunters while convincing broad sections of public opinion that they really did have something to hide. At the same time, the fact that senior government officials like Harry Dexter White (the architect of the Bretton Woods system) and Alger Hiss (a key State Department figure at the Yalta conference) were plausibly accused of reporting to Soviet handlers gave conspiracy theories credence. To many, the idea that there was no contradiction between America's hegemonic interests and the construction of a postwar world based on ongoing cooperation with the Soviet Union—a commonplace among American intellectuals and policymakers during the war—now seemed either stunningly naive or else deliberately duplicitous.

After the outbreak of fighting in Korea in summer 1950, McCarthy took his anti-communist campaign to new heights. With one foot planted firmly within bipartisan party politics, McCarthy reached toward the

---

[4] John King Fairbank, quoted in Masuda Hajimu, *Cold War Crucible: The Korean Conflict and the Postwar World* (Cambridge, MA: Harvard University Press, 2015), 166.

construction of a fascist-type mass movement that was energized at raucous mass rallies and organized through networks of local right-wingers, media outlets, and police organizations. This emerging movement cut across party lines, challenging traditional leaderships in both major parties while winning backing from business elites, particularly those outside of the old-school ruling class networks. McCarthy's campaign, ably assisted by 'All-American' senator Richard Nixon, took aim at a broad and overlapping array of targets that included communists—both in the CPUSA and beyond—labor and civil rights activists, lesbians and gay men, feminists, and immigrants. His goal, however, was not simply to purge the American body politic, but to prepare it to wage a global war. This now seems overblown, but it did not look that way as American troops raced toward the Chinese border in late 1950 or as the People's Volunteer Army surged south the following winter in campaigns that seemed to many to presage a new world war.

When the war in Korea was running in their favor, General Douglas MacArthur and other American leaders had mulled the possibility of shifting the global balance of forces decisively in their favor through a hot overturn of the Chinese Revolution. Instead, they had been fought to a standstill and forced to settle for simply holding onto their client state in South Korea. After Korea, American planners rejected the idea of waging major land wars, opting instead for the global nuclear standoff envisaged by President Eisenhower's New Look strategy (see Chapter Two). As it became clear that there was no short-term possibility of overturning non-capitalist social relations in either China or the Soviet Union, Washington finally accepted the inexorable logic of waging a long cold war. This bitter pill, reflective of the real limits to the global hegemony established after the Second World War, was sweetened by the beginning of a long wave of capitalist expansion as the postwar rebuilding of Western Europe and Japan began to bear fruit.

As the end of the war in Korea opened a new conjuncture in world politics, McCarthy's efforts to reshape American domestic politics in preparation for world war appeared out of step with the broader needs of America's ruling elites. Suddenly, McCarthy's boorish brand of incipient fascism became an embarrassment, particularly after he launched an investigation into alleged Communist penetration of the military in late 1953. This probe, organized through the congressional Permanent Subcommittee on Investigations with the help of attorney Robert F. Kennedy, collapsed dramatically during the televised Army-McCarthy hearings in spring 1954. In November 1954, the Senate voted by a large majority to censure McCarthy, effectively shutting down his witch-hunting campaign. Over the next several years the Supreme Court under Chief Justice Earl Warren reestablished some of the key legal and constitutional provisions trampled at the height of the McCarthyite campaign including—in a landmark 1958 case involving radical artist Rockwell Kent—ruling that the government could not deny a passport on the grounds of a person's political beliefs.

The National Security State and the Imperial Presidency

The process of domestic adjustments to the challenges of global hegemony also drove changes to the structures of political power, leading in particular to the strengthening of the powers of the presidency and of the executive branch as a whole. Described by historian Mark Stoler as a "master opportunist who disliked rigid planning," President Roosevelt had run his wartime administration in a freewheeling and seemingly chaotic style marked an absence of clear lines of decision-making and accountability.[5] Beyond its characteristic method of competition, approximation, compromise, and short-term expediency, however, Roosevelt's wartime administration was informed by a set of ideas—part Wilsonian vision of liberal world leadership and part unvarnished pursuit of American predominance—that provided a central axis around which the apparent chaos revolved. This approach was well suited to the complex challenge of fighting a global war while simultaneously projecting the worldwide establishment of American military and political predominance. Above all, these tasks demanded tremendous flexibility and a willingness to accept risk, and they were accomplished by centralizing decision-making in the hands of the president himself, thus strengthening the power of the executive and accelerating the emergence of an 'imperial' presidency. At the same time, new agencies—including the Joint Chiefs of Staff and the Office of Strategic Services (forerunner of the Central Intelligence Agency)—brought military planning to the center of executive decision-making, partially displacing the State Department in the formulation of foreign policy.

Ideally structured for the wartime establishment of global predominance, this anarchic and often informal setup was less suited to the postwar consolidation of hegemony. Even before the end of the world war it was becoming clear, as Melvyn Leffler points out, that a "fusion" of "geopolitical, economic, ideological, and strategic considerations" was transforming traditional foreign policy goals into "national security imperatives" that would require careful, detailed, and centralized planning.[6] This shift required a formalization of executive power, and it implied not a diminution of the imperial presidency, but rather its relocation within the broader architecture of an emerging national security state. Signed into law in July 1947, the National Security Act established a National Military Establishment (later the Department of Defense) that combined the old War

---

[5]Mark A. Stoler, *Allies and Adversaries: The Joint Chiefs of Staff, the Grand Alliance, and U.S. Strategy in World War II* (Chapel Hill: University of North Carolina Press, 2000), 36.
[6]Melvyn P. Leffler, *Preponderance of Power: National Security, the Truman Administration, and the Cold War* (Stanford, CA: Stanford University Press, 1992), 24.

and Navy departments into a single executive body that also integrated the newly independent Air Force. The 1947 Act also founded the Central Intelligence Agency, formalized the Joint Chiefs of Staff—set up on an ad hoc basis in 1942—and created a new National Security Council (NSC). This powerful new body enabled the president and senior civilian and military policymakers to integrate all aspects of national security policy, or 'grand strategy,' in a centralized and systematic manner. It is hard to see Roosevelt, the consummate juggler, willing to be bound by the NSC's closely argued policy statements and precisely minuted decisions, but in this, as in much else, it fell to Truman and then to Eisenhower to transform wartime victory into sustainable postwar hegemony.

Eisenhower and the 'Middle Way'

Sustained American economic growth during the 1950s was accompanied by a continuation of the high levels of state spending that had begun under the New Deal and increased dramatically during the war. The end of the war saw government spending drop from its wartime high, but the state remained a major economic actor under Truman and his Republican successor, Dwight D. Eisenhower. Elected in 1952, Eisenhower asserted that it was the government's responsibility to provide "a floor over the pit of personal disaster," and his administration expanded many of the key social programs—including state pensions and unemployment benefits—initiated by his Democratic predecessors.[7] Alongside this substantial social spending, massive military expenditures also continued into the postwar, fueled by the war in Korea, the rapidly expanding nuclear arsenal, and the costs of maintaining a worldwide network of military bases and the forces deployed on them. The federal government also funded major infrastructural projects, including a new 40,000-mile interstate highway system. Launched in 1956 at a projected cost of $27 billion, 90 percent of the construction costs were to be funded by the federal government through new taxes on gas, tires, and other auto-related products that would be recouped over time by tolls levied on road users. As vice-president Richard Nixon assured state governors, the United States needed to embrace centralized "vision" and "comprehensive plans" while avoiding the so-called "blueprints for a regimented economy" typical of socialist planning.[8]

---

[7]Steven Wagner, *Eisenhower Republicanism: Pursuing the Middle Way* (Dekalb, IL: Northern Illinois University Press, 2006), 5.
[8]Teal Arcadi, "Partisanship and Permanence: How Congress Contested the Origins of the Interstate Highway System and the Future of American Infrastructure," *Modern American History*, 5 (2022), 61.

In the fifteen years after the Second World War, federal spending—of which well over two-thirds went to what Eisenhower would famously describe as the 'military-industrial complex'—helped to sustain economic growth by boosting effective demand and moderating cyclical downturns in the business cycle. Countercyclical spending had been advocated since the 1930s by British economist John Maynard Keynes, and although his social policies—and his name—remained anathema to many American politicians, their governments acted much as he had suggested. Government spending played a similar macroeconomic role in the revitalized economies of Western Europe, although here—given their subordinate place in the new world hierarchy and their ability to shelter under the American nuclear umbrella—money flowed into the social programs central to their new welfare states rather than into the military.

After the turbulent years of McCarthyism, Washington's post-Korea recognition of the protracted character of the Cold War and the onset of 'peaceful coexistence' with the USSR facilitated the development of an expansive domestic political consensus. Eisenhower epitomized this development, and he pictured himself following a middle way between the dwindling socialist, or social democratic wing of the Democratic Party and the increasingly marginalized McCarthyite wing of the Republicans.[9] That did not mean an end to political factionalism—the two-party system demands it—but it did imply the emergence of a broad (and broadly liberal) middle ground populated by mainstream politicians of both parties together with labor leaders, corporate spokespeople, and public opinion-formers. In this context, the meaning of liberalism itself was transformed, with a new faith in sustained economic growth as the key to social progress replacing the vocal hostility to capitalism typical of New Deal liberalism. Reform, as historian Alan Brinkley argues, gave way to pro-capitalist consumerism, anti-communism, and implicit confidence in America's leadership of a "rules-based" global order.[10]

President Eisenhower's claim to a middle way in domestic politics and the inter-related pursuit of a less confrontational policy toward the Soviet Union was ideologically reinforced by the December 1953 announcement that Washington would promote the non-military development of nuclear power both at home and around the world. Dubbed Atoms for Peace after Eisenhower's speech to the United Nations, this policy accelerated the development of a domestic nuclear power program—work began on the Shippingport power station in Pennsylvania in 1954—and also allowed the carefully controlled export of nuclear knowledge and technology

---

[9] Wagner, *Eisenhower Republicanism*, 5.
[10] Alan Brinkley, *The End of Reform: New Deal Liberalism in Recession and War* (New York: Vintage, 1995), 265–71.

to select countries. *Life* magazine saw Eisenhower "giving mankind a glimpse of salvation by statesmanship," and government spokespeople worked hard to promote the vision of the United States as the leader of a worldwide revolution in the peaceful development of nuclear technology.[11] In fact, practical steps lagged far behind enthusiastic propaganda, and the widely publicized poisoning of the crew of the *Lucky Dragon* by fallout from an American H-Bomb test in March 1954 (see Chapter Four) quickly allowed a more pessimistic nuclear narrative to reassert itself.

Innovation, Modernization, and the Cold War University

The explosive growth of America's wartime economy was intertwined with dramatic technological advances that were themselves a product of a deepening relationship between big business, government, the military, and university research institutes. This nexus, connecting scientific and technological innovation directly to product development and manufacture, laid the basis of the postwar military-industrial complex—or more accurately the military-industrial-academic complex. Led by Massachusetts Institute of Technology president Vannevar Bush, the government's wartime Office of Scientific Research and Development linked rapidly expanding research facilities—like MIT's Radiation and Servomechanisms laboratories and the Applied Physics Lab at Johns Hopkins—directly to the corporations like General Electric, Bendix, and IBM that could manufacture military useful devices from radar sets to proximity fuses. The development of the atomic bomb through the Manhattan Project was emblematic of these relationships: its cadre of refugee scientists initially ran the world's first atomic reactor beneath a University of Chicago sports facility, but it required the government-led mobilization of industrial resources on a vast scale to produce actual nuclear weapons.

With government funds shaping academic research agendas, this nexus deepened after the war. Further breakthroughs followed. In 1951, collaboration between the Navy and MIT's Servo Lab produced *Whirlwind*, the world's first digital computer, and the following year the first programmable machine tool was produced.[12] With lucrative contracts, research funding, and professional prestige at stake, this could be a cutthroat world as inventors and research labs battled to secure patent rights while key figures moved seamlessly through the interconnected worlds

---

[11] Mara Drogan, "The Nuclear Imperative: Atoms for Peace and the Development of U.S. Policy on Exporting Nuclear Power, 1953–1955," *Diplomatic History*, Vol. 40, No. 5 (2015), 952.
[12] "An Automatic Machine Tool," *Scientific American*, September 1, 1952.

of government, business, and the academy. With science and technology in the lead, other academic disciplines were drawn into what historian David Engerman describes as "close and confidential" relationships with various arms of the national security state.[13] Anthropologists, geographers, historians, linguists, and political scientists collaborated in the new field of area studies, producing detailed analyses of regions of the world newly of interest to Washington. This useful knowledge was intended to help American policymakers get a more detailed understanding of the world they now led, particularly in areas where conflict with 'communism' was thought to be at its sharpest.

University professors and their doctoral students worked closely with the Ford, Rockefeller, Carnegie, and other industry-funded foundations, whose massive resources and established ties to government helped to shape research agendas while creating the new scholarly curricula needed to support them. Ambitious research projects in both hard and social sciences required legions of well-educated researchers, making the massive postwar expansion of higher education a circular and self-justifying proposition. Faculty ranks were boosted by wartime refugees and by émigrés attracted by the prospect of well-paid and prestigious positions, while student numbers were swollen by the recruitment of overseas students, whose numbers doubled between 1950 and 1955.[14] More broadly, these shifts rested on a transformation in the class character of the student body as government grants to former soldiers under the 1944 Servicemen's Readjustment Act (the GI Bill) and a general rise in living standards combined to begin making higher education normative for the broad American middle class.

The implicit rationale for this massive expansion in knowledge production was that America—and Americans—needed to master the complex challenges of world leadership, tasks that required proficiency at everything from science and technology to geography and behavioral science. For the new hegemon, ostensibly objective knowledge *about* the world was inextricably tied to the task of *shaping* the world in ways that both explained and facilitated American predominance. Calls by a 1947 presidential commission for university curricula to abandon parochialism in favor of "world citizenship"—essentially the kind gauzy internationalism advocated by Henry Luce, Henry Wallace, and Wendell Willkie to popularize America's entry into the World War—concealed a more hard-edged hegemonic project.[15] World citizenship and a universal family of man were all well and good, but there was never any doubt over who sat at

---

[13]David Engerman, "Bernath Lecture: American Knowledge and Global Power," *Diplomatic History*, Vol. 31, No. 4 (2007), 603.
[14]Ibid., 608.
[15]Ibid., 607.

the head of the family table and set the house rules. As Michael Adas points out, American elites embraced the apparently paradoxical belief that "their nation's history was unprecedented and unique" while simultaneously claiming that "American institutions, ideas, and modes of organization" should serve as "models for all societies."[16]

As US hegemony took shape, specialists in the emerging fields of modernization and development studies argued that American technical know-how, backed by modest financial aid, could promote economic advance in the 'underdeveloped'—and now decolonizing—countries of the 'third world.' Modeled on the American-led reform of financial systems in Latin America and baked into the Bretton Woods system, this developmentalism also promised to combat the threat of Soviet influence in the post-colonial world. Announcing what became known as the Point Four aid program in January 1949 (see Chapter Four), President Truman presented this case, pointing to American pre-eminence in the "development of industrial and scientific techniques" and arguing that these skills, applied in the spirit of "democratic fair-dealing" and supported by "limited" material aid, could forge a "constructive program for the better use of the world's human and natural resources."[17]

To policymakers and newly minted modernization theorists, the Tennessee Valley Authority (TVA) seemed to offer a replicable model for development projects worldwide. This sprawling New Deal project used dams and hydroelectric power to promote economic growth and industrialization in America's rural South, and TVA-type schemes were soon proposed for the Indus, Jordan, Mekong, Nile, and Yangtze rivers. While many such projects collapsed in the face of national rivalries and Cold War tensions, their grandiose scale had a powerful appeal to newly emerging national elites. They were accompanied by numerous other projects designed to generate power, modernize infrastructure, and combat disease, while agricultural productivity was boosted through a 'green revolution' based on the use of genetically modified high yield varieties of wheat, rice, and other staples. Beginning with the late-war United Nations Relief and Rehabilitation Administration, much of this work was done by American specialists operating under the auspices of the United Nations, a move that reinforced claims to disinterested universalism.

American universities became deeply involved in development work in the 'third world' as modernizing missions fanned out across the world: in 1957, Turkey alone hosted technical assistance projects run under US government contracts by Georgetown University, New York University,

---

[16]Michael Adas, *Dominance By Design: Technological Imperatives and America's Civilizing Mission* (Cambridge, MA: Harvard University Press, 2006), 226.
[17]Truman, quoted in David Ekbladh, *The Great American Mission: Modernization and the Construction of an American World Order* (Princeton: Princeton University Press, 2010), 78.

and the University of Nebraska.[18] Crucially, universities also provided much of the theoretical underpinning for modernization. Government and foundation funding for area studies overlapped with this work, particularly at MIT, where the Center for International Studies (CENIS) was set up in 1952. CENIS leader Walt Rostow quickly emerged as a major proponent of modernization theory, and his 1958 book *The Stages of Economic Growth*—tellingly subtitled *A Non-Communist Manifesto*—offered a concise summary of its key concepts. Taking the development of the industrialized West as normative, Rostow outlined the economic and cultural steps that could propel 'traditional' societies along to road toward industrial 'takeoff.'

Modernization theory rested on the untroubled assumption that capitalist economic growth was a self-evident measure of human progress: as Truman put it in his Point Four address, "greater production is the key to prosperity and peace."[19] American economists developed the concept of Gross National Product (GNP) as the defining metric by which growth—and hence progress—could be measured and policy defined. Few stopped to ask what effects untrammeled capitalist growth might have on the people of the traditional societies it was held to benefit. Moreover, the interest of American policymakers and academics in modernization was deeply embedded in broader efforts to consolidate hegemony and contain the perceived threat from the Soviet Union. It is telling that in 1951, government aid programs were organized into the new Mutual Security Agency, a name that made explicit the connection between development and national security.[20] Diplomats quickly found that this unequivocal link undercut efforts to present the United States as a disinterested force for good, and in 1953 it was renamed the Foreign Operations Administration.

High Art and Soft Power

The powerful sense of American self-confidence and superiority that was rooted in wartime victory and sustained by the postwar boom was reflected in two key cultural phenomena: first, the world center of high art shifted from Europe to New York, and second, American popular culture flowed outwards along the highways of economic, military, and political power. The transatlantic migration of high art—and of the art market—began

---

[18] Ekbladh, *The Great American Mission*, 172.
[19] Ibid., 178.
[20] Corinna R. Unger, "American Development Aid, Decolonization, and the Cold War," in David C. Engerman et al. (eds.), *America and the World*, Vol. IV (Cambridge: Cambridge University Press, 2021), 196.

as artists and avant-garde intellectuals fled to the United States following the outbreak of war in Europe. At the same time, war and the booming American economy shattered the Depression-era convergence between political radicalism and cutting-edge art, drawing artistic modernism into a flourishing and highly commodified art market. American businessman Solomon R. Guggenheim and his niece Peggy were key figures in this process. After running galleries in London and Paris, Peggy Guggenheim returned to New York in 1941, where she oversaw the development of the family art collection while promoting the work of emerging American artists like Jackson Pollock. The intersection of top-flight European artists, talented and energetic young Americans, and a supercharged market complete with wealthy sponsors quickly produced a new and distinctively American style, known as abstract expressionism. Moving rapidly from rebellion to orthodoxy, works by painters like Pollock, Jasper Johns, and sculptor Alexander Calder were soon commanding stunning prices. Many individual artists were political radicals—according to critic Clement Greenberg, Pollock remained a "goddamn Stalinist"—but they shed the overt political charge that had marked the work of their Cubist, Dadaist, and Surrealist predecessors.[21] Irrespective of their personal views, America's avant-garde artists were marshaled in support of Washington's hegemonic project, with Jackson Pollock and others emerging—in critic Serge Guilbaut's words—as "nothing less than a liberal warrior in the Cold War."[22]

The transatlantic migration of high art was particularly evident in architecture. Here, the modernist ethic of flat surfaces, extensive use of glass, and an avoidance of ornamentation produced the International Style pioneered in interwar Europe by architects including Walter Gropius (Dutch), Le Corbusier (French), and Ludwig Mies (German). Their personal trajectories reflected broader patterns: Gropius and Mies both moved to the United States and did much of their later work there, while Le Corbusier co-designed the United Nations building in New York with Brazilian Oscar Niemayer. That building, a modernist icon and the physical embodiment of both universalist idealism and American hegemony, was widely imitated in numerous corporate headquarters around the world as an Americanized international style radiated outward. Meanwhile, 'modern art' was physically headquartered in New York in the Rockefeller-funded Museum of Modern Art and in architect Frank Lloyd Wright's stunning Guggenheim Museum, opened in 1959. Redolent with the promise of progress, American

---

[21]Clement Greenberg, quoted in Perry Anderson, *The Origins of Postmodernity* (London: Verso, 1998), 83.
[22]Serge Guilbaut, *How New York Stole the Idea of Modern Art: Abstract Expressionism, Freedom, and the Cold War*, trans. Arthur Goldhammer (Chicago: University of Chicago Press, 1983), 202.

modernism embodied the limitless self-confidence of an elite whose time has come, and in doing so it became the house style of the postwar boom.

While high art was taking root in New York, American popular culture was flowing out across the globe. In the "American Century," Henry Luce had envisaged "American jazz, Hollywood movies, American slang [and] American machines" as key elements of the United States' coming hegemony.[23] As with much else, the war accelerated the advance of this soft power as American troops armed with chewing gum, cigarettes, nylons, and chocolate served as vectors of cultural connectivity as well as of military predominance. Meanwhile, US aid—from the tanks and airplanes delivered through Lend-Lease to the food distributed by UNRRA and other relief agencies—showcased America's material prosperity. Abundance presented an unmistakable vision of American superiority in a world ravaged by war, hunger, and economic breakdown: as Reinhold Wagnleitner points out, American goods and the popular culture they materialized modeled powerfully attractive images of "freedom, casualness, vitality, liberality, modernity, and youthfulness."[24] The American movie industry was central to this process as Hollywood studios leveraged their enormous resources, deep pools of talent, and advanced technical capacities to shoulder aside national film industries battered by war and economic breakdown. As television began to cut into cinema attendance in the United States—in 1949 almost all the world's domestic TV sets were in America—global markets became even more important, and Hollywood became *the* cinema of an American-dominated world.[25]

American popular culture and the values of modernity, freedom, and democracy that it seemed to embody were critical to building popular acceptance of American hegemony, especially in Europe. Having helped to derail the radical insurgencies that might have pointed toward different and more communal visions of modernity, Moscow found it impossible to compete in the interlinked spheres of popular culture and the production of desirable consumer goods. Meanwhile, the American government intervened directly and consciously into this culture war, weaponizing American consumerism for service in Eastern Europe and beyond. Founded in 1942, the Voice of America radio station broadcast a carefully curated mixture of news, music, and reruns of popular American shows designed to highlight the contrast between the 'free world' and Soviet style 'slavery.' Ironically, jazz—the archetypal music of an African American population

---

[23] Henry Luce, "The American Century" (1941), reprinted in *Diplomatic History*, Vol. 23, No. 2 (1999), 169.
[24] Reinhold Wagnleitner, "The Empire of Fun, or Talkin' Soviet Union Blues: The Sound of Freedom and U.S. Cultural Hegemony in Europe," *Diplomatic History*, Vol. 23, No. 3 (1999), 515.
[25] Wagnleitner, "The Empire of Fun," 507.

that was still denied full legal equality—was seen as particularly emblematic of innovation and creative freedom in the capitalist West. Washington also sponsored numerous cultural initiatives, including academic and artistic conferences, art shows, cultural exchanges, and tours by jazz musicians. In some cases, Washington's role in promoting such events was clear, but often the CIA utilized fronts and intermediaries like the Congress for Cultural Freedom in order to channel covert funds to favored projects.

The relationship between Washington and the artists it sponsored was not always an easy one. In 1946, a traveling modern art exhibition designed to showcase American freedom and creativity was canceled amidst harsh political criticism. "If that's art, I'm a Hottentot," President Truman scoffed in knee-jerk racism after reviewing artworks selected for the exhibition.[26] Perhaps unsurprisingly given the cutting-edge nature of the art, many of the contributing artists were also discovered to hold left-wing political beliefs. After this debacle, respectable museum directors and the nonprofit American Federation of Arts were encouraged—and covertly funded—to take the lead in the overseas promotion of American art. Nevertheless, the tension between wanting to showcase American freedom while being concerned about where that free expression might lead was ever present.

A similar tension existed within popular culture, as economic prosperity and the expansion of higher education allowed the creation of the teenager, a new category of person living in the liminal space between childhood and adult world of work. Consumer products aimed at teenagers helped to create a youth culture marked by a rebellious challenge to social conformity. For most of the 1950s, rock 'n roll music and movies like Marlon Brando's *The Wild One* might discomfort older people, but they hardly offered a generalized challenge to social norms. By the end of the decade, however, new groups of youthful rebels—loosely known as the beat generation—were inspired by the civil rights movement to advance a broader and more political critique to American society. In particular, women began to mount a vocal challenge to oppressive and discriminatory social norms, beginning what would emerge more fully in the 1960s as the second wave of feminism.

Questions of race occupied a particularly critical place in this tension between promoting and fearing freedom. In 1956, the State Department began organizing tours of leading American jazz musicians to Eastern Europe and to 'Third World' countries where the government was keen to counter Soviet influence. Viewed as a uniquely American art form, jazz showcased Black musicians whose presence, tour organizers hoped, would project an image of racial equality that could blunt Soviet criticism of

---

[26]Michael L. Krenn, *Fall-Out Shelters for the Human Spirit: American Art and the Cold War* (Chapel Hill, NC: University of North Carolina Press, 2005), 43.

Jim Crow segregation. In 1956, trumpeter Dizzy Gillespie led a tour of the Middle East, followed by Benny Goodman and Dave Brubeck—white leaders of multi-racial bands—whose tours took them to Southeast Asia, Poland, Iran, and Iraq in 1957 and 1958. Goodman argued that differences of "race, creed, or color" were not "of the slightest importance among the best of jazz bands," and he believed that his State Department-sponsored tour had helped to counteract a Communist-inspired perception of racial injustice in the United States.[27] Black musicians may have felt differently. Many appreciated government sponsorship, and they certainly enjoyed the opportunity to meet fans and fellow musicians around the world, but none were unaffected by systemic racism back home. By the early 1960s, even Gillespie, a frequent participant in State Department tours, was predicting a "revolution" in the United States if Black demands for equality were not met.[28] As Petra Goedde points out, the United States Information Agency—the main sponsor of the jazz tours—learnt the "painful lesson" that it could "control neither the messenger nor the message when it sent its cultural ambassadors abroad."[29]

The Civil Rights Movement—A Second American Front in the Postwar Upsurge

In the early postwar years, progressive-minded American elites often viewed "Jim Crow" racial segregation as a "blot" on the national character or, as Cornell professor and member of the President's Committee on Civil Rights Robert E. Cushman put it, an "Achilles heel."[30] This sensibility reflected a growing realization in ruling-class circles that the existence of overt, entrenched, and legally sanctioned racial discrimination in the United States undercut Washington's ability to present itself as the champion of freedom and democracy worldwide. The 1947 report of the President's Committee made this linkage explicit, arguing that while American policy aimed to "make the United States an enormous positive influence for peace and progress throughout the world," racial discrimination at home was a "serious obstacle" to achieving that goal.[31] Jim Crow, in other words, was blocking

---

[27]Penny von Eschen, *Satchmo Blows Up the World: Jazz Ambassadors Play the Cold War* (Cambridge, MA: Harvard University Press, 2004), 44–5.
[28]Frank Kovsky, *John Coltrane and the Jazz Revolution of the 1960s* (New York: Pathfinder Press (1970) 1998), 206.
[29]Petra Goedde, "US Mass Culture and Consumption in a Global Context," in Engerman et al. (eds.), *America and the World*, 288.
[30]Mary L. Dudziak, *Cold War Civil Rights: Race and the Image of American Democracy* (Princeton: Princeton University Press, 2000), 5, 23, 29.
[31]Ibid., 80.

the full realization of American global hegemony. Given these stakes, a broad bipartisan agreement that blatant segregation would have to go quickly emerged. This did not imply a commitment to end highly profitable practices of racial discrimination in employment, housing, education, and other spheres of social life, and nor did it point toward the establishment of full legal and political equality for African Americans. But it did mean that the Truman and Eisenhower administrations, backed by the Supreme Court and supported by a broad array of opinion-formers, would take steps to begin to dismantle Jim Crow's most egregious features.

Legislative progress in this direction in the early postwar was effectively stymied by powerful Southern Democrats—or Dixiecrats—whose leader Strom Thurmond ran against Truman in the 1948 presidential election on the States Rights Party ticket. Blocked in Congress, Truman invoked executive authority to mandate the desegregation of the military in July 1948, a move that was linked to the reintroduction of the draft as the postwar remilitarization drive got underway. With Supreme Court backing, limited steps toward the desegregation of higher education followed, while Truman's Justice Department set in motion a challenge to the constitutionality of racial segregation in schools. Pushed forward by the National Association for the Advancement of Colored People (NAACP), this work culminated in the Supreme Court's landmark 1954 ruling in *Brown v. Board of Education in Topeka, Kansas* that segregated schools were inherently unequal and therefore unconstitutional. *Brown* gave government propagandists a powerful new weapon, and Voice of America was beaming the news into the Soviet Union within an hour of the verdict. Actual school desegregation was a different matter. A follow-up Supreme Court ruling in 1955 mandated that desegregation should advance 'with all deliberate speed,' a thin euphemism for 'slowly,' and one that gave defenders of Jim Crow time to rally local opposition to integration. Violent demonstrations against school desegregation followed, and in 1957 President Eisenhower responded to racist anti-integration mobs by sending federal troops to Little Rock, Arkansas to escort Black students into class at the local high school.

Despite resistance from racist officials and violent mobs, these steps, along with legal rulings securing the desegregation of local bus lines and other institutions, began to register real progress toward dismantling Jim Crow segregation. But none of this happened simply because elite Americans grasped that overt segregation was incompatible with the exercise of hegemony in a world wracked by anticolonial struggles. For America's rulers—including many who continued to hold deeply racist views—the problem of the segregationist "blot" on their country's image was not that Jim Crow existed, but that its existence could no longer be swept under the carpet. This new fact of world politics was the product of the increasingly self-confident refusal of millions of Black Americans to tolerate life under Jim Crow segregation and its more informal counterparts in the North, and their increasing willingness to take action to end it.

Rising resistance to Jim Crow had deep roots, including in the formation of a vibrant and resilient African American culture in Harlem and other places during the interwar years, but it was the immediate result of the wartime experience of millions of Black Americans. Some 1.25 million Blacks served in the military, a number roughly proportional to the size of the African American population.[32] Almost all served in segregated units that were assigned primarily to heavy, dangerous, but largely noncombatant roles. Despite the best efforts of the Jim Crow military, however, Black soldiers deployed abroad often interacted with white civilians—both Axis and Allied—who did not automatically treat them as second-class citizens. Moreover, their service was encouraged and promoted by widely read 'Negro' newspapers that viewed the defeat of fascism abroad and Jim Crow at home as two interlocking goals. As a result of these experiences, Black soldiers returning from the war were reluctant to resubmit to the daily indignities of racism and segregation: as one returning GI told a bus driver attempting to enforce segregated seating put it, "I fought by the side of white men and intend to sit by the side of white men also."[33] Even the sight of a Black man in uniform could provoke a violent response from those who read its implicit assertion of authority and demand for respect as a challenge to legal segregation. Even small acts of personal resistance could trigger vicious beatings and lynchings that were designed, as the Black-owned *Pittsburgh Courier* put it, to "put the returned Negro veteran in his place."[34] Between 1941 and 1946, at least twenty-eight active-duty soldiers were killed for refusing to submit silently to the humiliations of Jim Crow, and many more were suffered non-fatal gunshots, beatings, and imprisonment.[35]

Racist attempts to push African Americans back into their "place" unfolded in the context of broader wartime economic and social changes. During the 1940s, around 1.5 million African Americans left the largely rural South to work in booming war plants in cities like Detroit, Pittsburgh, Los Angeles, and Oakland. Arriving migrants faced discrimination in hiring—they were often placed in the heaviest and dirtiest jobs—and housing, and they also faced attacks by cops and racist mobs. But discrimination, beatings, and everyday racial prejudice stirred resistance, and in Harlem, New York, the police wounding of a Black soldier in August 1943 sparked a rebellion that gained control of the district before being beaten back by thousands of city police, National Guardsmen, and white vigilantes. Meanwhile, under pressure from a threatened march on Washington in

---

[32]T. Fujitani, *Race for Empire: Koreans as Japanese and Japanese as Americans during World War II* (Berkley: University of California Press, 2011), 209.
[33]Margaret A. Burnham, *By Hands Now Known: Jim Crow's Legal Executioners* (New York: W. W. Norton, 2023), 111.
[34]Dudziak, *Cold War Civil Rights*, 20.
[35]Burnham, *By Hands Now Known*, 109.

1941 organized by labor leader A. Philip Randolph of the Brotherhood of Sleeping Car Porters, the Roosevelt administration took executive action to outlaw racial discrimination in war plants. Weakly enforced by the new Fair Employment Practice Commission, these moves did not end racist hiring practices or job segregation, but they did give Black workers a lever with which to fight for integration into the industrial workforce. By the middle of the war, African Americans constituted a significant minority of the workforce in key industries, where unions like the United Auto Workers and the United Steelworkers often played an important role in combatting racial prejudice and promoting on-the-job integration.

The changing class composition and geographical location of the African American population, combined with the refusal of many Black GIs to return to Jim Crow segregation, helped to generate a powerful postwar spirit of resistance to racial discrimination. This popular upwelling was further inspired by anticolonial struggles unfolding around the world, news of which featured regularly in the Black press. This emerging movement for civil rights attracted talented and resourceful leaders like Dr. Martin Luther King Jr., but these figures were themselves shaped by the power of grassroots activism. In 1955–56, this popular resistance reached a new high point in Montgomery Alabama, where veteran labor leader E. D. Nixon and experienced young activists like Rosa Parks led a year-long boycott of the city's buses to protest their segregationist practices. This successful struggle exemplified the determined, bottom-up, and largely working-class character of what became known as the civil rights movement. Always a broad combination of activists and campaigns rather than a centralized organization, over the next decade this movement played a major role in American politics that culminated in the passage of the federal Civil Rights and Voting Rights acts in 1964–65, victories that in turn propelled further battles against racial injustice.

The civil rights movement was driven forward by a campaign of mass actions, including strikes, street demonstrations, boycotts, sit-ins, and other forms of nonviolent protest. For many activists, however, nonviolence was a tactical choice rather than an immutable principle, and they were often ready and willing to use more forceful means to defend their communities from racist attack. In 1947, armed African Americans faced down a Klu Klux Klan motorcade in Monroe, North Carolina. One participant in these events was former marine Robert F. Williams, who pointed to the leadership provided by "returned veterans who were very militant and who didn't scare easy."[36] Williams went on to form community self-defense squads in Monroe and to inspire similar developments elsewhere. Williams's actions

---

[36]Walter Rucker, "Crusader in Exile: Robert F. Williams and the International Struggle for Black Freedom in America," *The Black Scholar*, Vol. 36, Nos. 2–3 (2006), 22.

FIGURE 8.2 *A crowd of five thousand African Americans rally in the First Baptist Church during the Montgomery, Alabama bus boycott, February 27, 1956. Rally participants expressed their redoubled commitment not to ride city buses until the company ended its segregationist policies. (Photo: Bettmann/Getty.)*

in the late 1950s were inspired by the example of the Cuban revolution, an attraction—and a revolutionary convergence—that was deepened in a meeting with Fidel Castro in Harlem in 1960. In embracing Cuba, Williams advocated revolutionary change in the United States, and in doing so he helped to open the door to a new generation of militant African American leaders like Malcolm X.

Constructing the Good War

Despite the horrors of a struggle in which over 405,000 American soldiers were killed, along with 12,000 civilians—many of them merchant seamen—and the 75,000 workers who died in wartime industrial accidents, for many Americans the Second World War came to be remembered as a 'good war.' This was not a universal perception, but in contrast to the wars that both preceded and followed it, many believed that in the Second World War moral justice lay clearly and unambiguously on their side. Primed from early in the war by ideologues like Henry Luce, many also bought into a vision of American global hegemony as a project rooted in the worldwide extension of freedom and democracy. However flawed this vision may have been—and however imperialistic and exploitative the reality of the new world order—it profoundly shaped American understandings of the war and the world it created.

The power and resilience of the notion of a good war was also rooted in the lived experience of millions of Americans. While US casualties were enormous, they constituted a mere 0.32 percent of the prewar population; in contrast, Soviet losses accounted for around 15 percent of the population, while other combatant nations also suffered heavily. In addition, the United States suffered no damage to its buildings, farms, and infrastructure, and while wartime rationing was an annoyance, Americans experienced none of the wartime destruction, fear, and hunger that constituted daily life in much of the world. At the same time, many American workers and family farmers experienced rising real wages and incomes, while the economic gulf between the richest citizens and the poorest sections of society narrowed appreciably.[37] For many women, wartime work—and wartime wages—opened new vistas of opportunity and agency, while for African Americans war work and military service laid the basis for the intensified postwar struggle for full legal equality. These trends continued after the war, and they were embedded into the long economic upswing amid a rising tide of cars, refrigerators, televisions, and other consumer durables. In the minds of many Americans, the old class divisions of the 1930s were replaced with "middle-class" prosperity and visions of an "Affluent Society."[38]

This understanding of the Second World War as a good war, carefully and constantly reinforced by politicians, popular histories, and by films, novels, and TV shows, helped to naturalize America's postwar hegemony. Buttressed by anti-communist witch-hunts and by a concerted drive to narrow the space for dissent, it also underpinned broad support—or at least acquiescence—for the defense of the 'free world' in the deepening Cold War. That does not mean that Americans supported every action that their government took: as Marilyn Young shows, the war in Korea was remarkably unpopular, with just 37 percent of the public supporting it by 1952.[39] Nevertheless, while domestic support for specific policies might waver, the ideological legacy of the good war framed a broad and largely

---

[37]Neil A. Wynn, "The 'Good War': The Second World War and Postwar American Society," *Journal of Contemporary History* Vol. 31, No. 3 (1996), 469.
[38]Wynn, "The 'Good War,'" 468.
[39]Mark Philip Bradley and Mary L. Dudziak (eds.), *Making the Forever War: Marilyn B. Yong on the Culture and Politics of American Militarism* (Amherst, MA: University of Massachusetts Press, 2021), 55–6.

uncritical acceptance of American foreign policy that lasted deep into the postwar, only beginning to fray amid mounting opposition to the war in Vietnam in the late 1960s.

For Further Reading

Michael Adas, *Dominance by Design: Technological Imperatives and America's Civilizing Mission* (Cambridge, MA: Harvard University Press, 2006).

Mark Philip Bradley and Mary L. Dudziak (eds.), *Making the Forever War: Marilyn B. Yong on the Culture and Politics of American Militarism* (Amherst, MA: University of Massachusetts Press, 2021).

Alan Brinkley, *The End of Reform: New Deal Liberalism in Recession and War* (New York: Vintage, 1995).

David Ekbladh, *The Great American Mission: Modernization and the Construction of an American World Order* (Princeton: Princeton University Press, 2010).

David Engerman, "Bernath Lecture: American Knowledge and Global Power," *Diplomatic History*, Vol. 31, No. 4 (2007).

Serge Guilbaut, *How New York Stole the Idea of Modern Art: Abstract Expressionism, Freedom, and the Cold War*, trans. Arthur Goldhammer (Chicago: University of Chicago Press, 1983).

David M. Kennedy, *The American People in World War II* (Oxford: Oxford University Press, 1999).

Art Preis, *Labor's Giant Step: The First Twenty Years of the CIO, 1936–1955* (New York: Pathfinder Press, 1971).

Ellen Schrecker, "McCarthyism: Political Repression and the Fear of Communism," *Social Research*, Vol. 71, No. 4 (2004).

Corinna R. Unger, "American Development Aid, Decolonization, and the Cold War," in David C. Engerman et al. (eds.), *America and the World*, Vol. IV (Cambridge: Cambridge University Press, 2021).

Penny M. Von Eschen, *Satchmo Blows Up the World: Jazz Ambassadors Play the Cold War* (Cambridge, MA: Harvard University Press, 2004).

Reinhold Wagnleitner, "The Empire of Fun, or Talkin' Soviet Union Blues: The Sound of Freedom and U.S. Cultural Hegemony in Europe," *Diplomatic History*, Vol. 23, No. 3 (1999).

Neil A. Wynn, "The 'Good War': The Second World War and Postwar American Society," *Journal of Contemporary History* Vol. 31, No. 3 (1996).

From World War to Postwar: Some Conclusions

The Second World War ended unevenly, moving quickly toward peace—or at least some semblance of it—in some places, while in others unspooling into revolutions, anticolonial revolts, and regional conflicts, some of which continued for decades. Around the world, urban workers, peasant farmers, and citizen soldiers seized on moments of collapse or transition to press their own claims in a wave of strikes, mutinies, and uprisings. These ragged endings of world war necessarily shaped the untidy beginnings of the postwar, and they, rather than simply the world war in its narrowest sense, constituted the contours of the new global order. Unfolding at different speeds in different parts of the world and dyssynchronous across the interlocking spheres of diplomatic, political, military, social, and economic life, the consolidation of the postwar took at least a further decade after the formal end of the great power conflict in September 1945. This expansive timeline underscores the fact that these were *processes* of transition rather than simply jumps from one clearly defined state called 'war' to another called 'peace.' This understanding also highlights the fact that the ultimate shape of the postwar world was not teleologically determined, but instead involved the contested and often bloody resolution of clashes between conflicting social forces and the foreclosure of other hopes, plans, and aspirations.

The single most important world-level consequence of this extended process was the establishment and consolidation of America's global hegemony, qualified though it was by the expansion of the Soviet Union, the Chinese Revolution, and by the instability generated by anticolonial revolt. Nevertheless, it took time to translate America's decisive military victory, including the defeat of its Italian, German, and Japanese rivals and the reduction of its British and French allies to the status of second-rank powers, into new structures of global predominance. Hegemony, it becomes clear, is not a *thing*, a crown or mantle that can be given, taken, or transferred from one power to another, but is instead a complex set of *relationships* that take time to construct, organize, and solidify.

The United States had emerged as the world's leading industrial economy by the early 1900s and it achieved global financial predominance after the First World War, and while battered by the Great Depression, these steps laid the basis for the rapid and dramatic expansion of the American economy during the Second World War. The arrival of American military power was even more explosive, with entirely new weapons systems—including strategic bombers, fleets of aircraft carriers, and atomic bombs—helping to take it from a second-rank military power to one of unprecedented global strength and reach in just four short years. By the end of the war, American military power was underpinned by a world-circling network of bases, and in the immediate postwar entire fleets were permanently stationed overseas for the first time. Even before the fighting ended, Washington had started to leverage this hard power to begin creating both a new world economic order—based on free trade and the US dollar—and a new political order, based on formally equal nations-states. Washington's success on these fronts, registered at Bretton Woods and at the founding conference of the United Nations in San Francisco, was underpinned by the wartime consolidation of its leadership of a block of Latin American nations. With its intertwined economic, military, political, and cultural dimensions, this regional hegemony modeled key aspects of the coming world-system and was indispensable to its creation.

While the world-level treaties and organization adopted at the end of the world war reflected the vast wartime expansion of American power, it took time to assemble and organize the dense networks of new relationships necessary to give hegemony real depth and content. This process of assuming or growing into hegemony turned out to be much more protracted and more complex than Washington had anticipated. In relation to Britain, for example, American leaders soon walked back their initial impulse simply to sideline the former hegemon, a proposal that resulted in the rapid suspension of Lend-Lease in summer 1945. Instead, Washington recognized that Britain's postwar recovery, along with that of other large and industrialized countries in Europe and Japan, was critical to the broader reconstruction of the world capitalist economy. That reconstruction, it turned out, would require the large-scale mobilization of American economic aid and capital investment, and in this context the plans for free trade and currency convertibility adopted at Bretton Woods could only be realized incrementally and over time.

As it began to navigate the complexities of the postwar world, Washington also recognized that it needed to draw on Britain's long experience of imperial governance and on its continued overseas military power. This was particularly important in Southeast Asia, the Middle East, and Sub-Saharan Africa, key regions where US forces were not yet embedded. In this context, Washington made a sharp turn away from the wartime promises of national self-determination enshrined in the Atlantic Charter and expressed in vague plans to replace colonial rule with UN trusteeship, and instead backed the re-establishment of European colonialism in Southeast Asia and its maintenance in Africa and elsewhere. This abrupt shift does not necessarily mean that Henry Luce, Henry Wallace, and Wendell Willkie were acting in bad faith when they advocated for a homogeneous and postcolonial world of nation-states under the United States' leadership. Their collective early-war envisioning of an "American Century" helped to convince many Americans of the efficacy—and even the moral grandeur—of the United States' coming hegemony, but it always glossed the hard-edged power upon which this new order would be based. Much of Washington's wartime claim to moral leadership—like Roosevelt's hints of support for Moroccan independence and the promises of UN trusteeship—lived within this ambiguity, but as the end of the war approached, harsher and less morally appealing policies came to the fore. This shift, however, could be conveniently repackaged as critical to the defense of the 'free world' against Communism.

In this way, the emerging American hegemon drew on the colonial power and prestige of Britain, France, Belgium, and Holland to buttress its position at a time when US policymakers were focused on crises in Europe and Asia. As a consequence, the postwar decade was in some ways a US-British global dyarchy, or system of two-party governance, with the United States only stepping fully into its hegemony in the mid-1950s. In reality, of course, the parties were far from equal, but recognizing the diarchic character of the immediate postwar decade helps us to see the transfer of hegemony as an extended process that combined collaboration and competition, rather than as a single event simultaneous with the end of the war.

While Washington's hegemony took a decade to consolidate, its true globality was qualified from the beginning by the expansion of Soviet power into Eastern Europe and by the rapidly escalating civil war in China. These challenges to American predominance were not fundamentally centered on an expansion of communism as a political ideology; instead, the extension of non-capitalist economic relations into Eastern Europe and then their establishment in China necessarily ripped vast potential markets—and hence vast potential profits—from the reach of American business. This situation was a direct product of Washington's wartime decisions to rely on the Soviets to carry the ground war against Germany and to fight a war against Japan that did not involve launching American land armies into China. The point is not that these strategic decisions were wrong; after all, the air-sea war and the massive economic growth that produced it brought the United States crushing victories. Instead, these strategic choices brought with them unintended consequences for the postwar world. Moreover, these consequences were magnified by contingent factors, including the fact that the great GI mutiny blocked the large-scale deployment of US troops to China after the Japanese surrender, thereby undercutting Washington's ability to impose postwar order there.

By summer 1945, American leaders were already well aware of degree to which the expansion of Soviet power would limit their global predominance, but with the exception of a few hotheads, they accepted the political and military impossibility of rolling back Moscow's control of Eastern Europe by military—or hot—means. Instead, Washington quickly developed plans to 'contain' the Soviet Union by exercising constant but cold military pressure with the aim of weakening it to the point at which a more forceful intervention might become possible. In this light, the rapid deepening of the Cold War in the immediate postwar years registered the *limits* of American power, not its overwhelming strength. As the hub of prewar world politics and the place where the divide between the presence and absence of America's postwar predominance was sharpest, Europe inevitably emerged as the epicenter of the Cold War. Given the global scope of American ambition, the deadly potential of the nuclear standoff with the USSR, and Washington's universalizing claim to be acting on behalf of human freedom worldwide, the Cold War necessarily played a key role in shaping the structure of world politics as it intersected with local, national, and regional issues. In many ways, 'Cold War' became synonymous with 'postwar,' giving shape and definition to an entire period of history. As I have argued in these pages, however, it is more accurate to see the Cold War as an *element* of the postwar, a key constituent of world politics, but by no means the sole one. Viewing the Cold War as a US-Soviet conflict centered in Europe helps to make it clear that while this contest necessarily impinged on developments elsewhere in the world, it neither defined the origins of national or class struggles elsewhere in the world, and nor did it overdetermine their outcomes. So, for example, while the American-sponsored coups in Iran in 1953 and in Guatemala the following year were certainly conceptualized and justified in Cold War terms, they were fundamentally driven by Washington's response to national and regional-level challenges that had nothing directly to do with Moscow or with the alleged expansion of its brand of 'Communism.'

Thinking about the Cold War in this way is particularly useful in helping to understand the significance of the great worldwide wave of popular protest that begin in the last years of the world war and continued into the early 1950s. The individual links in this interconnected series of protests and uprisings—from strikes and military mutinies to the election of social democratic and 'progressive' governments and anticolonial insurrections—all had specific modalities and discrete causalities. Nevertheless, their participants shared a common conviction that the end of the world war opened new possibilities to fight for better wages and living conditions, sweeping land reform, an end to racial discrimination, the overturn of colonial rule, or simply—and most profoundly—for a more just and equal society.

An tremendous worldwide expression of popular agency, these struggles played a major role in shaping the emergence of the postwar world, particularly in China, where a popular revolution prevented the consolidation of a capitalist and pro-American nation-state, and throughout

Southeast Asia, where anticolonial revolts disrupted the re-establishment of direct colonial rule. Nevertheless, while popular uprisings flared across Europe and mass anticolonial movements challenged colonial rule from the Middle East to India and Sub-Saharan Africa, it was only in China, Vietnam, and Yugoslavia that insurgencies led to the establishment of governments willing to make a decisive break with capitalism. The role of pro-Moscow Communism was crucial here. Many political forces that called themselves communist participated in these struggles and helped to lead them, but parties that looked to the Soviet Union for leadership generally exercised a moderating influence, seeking to avoid confrontations that might disrupt Moscow's hopes of securing ongoing postwar collaboration with the United States. In some places—such as Greece—Moscow stood aside as British- and American-backed forces crushed popular revolts, while from Italy to Indonesia, pro-Soviet Communist parties used their considerable influence to moderate insurrectionary movements and channel them into safe bourgeois-democratic channels. In northern Korea, meanwhile, Soviet moves to dispel the radical energy embodied in the formation of the Korean People's Republic paralleled those of American occupation forces in the south. Not surprisingly, Moscow also sought to blunt advancing revolutions in China, Vietnam, and Yugoslavia, either by proposing partitions or by locking Communist parties into coalition governments. In these three cases, however, stubborn and battle-hardened national leaderships acting under tremendous popular pressure bucked Moscow's control, leading to revolutionary victories and the establishment of non-capitalist states. Ironically, these popular revolutionary victories also fractured the unity of a Communist world movement that had presented a façade of homogeneity since the great Stalinist purges of the 1930s.

The policies and actions of pro-Moscow Communists were not the only factor in determining the outcome of the postwar revolts. Nevertheless, it is safe to say that without Soviet cooperation, initially secured at the Tehran conference in November 1943, the road to the formation of stable postwar capitalist states in Europe and beyond would have been much longer and more difficult. Moreover, Moscow's single-minded and nationalistic focus on securing its own defenses meant that in the early postwar it had very little interest—and often even less purchase—in politics in the colonial world or in Latin America. In contrast to the years after the First World War, when Bolshevik revolutionaries organized the Communist International (or Comintern) in an attempt to advance worldwide revolution, during the long Second World War the Soviet government and those who followed its lead acted as primarily as forces for stability. As a token of their good intentions toward the West, the Comintern was dissolved in 1943. Moreover, despite the abrupt and thoroughly disastrous turn toward armed insurrection launched by the newly formed Cominform in 1947, by the early 1950s Soviet leaders had returned to the pursuit of accommodation and peaceful coexistence with the capitalist world.

The stabilization of US-Soviet relations in the mid-1950s—registered in the consolidation of partitions in Germany, Korea, and Vietnam and in the emerging architecture of nuclear standoff—overlapped with the completion of long-terms shifts in the relationship between the major capitalist states. By the mid-1950s, British, French, and Dutch efforts to stem the anti-colonial dynamics unleashed by the war had largely failed, and from Palestine, Indonesia, and Indochina to India and—increasingly—Africa, retreat from empire had become the dominant theme. Far from buoying the revival of the metropoles, as European governments had hoped, empire had become a costly drain on their resources. At the same time, burgeoning popular nationalism in Egypt and throughout the Middle East was undercutting British claims to regional leadership, and in this context the 1956 Suez Crisis signaled the end of the postwar dyarchy. At the same time, Washington accelerated the recalibration of its relationships with the newly emerging postcolonial nation-states, beginning in Indonesia in the early 1950s and culminating after 1957 in the cascading emergence of new countries in Africa. While American policymakers continued to support specific imperial positions—including its own colonies in Puerto Rico and across the Pacific, the period of generalized backing for European colonialism was drawing to a close.

These political shifts marked the consolidation of American global hegemony—with all its qualifications and discontents—and in this sense they also registered the generalized emergence of the postwar. Within the polarized framework of the Cold War and its nuclear standoff, the partition of Europe was firmly entrenched and would remain so until popular revolts toppled the Stalinist regimes in the late 1980s. In Asia, the Korean war marked the end of large-scale postwar fluidity and signaled Washington's grudging—and unofficial—acceptance of the existence of the People's Republic of China. This is not to suggest that peace had broken out: indeed, the partitioned successor states of former French Indochina would enjoy only a brief mid-decade respite before a renewed push for national reunification prompted an expanded US military presence and the beginnings of the country's long 'American War.'

The political consolidation of American hegemony—and hence of the postwar more broadly—was underpinned by the opening of a protracted period of capitalist expansion. As huge flows of American aid and investment capital jump-started economic recovery in Europe and Japan, the free trade-based and dollar denominated world economic system envisaged at Bretton Woods finally began to function. As it did so, world capitalism entered an upswing that began in the early 1950s and continued unabated into the late 1960s.[1] Driven by what environmental historian J. R. McNeill refers to as the "motown cluster," a nexus of technological innovation, giant monopoly corporations, and large-scale assembly line production named

---

[1] The United Nations, *World Economic and Social Survey 2017* (New York: United Nations, 2017), Chapter II, esp. 24.

after the iconic center of the automobile industry in Detroit, the protracted postwar boom assured a virtually uninterrupted period of year-on-year growth in all the major capitalist countries.[2] In the United States, real gross domestic product per capita rose by around 20 percent during the 1950s, underpinning social stability—with the important exception of the struggle for racial equality—and generating a broad sense of confidence, progress, and relative prosperity. This mood was reflected in a sharp uptick in the birthrate, long suppressed by Depression and war, producing a significant postwar 'baby boom.' In the United States, Western Europe, and Japan, this long economic upswing has been described by some commentators as a golden age of capitalism: in France, it is known simply as *Les Trente Glorieuses*, or the "thirty glorious years."[3]

The view from what was being referred to as the underdeveloped or Third world was far less rosy. Here, a long-term postwar decline in the price of exported primary products—raw materials and food—relative to the cost of imported manufactured goods worked to lock the countries of Latin America and the newly independent postcolonial nation-states in Asia and Africa into long-term relationships of unequal trade and deep indebtedness. Moreover, beyond a handful of showcase projects, the promise of modernization and industrial development that had helped to secure Latin American and 'Third World' support for the new American-led world order came to very little. Instead, the consolidation of American predominance was intertwined with the deepening of semi-colonial relationships between the new imperial metropole and its regional clients that were reinforced by the operation of the World Bank and the International Monetary Fund. Meanwhile, the motown cluster's insatiable demand for energy reshaped physical and human landscapes around the world and quickened the anthropogenic acceleration of climate change. Even as American hegemony was being consolidated in the mid-1950s, it was already becoming clear to scientists working on projects funded by the American Petroleum Institute and Humble Oil (now ExxonMobil) that increased concentrations of atmospheric CO_2 produced by burning fossil fuels would have dramatic long-term impacts on the environment. Not surprisingly, given their own short-term interests, oil industry bosses chose to suppress these findings.[4]

*

---

[2] J. R. McNeill, *Something New Under the Sun: An Environmental History of the Twentieth-Century World* (New York: Norton, 2000), 296–7.
[3] Jutta Bolt et al. (2014), "GDP per capita since 1820," in Jan Luiten van Zanden et al. (eds.), *How Was Life?: Global Well-Being since 1820* (Paris: OECD Publishing, 2014), 67.
[4] Benjamin Franta, "Early Oil Industry Knowledge of CO_2 and Global Warming," *Nature Climate Change*, Vol. 8 (December 2018), 1024–5.

This book opened with American diplomat James Dunn's prescient observation that in summer 1944 Italy had already begun to enter its "post-war period" even as military combat and popular insurgency raged across the northern part of the country. After Italy, Dunn went on to play a significant role in helping Washington to navigate the protracted worldwide transition from war to postwar. From April to June 1945, he was a delegate to the founding conference of the United Nations, where he mobilized support for the maintenance of French colonial rule in Indochina and elsewhere. A fierce anti-communist, Dunn served as chief political advisor to the American delegation at the Potsdam conference in July 1945, a key site at which the Cold War division of Europe took shape. From 1946 to 1952, Dunn was Washington's ambassador to Italy, where he oversaw the covert campaign that helped to secure the Christian Democrat's critical victory over the Italian Communist Party in the April 1948 general election. From Rome he moved on to Spain, where he negotiated the 1953 pact that restored relations with Franco's rightist regime—an "important bulwark in the defense of the West," as he put it—and secured American use of three key military bases.[5] Dunn's final ambassadorial posting was to Brazil, where he worked to strengthen US ties with Vargas's successor Juscelino Kubitschek, a relationship that unfolded within the framework of a common commitment to fight Communism.

In many ways, Dunn's role in the protracted process by which military victory was leveraged to create a consolidated—if qualified—global hegemony epitomizes the transition from world war to postwar. Through the work of Dunn and his colleagues, former enemies were rehabilitated as subordinate allies, Communism was 'contained,' neocolonial relationships with Third World countries were solidified, and the dense and worldwide webs of economic, military, political, and cultural connections that sustained hegemony were forged. By the time James Dunn retired in 1956, this work had been largely accomplished. At the same time, the consolidation of American hegemony necessarily rested on the negation—or at least the abridgement—of the hopes and aspirations that had driven the great postwar wave of protests, uprisings, and insurgencies. Given continuing conditions of exploitation, oppression, and injustice, however, rebellion had been temporarily stilled, not permanently crushed: the mid-1950s did see the consolidation of American predominance amid relative global stability, but on January 1, 1959—just two years after Dunn's retirement—Fidel Castro's guerrilla army marched into Havana. Even at the moment of its completion, the limits of America's global hegemony were revealed in graphic new ways.

---

[5]Dunn, quoted in Camille M. Cianfarra, "Spanish Tie's Need Cited by U.S. Envoy," *New York Times*, April 11, 1953, 11.

INDEX

Acheson, Dean 122
Acker, Achille van 140
Adenauer, Konrad Herman
 Joseph 141–42, 149
Afghanistan 114, 117, 121
African Americans 22, 34, 69, 215,
 228, 240–45
 military service 69, 243–44
 wartime migration 22, 243–44
 See also, civil rights movement.
African National Congress (ANC) 187
agriculture 82
 in Africa 176, 186
 collectivization 40, 45, 56, 62,
  88–90
 in Eastern Europe 40, 45, 46, 57, 62
 in Latin America 191, 208, 211,
  215–16
 land reform 72, 98, 130, 211–12
 United States 24, 28, 198, 246
 wartime transformation 176
Albania 38, 45, 49, 56
Alemán, Miguel 204
Algeria 145, 160–61, 172, 177, 182
 See also, Sétif Massacre.
All-India Muslim League 111–12
Allied Military Governments and
 Control Commissions 5–6,
 17–18, 44, 132
 Austria 52
 France 140
 Germany 17, 51–52, 132
 Italy 1, 17–18, 21, 127–31
 Japan 17, 137–39
al-Quwatli, Shuri 160, 167
aluminum and bauxite 24–25, 96, 155,
 184–85, 195, 215, 217–8
Ambon 101
America. *See* United States.

"American Century" (Henry Luce) 34,
 134, 227, 239, 251
Andaman Islands 96
Angola 187
Anglo-American alliance 19–21, 70,
 128, 134, 139, 146, 166, 174
 tensions within 21–22, 28–29, 131,
 128
Anglo-Iranian Oil Company (AIOC)
 25, 163–65, 167, 169
 See also, oil.
anthropogenic climate change 255
anti-colonial uprisings 6–7, 35, 93–95,
 107, 124, 143, 157, 242, 244,
 249, 252–53
 in Africa 160, 178, 181–84, 185,
 187
 in Caribbean 216–19
 character of 98, 107, 113, 119,
 252–53
 international solidarity 105, 151
 in Middle East 172
 in Southeast Asia 6, 93–95, 100,
 102–3, 105, 115–116, 177, 253
 See also, United States,
 anticolonialism of.
anti-Semitism 50, 56, 132, 169–70
Arab-Israeli War (1948–49) 170
Arab League 161, 168, 170, 171
ARAMCO (Arabian American Oil
 Company) 167
Árbenz, Juan Jacobo 210–11
architecture and 'International Style,'
 32, 238
Argentina 28, 194–95, 196, 198–99,
 202–3, 205, 206–10
art and the art market 237–39
Asian-African Conference (Bandung,
 1955) 115, 118

Asian Relations Conference (Delhi, 1947) 114–15
Atlantic Charter 31, 34, 95–96, 119, 195, 251
Atomic bomb. *See* nuclear weapons.
'Atoms for Peace,' 233
Aung San 103, 106
Australia 21, 28, 99, 111, 120, 123, 131, 154–56, 179
Australia, New Zealand, United States Security Treaty (ANZUS, 1951) 123, 155
Austria 44, 52
Austro-Hungarian Empire 2, 6, 44
autarky and autarkic-colonial projects 4, 5, 19, 82, 194
Axis alliance 3–5, 18, 28, 38, 41, 159 (*see also individual countries*)
   and Latin America 192, 194–95, 197–98, 201
   and regional autarkies 3–5, 19, 82
Azerbaijan 162–64

Badoglio, Marshal Pietro 1, 127–28, 131
Baghdad Pact (1955) 174
Baltic States 3, 38, 42, 45
Bandung Conference. *See* Asian-African Conference (1955).
Bangladesh 113
Baruch, Bernard, and Baruch Plan 53–54
Batista, General Fulgencio 204, 207, 210, 219–20
Battle of the Bulge (1944) 43
bauxite. *See* aluminum.
Belgian Congo 179, 187
Belgium 43, 133, 140, 147, 251
Belorussia 42, 45, 49–50
Beneš, Edvard 47, 55–56
Bengal 109, 111, 112, 113
Berlin, blockade and airlift (1948–49) 52, 148
Bikini Atoll 54, 123
birth rate 255
'black markets,' 18, 35, 77
Bolivia 196, 204, 207, 211–12
Borneo 107, 114
Bose, Subhas Chandra 96, 109

Bracero Program 198
Brando, Marlon 240
Brazil 15, 194, 196–98, 200, 202–5, 206–8, 209, 256
Brazzaville Conference (1944) 178
Bretton Woods Conference (1944) 28–31, 42, 70, 114, 147, 152–53, 157, 199, 200–201, 213, 229, 236, 250, 254
British Commonwealth 17, 107, 156, 178–79, 216, 218
British Empire 4–5, 20, 29, 70, 111, 152–53, 156, 169, 177–80, 182–88, 200, 254 (*see also* British-Imperial military forces)
   dominions and 'dedominionization,' 8, 28–29, 31, 109–13, 123, 154–56, 179
   nationality laws in 156, 179
   postwar plans for 102, 153, 159–62, 177–79, 254
   retreat from 254
British Guiana (Guyana) 24, 215–17, 219
British-Imperial military forces,
   in African 15, 176–77, 179
   demobilization protests 69, 151
   in Europe 44, 142
   Indian Army 93, 109, 111
   in Middle East 159–61, 172–74, 197
   in Pacific 21, 71
   Royal Indian Navy 69, 109–10
   in Southeast Asia 93, 98, 103, 105, 119
British Somaliland 144, 180
Brown v. Board of Education of Topeka, Kansas, 242
Broz, Josip. *See* Tito.
Buddhism 107
'buffer states,' in Eastern Europe 38–39, 42, 56–57, 61, 65
Bulgaria 38, 42, 45, 47, 56, 142, 166
Burma (Myanmar) 21, 69, 74, 96, 102–3, 105–9, 111, 114, 117, 121, 124, 153, 177
   ethnic minorities in 106, 113

Camacho, Manuel Ávila 198
Campos, Pedro Albizu 215

Canada 24–25, 28, 59, 111, 131, 152, 154–56, 179, 215, 218
   military 44, 154–55
   Quebec 24, 154, 156
   relations with US 155–56
capitalism 6, 39–40, 63, 117, 152, 206, 213
   debt 121, 214, 255
   'free market' 37, 201, 213–14
   overturn of 41, 60, 116, 133, 253
   postwar boom 13, 20, 27, 133, 146–48, 156–58, 226, 232–33, 234, 246, 254–55
   United States 13, 20, 26–28, 34, 233, 246
   world system 27–31, 40, 117, 157, 250
Cárdenas, Lázaro 157, 198, 220
Caribbean 8, 15, 17, 22, 25, 31, 167, 192–93, 195, 199, 215–19
   (*see also individual colonies and countries;* West Indian Federation)
Caribbean Labor Congress 215, 217.
Castro, Fidel 219–21, 245, 256
Central African Federation (1953–63) 183
Central Intelligence Agency (CIA) 115, 145, 164–65, 211, 231–32, 240, 256
Ceylon (Sri Lanka) 105, 112–13, 121
Chiang Kai-shek 18, 69–71, 73–74, 76–77, 79, 82, 84, 116, 123
Chicago Convention on International Civil Aviation (1944) 200
Chile 203, 209, 211, 212–14
China,
   civil war and revolution 3, 7, 37, 59, 69–82, 87, 91, 106, 116–19, 153, 228–30, 249, 253
   economy 70, 80–81, 87–90
   'four policemen,' 21, 31, 69–71, 73–75, 119
   Guomindang (Nationalist) government 3, 18, 37, 69–73, 75–78, 116
   Japanese invasion and occupation 3, 18, 70–72, 96–97
   in Korean War 82, 86–87, 230

   Peoples' Republic 79–82, 85, 229, 254
   Republic of (Taiwan) 79, 82, 86, 90–91, 121, 123
Chinese Communist Party 3, 37, 71–81, 89–90, 118
   consolidates rule 80–82, 87–91
   land reform and peasant base 72, 76–78, 80–81
Churchill, Winston S. 22, 44, 54, 111, 131, 142, 153
civil rights movement (US) 187, 230, 240, 241–45
   and decolonization 244
climate change 255
coal and coal miners 47, 49, 61, 147, 152, 154–55, 209, 223
Coca-Cola 14, 34, 134, 168
Cold War,
   definition 6–8, 53, 65, 91, 214, 252–253
   intensification of 32, 53–55, 77, 95, 120, 132, 202, 227
Colombia 30, 204
Comecon (Council for Mutual Economic Assistance) 57, 91
'comfort women.' *See* Prostitution and forced sex work.
Cominform (Information Bureau of Communist and Workers' Parties) 55–56, 62, 77, 100–101, 116, 118, 143, 145, 253
Communist International (Comintern) 55, 133, 253
Communist Parties 3, 6, 41, 55–56, 64, 107–8, 116, 118, 128, 136, 192, 206–7, 209–10, 220, 253
   (*see also individual countries;* Cominform; Comintern; Stalinism)
Computers 234
Congress for Cultural Freedom 115, 240
Conservative and Christian Democrat parties 128, 140–42, 144–45, 147, 151, 153, 256
copper 175–76, 183, 214
Costa Rico 194, 196, 200
Cuba 195–96, 200, 203, 204, 207, 210, 215
   Cuban Revolution 219–21, 245, 256

Curtin, John 155
Cyprus 161
Czechoslovakia 42, 44–47, 55–56, 61, 65, 170, 172, 211
  Communist Party (KSČ) 46–47, 56, 61

D-Day landings 139
decolonization 2–3, 32–34, 37–38, 104, 111, 114, 119, 181–84, 188, 218–19
  American policy toward 32, 34, 36, 37–38, 119, 184–85
De Gasperi, Alcide 128
De Gaulle, General Charles 134, 136, 139–40, 144–45, 160–61, 177–78
  and 'grandeur' 139, 145
demobilization crisis (1945–46) 3, 67–69, 76, 81, 102, 110, 148, 151, 154, 186, 225
denazification and postwar purges 51, 135, 137–38
development. *See* modernization in global South.
Diem, Ngo Dinh 106, 124
Điên Biên Phủ, Battle of 106
Displaced Persons (DPs) 3, 132, 169
dollar (US currency) 29–30, 91, 152–53, 157, 178, 200, 214, 250, 254
Dominican Republic 194–96, 207–8, 212, 215
Du Bois, W. E. B. 181
Dulles, John Foster 174
Dunn, James 1, 8, 145, 256
Dutch East Indies. *See* Indonesia.
Dutch Empire 93, 97–101, 103, 120, 254
Duvalier, François 192

Eastern Europe 3–5, 38, 45, 70, 81, 84, 132, 153
  idea of 38, 45
  popular revolts in 45–48, 61–63
  Soviet power in 6–8, 37, 43, 51, 53, 55–65, 207, 249, 251–52
  US propaganda toward 239–41
Ecuador 196, 200, 203–4

Egypt 15–16, 18, 28, 62, 159, 161, 168, 170, 171–72, 197, 254
  Suez Crisis (1956) 161, 172–74, 187, 254
Eisenhower, Dwight D. 59, 123, 172–75, 230, 232–34, 242
Empire Windrush, HMT 217–18
Eritrea 180
Estimé, Dumarsais 192
Estonia. *See* Baltic States.
Ethiopia 28, 176, 179–80
Europe. *See* Eastern Europe; Western Europe.
European Coal and Steel Community 147
European Recovery Program (ERP or 'Marshall Plan') 49, 52, 55, 121, 133, 146–47, 178

famine 3, 18, 38, 40, 70, 72, 88–90, 96, 102, 109, 176
farms and farming. *See* agriculture.
Farouk I, King of Egypt 159, 161
Federal Republic of Germany (West Germany) 51–52, 59–60, 132, 142, 147–49, 171
Finland 45, 49
the First World War 2, 22, 33, 39, 41, 50, 133, 141, 159, 169, 250, 253
Five-Year Plans. *See* socialized economies and economic planning.
food and food production. *See* agriculture.
forced migrations 3, 49–50, 70, 79, 111–12, 132, 142, 170–71
forced workers 3, 16, 59, 96, 132, 176, 178
Ford Motor Company 23, 168, 235
France, (*see also* French Empire and Union)
  American policy toward 104, 139, 251
  Communist Party (PCF) 136, 139–40, 145, 182
  postwar politics 31–32, 55, 114, 123, 131, 133–34, 139–41, 143, 145–47, 171, 255

INDEX

in the Second World War 4, 18, 21–22, 28, 41, 132, 134, 136, 139–40, 159–60, 176–77
  Vichy government 134, 139, 159, 176
Franco, General Francisco 150–51, 256
Franklin D. Roosevelt, USS 35
Free India Movement 96, 109
free trade 17, 28–29, 31, 33, 42, 73, 147, 152, 200, 250, 254
French Empire and Union 4, 95, 103–5, 175–78, 181–82, 185, 251, 254
French Equatorial Africa 176
French West Africa 175–76, 177, 178

Gaddis, John Lewis 7
General Agreement on Tariffs and Trade (GATT) 29, 157
Geneva Conference (1954) 106
Geneva Convention 97
Geneva Summit (1955) 64
German Democratic Republic (East Germany) 52, 57, 59, 61
Germany (*see also* Federal Republic of Germany; German Democratic Republic) 52, 133, 147, 196–97
  postwar occupation and partition 3, 17, 42, 49–53, 55, 60, 79, 132–33, 135, 141–42, 252, 254
  in the Second World War 3–6, 13–14, 18–19, 22–23, 37–39, 41, 43–48, 70, 74–75, 96, 195–97, 251
Gillespie, John Birks 'Dizzy' 241
globalization 15–16, 254–55
Gold Coast (Ghana) 15, 176, 177, 181–85, 188, 217
gold and gold standard 29, 152, 175, 185, 200
Gomułka, Władysław 56, 62
'good war.' *See* Second World War.
governments-in-exile (the Second World War) 28, 31, 46, 48, 104, 139–40, 142
'Grand Alliance' (UK, US, USSR, 1941–45) 39, 41, 50–51, 55, 73, 195, 208
  postwar continuation 39, 73, 76–77, 100, 108, 163, 227
Great Depression 25, 28–29, 33, 73, 193, 238, 250, 255

Greater East Asia Conference (1943) 96
Greater East Asia Co-Prosperity Sphere 83, 96–97, 102, 115
'Greater Indonesia' 107, 114
Greece 3, 34, 55, 131, 142–43, 253
  Communist Party (KKE) 142–43
Greenland 15
Green Revolution 236
Guam 15, 33, 122, 148
Guatemala 194, 196, 204
  military coup (1954) 210–11, 213, 252
Guevara, Ernesto 'Che' 220
Guggenheim, Solomon R. and Marguerite 'Peggy' 238
Guinea 182–83, 185
gulag prison system (USSR) 40, 45, 57, 61

Haile Selassie, Emperor 179–80
Haiti 191–92, 203, 215
Hatta, Mohammad 93, 96, 100
Hawai'i 15, 122
hegemony, United States 4–6, 8, 19–22, 28–29, 31–35, 37–38, 43, 81–82, 95, 119–20, 147, 161–62
  Anglo-American dyarchy 20–21, 31, 153, 161–62, 166, 168, 174–75, 250–51, 254
  complexity of exercise 148, 157, 250
  domestic support for 226, 235–36, 245–47, 251
  establishment 157, 168, 174–75, 193, 254, 256
  in Latin America 199–200, 250
  limits 6, 38, 65, 81, 91, 153, 230, 249–52, 256
Hindus 30, 111–12
Hirohito, Emperor of Japan 137
Hitler, Adolf 44, 141
Ho Chi Minh 102, 105
Holland 25, 195, 251 (*see also* Dutch Empire)
  crisis in army 99
Hollywood and US cinema 239, 246
Holocaust 3, 18, 39, 50, 132, 169–70
homosexuals 230

Hong Kong 71, 79, 82, 85, 91
Houphouët-Boigny, Félix 182
Hukbalahap (People's Anti-Japanese Army) 68–69, 108, 122
'Hump,' (India-China Ferry route) 74
Hungary 38, 42, 45, 47–48, 61
    Revolution (1956) 62–63, 64, 174
Hyderabad 113, 117
hydroelectric power 24, 86, 155, 172, 184–85, 236

Ibn Saud, King of Saudi Arabia 25, 167
Iceland 15, 59, 195
Idris as-Senussi, King of Libya 168
India 28, 31 (see also Indian National Congress)
    British colonial rule 28, 30–31, 109, 111–113, 153, 253–54
    Communist Party 116
    economy 111, 114, 117, 121–22
    independence and partition 62, 70, 101, 111–14, 119, 253–54
    postwar strikes and protests 69, 99, 109–10, 151
    relations with United States 34, 119, 121–23
Indian Army. See British-Imperial military forces.
Indian National Army (INA) 109
Indian National Congress (INC) 96, 109, 111–12, 116
Indochina. See Vietnam.
Indonesia,
    Communist Party (PKI) 100–101, 116–18, 120, 253
    national revolt and war 3, 69, 93–101, 102, 108, 254
    postcolonial government 62, 93, 96, 101, 103, 107, 113, 114, 118, 121, 254
    US policy toward 95, 101, 122–23
International Bank for Reconstruction and Development (IBRD) 30–31, 200–201
International Civil Aviation Conference (1944) 15, 200
International Monetary Fund (IMF) 29, 200, 255

Iran 16, 25, 28, 34, 42, 114, 162–67, 171, 174
    US-backed coup 163, 164–65, 211, 252
Iraq 16, 28, 114, 159, 161, 169–70, 171, 174–75, 241
Irgun 169
Israel 170–71 (see also Palestine)
    and Holocaust 50, 169–170
Italy
    Allied invasion and occupation 1–3, 13, 17–18, 21, 127–31, 139, 197
    Communist Party (PCI) 1, 2, 55, 128–30, 133, 135–36, 141, 144–45, 209, 256
    popular revolts in 1, 2, 127–30, 141, 253
    postwar governments 1, 2, 127–28, 130–32, 134, 140, 144–45, 209, 256
    postwar reconstruction 32, 34, 130–36, 147, 256
    in the Second World War 1, 3–5, 13, 19, 111, 127–31, 133, 193, 197, 256
Ivory Coast 182

Jagan, Cheddi 217
Jamaica 24, 25, 215, 217–19
Japan,
    Communist Party (JCP) 136, 138
    economy 25, 82–83, 96, 144, 156–57, 254–55
    place in postwar order 120, 143–44, 156
    postwar labor upsurge 131, 138–39, 144
    postwar reform and governments 82, 131–34, 137–39, 141, 143–44
    in the Second World War 2–5, 11–14, 18–19, 51, 70–75, 82–83, 93–96, 99, 102–6, 109, 143–44, 153, 223, 249–51 (see also Greater East Asia Co-Prosperity Sphere)
    US occupation 17–18, 120, 131–35, 137–39, 143–44, 148–49
Japanese Surrendered Personnel (JSP) 97, 105

Java 97–99, 101
jazz music 239–41
Jews 50, 56, 132, 169–70 (*see also* anti-Semitism; Holocaust)
  'national home' in Palestine 169

Karen people 106–7, 113
Kashmir 113
Kennan, George F. 51, 53, 166, 212
Kennedy, Robert F. 230
Kenya 175–77, 181, 183
Keynes, John Maynard 30, 200, 233
Khrushchev, Nikita 62–64, 90, 117
Kim Il-sung 83, 85
King, Martin Luther Jr. 244
King, William Lyon MacKenzie 155
Korea
  Japanese colony 75, 82–83
  occupation and partition 75, 83, 84–87, 122, 253–54
  popular revolt 2, 83–85, 253
  war in 59, 82–88, 117, 120, 122–23, 148–49, 168, 186, 228–30, 232–33, 246, 253–54
Kurds. *See* Republic of Mahabad.
Kuwait 161, 167

Labour Party (UK) 70, 111, 151–54, 161, 170, 178, 180
land reform. *See* agriculture.
Latin America, (*see also individual countries*)
  Cold War and 202, 209, 214
  Communist Parties in 206–7, 209–10, 253
  economic conditions 194, 196–97, 214, 255
  popular militancy 3, 191–92, 202–5, 221
  postwar politics 205–14
  US policy toward 24, 29, 36, 192–202, 207–8, 212–14, 236, 250
Latvia. *See* Baltic States.
League of Nations 31, 33, 159, 169
Lebanon 159–60, 167, 175
Lend-Lease 4, 15–16, 21–22, 28, 34, 105, 152, 162, 167, 170, 180, 197, 207, 239, 250
Lenin, Vladimir Ilyich 39, 41, 50, 118

liberal internationalism 18, 30, 33–34, 233
Liberia 28, 179
Libya 42, 168
Lithuania. *See* Baltic States.
Luce, Henry R. 34, 134, 227, 235, 239, 246, 251

MacArthur, General Douglas 11–12, 17, 74, 84, 86, 104, 119, 137, 155, 230
Macmillan, M. Harold 174, 188
Madagascar 175–76
Madiun putsch (1948) 101, 117, 120
Magsaysay, Ramon 124
Malaka, Tan 97–98, 100–101, 108
Malawi 181, 183
Malaya 69, 96–97, 102–3, 105, 107–9, 114, 116–17, 122
Malcolm X. 245
Manchukuo. *See* Manchuria.
Manchuria,
  in Chinese Revolution 76–77, 83, 88
  in the Second World War 4, 18, 71, 73, 75–76, 83
Mandela, Nelson Rolihlahla 187
Manhattan Project 14, 24, 234
Manley, Norman Washington 217–18
Mao Zedong 18, 73, 76, 79, 90, 118
Marianas Islands 28, 74, 122 (*see also* Trust Territories of the Pacific)
Marshall, General George C. 76–77, 81, 146, 196, 229
Marshall Islands 15, 123 (*see also* Trust Territories of the Pacific)
Marshall Plan. *See* European Recovery Program.
Marxism 40, 182, 191, 206, 220
Massachusetts Institute of Technology (MIT) 234, 237
Mazey, Emil 68, 225
McCarthy, Senator Joseph R. and 'McCarthyism' 91, 228–30, 233
Mexico 25, 194, 198, 200, 202–4, 206, 209–10 (*see also* Bracero Program)
Micronesia 15, 17 (*see also* Trust Territories of the Pacific Islands)

Middle East 16–17, 25, 30, 34, 166–75
(*see also individual countries*)
    popular anticolonialism in 37, 159–66, 168–72
Middle East Supply Center (MESC) 16, 28, 161, 168
'military-industrial complex' 19, 26, 233–34
Missouri, USS 11–13, 166
'modernization' in global South 16–17, 29–31, 117, 121–22, 172, 175, 197, 200–201, 206, 236–37, 255
Mohammad V, Sultan of Morocco 34
Mongolia 74–75
Montgomery bus boycott (1955–56) 244
Montreux Convention Regarding the Regime of the Straits (1936). *See* Turkish Straits.
Morocco 34, 160–61
Mosaddeq, Mohammed 164–65, 167, 211, 220
Mozambique 187
Muslims 95, 110, 111–12, 113
Mussolini, Benito 1, 44, 127, 129, 174
Mutually Assured Destruction (MAD) 59

Naga people 113
Nakba (Catastrophe) 170
Naples 15, 18, 127–28, 149
Nasser, Colonel Gamal Abdel 171–75, 184, 220
National Association for the Advancement of Colored People (NAACP) 242
National Liberation Front (FLN, Algeria) 161
National Security Act (1947) 231–32
National Security Council 59, 148, 175, 184, 232
    NSC-68, 59, 86, 120, 148
Nazi party and government (Germany) 5, 19, 38, 41, 46–47, 51–52, 56, 96, 132, 141
Nehru, Jawaharlal 114, 116–17, 121, 123, 220
neocolonialism 105, 112, 114, 119, 122, 149, 168, 179–84, 216, 219, 255–56

Netherlands East Indies. *See* Indonesia.
neutrality and neutralism 42, 49, 51–52, 60, 95, 121–22, 168, 195, 199, 207
New Deal 121, 194, 196, 227–28, 232–33, 236
New Guinea 21, 74, 155
New Zealand 28, 44, 123, 154–56, 179
Nicaragua 200, 207
Nigeria 175–76, 183
Nixon, E. D. 244
Nixon, Richard M. 174–75, 184, 230, 232
Nkrumah, Kwame 182–85, 217
Non-Aligned Movement 62, 115, 123
North Africa 4, 19, 111, 160–61, 168, 175 (*see also individual colonies and countries*)
North Atlantic Treaty Organization (NATO) 59, 62, 64, 123, 148–51, 168, 180
Northern Rhodesia (Zambia) 175, 183, 187
Norway 49
nuclear power 114, 146, 171, 233
nuclear weapons 4–5, 11, 14, 54, 59, 123, 146, 229, 234
    United States 4, 11, 14, 35–36, 53–54, 59–60, 90, 122–23, 168, 232
Nuremberg Trials 135
Nyasaland (Malawi) 183

Office of Coordinator of Inter-American Affairs (OCIAA) 195, 200–201
Ogaden 179–80
oil,
    British companies 25, 152, 162–65, 167, 169 (*see also* Anglo-Iranian Oil Company)
    Latin America and Caribbean 25, 167, 198, 210, 212, 215, 218, 220
    Middle East and Iran 25, 161–65, 167–168, 174
    oilfield workers 163, 165, 209, 215, 223

INDEX

Soviet 42, 47, 49, 163–64, 220
United States companies 4, 25, 165, 167–68, 171, 198, 220, 255 (*see also* ARAMCO)
world market for 25, 164, 167, 169, 174
Okinawa 13, 15, 122, 144, 148
Osmeña, Sergio 104
Ottoman Empire 2, 50, 159, 169
overseas aid (*see also* European Recovery Program; Lend-Lease; Point Four Program; modernization; United Nations Relief and Rehabilitation Administration)
    Soviet 81, 117–18, 185, 211, 220–21
    United States 1, 28, 32–34, 59, 76, 105, 120–122, 143, 180, 195, 213, 236–37, 250, 254

Pact of Madrid (1953) 151, 256
Padmore, George 182–83
Pahlavi, Mohammad Reza, Shah of Iran 162–65
Pakistan 111–13, 115, 121, 123, 174
Palestine and Palestinians 50, 161, 168–71, 254 (*see also* Israel; Nakbah)
Pan-Africanism 181–84, 188
Pan-African Congress (Manchester, 1945) 181
Panama 195, 200, 202–4
Pan American Airlines 15, 196–97
Pan-American conferences 195, 200–202, 207, 213
Pan-American Security Zone 195
Pan-Arabism and Arab nationalism 159, 161, 170–71, 174–75, 254
Pan-Asianism 96, 114–15
Pan-Slavism 50
Papua 113
Paraguay 196
Paris Commune (1871) 2
Paris Peace Treaties (1947) 49, 133
Parks, Rosa Louise McCauley 244
partition
    China 73, 78–79
    Germany 51–53, 55, 57, 71, 79, 141, 146, 254

India 111–12
Korea 84, 254
Palestine 170
South Africa 186
Vietnam 106, 254
Patton, General George S. 53, 132
'peaceful coexistence' 63–65, 101, 115, 117–18, 233, 253
Pearl Harbor, Japanese attack on (1941) 4, 18, 73, 192
'people's democracies' 42, 46–47, 55–56, 76, 136–37
People's Republic of China. *See* China.
People's Republic of Korea (PRK). *See* Korea.
Perón, General Juan Domingo 199, 205–7, 209–10, 220
Persian Gulf and Gulf states 15, 161–62, 167
Peru 200, 204, 206, 208, 210
Peter I, King of Yugoslavia 48
Philippines
    Hukbalahap insurrection 3, 33, 68–69, 108, 122
    independence under Japan 96
    independence under US 15, 28, 33, 96, 104, 115, 119–21, 123–24
    and US military 15, 17, 74, 104, 122, 148, 155
Pierlot, Hubert 140
Pishevari, Ja'far 162–64
Point Four program (1949) 121–22, 213, 236–37
Poland 3, 46, 48, 50–51, 55, 57–58, 62, 65, 146, 241
    in the Second World War 38–39, 41–43, 45
Pollock, Jackson 238
Portugal and Portuguese colonies 15, 113–14, 187
Potsdam Conference (1945) 50–51, 75, 105, 256
prisoners of war 3, 45, 57, 86–87, 97, 109, 132 (*see also* Indian National Army; Japanese Surrendered Personnel)
prostitution and forced sex work 18, 83, 138, 149

Provisional Government of Free India (1943–1945) 96, 109
Puerto Rico 33, 215–17, 254

Qavam, Amad 163–64
'Quit India' movement (1942) 109, 111, 116

Randolph, A. Philip 244
Rassemblement Démocratique Africain (RDA) 182
refugees 3, 70, 79, 132, 142, 171, 235, (*see also* Displaced Persons; forced migrations)
reparations 39, 51–52, 75, 141
Republic of Mahabad 162–64
Reuther, Walter P. 223
Rockefeller, Nelson A. 195, 201–2, 213
Romania 38, 42, 45, 47
Rome, US capture of (1944) 1, 128
Rosenberg, Ethel and Julius 229
Roosevelt, Franklin D. 15, 20–22, 34, 43–44, 167, 180, 193, 196, 244
    and China 69–70, 74, 104, 119
    colonial policy 34, 95, 103–4, 114, 119, 160
    leadership style 20–21, 44, 231–32
Roxas, Manuel 104
Royal Indian Navy mutiny (1946) 69, 109–12
rubber 96, 102, 112, 176, 179, 191
Russia and Russian Empire 2, 40, 50, 53, 90
Russian Revolution (1917) 6, 40, 43, 90, 116, 133, 253

Saudi Arabia 25, 28, 167, 170–71
the Second World War
    character 3–5, 18–19, 70, 73–74, 91, 249–50
Sékou Touré, Ahmed 182, 185
'semi-colonial' relations. *See* neocolonialism.
Senegal 178, 181
Senghor, Léopold Sédar 178, 181–82
Serbia 48
Servicemen's Readjustment Act, (GI Bill) 27, 235

Sétif Massacre 160
Shan people 106–7, 113
shipping and shipbuilding 15–16, 23, 97, 102, 166, 176, 195
Sicily 127
Sikhs 109, 112
Singapore 105, 107
Sino-Soviet split 90–91, 118
Sino-Soviet Treaty of Friendship and Alliance (1945) 76
Sino-Soviet Treaty of Friendship, Alliance, and Mutual Assistance (1950) 89
Slovakia 38, 46
socialized economies and economic planning 3–4, 40–43, 48, 57–58, 61, 87–91, 117–18, 230
South East Asia Command (SEAC) 119
South East Asia Treaty Organization (SEATO) 123, 155
South Rhodesia (Zimbabwe) 183, 187
South Sakhalin and Kuril Islands 75
South West Africa (Namibia) 187
Spain 58, 150–51, 256
Sputnik 64
Stalin, Joseph 7, 40–42, 44, 56, 61–62, 101, 142, 163–64
    and China 73, 79, 89
    'destalinization' 62
    and postwar Europe 104, 128, 136, 142
Stalinism 9, 39–42, 50, 58, 116, 206, 220, 254 (*see also* Communist Parties)
    crisis of 60–65, 90–91
steel mills and steel workers 13, 88, 90, 117, 147, 152, 185, 197, 223, 225, 244
Sterling and 'sterling area' 29, 91, 152–53, 157, 174, 178, 199
strategic bombing 4, 11, 14, 19, 51, 74, 85–86, 131–32, 138, 141, 152
Struggle Front (Indonesia) 100, 108
Sub-Saharan Africa, (*see also individual colonies and countries*)
    Cold War in 179, 184–5
    decolonization 181–84, 188, 254–55

popular radicalization in 3, 5, 175–76, 182, 253
'second colonial conquest' of 24, 153, 175–79, 254
US policy toward 179–81, 184–85, 250–51
wartime mobilization 24, 176–77
sugar and sugar workers 215–16, 220
Sukarno 93, 96, 100–101, 107, 114, 117, 120, 123, 220
Sumatra 97–99, 101
Supreme Commander Allied Powers (SCAP) 137–38, 144
Surabaya, Battle of (1945) 93–95, 98
Surinam 24, 195, 215
Sweden 49
Syngman Rhee 84, 86
Syria 28, 159–60, 167, 169–70, 174

Taft-Hartley (Labor-Management Relations Act 1947) 225–27
Taiwan (Formosa) 74, 79, 82, 86, 90–91, 121, 123
Taiwan Straits Crisis (1958) 90
Tamils 112
Tehran Conference (1943) 41, 48, 104, 128, 253
television 35, 157, 239, 246
Thailand 96, 115, 121, 123–24
Thakin Nu 106, 117, 124
'Third World' 7–8, 30, 174, 221, 236, 240, 255–56
Thorez, Maurice 136
tin and tin miners 96, 102, 176, 204, 211–12
Tito (Josip Broz) 44, 48, 76, 79, 143
'Titoism' 56
Togliatti, Palmiro 128
Tokyo war crimes trials 135
Transjordan (Jordan) 161, 169–71, 236
Travancore 114
Treaty of San Francisco (1952) 133, 144
Trieste Crisis (1945) 44, 50, 53, 79, 144, 166
Trinidad 215, 217–19
Trotskyist parties 40, 61, 100, 108, 112

Trujillo, Rafael Leónidas 194, 212
Truman Doctrine (1947) 55, 143, 226
Truman, Harry S. 35–36, 44, 53–55, 77, 81, 93, 121, 149, 170, 225–28, 232, 236–37, 240, 242
Trust Territories of the Pacific Islands 15, 33, 122, 148, 254
Tunisia 160–61
Turkey 166, 168, 171, 174, 236
Turkish Straits Crisis 42, 166

Ukraine 3, 39–40, 42, 45, 49–50
Union of African States (1958–63) 183
Union of South Africa 28, 156, 176–77, 179, 185–87
Union of Soviet Socialist Republics (USSR) (*see also* Stalinism)
  character of 4, 9, 39–42, 117–18, 163, 206–7
  economy 40–41, 57–58, 62, 71, 75, 88, 163
  in Eastern Europe 3, 6–7, 37–65, 84, 251
  policy toward Africa 179–80, 184–85
  policy toward China and Korea 71, 73–78, 81–89
  policy toward Latin America and Caribbean 21, 209–11, 217, 220–21
  policy toward Middle East 162–66, 170–72
  policy toward Southeast Asia 100–101, 108–8, 115–18
  policy toward Sub-Saharan Africa 179–81, 184–85
  policy toward Western Europe 128, 136–37, 141–43, 149, 253
  postwar foreign policy 6, 31, 38–39, 63–65, 100–101, 185, 253–54 (*see also* Grand Alliance)
  in the Second World War 4, 6–7, 13, 18, 22, 31–32, 37–39, 41–49, 52, 71, 128, 246, 251 (*see also* Grand Alliance)
United Arab Republic (1958–61) 174

United Auto Workers union (UAW) 68, 223, 225, 244
United Fruit Corporation 211
United Kingdom, (*see also* British Empire; British-Imperial military forces)
  domestic politics and welfare state 70, 131, 151–54, 156
  economy 29–30, 103, 152–53, 197–98, 200
  relations with US 15, 21–22, 31–32, 127–28, 131, 152–54, 171–75, 249–51
  in the Second World War 4–5, 15, 119, 127–28, 132, 140, 142, 159–60, 249
United Mine Workers of America (UMWA) 27, 224
United Nations
  founding 31, 36, 195, 201–2, 213, 250, 256
  in Korean War 82, 85–86
  in postwar 53, 91, 101, 151, 163, 170–71, 180, 216, 233, 238
  Security Council 31–32, 53, 70, 82, 85, 170
  trusteeship 15, 33, 104, 122, 144, 251
  wartime alliance 31–32, 70, 114, 193, 195–96, 200
United Nations Atomic Energy Commission 53
United Nations Monetary and Financial Conference. *See* Bretton Woods Conference.
United Nations Relief and Rehabilitation Administration (UNRRA) 32–33, 72, 77, 130, 134, 146, 236, 239
United States Air Force 54, 59–60, 160, 168, 232, 250
United States Navy 11, 23, 35, 60, 122, 148–49, 168, 180
United States of America, (*see also* African Americans; civil rights movement; hegemony)
  and 'air-sea' war 4, 15, 19, 74, 251
  'anti-colonialism' of 95, 103–4, 119, 160–61, 181–82, 251–52, 254
  domestic politics 223–46
  demobilization protests 67–69, 76, 81, 102, 148, 186, 225, 251
  economy 13–14, 22–31, 34–35, 104, 216, 226, 232–33, 234, 246, 250
  overseas military bases 14–15, 54, 122, 148–51, 168, 180, 197–99, 202–203, 215, 232, 250
  policy toward Africa 179–82, 184–85, 254
  policy toward China 73–77, 81–82, 228–30, 251–52, 254
  policy toward Latin America 191–200, 205–8, 212–14, 250
  policy in Middle East 163, 164–68, 171–75, 211, 252
  postwar military expansion 59–60, 85–87, 122–23, 148–51, 230–32, 242, 250, 252
  'soft power' of 34, 134, 149, 195, 239–41, 246
universities and expansion of higher education 17, 121, 157, 181, 234–37
uranium 14, 59, 179, 186
urbanization 23, 176, 203
Uruguay 209

Vargas, Getúlio 194, 196, 199, 204, 206–9, 220, 256
Venezuela 25, 200, 210, 213
Victor Emmanuel III, King of Italy 127
Vietnam 69, 96–97, 102–108, 120, 161, 254–56
  US policy toward 95, 104–6, 120–121
  'Vietnam War' (1955–75) 7, 99, 124, 247, 254
Volksdeutsche, 49–50, 132, 142

Wafd Party (Egypt) 159
Wallace, Henry A. 34, 227, 235, 251
Warsaw Pact 60, 63–64
Warsaw Uprising (1944) 46
Westad, Odd Arne 7–8, 221
Western Europe, (*see also individual countries*)
  character of postwar democracy 133–36
  economic integration 146–47, 153–54

postwar restabilization 3, 6, 54, 56, 64, 130–36, 142–49, 156–57, 230–33, 255
  US bases in 149–51
West Indian Federation 216–19
White, Harry Dexter 196, 229
Williams, Eric Eustace 217–19
Williams, Robert F. 244–45
Willkie, Wendell L. 34, 227, 235, 251
Women,
  in armed forces 37, 48, 58, 67, 109
  economic mobilization 22, 25, 185, 224, 226, 246
  political mobilization 34, 47–48, 102–3, 108–9, 116, 130, 137, 191, 204, 240
  social status 25, 58, 72, 83, 89, 108, 134, 137, 157, 240
  violence against 47, 51–52, 75, 83, 86, 138, 141, 216 (*see also* prostitution and forced sex work)

World Bank 30, 121, 184, 255
  as 'good war' 4–5, 17–18, 237–39, 245–47
  in Latin America and Caribbean 192–93, 202–3, 215–216, 219
  physical destruction 3, 18–19, 38–39, 70, 96, 102, 131–32, 156, 245–46
  'ragged ends' in Asia 96–97, 101, 102, 119–20, 123

Yalta Conference (1945) 43–44, 51, 229
Yugoslavia 28, 38, 42, 44–45, 48–49, 58, 108, 143–44, 253 (*see also* Tito)
  revolution 58, 72–73, 76, 253
  split with USSR 56, 62, 91, 143

Zhdanov, Andrei 55, 116
Zhou Enlai 115, 118
Zog I, King of Albania 49